The Political

Communication

Reader

Edited by

**Ralph Negrine
and James Stanyer**

Routledge
Taylor & Francis Group

LONDON AND NEW YORK

First published 2007
by Routledge
2 Park Square, Milton Park, Abingdon, Oxon OX14 4RN

Simultaneously published in the USA and Canada
by Routledge
270 Madison Ave, New York, NY 10016

Routledge is an imprint of the Taylor & Francis Group, an informa business

Typeset in Perpetua and Bell Gothic by
Florence Production Ltd, Stoodleigh, Devon
Printed and bound in Great Britain

British Library Cataloguing in Publication Data
A catalogue record for this book is available from the British Library

Library of Congress Cataloging in Publication Data
The political communication reader/edited by Ralph Negrine and
James Stanyer.
  p. cm.
1. Mass media – Political aspects.   2. Communication – Political aspects.
I. Negrine, Ralph M.   II. Stanyer, James.
P95.8.P643 2007
302′.23 – dc22   2006038496

ISBN10: 0–415–35935–X (hbk)
ISBN10: 0–415–35936–8 (pbk)

ISBN13: 978–0–415–35935–1 (hbk)
ISBN13: 978–0–415–35936–8 (pbk)

The Political Communication Reader

The Political Communication Reader gathers together key writings on political communication from a range of leading authors, examining both conventional approaches and the newer realities of mediated political communication in advanced industrial democracies.

By drawing the boundaries of political communication as broadly as possible, this Reader offers a comprehensive overview of the key areas of debate, discussion and research within the field. The selected texts – each of which has been chosen because it has made a significant contribution to our understanding of the issues under consideration – have been organised into eight sections, whose content ranges from macro-level explorations of the place of the media in contemporary societies to micro-level examinations of the way the media play a part in civic and political life. Each section deals with issues and concerns that have a continuing importance and contemporary significance, including:

- the exercise of power, media and democracy
- the media and elections
- media effects
- political participation and the media
- the personalisation of politics
- new technologies and the reshaping of political communication.

This is an invaluable text for all students of the media, politics and communication studies.

Ralph Negrine is Professor of Political Communication at the Department of Journalism Studies, University of Sheffield. His research interests are in political communication and media policy. Recent publications include *Television and the Press Since 1945* (1999), and *The Communication of Politics* (1996). He is also co-editor of *The 'Professionalization' of Political Communication* (2007).

James Stanyer is Lecturer in Communication and Media Studies at the Department of Social Sciences, Loughborough University. His research focuses on developments in political communication in advanced industrial democracies. His work has appeared in a wide range of academic journals and he has also authored two books, *The Creation of Political News* (2001) and *Modern Political Communication* (2007).

Contents

SECTION 2
Media and political advocates

SECTION 3
Election campaigns

Illustrations

Figures

Tables

Acknowledgements

This book would not have been possible without the help of numerous people and institutions. A special thank you goes to Charlotte Wood, Sarah Fry and the team at Routledge for being patient, understanding and extremely helpful during the preparation of the book. We would like to thank Chris Cudmore for seeing the potential of the project, former colleagues at the Centre for Mass Communication Research and colleagues in the Department of Social Sciences, Loughborough and the Department of Journalism Studies, Sheffield for their support. We are particularly indebted to those who aided in the scanning of the various articles and book chapters. Mark Maynard at Leicester University and Peter Riley-Jordan at Loughborough University deserve a mention for all their patience and hard work.

A special mention should also go to Fleur and Angie (and Jonathan) for their constant support throughout the time spent producing this book.

Permissions

W. Lance Bennett (2003) 'Communicating Global Activism: Strengths and Vulnerabilities of Networked Politics', *Information, Communication & Society*, 6 (2), pp. 143–68. Reproduced by permission of the author and Taylor & Francis. www.tandf.co.uk/journals.

From *Smart Mobs: The Next Social Revolution*, by Howard Rheingold. ISBN 0738206083. Copyright © 2003 by Howard Rheingold. Reprinted by permission of Basic Books, a member of Perseus Books, LLC and Brockman, Inc.

Tiffany Danitz and Warren P. Strobel (2001) 'Networking Dissent: Cyber Activists Use the Internet to Promote Democracy in Burma'. From John Arquilla and David Ronfeldt (eds), *Networks and Netwars: The Future of Terror, Crime, and Militancy*. Copyright 2001 by Rand Corporation in the format of Other Book via Copyright Clearance Center.

Michael Cornfield, Jonathan Carson, Alison Kalis and Emily Simon (2005) 'Buzz, Blogs, and Beyond: The Internet and the National Discourse in the Fall of 2004', *Pew Internet & American Life Project*, 16 May, www.pewinternet.org. Reproduced by kind permission of the Pew Internet Project.

Darren Wallis 'Democratisation, Parties and the Net: Mexico – Model or Aberration', from Rachel Gibson, Paul Nixon and Stephen Ward (eds), *Political Parties and the Internet: Net Gain?* Copyright © 2003 Routledge. Reproduced by permission of Taylor & Francis Books UK.

M. Margolis and D. Resnick, *Politics as Usual: The Cyberspace 'Revolution'*, pp. 207–12 Copyright © 2000 Sage Publications, Inc. Reprinted by permission of the publisher.

Ralph Negrine and James Stanyer

POLITICAL COMMUNICATION TRANSFORMED?

T HIS READER APPEARS at a time when political communication in advanced industrial democracies is in a state of flux. What could be called the traditional model of political communication, based on limited and regulated channels of electronic communication, a stable press, and mass audiences with identifiable party loyalties, is giving way to a new, more decentralised and pluralised, structure – one characterised by fragmentation and uncertainty. To appreciate this transformation, it is important for students of political communication to be familiar not only with latest developments in the field but also with some of the traditional concerns.

What is political communication?

Before detailing the structure of this Reader, it is important to outline briefly what is meant by political communication. There have been numerous attempts to define it (see, for example, Wolton, 1990; or Blumler and Gurevitch, 1995). A simple definition might be: all communication between social actors on political matters – interpersonal and mediated. That said, in the main, scholarly research on political communication has focused on the production and dissemination of political messages in the national mass media and their impact on citizen audiences. Political communication can be seen in this sense as involving three sets of actors – media institutions, political institutions and citizen publics – in a bounded political territory, usually a liberal democracy. This tripartite configuration is a useful starting point but, of course, it conceals complex and evolving interrelationships and dynamics.

Defining the boundaries of the field

Traditionally the boundaries of political communication research have been quite narrowly defined. The field has been concerned with the production of political messages and their impact, especially during election campaigns. As the field has matured, so the focus of those working within it has broadened. Indeed, at the start of the twenty-first century there are difficulties in defining where the boundaries of the field of study lie (Dahlgren, 2004). The traditional focus remains: for example, researchers continue to deal with processes of communication that relate to political matters, and, at a very broad and general level, examine the distribution and maintenance of power in democratic societies. However, in addition to this traditional focus, the process of socio-economic and technological change has generated new areas to explore and new challenges for the field as a whole. For instance, the issue of power has been central to the study of political communication. However, the increasing visibility of elites and the pluralised flow of information in the multi-channel democracies means the position of political elites has never been more vulnerable. New technologies have opened up opportunities for once marginalised voices to enter the public sphere and contest the definitions of the powerful. This Reader seeks to draw the boundaries as broadly as possible, incorporating new issues and debates in the field. One outcome of this fairly loose definition of what the study of political communication comprises is the opportunity to include within it a whole range of topics that might otherwise be excluded if a traditional narrow definition was adopted.

The selection

It is the recognition that political communication is a broad field that informs, in part, the selections that are included in this Reader. The selection also seeks to reflect some of the traditional research concerns. For example, the section on media effects (Section 5) draws on some of the key pieces of research on the subject produced over the past fifty years. Inevitably, considerations of length and accessibility have also played their parts in making the selection, but the aim has remained constant – namely, to offer readers a selection of texts on key aspects of the study of political communication. Some of these are obvious, some are less so, but when taken together they hopefully provide a considered view of the main elements in this field of study.

In very general terms, the texts range from macro-level explorations of the place of the media in contemporary societies (Section 1, 'Media and democracy', for example) to micro-level examinations of the way the media play a part in civic and political life (Section 8, 'New media, new politics'). In between, the extracts include such topics as election campaigns and campaigning, the personalisation of politics, the onset of the new media, and the place of weblogs in contemporary politics, to name but a few.

The structure of the Reader

Each of the eight sections tackles a set of topics that are central to understanding political communication in contemporary liberal democracies. There is, of course, some overlap but the following represent the key themes of this Reader.

The exercise of power

It is perhaps difficult to avoid the conclusion that, despite the need for a broad understanding of the contours of this field of study, political communication concerns itself with aspects of power: how power is achieved and how it is maintained, and how those who seek power, or seek to alter the distribution of power, engage with the media in order to do so. This explains the inclusion of the following three sections: Section 1, 'Media and democracy'; Section 2, 'Media and political advocates'; and Section 3, 'Elections and campaigns'.

Section 1, 'Media and democracy', is perhaps the most general in scope and is primarily concerned with the need to understand where media organisations are located and what roles they play, or should play, in mature democracies. Are they simply vehicles that are used by those in power to maintain their positions? Are media organisations part of a complex of powerful institutions that are somehow distinct or separate from the public or citizens? Are they beholden to political institutions or to their economic masters? And, much more generally, Section 1 concerns the need to understand the range of accounts that all contribute to an explanation of the role of the media in democratic societies.

Such questions throw up many answers and these are reflected in the selection of texts. Beginning with a short extract from **Lippmann**'s *Public Opinion*, Section 1 includes well-established critiques of the media (for example, **Klaehn**'s discussion of the 'propaganda model' applied by Edward Herman and Noam Chomsky) as well as accounts that offer a more institutionalised perspective on the arrangements that sustain the media and political actors in society (for example, **Swanson**'s (1997) piece on the 'political-media complex'). In these, and the other extracts included in Section 1, there is an opportunity to interrogate different approaches to the study of the media – some of these highlight economic imperatives and ownership, others institutional arrangements, still others provide insights on the need to reformulate how we understand the role of the media over the last fifty years.

Taken together, these extracts produce a set of questions about the media and democracy that require careful thought. More importantly, perhaps, these questions can frame other questions about the study of political communication itself. For example, how useful is it to study micro-level aspects of the media, if the role of the media is circumscribed by an external, overarching and often hidden dimension? How useful is it to study elections, say, if the media never question fundamental aspects of the organisation of elections (e.g. majoritarian, first-past-the-post, funding) or the legitimacy of the process itself or its outcomes (e.g. as a consequence of low turnouts)?

The point to note is that no study of political communication can avoid high-lighting the larger context within which the communication of politics takes place. After all, the media – newspapers, television, the Internet – are part of economic, cultural and political landscapes and these may, at some level and in some way, circumscribe what they do and how they do it.

If Section 1 alerts us to macro-level issues and themes, Sections 2 and 3 offer more specifically targeted accounts of how we may need to explore the role of the media: first, in relation to the media's counterparts in the practice of political communication (namely, the politicians and other actors that play a part in drawing together the main issues and themes that populate our media), and, second, elections and campaigns.

Campaign communication

Section 3 focuses on elections, with two clear themes. The first is the more general one as it addresses the 'meanings' and 'purposes' of elections and their coverage. In the first piece, Katz (1972) asks the questions that are often overlooked: why is election coverage constructed in the way that it is, and who benefits from it? Is this the best way to meet the 'needs' of the citizen or are there better ways? While such questions bring forth a variety of answers, these can be read in a number of other contributions found in this Reader. For example, Jamieson's piece (1992) highlights the more negative aspects of presidential campaigning – is that really to the benefit of the citizen? – and Semetko et al. (1991) explore the ways in which agendas are formed in the interaction between political parties and media. The possible impact of media coverage on levels of cynicism and turnout are touched on by Capella and Jamieson (1997); as well as by Patterson (2002) and Putnam (2000) in Section 6.

But the concern with the role of the media in election coverage as exemplified in the extract from Katz (1972) must be accompanied by more focused work on how elections are covered in practice and what sorts of influences have made that coverage what it is. Jamieson's (1992), for example, does the former, but the latter is dealt with in the other pieces in Section 3, pieces that explore how election practices have converged and are converging around such themes as 'Americanisation' and 'modernisation'.

Evolution of campaign communication

The presence of many pieces on election campaigns – in Sections 3 and 4 – can be justified by the fact that the study of elections plays such an important part in the study of political communication. Election campaigns are political events per se. They involve key political actors contesting power and they bring to the fore the processes through which those in power – or those who seek power – attempt to mobilise and persuade the voters. In the pre-television (and pre-Internet age), such activities were comparatively simple in their organisation and execution. The advent of television and the Internet, changes in the make-up of political parties, processes of voter de-alignment, the development of new techniques of campaign, communication and marketing, among other developments, have immensely complicated the whole nature of campaigning.

While it would be too simplistic to attribute any of these changes to specific causes, the overall effect of change has been to recast the nature of campaigns and campaigning. When Sections 3 and 4 are read together one can get a better sense of how campaigns and campaigning has changed and what reasons are put forward to explain that change. In other words, if we were seeking to understand how election campaigns are organised and run – and why they are the way that they are – what would we need to examine? The answers include: processes of 'Americanisation' and 'modernisation' (both in Section 3) but also 'professionalisation', the introduction of new techniques derived from commercial practices, the globalisation of campaigns through the employment of consultants, new ways of thinking about campaigning and how parties may need to 'market' themselves, and the possible impact of these on such things as allegiance, membership of political parties and levels of turnout.

As for explanations of this transformation, there are several that can be put forward, ranging from **Blumler and Kavanagh**'s (1999) exploration of changes in political communication over the last century (in Section 1), to **Norris**'s notion of the postmodern campaign (in Section 3), and to **Scammell**'s (1998) considered account of why the practice of 'marketing' is so important in understanding the conduct of elections (in Section 4). Sections 3 and 4, therefore, complement one another and offer a range of texts that cover contemporary concerns about how election campaigns are run, why they are run as they are and the possible implications of this on voters' allegiances and preferences.

Globalisation

While the material in these sections is essentially taken from US and UK studies, the lessons that can be drawn are of much wider significance. This is so, in part, because some of these themes are in fact derived from comparative studies that, in turn, draw on the experiences of other countries. **Mancini**'s (1999) piece on professionalisation, for example, reflects on the Italian experience, **Negrine and Papathanassopoulos** (1996) contrast the UK and Greek experience, and the extract from **Plasser and Plasser**'s (2000) study of political consultants is itself part of an international study of the consulting 'industry'. In other words, what appears at first sight to be a US- and UK-centred discussion is in fact a discussion drawn from a wider set of examples and thus has a much wider relevance. It should follow, therefore, that part of the task of Section 4 is to identify those sets of issues that can be used for exploring the nature of campaigns and campaigning in a range of non-Anglo-American contexts. To quote from a recent volume on political communication: 'in the twenty-first century we are confronted with developments in the realm of politics and mass communications that rule out the conception of political communication as a phenomenon that could be defined within singular national, cultural, or linguistic boundaries. In fact, the challenge today is to face the developments and consequences arising from the modernization and globalization of political processes' (Pfetsch and Esser, 2004: 4).

Political advocates and media relations

Unlike the three sections that concentrate on macro-level issues, including those related to election campaigns and campaigning, Section 2 moves the focus towards different sets of relationships between the media and a range of actors. **Blumler and Gurevitch**'s (1995) piece explores the relationship between politicians and the press and the different roles that each takes on in the process of news-making. **Timothy Cook**'s (1998) piece similarly touches on such high-level considerations, but his piece addresses the broader question of how we are to understand the media in the political system. By looking at the process of news-making, Cook suggests that the media are implicated in the political process and must be seen as *part* of the political system and also as a political institution – not simply as something external to it, representing it, covering it and fundamentally separate from it.

Why these insights are important becomes clear in the other extracts in Section 2. **Wolsfeld** (1997) looks at how careful and considered use of the media brings with it political power, although that institutional power can be challenged by outsiders, in this case Palestinians fighting in the first Intifadah. **Hallin** (1994) looks at how, and why, elite opinion moved against the war in Vietnam; and **Manheim** (1994) at how different actors have come to learn to use the media to their advantage. What these extracts show is that far from being isolated and impartial systems of communication, the media can be employed by individuals and groups to their advantage. When those individuals and groups are part of the political world, the consequences are political in character and outcome.

Media effects

If the first four sections of this volume explore the macro-level nature of the study of political communication, Section 5 turns to the question of 'media effects'. When considerations of 'media effects' are raised, particularly in the context of political communication, the overwhelming interest lies in the sorts of direct 'effects' – effects understood as changes in voting behaviour as a direct and causal outcome of media content, for example. Often there are too many other variables to take into account – ranging from occupational through to experiential ones – to allow for such a narrow definition of effects to be identified in studies. Nonetheless, it would be wrong to suggest that studies do not tackle these sorts of topics and that they do not arrive at some sets of conclusions about such 'effects'. On the other hand, it would also be wrong to suggest that these were the *only* effects of the media to warrant consideration. In a sense, the texts in Section 1 (for example, from Lippmann) also discuss 'effects' but in a different and more global, albeit general, understanding of the term.

Section 5, therefore, consists of several texts that touch on fairly general understandings of media 'effects' as well as the more specific and narrowly defined ones. Effects research is perhaps the most well-established area of political communication research which has produced diverse and often contradictory findings. In **Lazarsfeld** *et al.* (1969) we have what became the dominant canon of post-war media effects research, the reinforcement doctrine. The power of the media to reinforce existing voting behaviour is also the conclusion of **Norris** *et al.*'s (1999) research on the impact of the press on voting behaviour in the UK.

One of the first attempts to rethink the impact of the media was **McCombs and Shaw**'s (1972) study of agenda setting. If the media do not tell voters *what* to think, they may tell voters what to think *about*. This point is central to debate on the media's agenda-setting function, and taken up in the extract from McCombs and Shaw's study. A similar interest in the cognitive impact of campaigns can be seen in the work of **Lewis** *et al.*, (1992) who argue that the media can misinform the electorate on certain issues. For **Capella and Jamieson** (1997) and **Iyengar** (1991), it is not the presence of an issue in the news that is important, but the way that issue is framed. Capella and Jamieson (1997) ask whether the news media's framing of politics creates cynicism, so debasing political discourse, and Iyengar (1991) questions whether the media's framing of political issues makes it more difficult to identify who is 'responsible' for actions such as terrorism.

The Langs' (1953) study of the MacArthur Day march in the 1950s raises the spectre of television's more general 'effects' on political behaviour – individual, collective and elite – but its inclusion here within a discussion of 'media events' highlights the ways in which television's role in granting ceremonial legitimacy to events goes some way to constructing a political spectacle and a spectacle with political consequences: we, as individuals and we as publics, respond to these in particular ways. The significance of this study is highlighted in the section from **Katz and Dayan**'s (2003) critical reappraisal of the study and it emphasises its continued importance today. If the extracts from studies by the Langs and Katz and Dayan alert us to the larger question of the 'effects' of television on the political system and on political behaviour, so do some other extracts in this section.

In these seven pieces, the themes move back and forth from general 'effects' to more specific ones, from a focus on collectivities to one on individuals. The point, though, is to be alert to an understanding of effects that goes beyond a single and narrowly defined one as impacting on individuals (and at election times only!).

The media and political engagement

Section 6 examines how individuals engage (or not) with the political process and the processes of political communication. Beginning with an extract from **Putnam**'s (2000) study *Bowling Alone*, the theme of this section is whether the media enhances or hinders political engagement and how it does so. Putnam suggests that television, among other things, has had an impact on political engagement, and **Patterson**'s study of 'the vanishing voter' points to a similar trend of non-engagement. The other extracts in this section illustrate engagement with mediated politics: from young people and how they learn and communicate about politics (**Buckingham**, 2000) to participation in television's political output (**Jones**, 2005; **McNair** *et al.*, 2003).

Personalisation

If the first six sections in this volume deal with more 'traditional' understandings of politics and political communication, namely, as an interest in institutions and political actors, Section 7 begins to move the focus away from this and towards less traditional forms such as personalities or celebrities, and scandals in the realm of politics. In other words, Section 7 takes us back to questions of television's role in changing the nature of political discourse and of the polity generally and highlights the ways in which the issues of personality and celebrity have now become a part of the political landscape. If the more traditional interest has lain in the idea of 'rational' debate and rational decision-making, this section turns our attention to the ways in which personality and celebrity have intruded into political debate and, to some extent, distorted more 'traditional' news values in the realm of politics and the political. Three of the six extracts deal with political scandals and the way they now are often the staple of political coverage; the other three extracts offer insights into different aspects of celebrity. For example, one extract looks at the ways in which Bill Clinton's image was constructed and the meaning of personality politics, while the other two pick up the theme in different ways. **West and Orman** ((2003) examine the meaning of celebrity politics in a general way, whilst **Glynn** (2000) tries to explain the election of Jesse 'the Body' Ventura in a media-saturated celebrity-obsessed age.

The interest in political communication evidenced in Section 7 is a world away from the interest in electoral behaviour or coverage of parliaments and political parties, yet it signals the much wider understanding of politics that we now have (and need to work with). Section 7 also offers a link to the extracts that feature in Section 8 which themselves draw our attention to 'new politics' in the context of 'new media'.

New media

Perhaps inevitably, no discussion of political communication in the twenty-first century would be complete without a detailed discussion of the Internet and the way in which it has changed both political behaviour and the production of political content. Many dimensions of this new medium in the field of communication remain little understood at present. For example, research shows that more people are getting their political news from websites and that traditional media are suffering as a consequence, but we still do not know enough how individuals navigate the web to get political content or how they receive/decode such content. Much work remains to be done in this area, as the web becomes established – it is still comparatively 'new' – but Section 8 shows that when it comes to use of the web, social and political movements have already established a pattern of working and have already learned how to use it to their advantage.

Using the web in new and different ways is the theme of most of the extracts in Section 8: the use of blogs, cyberactivists, and the discussion of 'smart mobs' all point towards a future where new patterns of communication (using the web) are increasingly established to connect people and to mobilise. By creating networks and linking people through the web, so bypassing the traditional media, new forms of action can be engendered and new challenges to the status quo can be made. Whether or not these new patterns of activity will overturn existing patterns rather than simply emphasise the continuities with the present is the theme of the final pieces in this section (**Margolis and Resnik**, 2000; Wallis, 2003). It is perhaps obvious that the well-established and the well-funded will tend to exploit the new forms of communication most – a point underpinning Margolis and Resnick's work – but it is perhaps too negative an analysis to suggest that it will be 'business as usual'.

The eight sections offer, therefore, an overview of the field of political communication. The extracts themselves highlight particular visions of the field. Issues of space have inevitably meant that certain areas have not been well served by this selection. For example, more could have been included about representations – of groups, individuals, nations even – and more could have been added to the discussion of audience reception of political content. That said, it is worth pointing out that some of our extracts touch on these issues. In respect of representations, the discussions in Sections 1 and 2 focus on the production of content. While they do not highlight specific representations they hint at who is involved in the production of political content and who is likely to benefit from that process. Similarly, although there is no section explicitly on audience reception, the discussions in Sections 5 and 6 illustrate how individuals and citizens make sense of politics and how the role of the media may have had a part to play in levels of engagement, in the comprehension of political news, and of content more generally.

These cross-references underpin one of the key points that readers of this volume should be alert to, namely, that while each individual section highlights particular issues and themes, the eight sections, when taken together, provide a wealth of material that contributes to a rounded understanding of this important field of study.

References

Blumler, J.G. and Gurevitch, M. (1995) *The Crisis of Public Communication*, London: Routledge.

Dahlgren, P. (2004) 'Theory, Boundaries and Political Communication: The Uses of Disparity', *European Journal of Communication*, 19 (1): 7–18.

Pfetsch, B. and Esser, F. (2004) 'Comparing Political Communication: Reorientations in a Changing World', in F. Esser and B. Pfetsch (eds) *Comparing Political Communication: Theories, Cases, and Challenges*, Cambridge: Cambridge University Press.

Wolton, D. (1990) 'Political Communications: The Construction of a Model', *European Journal of Communication*, 5 (1): 9–28.

SECTION 1

Media and democracy

THE 'BIG' QUESTIONS about the role of the media in the democratic process form the subject of the eight extracts in this section. Some of these extracts, including those by **McChesney**, **Klaehn** and **Sparks**, take an approach that highlights questions of economics and of ownership in particular. **Sparks** raises these questions by drawing on the experience of newly democratised East European countries, so offering a different lens through which to ask familiar questions. By contrast, **Swanson**'s piece also highlights the relationship between politics and media, but this time through a more institutional perspective taken from the study of the media in American politics. By suggesting that there is a political-media complex, Swanson also raises questions about how we need to understand the full picture.

The remaining four extracts touch on other aspects of the 'big' questions. Have the media become too powerful? Do the media 'overshadow' and distort the nature of politics? These questions are tackled by **Mazzoleni and Schultz**, while **Blumler and Kavanagh** provide an overview of how the relationship between media and politics – so central to many of the extracts here – has shifted over the last fifty years, as new media and different ways of dealing with politics and politicians have begun to alter how things are done. **Curran**, by contrast, asks whether the media can be altered to provide a better and more critical stance on the democratic process.

The very first extract (a short one at that), from **Lippmann,** points out how the study of politics and the media needs to be alert to power – those who have it, and how they can use the media to their advantage.

All these extracts, in their own way, illustrate why the study of political communication must take account the larger context within which the media are located.

Chapter 1

Walter Lippmann

PUBLIC OPINION

Source: Walter Lippmann (1997 edition) *Public Opinion,* New York: Free Press Paperbacks (Simon & Schuster), pp. 157–8. First published in 1922.

THE CREATION OF CONSENT is not a new art. It is a very old one which was supposed to have died out with the appearance of democracy. But it has not died out. It has, in fact, improved in technic, because it is now based on analysis rather than on rule of thumb. And so, as a result of psychological research, coupled with the modern means of communication, the practice of democracy has turned a corner. A revolution is taking place, infinitely more significant than any shifting of economic power.

Within the life of the generation now in control of affairs, persuasion has become a self-conscious art and a regular organ of popular government. None of us begins to understand the consequences, but it is no daring prophecy to say that the knowledge of how to create consent will alter every political calculation and modify every political premise.

Chapter 2

Robert McChesney

RICH MEDIA, POOR DEMOCRACY

Source: Robert McChesney (1999) *Rich Media, Poor Democracy*, Illinois: University of Illinois Press, pp. 1–7, 76–7.

Introduction

The media-democracy paradox

OUR ERA RESTS UPON a massive paradox. On the one hand, it is an age of dazzling breakthroughs in communication and information technologies. Communication is so intertwined with the economy and culture that our times have been dubbed the Information Age. Sitting high atop this golden web are a handful of enormous media firms – exceeding by a factor of 10 the size of the largest media firms of just fifteen years earlier – that have established global empires and generated massive riches providing news and entertainment to the peoples of the world. [. . .] Independent of government control, this commercial media juggernaut provides a bounty of choices unimaginable a generation or two ago. [. . .]

[. . .]

On the other hand, our era is increasingly depoliticized; traditional notions of civic and political involvement have shriveled. Elementary understanding of social and political affairs has declined. Turnout for US elections – admittedly not a perfect barometer – has plummeted over the past thirty years. [. . .] It is, to employ a phrase coined by Robert Entman, "democracy without citizens" (Entman, 1989).

By conventional reasoning, this is nonsensical. A flowering commercial marketplace of ideas, unencumbered by government censorship or regulation, should generate the most stimulating democratic political culture possible. The response comes that the problem lies elsewhere, that "the people" obviously are not interested in politics or civic issues, because, if they were, it would be in the interests of the wealthy media giants to provide them with such fare. There is an element of truth to that reply, but it is hardly a satisfactory response. Virtually all defenses of the commercial media system for the privileges they receive – typically made by the media owners themselves – are based on the notion that the media play an important, perhaps a central, role in providing the institutional basis for having an informed and participating citizenry. If this is, indeed, a democracy without citizens, the media system has much to answer for.

I argue [in the original publication] that the media have become a significant *antidemocratic* force in the United States and, to varying degrees, worldwide. The wealthier and more powerful the corporate media giants have become, the poorer the prospects for participatory democracy. I am not arguing that *all* media are getting wealthier, of course. Some media firms and sectors are faltering and will falter during this turbulent era. But, on balance, the dominant media firms are larger and more influential than ever before, and the media *writ large* are more important in our social life than ever before. Nor do I believe the media are the sole or primary cause of the decline of democracy, but they are a part of the problem and closely linked to many of the other factors. Behind the lustrous glow of new technologies and electronic jargon, the media system has become increasingly concentrated and conglomerated into a relative handful of corporate hands. This concentration accentuates the core tendencies of a profit-driven, advertising-supported media system: hypercommercialism and denigration of journalism and public service. It is a poison pill for democracy.

Nor is the decline of democracy in the face of this boom in media wealth a contradiction. The media system is linked ever more closely to the capitalist system, both through ownership and through its reliance upon advertising, a function dominated by the largest firms in the economy. Capitalism benefits from having a formally democratic system, but capitalism works best when elites make most fundamental decisions and the bulk of the population is depoliticized. For a variety of reasons, the media have come to be expert at generating the type of fare that suits, and perpetuates, the status quo. I argue that if we value democracy, it is imperative that we restructure the media system so that it reconnects with the mass of citizens who in fact comprise "democracy." The media reform I envision (and write about here), can take place only if it is part of a broader political movement to shift power from the few to the many. Conversely, any meaningful attempt to do this, to democratize the United States, or any other society, must make media reform a part (though by no means all) of its agenda. Such has not been the case heretofore.

[The original publication], then, is about the corporate media explosion and the corresponding implosion of public life, the rich media/poor democracy paradox. [. . .]

[. . .]

A major theme [of the original publication] is that the rise of *neoliberalism* is a main factor that accounts for the corporate media boom, on the one hand, and the collapse of democratic political life on the other hand. Neoliberalism refers to the policies that maximize the role of markets and profit-making and minimize the role of nonmarket institutions. It is the deregulation provided by neoliberalism that has been instrumental in allowing the wealthy media corporations to grow and prosper as they have. Likewise, neoliberalism is a political theory; it posits that society works best when business runs things and there is as little possibility of government "interference" with business as possible. In short, neoliberal democracy is one where the political sector controls little and debates even less. In such a world political apathy and indifference are a quite rational choice for the bulk of the citizenry, especially for those who reside below the upper and upper-middle classes.

[. . .]

The media/democracy paradox [. . .] has two components. First, it is a political crisis. I mean this in two senses. On the one hand, the nature of our corporate commercial media system has dire implications for our politics and broader culture. On the other hand, the very issue of who controls the media system and for what purposes is not a part of contemporary political debate. Instead, there is the presupposition that a profit-seeking, commercial media system is fundamentally sound, and that most problems can be resolved for the most part through less state interference or regulation, which (theoretically) will produce the magic elixir of competition. In view of the extraordinary importance of media and communication in our society, I believe that the subject of how the media are controlled, structured, and subsidized should be at the center of democratic debate. Instead, this subject is nowhere to be found. This is not an accident; it reflects above all the economic, political, and ideological power of the media corporations and their allies. And it has made the prospect of challenging corporate media power, and of democratizing communication, all the more daunting.

The second component of the media/democracy paradox concerns media ideology, in particular the flawed and self-serving manner in which corporate media officers and their supporters use history. The nature of our corporate media system and the lack of democratic debate over the nature of our media system are often defended on the following grounds: that communication markets force media firms to "give the people what they want"; that commercial media are the innate democratic and "American" system; that professionalism in journalism is democratic and protects the public from nefarious influences on the news; that new communication technologies are inherently democratic since they undermine the existing power of commercial media; and, perhaps most important, that the First Amendment to the US Constitution authorizes that corporations and advertisers rule US media without public interference. These are generally presented as truisms, and nearly always history is invoked to provide evidence for each of these claims. In combination these claims have considerable sway in the United States, even among those who are critical of the social order otherwise. It is because of the overall capacity of these myths, which are either lies or half-truths, to strip citizens of their ability to comprehend their own situation and govern their own lives that I characterize these as "dubious" times in the book's subtitle [original publication].

[. . .]

Conclusion

The clear trajectory of our media and communication world tends toward ever-greater concentration, media conglomeration, and hypercommercialism. The notion of public service – that there should be some motive for media other than profit – is in rapid retreat if not total collapse. The public is regarded not as a democratic polity but simply as a mass of consumers. Public debate over the future of media and communication has been effectively eliminated by powerful and arrogant corporate media, which metaphorically floss their teeth with politicians' underpants. It is, in short, a system set up to serve the needs of a handful of wealthy investors, corporate managers, and corporate advertisers. Its most important customers are affluent consumers hailing from the upper and upper-middle classes. The system serves the general public to the extent that it strengthens and does not undermine these primary relationships. Needless to say, the implications for democracy of this concentrated, conglomerated, and hypercommercialized media are entirely negative. By the logic of my argument, the solution to the current problem of US media demands political debate and structural reform. [. . .]

Reference

Entman, R.M. (1989). *Democracy Without Citizens: Media and the Decay of American Politics.* New York: Oxford University Press.

Chapter 3

Jens Klaehn

A CRITICAL REVIEW AND ASSESSMENT OF HERMAN AND CHOMSKY'S 'PROPAGANDA MODEL'

Source: Jens Klaehn (2002) 'A Critical Review and Assessment of Herman and Chomsky's "Propaganda Model"', *European Journal of Communication*, 17 (2): 147–82.

Abstract

MASS MEDIA PLAY an especially important role in democratic societies. They are presupposed to act as intermediary vehicles that reflect public opinion, respond to public concerns and make the electorate cognizant of state policies, important events and viewpoints. The fundamental principles of democracy depend upon the notion of a reasonably informed electorate. The 'propaganda model' of media operations laid out and applied by Edward Herman and Noam Chomsky in *Manufacturing Consent: The Political Economy of the Mass Media* postulates that elite media interlock with other institutional sectors in ownership, management and social circles, effectively circumscribing their ability to remain analytically detached from other dominant institutional sectors. The model argues that the net result of this is self-censorship without any significant coercion. Media, according to this framework, do not have to be controlled nor does their behaviour have to be patterned, as it is assumed that they are integral actors in class warfare, fully integrated into the institutional framework of society, and act in unison with other ideological sectors, i.e. the academy, to establish, enforce, reinforce and 'police' corporate hegemony. [. . .]

Herman and Chomsky's PM (Propaganda Model), initially referred to as a 'general theory of the Free Press', contends that America's elite agenda-setting media play an important role in establishing cultural hegemony, primarily by establishing a general framework for news discourse that is typically adhered to by lower-tier media.

[. . .]

The PM contends that the agenda-setting media function as mechanisms of propaganda in several ways. The elite media determine what topics, issues and events are to be considered 'newsworthy' by the lower-tier media and establish the general premises of official discourse. Furthermore, elite media establish limitations on the range of debate and general boundaries for subsequent interpretation (Herman and Chomsky, 1988: 1–2).

[. . .]

First and foremost, the PM constitutes an institutional critique of media performance. Herman and Chomsky argue that media serve the political and economic interests of dominant elites and charge that 'the workings of the media [. . .] serve to mobilize support for the special interests that dominate the state and private activity' (Herman and Chomsky, 1988: xi).

> Perhaps this is an obvious point, but the democratic postulate is that media are independent and committed to discovering and reporting the truth, and that they do not merely reflect the world as powerful groups wish it to be perceived. Leaders of the media claim that their news choices rest on unbiased professional and objective criteria, and they have support for this contention within the intellectual community. If, however, the powerful are able to fix the premises of discourse, to decide what the general populace is allowed to see, hear, and think about, and to 'manage' public opinion by regular propaganda campaigns, the standard view of how the system works is at serious odds with reality.
>
> (Herman and Chomsky, 1988: xi)

The PM argues that regularities of misrepresentation in news accounts flow directly from concentration of private power in society. It holds that elite media interlock with other institutional sectors in ownership, management and social circles, effectively circumventing their ability to remain analytically detached from the power structure of society, of which they themselves are an integral part. The net result of this, the authors contend, is self-censorship without any significant coercion. Media performance is understood as an outcome of market forces.

[. . .]

The PM argues that media serve 'political ends' by mobilizing bias, patterning news choices, marginalizing dissent, by allowing 'the government and dominant private interests to get their messages across to the public'[1] (Herman and Chomsky, 1988: 2).

According to this framework, media serve to foster and reinforce an intellectual and moral culture geared towards protecting wealth and privilege 'from the threat of public understanding and participation' (Chomsky, 1989: 14) [. . .]

Market forces in action: the five 'filter elements' (constraints) explained

Herman and Chomsky (1988: 1–35) argue that the 'raw material of news' passes through a series of five interrelated filter constraints, 'leaving only the cleansed residue fit to print'. These filter elements continuously 'interact with and reinforce one another' and have multilevel effects on media performance (Herman and Chomsky, 1988: 2). The five filter elements are:

> [. . .] (1) the size, concentrated ownership, owner wealth, and profit orientation of the dominant mass-media firms; (2) advertising as the primary income source of the mass media; (3) the reliance of the media on information provided by government, business, and 'experts' funded and approved by these primary sources and agents of power; (4) 'flak' as a means of disciplining the media; and (5) 'anti-communism' as a national religion and control mechanism.
>
> (Herman and Chomsky, 1988: 2)

The first filter constraint emphasizes that media are closely interlocked and share common interests with other dominant institutional sectors (corporations, the state, banks) (Herman and Chomsky, 1988: 3–14). As Herman and Chomsky point out: 'the dominant media firms are quite large businesses; they are controlled by very wealthy people or by managers who are subject to sharp constraints by owners and other market-profit-oriented forces' (Herman and Chomsky, 1988: 14).

The second filter highlights the influence of advertising values on the news production process. To remain financially viable, most media must sell markets (readers) to buyers (advertisers). This dependency can directly influence media performance [. . .].

[. . .]

The third filter notes that dominant elites routinely facilitate the news-gathering process: providing press releases, advance copies of speeches, periodicals, photo opportunities and ready-for-news analysis (Herman and Chomsky, 1988: 19). Thus, government and corporate sources are attractive to the media for purely economic reasons. Such sources are favoured and are routinely endorsed and legitimized by the media because they are recognizable and viewed as prima facie credible. Information provided to the media by corporate and state sources does not require fact checking or costly background research and is typically portrayed as accurate.

In sum, Herman and Chomsky highlight not only the symbiotic nature of the relationship between journalists and their sources, but the reciprocity of interests involved in the relationship. The third filter constraint stresses that the opinions and analyses that are expounded by corporate and state sources are adapted to dominant class interests and market forces (Herman and Chomsky, 1988: 23; see also Martin and Knight, 1997: 253–4). [. . .] Dissenting views are frequently excluded from public forums. In this way, core assumptions that cannot stand up to factual analysis can find widespread support.

[. . .]

Importantly, the authors contend that preferred meanings are structured into news discourse as a result of the dominance of official sources who are identified as 'experts'. In this way, news discourse 'may be skewed in the direction desired by the government and "the market"' (Herman and Chomsky, 1988: 23). Concurrently, the '*preferred*' meanings that are structured into news discourse are typically 'those that are functional for elites' (Herman and Chomsky, 1988: 23).[2]

Flak, the fourth filter, means that dominant social institutions (most notably the state) possess the power and requisite organizational resources to pressure media to play a propagandistic role in society. [. . .]

[. . .]

In sum, the authors maintain that there are powerful interests that routinely encourage right-wing bias in media (Herman and Chomsky, 1988: 27–8).

According to the PM, these filter constraints are the most dominant elements in the news production process, and they continuously interact with one another and operate on an individual and institutional basis (Herman and Chomsky, 1988: 2; Rai, 1995: 40). According to Herman and Chomsky, the filter constraints excise the news that powerful interests deem *not* fit to print.

Since the publication of *Manufacturing Consent*, the demise of communism in the former Soviet Union has brought about radical changes in the world political landscape. According to Chomsky, the last filter, that of anti-communism, still functions in the post-Cold War world, but has been replaced with a dichotomy of 'otherness'. Chomsky (1998: 41) explains that:

> [. . .] it's the idea that grave enemies are about to attack us and we need to huddle under the protection of domestic power. You need something to frighten people with, to prevent them from paying attention to what's really happening to them. You have to somehow engender fear and hatred, to channel the kind of fear and rage – or even just discontent – that's being aroused by social and economic conditions.[3]

Ed Herman concedes that the filter perhaps should have been originally termed 'the dominant ideology', so as to include elements of the dominant ideology that are referred to at various points throughout *Manufacturing Consent*; such as the merits of private enterprise, or the benevolence of one's own government (Herman, cited in Wintonick and Achbar, 1994: 108). In the end, however, anti-communism was selected, primarily because the authors wished to emphasize the ideological elements that have been most important in terms of disciplinary and control mechanisms. As it is laid out in *Manufacturing Consent*, the description of the fifth filter is vague and is already veering towards the newly revised definition. [. . .]

[. . .]

Herman (2000) suggests that the 'potential weakening' of the fifth filter mechanism/constraint in the contemporary political-economic landscape is 'easily offset by the greater ideological force of the belief in the "miracle of the market" (Reagan)'.[4]

Herman and Chomsky state that these five filter constraints capture the essential ingredients of the PM. The authors argue that there is 'a systematic and highly political dichotomization in news coverage based on serviceability to important domestic power interests' (Herman and Chomsky, 1988: 35). Herman and Chomsky contend that this dichotomy is routinely observable in 'choices of story and in the volume and quality of coverage' (Herman and Chomsky, 1988: 35). They maintain that choices for publicity and suppression are bound to the five filter constraints just outlined. The authors argue that media shape public opinion by controlling how ideas are presented, and also by limiting the range of credible alternatives. Herman and Chomsky write that:

> The five filters narrow the range of news that passes through the gates, and even more sharply limit what can become 'big news,' subject to sustained news campaigns. By definition, news from primary establishment sources meets one major filter requirement and is readily accommodated by the mass media. Messages from and about dissidents and weak, unorganized individuals and groups, domestic and foreign, are at an initial disadvantage in sourcing costs and credibility, and they often do not comport with the ideology or interests of the gatekeepers and other powerful parties that influence the filtering process.
>
> (Herman and Chomsky, 1988: 31)

Notes

1   Herman and Chomsky (1988: xii) describe the PM as a 'guided market system' within which the *guidance* is 'provided by the government, the leaders of the corporate community, the top media owners and executives, and the assorted individuals and groups who are assigned or allowed to take constructive initiatives'.
2   Herman (2000) writes that: 'Studies of news sources reveal that a significant proportion of news originates in public relations releases. There are, by one count, 20,000 more public relations agents working to doctor the news today than there are journalists writing it.'
3   The filter constraint suggests that media generate fear. It also suggests that media redirect fear that already exists. See Chomsky (1997a: 91–1) for further discussion of the latter.
4   See McMurtry (1998) and Dobbin (1998) for evidence of this.

References

Chomsky, Noam (1989) *Necessary Illusions: Thought Control in Democratic Societies*. Toronto: CBC Enterprises.

Chomsky, Noam (1997a) *Class Warfare*. Interviews with David Barsamian. Vancouver: New Star.

Chomsky, Noam (1998) *The Common Good*. Interviews with David Barsamian. Berkeley, CA: Odonian.

Dobbin, Murray (1998) *The Myth of the Good Corporate Citizen: Democracy Under the Rule of Big Business*. Toronto: Stoddart.

Herman, Edward, S. (2000) 'The Propaganda Model: A Retrospective', *Journalism Studies* 1(1): 101–12.

Herman, Edward, S. and Chomsky, Noam (1988) *The Manufacturing of Consent: The Political Economy of the Mass Media*. New York: Pantheon.

McMurtry, John (1998) *Unequal Freedoms: The Global Market as an Ethical System*. Toronto: Garamond Press.

Martin, M. and Knight, G. (1997) *Communication and Mass Media: Culture, Domination and Opposition*. Toronto: Prentice Hall.

Rai, M. (1995) *Chomsky's Politics*. New York: Verso.

Wintonick, P. and Achbar, M. (1994) *Manufacturing Consent: Noam Chomsky and the Media*. Montreal: Black Rose.

Chapter 4

Colin Sparks

MEDIA THEORY AFTER THE FALL OF EUROPEAN COMMUNISM
Why the old models from East and West won't do anymore

Source: Colin Sparks (2000) 'Media Theory after the Fall of European Communism: Why the Old Models from East and West Won't Do Anymore', in J. Curran and M.-J. Park, *De-Westernizing Media Studies*, London: Routledge, pp. 35–49.

What comes after communism?

[. . .]

IT IS ENTIRELY TRUE to say that what comes after communism is capitalism, but the nature and form of the capitalism that has emerged in the former communist countries are distinctive. This invites a different perspective on the nature of the relationship between politics and economics from what one might derive from evidence drawn from the US in the 1950s. In country after country, there is very strong evidence, particularly with regard to the mass media, of the close interrelationship between political and economic power.

We may take as an example to illustrate these realities the Hungarian "media wars" that broke out shortly after the first democratic elections in that country, in 1990. Media conduct during the two rounds of elections had been regulated by an agreement between all of the political parties, including both the communists and their opponents (Korosenyi 1992: 76). As part of the deal, it had been agreed that the President of the Republic had the power to appoint the heads of both Hungarian Radio and Hungarian Television, but that the candidates were nominated by the Prime Minister in order to maintain political balance (Kovats and Tolgyesi 1993: 40–4). The first director of Hungarian radio was a well known journalist, Gomhdr, and the first director of Hungarian Television (MTV) was a famous dissident sociologist, Elemer Hankiss, who was generally believed to be close to the new Prime Minister, Antall of the Hungarian Democratic Forum (MDF) (Cunningham 1994: 4).

Despite these close links, there was soon a sharp conflict between the MDF and the leaders of both radio and television. The basic charge was that they were attempting to pursue independent policies, and were thus not sympathetic enough to the policies, and in particular the strongly nationalist orientation, of the new government. The government mobilized their supporters, both inside and outside of parliament, against the two directors, in an attempt to force them to resign. A large part of the opposition came to the support of the men, and a full-scale political struggle developed. Eventually, after a long battle, the government won, and both men were forced out at the end of 1992. The overall effect of all of this was to make the direction of television and radio an intensely political issue. The MDF used its new control to sack any journalists suspected of political unreliability and to attempt to turn radio and television into reliable vehicles for their ideas. As it turned out, despite this control of broadcasting, the MDF lost the 1994 elections very heavily, and were followed by a government dominated by the Hungarian Socialist Party (the communist successor party), under the former Stalinist enthusiast Horn. He followed the precedent established by his immediate predecessors and intervened regularly in the appointment of senior broadcasters (Oltay, 1995).

Although the Hungarian case is the best known and most protracted of the struggles to subordinate broadcasting to the government of the day, it is part of a more general pattern in the region. [. . .]

[. . .]

Newspapers, having operated in a much less regulated environment, do not everywhere display the same pattern of continuing close relations with politicians, but they do provide very clear evidence about the political nature of issues of ownership. [. . .]

It should not be imagined that the readiness of businessmen to dabble in politics, and of politicians to court friendly relationships with particular business groups, is the product of "naive" politicians unused to democratic societies, or of "inexperienced" businessmen new to the idea of the market. In the whole region, there has been a very strong element of foreign ownership in both press and broadcasting. This was an important element in Czech broadcasting and in the Hungarian press, where they continue to have a major influence, particularly in the new tabloid market (Gulyas 1998). These foreign owners have been sophisticated enterprises, sometimes very large ones, with considerable experience in operating in conditions of capitalist democracy, but they also have been deeply involved in the alliances with local forces and have played the game of political capital without any apparent hesitation. The basis for the alliances that are so common in this field, and of which CME is such a prominent exponent, is precisely that the Western company brings expertise in programming and production, and sometimes the necessary financial resources, while the local company brings the political contacts needed for success. Such alliances, of course, are always strained and are often fragile. Sometimes, as in the case of Nova TV, the foreign owners have ended up in sole control. Sometimes, as in the case of the alliance between CME and the Polish company International Trading and Investment Holdings, the locals have come out on top (Dziadul and Drazek

1999: 1). What there is no evidence of, however, is that Western business, whether as partners or as sole owners, have refused to adopt the appropriate rules of societies in which capital and politics are closely intertwined.

There is a continuing and mutually supportive relationship between businessmen and politicians. This arises not from inexperience or ignorance, but from the nature of the transition itself. Not only did the politicians in the region help their friends to win important competitive positions in the new market economy, but they also continue to exert considerable influence over the media. The media, in turn, tend to rely on relationships with politicians to gain advantages in the competitive struggle for survival and profit.

A moment's reflection, however, suggests to us that this situation of close links between political and economic actors is very far from being some strange aberration unique to post-communist countries. [. . .]

[. . .]

In summary, one of the main lessons learned from the fall of communism is that the fundamental opposition, in terms of the mass media fulfilling a role of informing the citizens of a state about its government, is not between commercial media and political media. These two forces may relate to each other in a number of ways. Sometimes they are in conflict, sometimes in concert. They both follow a logic that places them on the side of power. [. . .]

Outbreaks of (much more interesting) democracy

The final lesson learned from the fall of communism concerns the limitations of this logic of power. The media before the fall of communism were large-scale, hierarchically organized, bureaucratic establishments in which there were elaborate procedures for ensuring acquiescence to the will of the directorate. The media after the fall of communism are still large-scale, hierarchically organized, bureaucratic establishments in which there are elaborate procedures for ensuring acquiescence to the will of the directorate. Of course, there are very important differences. We may note particularly those arising from the fact that there are now competing sources of power that make for much more open conflict and public debate. These differences, however, should not be allowed to obscure the fact that in both cases most media workers, let alone the citizens who make up their audience, are systematically excluded from determining the policy and direction of the media.

This was not the necessary and inevitable outcome of the events of 1989, and indeed it was not the outcome that was desired by all of the opposition. As remarked above, many of the oppositional forces in communist regimes wanted to "create a civil society." This dream came in several different versions, but in many of them the idea was to extend the control that ordinary people had over the institutions that structured their social life. In these perspectives, there would be a much more radical revision of the structures of power, the mass media included, than simply the replacement of communist bureaucrat by capitalist entrepreneur.

[. . .]

There was thus, in the revolutions of 1989, as much as in any other great revolutionary upheaval, the promise of a more thoroughgoing and popular democracy than the one that prevails in capitalist countries. It is one of the marks of the limits of the events of 1989 that these shoots of citizen's power were crushed in the interests of the new capitalists and political elite. Certainly, Central and Eastern Europe are politically free today compared to their communist past, in the same way as Spain and Portugal are politically free today compared to their fascist past. But this is a democracy negotiated by elite groups, organized for the benefit of elite groups, and demarcated by the interests of those elite groups.

The lessons for media theory in all of this is that discussions of democracy and the media, however that relationship may be formulated, miss the point if they concentrate on the sterile debate between state and market, bureaucrat and entrepreneur. Those are real differences, but both terms in the debate are the enemies of popular expression and popular democracy. The attention of students of the media interested in finding ways in which they may be democratized would be better directed at the relationships between the media and their audiences, and the fault lines within media organizations between those who give orders and those who are forced to take them. [. . .]

References

Cunningham, J. (1994) The "Media War" in Hungary. London: European Film and Television Studies.

Dziadul, C. and Drazel, E. (1999) "CME pulls out of Poland," TV East Europe, January 23: 1–2.

Gulyas, A. (1998) "Tabloid newspapers in post-communist Hungary," Javnost / The Public, 5(3): 65–77.

Korisenyi, A. (1992). The Hungarian Parliamentary Elections of 1990. In A. Dozoki, A., Korisenyi and G. Schopflin (eds) Post-Communist Transitions: Emerging Pluralism in Hungary. London: Pinter.

Kovats, I. and Tolgyesi, J. (1993) On the Background of the Hungarian Media Changes. Media in Transition: An East-West Dialogue. Budapest-Ljubljana: Communication and Culture Colloquia.

Oltay, E. (1995) "The Return of the Former Communists," in Transition: 1994 in Review Part One. Prague: Open Media Research Institute.

Chapter 5

James Curran

RETHINKING MEDIA AND DEMOCRACY

Source: James Curran (2000) 'Rethinking Media and Democracy', in J. Curran and M. Gurevitch (eds), *Mass Media and Society*. London: Edward Arnold, pp. 120–54.

Free market watchdog

THE PRINCIPAL DEMOCRATIC ROLE of the media, according to liberal theory, is to act as a check on the state. The media should monitor the full range of state activity, and fearlessly expose abuses of official authority.

This watchdog role is said to override in importance all other functions of the media. It dictates the form in which the media system should be organized. Only by anchoring the media to the free market, in this view, is it possible to ensure the media's complete independence from government. Once the media becomes subject to public regulation, it may lose its bite as a watchdog. Worse still, it may be transformed into a snarling Rottweiler in the service of the state. [. . .]

Market liberals had only accepted more extensive regulation of broadcasting on the grounds that the limited number of airwave frequencies made it a 'natural monopoly' (Royal Commission on the Press, 1977: 9; see also Horwitz, 1991). When the number of television channels multiplied [. . .] this 'special case' was undermined. What was right in principle for the press was now applicable, it was argued, to broadcasting. Television should be set free. [. . .]

Time-worn arguments

The traditional public watchdog definition of the media thus legitimates the case for broadcasting reform, and strengthens the defence of a free market press. At first glance, this approach appears to have much to commend it. After all, critical surveillance of government is clearly an important aspect of the democratic functioning of the media. [. . .]

However this argument is not as clear-cut as it seems. While the watchdog role of the media is important, it is perhaps quixotic to argue that it should be paramount. This conventional view derives from the eighteenth century when the principal 'media' were public affairs-oriented newspapers. By contrast, media systems in the early twenty-first century are given over largely to entertainment: Even many, so-called 'news media' allocate only a small part of their content to public affairs – and a tiny amount to disclosure of official wrong-doing.[1] In effect, the liberal orthodoxy defines the main democratic purpose and organizational principle of the media in terms of what they do *not* do most of the time.

The watchdog argument also appears time-worn in another way. Traditionally, liberal theory holds that government is the sole object of press vigilance. This derives from a period when government was commonly thought to be the 'seat' of power and main source of oppression. However, this traditional view takes no account of the exercise of economic authority by shareholders. A revised conception is needed in which the media are conceived as being a check on *both* public and private power.

This modification diminishes the case for 'market freedom' since it can no longer be equated with independence from all forms of power. [. . .] The issue is no longer simply that the media are compromised by their links to big business: the media *are* big business. [. . .]

[. . .]

Market suppression

[. . .]

(What all these examples point to) is the inadequacy of the liberal model which explains the media solely in terms of market theory. The media are assumed to be independent, and to owe allegiance only to the public, if they are funded by the public and organized through a competitive market. This theory ignores the many other influences that can shape the media, including the political commitments and private interests of media shareholders, the influence exerted through news management and the ideological power of leading groups in society. In short, this extremely simplistic theory fails to take into account the wider relations of power in which the media are situated. [. . .]

State control

If private media are subject to compromising constraint, so too of course are public media. There is no lack of examples where public broadcasters have acted as little more than mouthpieces of government (Downing, 1996; Sparks, 1998; Curran and Park, 2000). [. . .]

However, a qualifying note needs to be introduced at this point. The radical media literature is bedevilled by system logic which assumes that state controlled media serve the state and corporate-controlled media serve business corporations. This ignores, or downplays, countervailing influences. Privately owned media need to maintain audience interest in order to be profitable; they have to sustain public legitimacy in order to avoid societal retribution; and they can be influenced by the professional concerns of their staff. All these factors potentially work against the subordination of private media to the political commitments and economic interests of their shareholders. Likewise, the long-term interest of public broadcasters is best served by developing a reputation for independence that wins public trust and sustains political support beyond the duration of the current administration. [. . .]

[. . .]

The political culture of liberal democracies is very alert to the threat posed by governments to the freedom of public media, but is much less concerned about the threat posed by shareholders to the freedom of private media. [. . .] Elaborate checks and balances have been established in old liberal democracies to shield public media from the state. Yet, equivalent checks have not yet been developed to shield private media from their corporate owners.[2]

In sum, an unthinking, catechistic subscription to the free market is not the best way to secure fearless media watchdogs that serve democracy. Instead, practical steps should be taken to shield the media from the corruptions generated by *both* the political and economic system. [. . .]

[. . .]

Idealist legacy

A critical revision needs to think further not only about the functioning of the public sphere, but also about the idealist premises of liberal theory. The traditional justification for media pluralism – that truth will automatically confound error in open debate – now seems implausible. [. . .] [Such] reservations [are] based on distortions in the distribution of information and the subjective element in making judgments. [. . .] To these misgivings should be added a further reservation: the 'best' argument, in the sense of one best supported by evidence and logic, does not necessarily prevail against arguments that have more publicity and are more congenial to those in power. Yet, the liberal idea that media should offer a plurality of opposed opinion still seems essential, and defensible, for other reasons. It is a way of promoting not truth but public rationality based on dialogue; not rule devoid of error but a system of self determination informed by freedom, choice and a tradition of independence that comes from civic debate.

This raises the question of how media plurality should be conceptualized. The traditional liberal approach, still dominant in American jurisprudence, is to equate it with the free trade of ideas. This has given rise to the rule-of-thumb yardstick which measures media pluralism in terms of the number of competing media outlets or the division of market shares. The assumption is that if there is a significant level of competition, there is no lack of pluralism. [. . .]

This ignores where opinion comes from, and brackets out the question of social access. [. . .]

For this reason, pluralism cannot just be equated with competition. It needs to mean more than this: namely, media diversity supported by an open process of contest in which different social groups have the opportunity to express divergent views and values. This broader definition implies a commitment to extending freedom of expression, broadening the basis of self-determination, and promoting equitable outcomes informed by awareness of opposed opinions and interests. [. . .]

An alternative approach

If the conventional liberal approach has a number of flaws, how might it be replaced with something better? Perhaps the first step in rethinking liberal theory is to break free from the assumption that the media are a single institution with a common democratic purpose. Instead, different media should be viewed as having different functions within the democratic system, calling for different kinds of structure and styles of journalism.

[. . .]

A democratic media system needs, therefore, to have a well-developed, specialist media tier, serving differentiated audiences, which enables different social groups to debate issues of social identity, group interest, political strategy and normative understanding on their own terms. For some subordinate groups in particular this will be liberating because they will have the space and media arsenal to question social arrangements that restrict the social resources available to them and curtail their life chances. They will also be empowered by being able to question dominant discourses that legitimate their subordination, and will be in a position to develop alternative arguments that advance their interests.

This specialist tier also has a secondary democratic purpose of enhancing the political effectiveness of different social groups. It should include media that assist collective organizations to recruit support; provide an internal channel of communication and debate for their members; and transmit their concerns and policy proposals to a wider public. In other words, the representative role of the media includes helping civil society to exert influence on the governmental system.

Above this specialist sector is a general media sector, reaching heterogeneous publics. This should be organized in a way that enables different groups in society to come together and engage in a reciprocal debate. [. . .]

[. . .]

Built into this conception of a democratic media system is a desire to maintain some kind of equilibrium between conflict and conciliation, fragmentation and unity. The intention is to create spaces in which differently constituted groups can communicate effectively with themselves in order to facilitate the self-organization needed to advance their sectional interests. At the same time, these divergent groups need also to be brought into an arena of common discourse where reciprocal debate can take place in order to facilitate an agree compromise. Informing this approach is the hope that tacit acceptance of an inegalitarian social order will be replaced by an informed, unbiddable public, in which powerful economic forces are confronted by well-organized political ones. [. . .]

Notes

1   Estimates for the proportion of public affairs content in mass media are provided by Curran and Seaton (1997); Strid and Weibull (1998); and Neuman (1986) quoted in Abramson (1990).

2   In this context it is worth noting that the *Observer*, when it was owned by Lonrho, was different from most privately owned media in having 'independent directors' largely selected by staff who played a key role in resisting corporate corruption.

References

Abramson, J. (1990) 'Four Criticisms of Press Ethics' in J. Lichtenberg (ed.) *Mass Media and Democracy*. New York: Cambridge University Press.

Curran, J. and Seaton, J. (1997) *Power Without Responsibility. The Press and Broadcasting in Britain*. London: Routledge.

Curran, J. and Park, M-J. (2000) *De-Westernising Media Studies*. London: Routledge.

Downing, J. (1996) *Internationalising Media Theory*. London: Sage.

Horwitz, R. (1991) 'The First Amendment Meets Some New Technologies: Broadcasting, Common Carriers, and Free Speech in the 1990s', *Theory and Society*, 20(1): 21–72.

Neuman, W. (1986) *The Paradox of Politics*. Cambridge, MA: Harvard University Press.

Royal Commission on the Press, 1974–77 Final report. (1977) HMSO.

Sparks, C. (1998) *Communism, Capitalism and the Mass Media*. London: Sage.

Strid, I. and Weibull, L. (1988) *Mediasveridg*. Goteborgs: Gotesborgs University Press.

Chapter 6

Gianpietro Mazzoleni and Winfried Schulz

'MEDIATIZATION' OF POLITICS
A challenge for democracy?

Source: Gianpietro Mazzoleni and Winfried Schulz (1999) '"Mediatization" of Politics: A Challenge for Democracy?', *Political Communication*, 16: 247–61.

[. . .]

THE SUCCESSFUL PERFORMANCE of Silvio Berlusconi, a media tycoon, in the 1994 Italian general elections; and the 1997 electoral victory of Labour leader Tony Blair in the United Kingdom, [. . .] provided ammunition to critics who blamed the "media complex" for distorting the democratic process. The catch-words of the debate about media power triggered especially in European political communication scholarship by such cases—"videocracy," "démocratie médiatique," and even "coup d'état médiatique"—all are symbolic depictions of the feared consummation of improper developments in the relationship of media and politics. In its concrete declension, a media-driven democratic system is thought to cause the decline of the model of political organization born with the liberal state, as the political parties lose their links with the social domains of which they have been the mirrors and with the interests the parties traditionally have represented.

Critics' concern for the excessive power of the media expanding beyond the boundaries of their traditional functions in democracies focuses mainly on the "irresponsible" nature of the media complex: While the political parties are accountable for their policies to the electorate, no constitution foresees that the media be accountable for their actions. Absence of accountability can imply serious risks for democracy, because it violates the classic rule of balances of power in the democratic game, making the media (the "fourth branch of government") an influential and uncontrollable force that is protected from the sanction of popular will.

According to critics, the media have distorted the political process also by turning politics into a market like game that humiliates citizens' dignity and rights and ridicules political leaders' words and deeds (Entman, 1989; Jamieson, 1992; Patterson, 1993; Sartori, 1997). Critics argue that the media's presentation of politics in the United States as well as in many other countries—as "show-biz" based on battles of images, conflicts between characters, polls and marketing, all typical frenzies of a journalism that is increasingly commercial in its outlook—has diminished if not supplanted altogether debate about ideas, ideals, issues, and people's vital interests and has debased voters by treating them not as citizens but rather as passive "consumers" of mediated politics.

Critics' concerns extend to the newest media to enter the arena of political communication [. . .]. Because they create the possibility of direct and instant "electronic democracy," the new media have given rise to several fears described by critics: Traditional democratic institutions of representation will be undermined or made irrelevant by direct, instant electronic communication between voters and officials; the new media will fragment the electorate, eroding the traditional social and political bonds that have united the polity; political parties will lose their function as cultural structures mediating between the people and the government; shrewd, unprincipled politicians will find it easier than before to manipulate public opinion and build consensus by using new information technologies and resources; and the new media can facilitate the spread of populist attitudes and opinions.

In short, critics' regard conventional mass communication and new communication technologies as sharing what could be described as a "mutagenic" impact on politics, that is, the ability to change politics and political action into something quite different from what traditionally has been embodied in the tenets of liberal democracy. Without depreciating the validity of the critical, somewhat apocalyptic positions of those who see the media as one of the most crucial factors in the crisis of politics and political leadership in postmodern democracies, it is our argument here that the increasing intrusion of the media in the political process is not necessarily synonymous with a media "takeover" of political institutions (governments, parties, leaders, movements). Moreover, media intrusion cannot be assumed as a global phenomenon, because there are very significant differences between countries in this respect. Recent changes that have occurred in the political arenas around the world cannot be explained as reflecting some common pattern of "media-driven democracy." Instead, the concept of "mediatization" of politics is a more sensible tool for addressing the question of whether the media complex endangers the functioning of the democratic process.

Mediatization is, in fact, a phenomenon that is common to the political systems of almost all democratic countries, where it has taken different shapes and developed at different speeds. However, it has in all cases proved impossible to contain because the media have assumed the character of "necessity" in the political domain. The mass media are not mere passive channels for political communicators and political content. Rather, the media are organizations with their own aims and rules that do not necessarily coincide with, and indeed often clash with, those of political communicators. Because of the power of the media, political communicators are forced to respond to the media's rules, aims, production logics, and constraints (Altheide & Snow, 1979). One of the most significant results is that politicians who wish to address the public must negotiate with the media's preferred timing, formats, language, and even the content of the politicians' communication. (Dayan and Katz, 1992) Some even hypothesize that legitimacy of the exercise of power increasingly might lie in the ability of rulers to communicate through the media. (Cotteret, 1991)

[. . .]

Critics' argument that the media are taking over political actors in the political process calls for an assessment of the empirical evidence in a variety of national contexts in order to determine whether the general trend is toward a "media-driven republic," as critics claim, or toward innocuous forms of "mediatized democracy," as we argue. [. . .]

Mediatization processes

The process of mediatization of political actors, political events, and political discourse is a major trend in political systems of the 1990s. It is a phenomenon that dates back at least to the introduction of television, but it has certainly gained speed with the expansion and commercialization of media systems and the modernization of politics.

The term *mediatization* [. . .] is distinguished from *mediation*, which refers in a neutral sense to any acts of intervening, conveying, or reconciling between different actors, collectives, or institutions. In this sense, mass media can be regarded as a mediating or intermediary agent whose function is to convey meaning from the communicator to the audience or between communication partners and thereby sometimes substitute for interpersonal exchanges. [. . .]

[. . .]

Nowadays more than ever, politics cannot exist without communication. [. . .] Politics increasingly has been molded by communication patterns. There is no doubt that much "politics of substance" is still practiced away from media spotlights, behind the scenes, in the discreet rooms of parliament and government. Yet, politics by its very nature, and independent of its substantive or symbolic value, sooner or later must go through the "publicity" stage, which entails use of the media (for example, to make known the terms of a policy decision), resort to the means of persuasion, and exposure to scrutiny by the press.

To characterize politics as being *mediatized* goes beyond a mere description of system requirements. Mediatized politics is politics that has lost its autonomy, has become dependent in its central functions on mass media, and is continuously shaped by interactions with mass media. This statement of the mediatization hypothesis is based on observations of how mass media produce political content and interfere with political processes. [. . .] Of the processes that have been identified as contributing to the mediatization of politics, the following are among the most important.

First, in their news reporting, mass media present only a highly selective sample of newsworthy events from a continuous stream of occurrences. [. . .]

[. . .]

Second, [. . .] modern democratic states are characterized by mediatized participation. Mass media construct the public sphere of information and opinion and control the terms of their exchange. [. . .] In the same way that media select and frame events, the media select which actors will receive attention and frame those actors' public images. [. . .]. In addition to conferring status upon actors by giving them attention, the media also assign political relevance and importance to social problems by selecting and emphasizing certain issues and neglecting others.

Third, "media logic" (Altheide & Snow, 1979), the frame of reference within which the media construct the meaning of events and personalities they report, increasingly has come to reflect the commercial logic of the media industry, mixing the structural constraints of media communication with the typical aims of commercial communication activity. One major implication for politics is the "spectacularization" of political communication formats and of political discourse itself. The adaptation of political language to the media's commercial patterns has been observed in three domains: (a) the communication "outlook" of political actors, be they the government, the parties, leaders, or candidates for office; (b) the communication techniques that are used; and (c) the content of political discourse. [. . .]

[. . .]

Fourth, since the mass media's attention rules, production routines, selection criteria, and molding mechanisms are well known in the world of politics [. . .] political actors know and are able to adapt their behavior to media requirements. [. . .] In other words, we are facing a symbiotic relationship that is characterized by a mediatization of politics and, at the same time, politicians' instrumental use of mass media for particular political goals. The use of methods for engineering public opinion and consent, such as political opinion polling, marketing strategies, proactive news management, and spin doctoring—which have been studied and discussed extensively in recent years—is indicative of this phenomenon.

Finally, the mass media have genuine, legitimate political functions to perform in voicing a distinct position on an issue and engaging in investigative reporting to perform their watchdog or partisan role. News partisanship is a European tradition that goes back to the close linkages between newspapers and political parties in the 19th century. It is still quite common that a newspaper's editorial position colors its news coverage, and broadcast journalism has adopted this style in many European countries. However, journalistic partisanship becomes particularly problematic under two conditions: (a) when the political beliefs of journalists deviate substantially from the beliefs of their news audiences, which seems to be the case in countries like Italy and Germany where journalists view themselves as more liberal than their audience (Patterson & Donsbach, 1996), and (b) when the mass media exaggerate their control functions and focus excessively on the negative aspects of politics, which also is an obvious trend on the European scene. [. . .]

Conclusion

Do [. . .] transformations in the societal, political, and media domains provide evidence to support the concerned alarms of an irresistible drift toward a "media-driven democracy"? Or do these trends provide evidence for our hypothesis that the "third age" of political communication witnesses an intense yet harmless process of mediatization of politics?

[. . .]

[. . .] the evidence is far from clear cut; it seems to offer support for both interpretations. However, the core of the phenomenon allows us to argue that critics' apocalyptic views are probably based on misinterpretation of the real latitude or extent of certain key trends. In other words, some of the scholarly research in political communication that has led to critics' alarm seems too focused on the distortions produced by the "media-politics complex" in the United States and tends to infer from the US experience that there is a global decline of democratic institutions assaulted by intrusive media. In fact, despite general trends, the experiences of other countries have been significantly different from the experience of the United States. Moreover, some proponents of critical perspectives seem to have difficulty in distinguishing between phenomena that reflect the sheer "mediatization" of politics and phenomena that raise legitimate concerns.

[. . .]

In conclusion, political systems in most liberal democracies are facing momentous changes on the communication front that raise serious challenges to the old order. [. . .] Excessive mediatization of political leadership and political practice, citizens forced to become consumers and spectators, and fragmentation of political participation induced by the new information and communication technologies all can distort the proper functioning of democracy. But to maintain that we are heading toward a media-driven democracy, that is, toward the dissolution of the primacy of politics in the polis, is an unwarranted conclusion relying on erroneous estimates of phenomena that are simply connatural to modern politics, largely and deeply interwoven with communication. In brief, "media politics" does not mean "politics by the media." [. . .]

References

Altheide, D.L., & Snow, R.P. (1979) *Media Logic*. Beverly Hills, CA: Sage.

Cotteret, J.-M. (1991) *Gouverner c'est paraître* [Governing is appearance]. Paris: Presses Universitaires de France.

Dayan, D., & Katz, E. (1992) *Media Events: The Live Broadcasting of History*. Cambridge, MA: Harvard University Press.

Entman, R.M. (1989) *Democracy Without Citizens: Media and the Decay of American Politics*. New York: Oxford University Press.

Jamieson, K.H. (1992) *Dirty Politics: Deception, Distraction, and Democracy*. New York: Oxford University Press.

Patterson, T.E. (1993) *Out of Order*. New York: Knopf.

Patterson, T.E. & Donsbach, W. (1996) 'New Decisions: Journalists as Partisan Actors', *Political Communication*. 13: 455–68.

Sartori, G. (1997) *Homo videns: Televisione e post-pensiero* [Television and the end of Homosapiens]. Bari, Italy: Laterza.

Chapter 7

David Swanson

THE POLITICAL-MEDIA COMPLEX AT 50

Source: David Swanson (1997), 'The Political-Media Complex at 50: Putting the 1996 Presidential Campaign in Context', *American Behavioural Scientist*, 40 (8): 1264–82.

[. . .]

IT IS HELPFUL TO PLACE the [1996 presidential] campaign in a broader context. One such larger context that has proven to be useful is an institutional perspective that focuses on tracking over time the continually evolving relationship between politics and journalism, and understanding how this relationship influences the conduct of campaigns, the practices of campaign journalism, and the response of the voters. Indeed, many of the components of campaigns that are of greatest interest to scholars and the public – from political advertising to the ways in which politicians and journalists attempt to manipulate each other to the effects of political debates – are shaped by the fundamental relationship between candidates, their campaigns, and the news media. This is why some of our most acute analysts have identified the relationship between media institutions and the institutions of government and politics as the critical relationship that defines national systems of political communication (e.g., Blumler & Gurevitch, 1995; Garnham, 1992; Gurevitch & Blumler, 1990). [. . .]

The political-media complex

[. . .]
The political-media complex is a constantly evolving relationship between media institutions and the institutions of politics and government and the way in which

both relate to the public. [. . .] the idea is that in some respects, neither institution and its practices can be understood very well, or its rationality appreciated, apart from the other institution and its practices. The institutions of politics and journalism have quite different cultures, agendas, and institutional needs, and these sometimes place them in conflict. But they are interdependent, and thus their respective agendas and institutional needs provide incentives for cooperation as well as conflict. The origins of the modern political-media complex date back to the rapid social, political, and other changes that occurred in the period immediately following World War II, so among other things, the 1996 campaign allows us to observe what the political-media complex has become at roughly age 50.

The political-media complex is what we see today in part because it is the product of a particular history. The history of the electoral environment that political parties have faced in trying to accomplish their aims and of the circumstances and opportunities that have faced political candidates tells us a lot about why political campaigns do what they do these days. Parties and candidates have responded in quite rational ways to their profoundly altered circumstances over the past 50 years.

[. . .]

Television assumed prominence in the 1950s and 1960s as the public's main source of, first, entertainment and, later, information. Network television news and televised political advertising both came into their own in the 1960s, and television became the medium from which most Americans said they received most of their information about politics and government. Television thus offered a way of reaching more voters than had been possible before and, so, as the effectiveness of party appeals and organizations was declining, became the premiere medium for national and statewide campaigning.

In the 1970s, the transfer of the power to select candidates from party bosses and state conventions to the voters in primary elections required candidates to launch their campaigns before support was available from the party. Candidates did not need the approval of the parties to mount highly effective campaigns, using the resources of television especially, but they did need professional advice to use the medium to advantage and to raise the large sums required to discover the views of their target audiences, produce effective messages, and buy airtime. As a result, candidates began creating their own professional campaign staffs independent from party organizations.

As the ability of parties to deliver votes declined, the bases of political power began to tilt away from traditional sectional, class-, group-, and interest-based partisan divisions and toward the personal popularity across traditional cleavages of individual candidates and executive officeholders, popularity that, it was thought, had to be cultivated continuously by frequent and favorable media coverage. In consequence, the practices of campaigning and governing became steadily more intertwined over time with the priorities and interests of political journalism in what Blumler (1990) has called "the modern publicity process" (see also Franklin, 1994). That is, campaigning and governing became media-centered.

These changes in the institutional situation of the political parties go a long way toward explaining, across candidates and elections, the practices that have come to dominate the "politics" side of the political-media complex. Faced with an electoral environment in which voters' preferences, allegiances, and coalitions are volatile, temporary, and based on short-term opinions, parties and candidates have endeavored to cultivate support through marketing strategies.

[. . .]

In the same way, the history of political journalism and its institutions over the past 50 years explains many of the defining features of how journalists have come to cover presidential campaigns. On the media side, the story of the political-media complex has been, until fairly recently, mostly a story of the rise and dominance of television at the center of the national political process. For more than 20 years, the network news programs reigned as the most prized venue for political officials and aspirants. [. . .] With most Americans receiving most of their information about national campaigns from television, the conventions that television journalists developed for covering campaigns became important. [. . .] Thus the attributes that had long dominated American campaign journalism, such as focusing on campaign "horse races" and dramatizing electoral contests, assumed exaggerated forms in the conventions of television news (Sigelman & Bullock, 1991), leading critics and pundits to protest that the information being offered to viewers was inadequate and often irrelevant to responsible civic decision making. [. . .]

[. . .]

It was also during the 1960s and early 1970s that the modern dynamic of the political-media complex was consolidated. Favorable media exposure was seen as essential to electoral success when traditional partisan loyalties lost their ability to mobilize voters and politicians became more sophisticated at manipulating journalists in order to receive coverage. [. . .]

[. . .]

It became important to journalists that they demonstrate their independence from politicians' manipulations, and one result was a more interpretive style of campaign reporting. In this reporting style, candidates were given less opportunity to express their views in their own words [. . .] Instead, reporters took a more active role in mediating the candidates' words and actions for viewers in news stories that focused more on the reporters' opinions and less on reporting facts. [. . .]

[. . .]

Like political parties and candidates, the media institutions that produce mainstream political journalism also have faced a changing and unstable environment. The growing fragmentation of the audience due to the proliferation of new media outlets and forms and the absorption of traditional media into diversified parent corporations have increased the pressure on news organizations to compete for audiences and profitability in a marketplace in which it is increasingly difficult to do so, while in many cases reducing their resources. [. . .]

[. . .]

Mediating between institutional needs and individuals' choices are professional cultures. Both the institutions of politics and journalism contain professional cultures – that of the politician and party activist and that of the professional journalist – which include shared values and related canons of practice. Increasingly in the last few decades, these professional cultures have conflicted with the needs of the institutions they inhabit as the positions of the institutions have weakened. [. . .]

[. . .]

But there is a more fundamental set of tensions that structure the political media complex, and these are found in the interaction between the two institutions and their respective professionals. When we try to understand why campaigns are the way they are, or why political journalism has taken on its present characteristics, and how all of this came to be, we are drawn to these interactions in the vortex of the political-media complex. This is where institutional needs clash in a dynamic of both cooperation and competition, where there is an unending spiral of manipulation and resistance within a struggle for dominance, where politicians court the favorable attention of journalists while manipulating them and seeking ways to circumvent their mediation and reach the public directly, and where journalists seek access and cooperation from politicians while attempting to assert their independence and imperium ever more aggressively. And this occurs within the framework of institutions that have been weakened and challenged by a host of changes to which they constantly struggle to adapt.

The quality of political communication as it is shaped by the institutional needs and goals that interact within the political-media complex has received little praise and frequent condemnation. A common judgment is that despite the proliferation of information and news sources, voters are deluged with appeals and accounts that are not very helpful to responsible decision making, leaving them perhaps less informed than before (e.g., Bennett, 1991, 1992; Entman, 1989; Patterson, 1993). And the public's response has not been encouraging. Candidates and reporters alike have been blamed for high levels of cynicism and low levels of interest in campaigns.

An institutional perspective allows us to see how the actions and decisions of individual journalists, candidates, and others, and the events of particular campaigns, reflect at least in part these powerful underlying institutional forces. And this gives us a somewhat different viewpoint when we try to imagine how one or another feature of present practice might be changed for the better, or when we attempt to predict the future course of campaigning and political journalism. [. . .]

References

Bennett, W.L. (1991) *The Governing Crisis: Media, Money and Marketing in American Elections.* New York: St Martin's.

Bennett, W.L. (1992) 'White Noise: The Perils of Mass Mediated Democracy', *Communication Monographs, 59,* 401–406.

Blumler, J.G. (1990) Elections, the Media and the Modern Publicity Process. In Ferguson, M. (ed.), *Public Communication: The New Imperatives.* London: Sage, pp. 101–113.

Blumler, J.G., & Gurevitch, M. (1995). *The Crisis of Public Communication.* London: Routledge.

Entman, R.M. (1989) *Democracy Without Citizens: Media and the Decay of American Politics.* New York: Oxford University Press.

Franklin, B. (1994) *Packaging Politics: Political Communications in Britain's Media Democracy.* London: Edward Arnold.

Garnham, N. (1992) The Media and the Public Sphere. In C. Calhoun (ed.) *Habermas and the Public Sphere.* Cambridge: MIT Press, pp. 359–376.

Gurevitch, M. and Blumler, J.G. (1990) Comparative Research: The Extending Frontier. In D.L. Swanson and D. Nimmo (eds), *New Directions in Political Communication.* Newbury Park, CA: Sage, pp. 305–325.

Patterson, T.E. (1993) *Out of Order.* New York: Knopf.

Sigelman, L., & Bullock, D. (1991) 'Candidates, Issues, Horse Races, and Hoopla: Presidential Campaign Coverage, 1888–1988', *American Politics Quarterly,* 19, 5–32.

Chapter 8

Jay Blumler and Dennis Kavanagh

THE THIRD AGE OF POLITICAL COMMUNICATION
Influences and features

Source: Jay G. Blumler and Dennis Kavanagh (1999) 'The Third Age of Political Communication: Influences and Features', *Political Communication*, 16: 209–30.

[. . .]

SCHOLARS INCREASINGLY ARE sensing that profound changes in both society and the media may be giving birth to a new form of political communication system that is qualitatively different from its predecessors (Cook, 1998; Norris, Curtice, Sanders, Scammell, & Semetko, 1999; Wyatt, 1998). Not only are the avenues of political communication multiplying in a process that is becoming more diverse, fragmented, and complex, but also, at a deeper level, power relations among key message providers and receivers are being rearranged; the culture of political journalism is being transformed; and conventional meanings of "democracy" and "citizenship" are being questioned and rethought (Brants, 1998; Buckingham, 1997). The research community is therefore challenged to keep up with the evolving trends and avoid overcommitment to superseded paradigms. [. . .]

[. . .]

The phasing of political communication systems

Political communication in many democracies appears to have passed through three successive (if overlapping) phases in the postwar period. Each has pivoted on a distinctive organizing principle, although other influences have prevailed as well, and each has been caught up in a characteristic paradox.

Age 1

The first two decades after World War II have been termed "the 'golden age' of parties" (Janda & Colman, 1998, p. 612). In this period, the political system was regarded as the prime source of initiatives and debate for social reform; the party system was closely articulated to entrenched cleavages of social structure; and many voters related to politics through more or less firm and long-lasting party identifications. At this time of "high modernism" (as it has also been called), "Consensus was accompanied by a high level of confidence in political institutions" (Hallin, 1992, p. 17), and much political communication was subordinate to relatively strong and stable political institutions and beliefs. [. . .]
   [. . .]

Age 2

A new era dawned in the 1960s when limited-channel nationwide television became the dominant medium of political communication, while the grip of party loyalty on voters was loosening. Four transformations resulted.

One was a reduction in the frequency of selective patterns of exposure to party propaganda, since a medium of even-handed news, several-sided discussion, and free slots for most parties (paid commercials in the United States) afforded less scope for viewers consistently to tune in to their own side of the argument. Selectivity was also undermined by a decline in newspapers, clubs, and other organizations attached to the parties, especially in continental Europe (Kirchheimer, 1966).

Second, a medium constitutionally mandated to such nonpartisan norms as fairness, impartiality, neutrality, and measured choice was now the central platform for political communication. [. . .]

Third, television enlarged the audience for political communication by penetrating a sector of the electorate that was previously more difficult to reach and less heavily exposed to message flows. [. . .]

Fourth, a crucial channel of [. . .] short-term influences was thought to be television news. Its values and formats therefore had an increasingly far-reaching impact on the scheduling of political events (coordinated with news bulletin timings), the language of politics (through the crafting of soundbites and cultivation of more intimate styles of address), and the personalization of its presentation (with a sharper focus on top leaders).

To cope with the demands of a new medium, its larger audience, and a more mobile electorate, the parties had to work harder and learn new tricks. They accordingly adopted an array of tactics to get into the news, shape the media agenda, and project a preplanned "line" in press conferences, briefings, interviews, and broadcasts. [. . .]

Age 3

This still emerging phase is marked by the proliferation of the main means of communication, media abundance, ubiquity, reach, and celerity. [. . .]

New patterns and adaptations ensue for all involved in the political communication process [. . .]. In gist, it changes how people receive politics in ways that have been little studied so far. To politicians, the third-age media system must loom like a hydra-headed beast, the many mouths of which are continually clamoring to be fed. [. . .] For journalists, the news cycle has accelerated, since more outlets combined with increased competition across them piles pressure on all involved to keep the story moving and to find fresh angles on it. [. . .]

This age is more complex than its predecessors, molded more by conflicting cross currents than by a dominant tendency. Political communication during it is likely to be reshaped by five main trends, not all in harmony with each other. [. . .]

[. . .]

Intensified Professionalization of Political Advocacy. As the "third age" proceeds, the dependence of politicians on professional assistance is likely to increase further. [. . .] The new recruits (skilled personnel) have skills specific to the media and persuasive communications [. . .] they are the new elites of Anglo-American politics, the products of a media-saturated style of politics. They represent the politicians' professional approach to managing the media and resisting pressure from them. [. . .]

[. . .]

Increased Competitive Pressures. As media abundance advances, politics intended to inform, reveal, or persuade must vie for the attention of editors, reporters, and audiences in a far more competitive environment. [. . .]

[. . .]

Anti-Elitist Popularization and Populism. As a result of a third major development, the public sphere appears differently peopled than in the past. However protean and inchoate, this trend may be transforming relationships between political communicators and their publics.

Until recently, much political communication was a top-down affair. [. . .]

[. . .]

Since the early 1990s, however, strong currents of populism have been suffusing the world of both politics and the media. [. . .] In such conditions, paternalistic discourse is no longer an option. [. . .]

But whether the populist groundswell will mainly be empowering or merely symbolic, mainly redemptive or corrosive for civic communication, could depend in the end on the aims of its producers and on how it is received by audiences— on both of which we badly need more and better research. [. . .]

[. . .]

Centrifugal Diversification. A fourth area of potential consequence concerns the relationship of communication to community. In the heyday of Age 2, much political communication was centripetal. The most attractive mass medium offered relatively little choice. [. . .]

[. . .]

In the abundance of Age 3, however, there are more channels, chances, and incentives to tailor political communication to particular identities, conditions, and tastes. This reduces the size of the mass audience, both generally and for news. It facilitates the diversification of political communication forms (i.e., mass mediated vs. computerized; "old" vs. "new" political journalism; nationwide vs. subcultural discourse). It creates openings for previously excluded voices to express their views and perhaps even be noticed by mainstream outlets. It creates opportunities for would-be persuaders to seek more efficient impact by selectively focusing their communications on preferred population sectors. [. . .] In most modern societies, then, centripetal communication is to some extent retreating and centrifugal communication is advancing.

It is difficult to tell how far this process will extend and what its main political communication consequences could be. Its impact may vary cross nationally, depending on how far the societies concerned are themselves culturally segmented and polarized. For political communication research, however, the implications could be unsettling. The presumption of mass exposure to relatively uniform political content, which has underpinned each of the three leading paradigms of political effect—agenda setting, the spiral of silence, and the cultivation hypothesis—can no longer be taken for granted. At present, the following tendencies seem most discernible.

1. *Restored prospects of selective exposure.* These occur via the individual's own attitudes and allegiances, provided that they are absorbed into his or her social identity and that they are shared sufficiently widely to encourage and sustain media outlets catering to them.

2. *Readier pursuit of identity politics.* [. . .] in recent times, subgroup identities have become more meaningful for many people, have thrown up prominent spokespersons, and have given rise to new political claims and conflicts. Media abundance plays a part in this by providing more channels through which such claims can be voiced and support for them mobilized. [. . .]

3. *Multiplication of political agendas.* In the past, journalists were often consonant in their selection and framing of major political events and issues (Noelle-Neumann & Mathes, 1987). Although this may still be largely true of their responses to the top stories of the day, such conformism is less characteristic of certain issue areas that have attracted the concerted political and media strategies of astute protest groups.

4. *More cyber politics.* (The) impression of marginality could be fast overtaken [. . .] by the dynamic increase in Internet subscriptions, patronage, and applications in many Western societies. [. . .]

Thus, cyber politics could develop significantly in at least three directions in the not too distant future. It could become a campaign medium in its own right, not necessarily displacing but supplementing more traditional ones. It could become an important vehicle of interest group solidification and mobilization within and across national boundaries. And it could diversify the exposure to political communication of those regular users who enjoy exploring the access to a wider range of views and perspectives that the Internet affords. [. . .]

5. *Widening cultural gaps in society.* Bigger differences between those with access to ample stores of political material and the informationally deprived could arise from fragmentation of the news audience. [. . .]

6. *Reduced influence of "the political-media complex."* The combined inroads of populist programming, minority media, and cyber politics could gradually reduce the proportion of time and space for news events and opinions shaped by the political-media complex (Swanson, 1997). [. . .]

Audience Reception of Politics. [. . .] media abundance changes how political messages are received by audience members. A "pick and choose" culture emerges. [. . .]

All of this appears a quite new "ballgame" in which three significant issues arise:

1   *Audience structure.* Katz (1987) foresees a radical segmentation of the political audience arising from multichannel abundance, increased competition, and the disintegration of public service broadcasting. [. . .] Schulz (1997), however, finds little evidence of such segmentation in an analysis of the television channels patronized regularly and frequently by the members of a large German sample surveyed in 1995. Their viewing repertoires were more overlapping than segmented, often spanning both the public and private networks.

2   *Political effects.* [. . .] Media expansion and differentiation allow a wide range of problems, viewpoints, and informed analyses to be expressed somewhere in the system. And so long as that openness exists, not everyone has to pay attention to the public debate all the time: Extensive amounts of information and reasonable conclusions from it will trickle out through opinion leaders and cue givers to ordinary citizens, who can deliberate about it in their own face-to-face groups of family, friends, and coworkers. Schulz (1997), however, drawing on associations between cynicism and several different measures of exposure to television [. . .], considers that the new system encourages a "fragmented and 'peripheral' style of information reception" in which people are exposed to "the more spectacular, sensational and negative aspects of politics" and pick up "bits and pieces from different programs without contextualizing and digesting the information properly". But Bennett (1998) argues that public cynicism is less a response to television than to governments' inability to serve the needs of a less coherent and assured socioeconomic order.

3   *Popularization.* On the one side, there are what might be termed "critical traditionalists," who apply terms such as tabloidization and dumbing down to recent developments in the news media (Franklin, 1997). On the other side, what might be termed "popular culturalists" look more positively on the same developments [. . .]

References

Bennett, W.L. (1998) 'The civic culture: Communication, identity, and the rise of lifestyle politics', *PS: Political Science and Politics*, *31*, 741–762.

Brants, K. (1998) 'Who's afraid of infotainment?', *European Journal of Communication*, *13*, 315–335.

Buckingham, D. (1997) 'News media, political socialization and popular citizenship: Towards a new agenda', *Critical Studies in Mass Communication*, *14*, 344–366.

Cook, T.E. (1998) *The Future of the Institutional Media and the Future of American Politics*. Paper presented at the "Mediated Politics" workshop, University of Pennsylvania, Philadelphia.

Franklin, B. (1997). *Newszak and News Media*. London: Arnold.

Hallin, D.C. (1992) 'The passing of the "high modernism" of American journalism', *Journal of Communication*, 42(3), 14–25.

Janda, K., & Colman, T. (1998). 'Effects of party organization on performance during the "golden age" of parties', *Political Studies*, 46(3), 611–632.

Katz, E. (1987) *The New Media and Social Segmentation*. Paper presented at the "New Media and Conceptions of Communication" symposium, Heidelberg, Germany.

Kirchheimer, O. (1966) The transformation of the West European party system. In J. Palombara & M. Weiner (eds.), *Political Parties and Political Development* (pp. 177–200). Princeton, NJ: Princeton University Press.

Noelle-Neumann, E. & Mathes, R. (1987) 'The "event as event" and "the event as news": The significance of "consonance" for media effects research', *European Journal of Communication*, 2, 391–414.

Norris, P., Curtice, J., Sanders, D., Scammell, M. & Semetko, H. (1999) *On Message: Communicating the Campaign*. London: Sage.

Schulz, W. (1997) 'Changes of the mass media and the public sphere', *Javnost—The Public*, 4, 57–69.

Swanson, D.L. (1997). 'The political-media complex at 50: Putting the 1996 presidential campaign in context', *American Behavioral Scientist*, 40, 1264–1282.

Wyatt, R.O. (1998) 'After 50 years, political communication scholars still argue with Lazarsfeld', *Journal of Communication*, 48(2), 146–156.

SECTION 2

Media and political advocates

I N EXPLORING THE THEME of 'the media and political advocates', this
section seeks to highlight the ways in which the relationship between the media
and political actors provides an insight into the production of political news and
other content. If the previous section focused on bigger questions, this section offers
a set of extracts that look at specific relationships and the outcomes of those
relationships for understanding content.

The first piece by **Blumler and Gurevitch** is a study of the relationship between
journalists and politicians, the ways in which that relationship is established and
maintained, and how the tensions that derive from it are or can be resolved. The
relationship that their extract deals with is also at the heart of two other extracts,
those from **Cook** and **Hallin**. Cook's piece examines how we need to look at the
media as political institutions, not as separate from the political process, or simply
reflecting on that process, but actually being a party to it. The ways in which the
media deal with politicians and news makes them such institutions. Hallin's piece
– on the media and the coverage of Vietnam – explores the relationship between
media and politicians from a different angle altogether. By asking why opinion against
the war turned at a particular moment in time, Hallin touches on the links between
media and politicians, and the ways in which opinion moves back and forth between
the two.

The remaining four pieces also explore how the relationship between the media
and political actors impacts on news content, and how different actors can play a
part in the news-making process by careful and judicious use of different sources
of power. **Wolsfeld** draws on his study of Palestinians and the first intifada in their
struggles against the Israeli authorities; while **Schlesinger and Tumber** focus on
organisations in the public justice system. Both extracts illustrate how organisations
'outside' the 'traditional' political system can often offer challenges to it.

Both **Gandy** and **Manheim** show how actors use the media for their own purposes. Gandy sets out how journalists are 'subsidised' by having information made available to them for their use, whilst Manheim illustrates the growing interest in 'strategic public diplomacy', and the ways in which individuals, organisations and even governments can make judicious use of the media by careful public relations activities in order to generate positive images and opinion.

Overall, this section shows how the media are implicated in the political process and, while they can often have their way in the coverage of politics, they too can be used by those who are determined and knowledgeable about how to use them.

Chapter 9

Jay Blumler and Michael Gurevitch

POLITICIANS AND THE PRESS
An essay on role relationships

Source: Jay G. Blumler and Michael Gurevitch (1995) 'Politicians and the Press: An Essay on Role Relationships', in J. Blumler and M. Gurevitch, *The Crisis of Public Communication*, London: Routledge, pp. 25–44. First published in D.D. Nimmo and K.R. Sanders (eds) (1981) *Handbook of Political Communication*, Beverly Hills, CA: Sage, pp. 467–93.

[. . .]

An expanded framework

THE PRODUCTION OF POLITICAL communications is inherently complex. [. . .] we have developed an [. . .] analytical framework couched in the following summary terms: media-disseminated political communications derive from interactions between (1) two sets of mutually dependent and mutually adaptive actors, pursuing divergent (though overlapping) purposes, whose relationships with each other are typically (2) role-regulated, giving rise to (3) an emergent shared culture, specifying how they should behave towards each other, the ground rules of which are (4) open to contention and conflicting interpretation, entailing a potential for disruption, which is often (5) controlled by informal and/or formal mechanisms of conflict management. The following [. . .] outline some implications of each of these elements in turn.

Dependence and adaptation

Political communication originates in mutual dependence within a framework of divergent though overlapping purposes. Each side of the politician-media professional partnership is striving to realize certain goals *vis-à-vis* the audience; yet it cannot pursue them without securing in some form the co-operation of the other side. Sometimes they share certain goals – for example, addressing, and sustaining credibility with, as large an audience as they can. Usually the actors' purposes are in some tension as well: journalists are primarily aiming to hold the attention of a target audience through some mixture of alerting, informing, and entertaining them; politicians are primarily trying to persuade audience members to adopt a certain view of themselves, or of their parties or factions, and of what they are trying to achieve in politics.

Whatever the exact mixture of goals, each side needs the other and must adapt its ways to theirs. Politicians need access to the communication channels that are controlled by the mass media, including the hopefully credible contexts of audience reception they offer. Consequently, they must adapt their messages to the demands of formats and genres devised inside such organizations and to their associated speech styles, story models and audience images. Likewise, journalists cannot perform their task of political scrutiny without access to politicians for information, news, interviews, action and comment [. . .]

Thus, each side of the prospective transaction is in a position to offer the other access to a resource it values. The mass media offer politicians access to an audience through a credible outlet, while politicians offer journalists information about a theatre of presumed relevance, significance, impact and spectacle for audience consumption. Because such resources are finite, however, rivals inside each camp compete more or less keenly for them, further strengthening the pressures promoting a mutual adaptation. The scope and terms of politicians' access to the media depend not only on conventional limitations of time and space but also on the 'threshold of tolerance' audiences may have towards political messages. So in competing for favourable attention in the preferred 'slots', politicians adjust to perceived media values and requirements. But politicians also command scarce resources. Not only is the amount of informational raw material they can supply limited; it may also vary in quality – for example, a strong leak on a headline development is worth more than a speculative rumour about a more technical issue from a lower-placed source. Politicians are therefore in a position, especially when newsworthy, to 'ration the goodies', use them as bargaining counters, and direct reporters' attention to their pet themes. 'Pack journalism', which stems from a subtle mixture of (1) uncertainty about what really counts as political news and (2) anxiety not to miss something the competition will be carrying, intensifies the ensuing adaptations.

Of course, many of these factors operate as variables, not constants. Politicians vary in their need for media publicity. Similarly, journalists will be more anxious to cover certain politicians and events than others. [. . .] But despite such sources of variation, the forces of mutual dependence, competition and adaptation will tend most formatively to shape political communication about precisely those personalities and situations that receive the heaviest and most regular coverage in political news. [. . .]

Role relationships

The recurrent interactions that result in political communication for public consumption are negotiated, not by unsocialized individuals, but by individuals in roles whose working relationships are consequently affected by normative and institutional commitments. [. . .] What theoretical advantages flow from treating political communicators as occupants of roles, the terms of which guide their own behaviour and shape their relationships with and expectations of their counterparts in the message production process? These may be outlined from three perspectives.

First, such an approach explains the behaviour of political communicators by locating them in their respective organizational settings, where their roles are chiefly defined and performed. In the case of political journalists, role-anchored guidelines serve many functions. They provide models of conduct to be observed when contacting politicians or appearing before the public as 'representatives' of their organizations, whose standards they are supposed to display (Kumar, 1975). They steer activity in countless daily routines. [. . .] They are a source of support when conflict erupts. [. . .]

[. . .]

In contrast to professional journalists, many practising politicians are only part-time communicators. Even so, their media arrangements are often tended by full-time specialists with corresponding roles to match – press officers, publicity aides, campaign managers, speech writers, and so on. And when functioning as communicators, politicians also act out certain role prescriptions themselves: 'representing' the interests of a party, government or department of state; responding to the expectations of political colleagues, with whom their reputations can be strengthened or weakened by the quality of their public appearances; and addressing the electoral audience in a certain style. [. . .]

[. . .]

Second, a focus on roles as shapers and regulators of behaviour also connects the interactions of media professionals and partisan advocates to the surrounding socio-political culture. This helps to explain their patterned continuity over time and their variety across diverse societies. Thus, mass media structures, their organizational and professional ideologies, and their specific work practices are in every society specific to and shaped by its culture. Likewise, the structure and operations of the political institutions of society are products of the same cultural forces. [. . .]

[. . .]

Third, a reference to role conceptualization clarifies the partial plausibility of the adversary and exchange models and helps to reconcile their apparent opposition. On the one hand, exchange mechanisms are set in motion when performance of role obligations on either side requires the enlisting of co-operation from the other. On the other hand, adversarial relations are triggered when the role obligations of the two sides are such as to bring them into collision course with each other. [. . .]

Underlying sources of conflict

However tightly woven, the web of mutual need and shared understandings cannot eliminate conflict. In the preceding discussion we have characterized politicians and journalists as locked into a complex set of transactions which, though mutually beneficial, also include potentials for disagreement and struggle. Underlying the resulting disputes are certain role-related, and therefore abiding, sources of conflict

– ones that continually arise because they are part and parcel of a system of inter-
acting role partners whose purposes to some extent diverge.

First, the participants' differing organizational and professional role commitments
give rise to the *cui bono?* question of political communication: Who is supposed to
be its main beneficiary? All commonly recognize that multiple purposes will be served,
but their priorities are inevitably different. Politicians tend to regard the political
communication process predominantly as an agency of persuasion, available to
themselves (and their competitors) for mobilizing public support for their own causes
and views, rather than as a channel for more detachedly educating and enlightening
the electorate. [. . .] For media professionals, the scales of ultimate aims are
differently balanced. It is true that they often acknowledge politicians' special access
rights, particularly at election time. [. . .] Yet the principle of service to the audience
is an integral part of the professional ideology of media personnel in liberal-
democratic societies and is supposed to override the service proffered to other
interests. [. . .]

[. . .]

Second, different perceptions of the division of labour in the production of political
messages generate the 'agenda-setting' question of political communication: Who
should determine which definitions of political problems citizens will think and talk
about most often? [. . .]

[. . .]

Third, different ways of interpreting each other's roles give rise to a 'fixing-of-
responsibility' question about political communication: Who is to blame when it
goes wrong and proves unsatisfactory? [. . .]

[. . .]

The systematization of political communication:
consequences and policy implications

[. . .]

What principal consequences flow from such a system for the production of
political messages in competitive democracies? The answers are not all reassuring:

1. The system gives a rather privileged position in political communication output
to the views of already established power holders. [. . .]

[. . .]

2. The other side of the coin is that leading politicians get their say almost entirely
through formats devised and controlled by journalists. [. . .]

[. . .]

3. Meanwhile, the needs of the audience may be relegated to a back seat in
the political communication bus. This is because, in their preoccupation with a
complex of conflicting interests, mutual dependencies, and problems of second-
guessing each other, the two main sets of communicators may well lose sight of the
ordinary voter's concerns and come to behave largely in those ways that seem likely
to forge the most convenient accommodation to the other side's behaviour (Blumler,
1977). Fortunately, potentially strong antidotes to such a tendency can be found
in the journalistic ethic of audience service. Yet even this may be impoverished in

application by the hold of sharply stereotypical impressions of what the average audience member is like as a news-processing animal. [. . .]

[. . .]

4. Finally, much of a society's political news 'conveys an impression of eternal recurrence' (Rock, 1973). [. . .] This is not to imply that innovatory impulses are often stifled at birth; but that they may have to fight a steep uphill battle even to stand a chance of being tried. [. . .]

[. . .]

Such formidable blockages to innovation are worrying, not because novelty should be valued for its own sake, but because freshness of approach is indispensable when tackling the inherently difficult tasks of making political information palatable and political argument comprehensible to large masses of voters. [. . .]

References

Blumler, J. (1977) The Election Audience: An Unknown Quantity? In RAI/Prix Italia. *TV and Elections*, Torino: Edizioni Rai Radiotelevisione Italiana.

Kumar, K. (1977) Holding the Middle Ground: The BBC, the Public and the Professional Broadcaster. In Curran, J., Gurevitch, M. and Woollacott, J. (eds), *Mass Communication and Society*. London: Edward Arnold.

Rock, P. (1973) News as Eternal Recurrence. In Chen, S. and Young, J. (eds), *The Manufacture of News: Social Problems, Deviance and the Mass Media*. London: Constable.

Chapter 10

Timothy Cook

GOVERNING WITH THE NEWS
The news media as a political institution

Source: Timothy Cook (1998) *Governing with the News. The News Media as a Political Institution,* Chicago, IL: University of Chicago Press, pp. 12, 14–15, 86–7, 110–12, 140.

INTRODUCTION: WHY DON'T WE CALL JOURNALISTS POLITICAL ACTORS?

Trouble in paradigms

[. . .]

NEWSMAKING AND ITS PLACE in the political system is best conceived not as a linear, unidirectional process but as interactive and interdependent, the result of what I have (elsewhere) termed the negotiation of newsworthiness. Political actors and journalists (and only occasionally citizens) interact in a constant but implicit series of negotiations over who controls the agenda, what can be asked, where and how, and what a suitable answer will be.[1]

[. . .] officials and journalists each control important resources because of the duality whereby news is to be both important and interesting. Politicians dictate conditions and rules of access and designate certain events and issues as important by providing an arena for them. Journalists, in turn, decide whether something is interesting enough to cover, the context in which to place it, and the prominence the story receives. [. . .]

[. . .]

Whereas much research on the purported bias of the news media end up examining individual journalists and their individually held values and attitudes, an institutional approach stresses the roles that journalists and political actors occupy within their respective political and social systems. (I seek to establish two things.) First, the news media are not simply distinct organizations but make up a collective institution – a site of systematized principles of action enduring across time and supervising a central area of social and political life. Second, journalists' activities are not merely constrained, they are enabled if not constituted by such an institutional approach. [. . .] the media are treated as an institution by government, with subsidies and privileges available to a class of publications. The pressures of uncertainty as well as the rise of professionalism also push news organizations [. . .] to look alike. We can then speak not of the news media as organizations or as institutions in the plural, but as a single – and quite singular – institution. [. . .]

[. . .]

CHAPTER 5 THE POLITICAL NEWS MEDIA

[. . .]
How do the news media enter into the authoritative allocation of values? One way is by reinforcing political power or otherwise providing resources to official actors to pursue their agendas. Thus, many studies have suggested that the political role of the news media lies in augmenting the reach of those who are already politically powerful. In that sense, they would be primarily influential in buttressing official authority and less in the allocation of values.

But matters are not as simple as that. The news media are at least partially independent from their sources in producing the content of the news. Consequently, they may be able to influence who is authoritative, what the values of politics are, and which allocations are made. The news media share a similar fate with the three constitutional branches being partially independent from and partially dependent on other institutions for themselves to accomplish their own task.

In that sense, we can and should go beyond Easton's definition to contend that the news media are not just political; in the modern United States, they have become part of government.[2] [. . .]

What contribution do the news media then make to the governing process? [. . .] On one hand, the news does indeed work to emphasize official action and thereby to implicate the news media more deeply into government. On the other, the news presents and interprets such actions by means of agreed-upon production values, which contain an implicit politics therein that is not always so beneficial to those official actors. Consequently the news is the result of recurring negotiations between sources and newspersons, the daily results of which favor only certain authoritative allocations of values. [. . .]

[. . .]

Conclusion

What then is the politics of the American news media? What "authoritative allocation of values" flow out of the news media's involvement in political processes? [. . .]

[. . .]

The most abiding political bias of the news is, of course, its primary concentration on the events, ideas, preoccupations, strategies, and politics of powerful officials. This gravitation toward officialdom is what enables the news media to be not merely political but governmental. The availability and presence of the news media, both within their institutions and within government as a whole, provokes officials to think of them as a potential help to accomplish their goals and to assist the conversion of the news media into an "institution of governance."

But, as we have seen, that assistance rarely comes without a cost. Most important, the by-and-large private ownership of the news media and the increasing profit orientation of news organizations provides something of a counterweight to official power. Journalists apply standards of newsworthiness beyond importance in order to keep an audience interested, and therefore, to keep the viewership tuned in or the readership continuing to buy papers. The authority of officials, as represented in the news, depends, in no small part, on the ability and willingness of those political actors to fit their activities to the production values of the news. If they do not – as we have noted above – they run the risk of losing control of their agenda and/or being portrayed in negative terms. [. . .]

[. . .]

The news media thereby enter into what political scientist Richard Neustadt described as "separated institutions sharing power." Although the news often acts to reinforce official power, it also provides incentives to act in only particular ways. This is not to say that reporters are thereby agents of the citizenry checking political authority: far from it. Journalists' professional autonomy means that they are often unwilling to pay much attention to readers' judgments, particularly since they can claim that while readers may know what information they like, they may not know what information they need.[3] [. . .]

[. . .]

In addition to the official leanings of the news, then, there are a number of other biases maintained by the commercial pressure to attract and keep audiences that affect the "authoritative allocation of values." [. . .]

[. . .]

Moreover, reporters' simultaneous needs to craft a story from the material provided to them while distancing themselves from the political responsibility of airing this information means that they find ways to show that they are not mere extensions of the government and that they, as argued above, must figure out how to turn unpromising material into a story that will be worth printing or airing. [. . .]

[. . .]

The consequence has been a greater negativity in the news across the board and in journalist-initiated stories in particular.[4] Even generally positive stories can and do call attention to the contrived nature of the staged events and/or raise doubts about the motives of the actors (usually laid at the feet of pure politics) and their effectiveness. [. . .]

[. . .]

CHAPTER 6 THE USES OF NEWS: THEORY AND
(PRESIDENTIAL) PRACTICE

Conclusion: newsmakers in government

[. . .] an awareness of newsworthiness influences decisions of others on what to push and what to do; and though many press officers are mere spokespersons and "flacks," they may have to be involved in policy decisions if they can provide reporters with useful information. These press officers may be in but not of the political institution, given that they exhibit different recruitment patterns and fill a "boundary role"[5] that builds bridges to another occupant of a boundary role, the reporter at the newsbeat. So, not only do the news media act as political institutions. Official roles for dealing with the media and consequently the news media's interactions with government have become institutionalized in their own right.

This pattern has [. . .] held for other agencies within the executive and the two other branches of the federal government. All political institutions have personnel to deal with and often to guide news media coverage in an optimal direction. The trick here is that the very desire to exploit the news media in pursuit of one's own policy goals may only implicate the needs of news deeper into the process of governing. When we talk about "governing with the news," then, it may be that newsmaking helps political actors in the short run but pushes them toward particular issues, concerns, and events and away from others, to the point that news values become political values, not only within the news media but within government as well. [. . .]

Notes

1   The phrase "negotiation of newsworthiness" is from my *Making Laws and Making News*, p. 169. A fuller discussion of this position is in ibid., Chap. 1; and first published in Nimmo, D.D. and Sanders, K.R. (eds), *Handbook of Political Communication*. Beverly Hills: Sage, 1981, pp. 467–493. For a good study of this process at work in campaigns, see F. Christopher Arterton, *Media Politics: The News Strategies of Presidential Campaigns.* (Lexington, MA: Lexington Books, 1984).

2   I do not want to get enmeshed in the ongoing terminological battles over the meanings of "politics," "the polity," "government," "governance," and "the state." The latter term owes some of its recent popularity in political science and political theory, at least, to the ambiguous way in which it has been defined. Almost all will agree with a definition of "the state" that contains a neo-Weberian understanding of centralized and rationalized bureaucracies that exercise a monopoly over regulation, particularly over the means of violence and coercion. See, e.g., John A. Hall and G. John Ikenberry, *The State* (Minneapolis MN: University of Minnesota Press, 1989), pp. 1–2. Yet the boundary between state and civil society has always been difficult to specify, and as such authors admit, the state's power may not emanate from the state itself but from its coordination of other sources of power. Although most authors would see the state as a subset of government, even deleting institutions such as the legislature, others would argue that "the state must be considered as more than the "government.'" Alfred Stepan, *The State and Society.* (Princeton: Princeton University Press, 1978), p. xii. Given the uncertainty of the term and the unclear payoff its use would provide, I will not discuss here the media's relationship to "the state."

3   Reporters' patronizing attitudes toward – and unwillingness to learn more about – their audiences are well described in Darnton, "Writing News and Telling Stories", *Daedalus*, 104(2); Gans, *Deciding What's News*. New York: Vintage, 1979, Chap. 7; and Burgoon, J.K. Burgoon, M. and Atkin, A., *World of the Working Journalist*. New York: Newspaper Advertising Bureau, 1982, Chap. 5.

4   Patterson, *Out of Order*, presents the best information on the rising negativity of the news media. Elsewhere, a team of authors, including myself, showed that the coverage of candidates during the 1992 election campaign was significantly more negative in journalist-initiated stories. Whether journalists initiated the story also was the most consistent predictor across media of the tone toward he candidate; Just *et al.*, *Crosstalk*, p. 111.

5   See Blumler and Gurevitch, "Politicians and the Press," in Nimmo, D.D. and Sanders, K.R. (eds), *Handbook of Political Communication*. Beverly Hills: Sage, 1981, p. 485.

Chapter 11

Daniel Hallin

WE KEEP AMERICA ON TOP
OF THE WORLD

Source: D. Hallin (1994) *We Keep America on Top of the World*, London: Routledge, pp. 52–5.

Conclusion: objective journalism and
political support

THE CASE OF VIETNAM [. . .] does not support the thesis that the American news media shifted to an oppositional role during the 1960s and 1970s. There was, to be sure, a very substantial turn toward more critical coverage of US policy in Vietnam. But it is hard to argue that journalists began to take on an actively oppositional role; the professional ideology of objective journalism and the intimate institutional connection between the media and government which characterized American journalism before the turbulence of the 1960s and 1970s both persisted more or less unchanged.

That conclusion made, however, we are left with an important problem of how to account for the substantial change in news content over the course of the Vietnam War. The puzzle is the more acute as we have already rejected the most obvious alternative explanation: the mirror theory that changing news content reflected a changing course of events.

As paradoxical as it may seem, the explanation for the media's changing level of support for political authority during the Vietnam War lies in their constant commitment to the ideology and the routines of objective journalism. Tom Wicker of the *New York Times*, referring to the early 1960s, once observed that 'objective journalism almost always favors Establishment positions and exists not least to avoid offense to them.'[1] He was, as we shall see, essentially correct. But from the point of view of a particular administration and its policies, objective journalism can cut both ways politically. A form of journalism which aims to provide the public with a neutral record of events and which, at the same time, relies primarily on government officials to describe and explain those events obviously has the potential to wind up as a mirror not of reality, but of the version of reality government officials would like to present to the public. At the same time, objective journalism involves a commitment to the political independence of the journalist and to the representation of conflicting points of view. The journalist's relation to political authority is thus not settled in any definite way by the professional norms and practices of objective journalism. It is on the contrary something of a paradox for the journalist, and it is resolved in different ways depending on political circumstances.

Consider the early period of the Vietnam War, when coverage was by most measures heavily favorable to administration policy. How could coverage so imbalanced be reconciled with a conception of journalism which requires neutrality and balance on controversial issues? The one-sided character of news coverage in this period is not hard to understand if one simply keeps in mind that Vietnam was not yet a particularly controversial issue within the mainstream of American politics. There were debates in Congress over certain tactical questions – whether the military should have greater freedom in selecting bombing targets, whether enough was being done on the political and diplomatic fronts, and so on. But on the broad outlines of US policy there was still relatively little disagreement among the major actors of American politics. To reflect the official viewpoint did not seem in this context to violate the norms of objective journalism: it did not seem to involve taking sides on a controversial issue.

This consensus, of course, did not last forever. Its erosion became serious politically, by most accounts, about the middle of 1967, and was accelerated by the Tet offensive.[2] Given this change in the parameters of political debate it is perfectly reasonable to expect that the media, without abandoning objective journalism for some more activist and anti-establishment conception of their role, would produce a far higher quantity of critical news coverage. Here, then, is an explanation for the change in Vietnam coverage that seems to fit nicely both with the data on news content and with our knowledge of the institutional relations between the media and political authority: *the change seems best explained as a reflection of and a response to a collapse of consensus – especially of elite consensus – on foreign policy*. One journalist expressed it this way:

> As protest moved from the left groups, the anti-war groups, into the pulpits, into the Senate – with Fulbright, Gruening and others – as it became a majority opinion, it naturally picked up coverage. And then naturally the tone of the coverage changed. Because we're an Establishment institution, and whenever your natural constituency changes, then naturally you will too.[3]

It is useful to imagine the journalist's world as divided into three regions, each of which involves the application of different journalistic standards. The first can be called the sphere of consensus. This is the region of motherhood and apple pie; in its bounds lie those social objects not regarded by journalists and by most of the society as controversial. Within this region journalists do not feel compelled to present opposing views, and indeed often feel it their responsibility to act as advocates or ceremonial protectors of consensus values. The discussion of patriotism that marked coverage of the homecoming of the hostages after the Iranian crisis is a good example. So is the journalists' defense of the motives of US policy in Vietnam. Within this region the media play an essentially conservative, legitimizing role; here the case for a Gramscian model of the media as maintainers of the hegemony of a dominant political ideology is strong.

Beyond the sphere of consensus lies what can be called the sphere of legitimate controversy. This is the region where objective journalism reigns supreme: here neutrality and balance are the prime journalistic virtues. Election coverage best exemplifies the journalistic standards of this region.

Beyond the sphere of legitimate controversy lie those political actors and views which journalists and the political mainstream of the society reject as unworthy of being heard. It is, for example, written into the Federal Communications Commission's (FCC) Fairness Doctrine that '[it is not] the Commission's intention to make time available to Communists or to the Communist viewpoints.'[4] Here neutrality once again falls away and the media become, to borrow a phrase from Parsons,[5] a 'boundary-maintaining mechanism:' they play the role of exposing, condemning, or excluding from the public agenda those who violate or challenge consensus values,[6] and uphold the consensus distinction between legitimate and illegitimate political activity. The anti-war movement was treated in this way during the early years of the Vietnam period; so were the North Vietnamese and the Viet Cong, except during a brief period when peace talks were near completion.

All of these spheres, of course, have internal gradations, and the boundaries between them are fuzzy. Within the sphere of legitimate controversy, for instance, the practice of objective journalism varies considerably. Near the border of the sphere of consensus journalists practice the kind of objective journalism that involves a straight recitation of official statements; farther out in the sphere of controversy they become more willing to balance official statements with reactions from the opposition or with independent investigations of controversial issues.

Using this framework the major changes in Vietnam coverage can easily be summarized. First, the opposition to the war expanded, moving from the political fringes of the society into its mainstream – into the electoral and legislative arenas, which lie within the sphere of legitimate controversy. As this occurred the normal procedures of objective journalism produced increasing coverage of oppositional viewpoints; when a presidential candidate comes out against the war, as occurred for the first time at the New Hampshire primary in 1968, the opposition becomes not only a respectable but an obligatory subject for news coverage. The reader may recall that Miller, Erbring, and Goldenberg found most criticism of political authorities reported in post-Watergate newspaper coverage to be criticism of one political authority by another – of Congress by the president and vice versa. [. . .] Similarly, the data on television coverage of Vietnam show 49 percent of all domestic criticism of administration policy attributed to other public officials, compared with 16 percent which came from reporters in commentaries and interpretive comments, and 35 percent from all other sources, including anti-war activists, citizens in the street, and soldiers in the field.

Second, the sphere of consensus contracted while the sphere of legitimate controversy expanded. Not only did the media report the growing debate over the war, they were also affected by it. As the parameters of political debate changed, so did the behavior of the media: stories that previously had been reported within a consensus framework came to be reported as controversies; subjects and points of view that had been beyond the pale in the early years came to be treated as legitimate news stories. Neither the institutional structure nor the professional ideology of the media had changed substantially, but in a changed political environment these could have very different implications for the reporting of the news. The media did not shift to an oppositional role in relation to American foreign policy during the Vietnam War, but they did start to treat foreign policy as a political issue to a greater extent than they had in the early 1960s. This meant that the journalistic standards they applied were less favorable to administration policy-makers.

In short, then, the case of Vietnam suggests that whether the media tend to be supporting or critical of government policies depends on the degree of consensus those policies enjoy, particularly within the political establishment. In a limited sense, the mirror analogy is correct.[7] News content may not mirror the facts, but the media, as institutions, do reflect the prevailing pattern of political debate: when consensus is strong, they tend to stay within the limits of the political discussion it defines; when it begins to break down, coverage becomes increasingly critical and diverse in the viewpoints it represents, and increasingly difficult for officials to control.[8] This does not necessarily imply that the media's role is purely passive or unimportant. It seems likely, on the contrary – though the question of media impact is beyond the scope of this study – that the media not only reflect but strengthen prevailing political trends, serving in a time of consensus as consensus-maintaining institutions and contributing, when consensus breaks down to a certain point, to an accelerating expansion of the bounds of political debate.[9] If this interpretation is correct, however, the media are clearly intervening and not – as the oppositional media thesis implies – independent variables in the process by which political support is generated or broken down. One must therefore look to other factors besides the structure and ideology of the media for the more basic causes of the current crisis of confidence in American politics. [. . .]

Notes

1   *On Press*, New York, Viking, 1978, pp. 36–7.
2   Schandler, H.Y. (1977) *The Unmaking of a President: Lyndon Johnson and Vietnam.* Princeton, NJ, Princeton University Press.
3   Max Frankel of the *New York Times*, quoted in T. Gitlin (1980) *The Whole World is Watching: Mass Media in the Making and Unmaking of the New Left.* New York, Ballantine, p. 205.
4   Quoted in Epstein, J. (1974) *News From Nowhere.* New York, Vintage.

5   Parsons, T. (1978) *The Social System*. New York, Free Press.
6   Cf. Gans, H.J. (1979) *Deciding What's News*. New York, Pantheon.
7   Cf. Tuchman, G. (1978) *Making the News*. New York, Free Press.
8   Gitlin makes a similar argument, op. cit., ch. 10.
9   See here the recent work of Zaller, J. (1992) *The Nature and Origins of Mass Opinion*. New York, Cambridge University Press.

Chapter 12

Philip Schlesinger and Howard Tumber

REPORTING CRIME
The media politics of criminal justice

Source: P. Schlesinger and H. Tumber (1994) *Reporting Crime. The Media Politics of Criminal Justice*, Oxford: Oxford University Press, pp. 16–21.

CHAPTER 1 NEWS SOURCES AND NEWS MEDIA

Rethinking the sociology of journalism

[. . .]

Source-media relations

WE HAVE SET OUT to analyse the behaviour of political actors as news sources. Crucial to the study of news sources are the relations between the media and the exercise of political and ideological power, especially, but not exclusively, by central social institutions that seek to define and manage the flow of information in contested fields of discourse.[1] Inevitably, (in the present study) we focus on the institutions of the state's criminal justice apparatus and how these compete for media attention, both amongst themselves and with other, more or less institutionalized, sources of information. Although, as we shall show, official bodies do occupy a dominant position in shaping crime-reporting (as is the case in other journalistic fields), we shall also demonstrate that a fuller understanding of competition amongst sources requires us also to pose questions about non-official sources – a theme hitherto neglected.

[. . .]

News sources as 'primary definers'?

Much cited in debate about the power of sources has been the concept of 'primary definition' proposed by Stuart Hall and his colleagues in an analysis of 'the social production of news' that centres upon crime coverage.[2] The media are analysed by Hall *et al.* in terms of a theory of ideological power underpinned by a Gramscian conception of the struggle for hegemony between dominant and subordinate classes in capitalist societies. According to them, 'It is this structured relationship-between the media and its [*sic*] "powerful" sources – which begins to open up the neglected question of the ideological role of the media. It is this which begins to give substance and specificity to Marx's basic proposition that "the ruling ideas of any age are the ideas of its ruling class."'[3]

Hall *et al.* argue that the media give access to those who enjoy 'accreditation'. This is a resource limited to certain social groups which enjoy a special status as sources in virtue of their institutional power, representative standing, or claims to expert knowledge. Specific examples given are government Ministers and Members of Parliament (MPs), and organized interest groups such as the Confederation of British Industry (CBI) or the Trades Union Congress (TUC). As a consequence of professional practices of ascertaining source credibility, the media are held to be structurally biased towards very powerful and privileged sources who become 'over-accessed':

> The result of the structured preference given by the media to the opinions of the powerful is that these 'spokesmen' become what we call the *primary definers* of topics [. . .] [which] [. . .] permits the institutional definers to establish the initial definition or *primary interpretation* of the topic in question. This interpretation then 'commands the field' in all subsequent treatment and sets the terms of reference within which all further coverage of debate takes place.[4]

Primary definition, then, involves a primacy both temporal and ideological. This is a very strong argument indeed. Taken at face value, its import is that the structure of access *necessarily* secures strategic advantages for 'primary definers', not just initially but also subsequently, for as long as a debate or controversy lasts. It also asserts that counter-definitions can never dislodge the primary definition, which consistently dominates.

The assumptions just discussed are open to various criticisms. Here we set them out as analytical points, but as the empirical findings of this and other studies show, our critique is grounded in the actual relations between news sources and news media.

First, the notion of 'primary definition' is more problematic than it seems. The broad characterization offered above does not take account of contention between official sources in trying to influence the construction of a story. In cases of dispute, say, amongst members of the same government over a key question of policy, who is the *primary* definer? Or – and it goes against the very logic of the concept – can there be more than one?[5]

Second, the formulation of Hall *et al.* fails to register the well established fact that official sources often attempt to influence the construction of a story by using 'off-the-record' briefings – in which case the primary definers do not appear directly as such, in unveiled and attributable form.[6]

A third point concerns the drawing of the boundaries of primary definition. Do these shift, and if so, why? Hall *et al.* make reference to MPs and Ministers. Presumably, primary definition is intended to include all consensually recognized 'representative' voices. But access to the media is plainly not equally open to all members of the political class: Prime Ministers and Presidents routinely command disproportionate attention and politicians may also use media strategies to gain attention for themselves in competition with others.[7] There is nothing in the formulation of primary defining that permits us to deal with such inequalities of access amongst the privileged themselves.

Fourth, there is the unconsidered question of longer-term shifts in the structure of access. Writing in the late 1970s, it may have been obvious to talk of the CBI and TUC as major institutional voices. But with the disappearance of corporatism in Britain under successive Conservative governments, such interests have lost their one-time prominence. What this point reveals is the tacit assumption that certain forces are permanently present in the power structure. It is thus an atemporal model, underpinned by the notion that primary definers are simply 'accredited' to their dominant ideological place in virtue of an institutional location. But when these are displaced by new forces and their representatives, it becomes essential to explain their emergence.

Hall *et al.* go on to locate the media in the power structure thus:

> The media, then, do not simply create the news; nor do they simply transmit the ideology of the 'ruling class' in a conspiratorial fashion. Indeed, we have suggested that, in a critical sense, the media are frequently not the 'primary definers' of news events at all but their structured relationship to power has the effect of making them play a crucial secondary role in *reproducing* the definitions of those who have privileged access, as of right, to the media as 'accredited sources'. From this point of view, in the moment of news production, the media stand in a position of structured subordination to the primary definers.[8]

Thus, the media are characterized as a subordinate site for the reproduction of the ideological field; in effect, they are conceived as 'secondary definers'.

This now brings us to a fifth objection, which is that Hall *et al.* tend to overstate the passivity of the media as recipients of information from news sources: the flow of definitions is seen as moving uniformly from the centres of power to the media. Within this conceptual logic, there is no space to account for occasions on which media may themselves take the initiative in the definitional process by challenging the so-called primary definers and forcing them to respond. Relevant examples would be cases of investigative journalism dealing with scandals inside the state apparatus or in the world of big business, or when leaks by dissident figures force out undesired and unintended official responses, or when accidents occur and official figures are caught on the hop.[9] At times, too, it is the media that crystallize slogans or pursue campaigns that are subsequently taken up by the would-be primary definers because it is in their interests to do so.[10] Aside from seeing the media as excessively passive, this way of conceiving of their relations to news sources tends to elide the variations that exist within and between different news media. Access for 'alternative' viewpoints differs as between the press and television, and indeed, as between different newspapers.[11]

A sixth criticism concerns how the conception of 'primary definition' renders largely invisible the activities of sources that attempt to generate 'counter-definitions'. This rules out any analysis of the process of *negotiation* about policy questions between powerholders and their opponents that may occur prior to the issuing of what are assumed to be primary definitions. As we shall see, thinking about such brokerage as taking place within a policy arena does complicate the picture, even though access to that political space is undoubtedly limited. The essentially structuralist approach of Hall *et al.*, however, is profoundly incurious about the processes whereby sources may engage in ideological conflict prior to, or contemporaneous with, the appearance of 'definitions' in the media. It therefore tends to ignore questions about how contestation over the presentation of information takes place within institutions and organizations reported by the media, as well as overlooking the concrete strategies pursued as they contend for space and time.

Although Hall *et al.*'s approach fails to deal with a number of conceptual difficulties, there is still undoubtedly a strong case for arguing that the organization of journalistic practice *generally* promotes the views and interests of authoritative sources. This is a paramount finding of much of the sociology of journalism [. . .]. The key point is that because the conception of 'primary definition' resolves the question of source power on the basis of structuralist assumptions, it closes off any engagement with the dynamic processes of contestation in a given field of discourse.[12] It has the signal advantage of directing our attention to the exercise of definitional power in society, but it offers no account of how this is achieved as the outcome of strategies pursued by political actors. That is because 'primary definers' are seen as simply guaranteed access to the news media in virtue of their structural position. To sum up: 'primary definition', which ought to be an empirically ascertainable outcome, is held instead to be an a priori effect of privileged access.

However, the massive investments that have taken place in political public relations and marketing both by state agencies, and by a variety of other interests that aim to establish themselves as authoritative news sources, do require some explanation. Thinking of 'primary definition' as a resolved matter makes us incurious about source competition and what its implications for the workings of the public sphere might be. [. . .]

Notes and references

1   In personal correspondence reacting to an earlier version of this chapter, Herbert Gans notes: 'Emphasizing the role of sources is the best way, or perhaps the only one, to connect the study of journalism to the larger society . . .' (22 July 1988).

2   Hall, S., Critcher, C., Jefferson, T., Clarke, J., and Roberts, B., *Policing the Crisis: Mugging, the State, and Law and Order.* (London: Macmillan, 1978).

3   Ibid. 58.

4   Ibid., authors' emphases.

5   A classic instance of policy divisions within the state machine is illustrated in Daniel Hallin's study of the Vietnam war and the news media. See Hallin, D., *The 'Uncensored*

War': The Media and Vietnam (Oxford: Oxford University Press, 1986). More recently David Miller has shown the problems of applying the concept of 'primary definition' to a divided officialdom in Northern Ireland. See Miller, D., 'Official Sources and "Primary Definition": The Case of Northern Ireland', *Media, Culture and Society*, 15 (1993), 385–406.

6   The story of the prime-ministerial voice of the Thatcher years, Bernard Ingham, offers some instructive insights in this regard. See Harris, R., *Good and Faithful Servant: The Unauthorized Biography of Bernard Ingham* (London: Faber & Faber, 1990).

7   See Seymour-Ure, C., 'Prime Ministers' Reactions to Television: Britain, Australia and Canada', *Media, Culture and Society*, 11 (1989), 307–25; Hinkley, B., *The Symbolic Presidency: How Presidents Portray Themselves* (New York: Routledge, 1990).

8   Hall *et al.*, *Policing the Crisis*, 59, authors' emphasis.

9   For relevant studies see Murphy, D., *The Stalker Affair and the Press* (London: Unwin Hyman, 1991); Molotch, H. and Lester, M., 'News as Purposive Behavior: On the Strategic Use of Routine Events, Accidents and Scandals', *American Sociological Review*, 39 (1974), 101–12; Tumber, H., '"Selling Scandal': Business and the Media", *Media, Culture and Society*, 15: 345–61.

10   E.g. the press campaign over the 'seal plague' and its political impact. See Anderson, A., 'Source Strategies and the Communication of Environmental Affairs', *Media, Culture and Society*, 13 (1991), 459–76.

11   For relevant studies see Curran, J., 'Culturalist Perspectives of News Organizations: A Reappraisal and a Case Study', in Ferguson, *Public Communication*, 114–34; McNair, B., *Images of the Enemy* (London: Routledge, 1988); Schlesinger, P., Murdock, G., and Elliott, P., *Televising 'Terrorism': Political Violence in Popular Culture* (London: Comedia, 1983).

12   Hall has maintained his views on 'primary definition'. In the opening essay in a critical collection aimed at giving an 'adequate understanding' of media power to those at the receiving end, he put the argument in a less qualified, and therefore more revealing way: 'Some things, people, events, relationships always get represented: always centre-stage, always in the position to define, to set the agenda, to establish the terms of the conversation. Some others sometimes get represented-but always at the margin, always responding to a question whose terms and conditions have been defined elsewhere: never "centred". Still others are always "represented" only by their eloquent absence, their silences: or refracted through the glance or the gaze of others.' See Hall, S., 'Media Power and Class Power', in J. Curran, J. Ecclestone, G. Oakley, and A. Richardson (eds), *Bending Reality: The State of the Media* (London: Pluto, 1986), 9. Although he concedes that some 'marginal categories get "accessed" all the time' (ibid.), this is basically seen as window-dressing and not as the outcome of source strategies.

Chapter 13

Gadi Wolsfeld

MEDIA AND POLITICAL CONFLICT
News from the Middle East

Source: Gadi Wolsfeld (1997) *Media and Political Conflict. News from the Middle East*, Cambridge: Cambridge University Press, pp. 1–5, 16, 30, 55–7, 63–5, 69.

Introduction

[. . .]

[**THE FOCUS IN MEDIA** and political conflict] will be on the role of the news media in *unequal political conflicts*. These include all public confrontations between a government and at least one other antagonist in which the state (or one state) has a significantly superior amount of coercive resources at its disposal. [. . .] the news media are most likely to have an impact on just these types of conflicts and this is the reason for this choice. Nevertheless, many conflicts fall under this category: protests, terrorist acts, riots, rebellions, revolutions, and all-out wars between powerful countries and weaker ones. [. . .]

[. . .]

The theoretical model presented here is called the *political contest model*. [. . .] the best way to understand the role of the news media in politics is to view the competition over the news media as part of a larger and more significant contests among political antagonists for political control. [. . .]

[. . .]

The model rests on five major arguments. First, that *the political process is more likely to have an influence on the news media than the news media are on the political process.*

[. . .]

[. . .]

This does not mean that news media do not also influence the political process. They help set the political agenda, they can accelerate and magnify political success and failure, they can serve as independent advocates for victims of oppression, they can mobilize third parties into conflict, and they are central agents in the construction of social frames about politics. The press serves as a powerful catalyst for political processes and it is therefore essential to understand better how this catalyst operates. This cycle of influence, however, usually begins within the world of politics.

The second argument is that *the authorities' level of control over the political environment is one of the key variables that determine the role of the news media in political conflict.* [. . .]

[. . .] When authorities succeed in dominating the political environment, the news media find it difficult to play an independent role. When [. . .] authorities lack or lose control it provides the news media with a much greater array of sources and perspectives from which to choose. This offers important opportunities for challengers to promote their own frames to the press.

The third major argument is that *the role of the news media in political conflicts varies over time and circumstances.* [. . .]

[. . .]

The fourth argument is that *those who hope to understand variations in the role of the news media must look at the competition among antagonists along two dimensions: one structural and the other cultural.* [. . .] They compete over *access* to the news media and they compete over *media frames.* The model will use two dimensions of analysis [. . .] The *structural dimension* looks at the extent of mutual dependence between the antagonists and each news medium to explain the power of each side in the transaction. This offers important insights about which political actors are most likely to gain access to the arena. The *cultural dimension* [. . .] focuses on how norms, beliefs, and routines all have an influence on the construction of media frames of conflict. [. . .] political conflicts are also struggles over meaning in which support within the news media can lead to higher levels of support.

The fifth [. . .] argument is that *while authorities have tremendous advantages over challengers in the quantity and quality of media coverage they receive, many challengers can overcome these obstacles and use the news media as a tool for political influence.* [. . .]

When taken as a whole, these five arguments suggest a process that is neither linear nor constant. [. . .]

CHAPTER 1   THE STRUCTURAL DIMENSION: THE STRUGGLE OVER ACCESS

Translating political power into power over the news media

[. . .]

[. . .]

The power of a given antagonist over a given news medium is based on the antagonist's level of perceived news value on the one hand and the antagonist's need for the news media on the other: The higher the value and the lower the need the greater the likelihood of an antagonist having an influence on the press. This influence

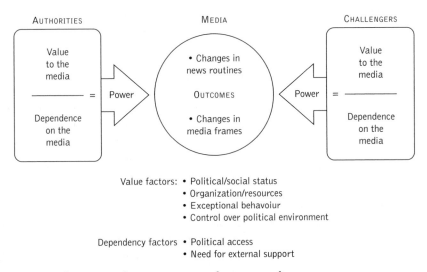

Figure 13.1   The power of antagonists over the news media

will be manifested in terms of more access and an increased ability to have one's preferred frames adopted by the news media. An outline of these initial principles is shown in Figure 13.1.

There are four major factors that increase the inherent news value of antagonists: their level of political and social status, their level of organization and resources, their ability to carry out exceptional behavior, and their level of control over the political environment. [. . .]

Summary

There are two [. . .] parts to this story. The first [. . .] is that political power brings important advantages to those who want to achieve exposure in the news media. Political power brings status, organization and resources, the ability to carry out exceptionally important behavior, and a reduced level of dependency on the press.

The second [. . .] is that despite these obstacles, challengers can and do compete. Authorities are never in full control of the political environment and these gaps provide important gateways for challengers to enter. The ability of the challengers to compete successfully with more powerful antagonists will depend to a large extent on their ability both to create and to exploit these opportunities. Some measure [of] success in this area will come to those challengers who can initiate and control events considered newsworthy, who find innovative ways to circumvent the powerful's control over the flow of information, and who make serious inroads among political elites.

Political successes and failures will often *precede* and *determine* success within the news media. The success of challengers in political mobilization will be reflected in their level of access to the news media that in turn will usually lead to a higher level of mobilization. Political control and control over the media are perpetually intertwined, for better, and for worse. [. . .]

[. . .]

CHAPTER 2 THE CULTURAL DIMENSION: STRUGGLE OVER MEANING

[. . .]

Summary

The cultural dimension of analysis attempts to explain the role of the news media in the struggle over meaning which characterises every political conflict. The media serve as *public interpreters* of events and as *symbolic arenas* for ideological struggle between antagonists. News stories about political conflicts are a form of social construction, in which some frames are more likely than others to serve as the underlying theme of news stories.

The construction of media frames of conflict is an interactive process in which the press attempts to find a narrative fit between incoming information and existing media frames. While the scope of incoming information is limited by both inside and outside forces, the data that do come in have an important influence on the construction process. The professional and political culture in each news medium also plays a significant role in this procedure by directing the search for relevant information and defining the range and tone of existing frames that can be applied to a given conflict.

As in the structural dimension [above], authorities have important advantages over theory challengers in the promotion of their frames to the news media. Their political power can be translated into cultural power through their ability to socialize journalists, and through their ability to plan, execute, and package events in ways that resonate within the professional and political culture of the news media. Challengers, however, can and do compete in the cultural realm. The news media have a large variety of frames waiting on the shelf for those activities who are skilled enough to construct an effective package and lucky enough to be promoting them at a time when the authorities are vulnerable to attack. In these cases the news media can play a critical role by legitimating oppositional frames that increase the status, resources, and power of challengers.

[. . .] The struggle over media frames is primarily a battle for political legitimacy, and the results of that contest have important consequences for the political process. [. . .]

CHAPTER 3 MEDIA INFLUENCE AND POLITICAL OUTCOMES

The power of the news media

Just as some political antagonists are more likely than others to have an influence on the news media, so some news media are more likely to have an influence on antagonists. The key to understanding these differences is to focus again on the notions of value and dependence. The greater the value of a given news medium to a particular antagonist and the smaller the medium's dependence on the information being provided, the more powerful the antagonist's influence. This point is made in graphic form in Figure 13.2, which provides the reverse perspective to the figure presented [on page 71 of this chapter]. [. . .]

[. . .]

Political outcomes

[. . .] The discussion (in this study) will focus [. . .] on transactional outcomes rather than effects. This formulation places antagonists on a more equal footing with the news media and serves to remind us that many outcomes are based on deliberate decisions made by the parties involved. The term "influence" is also preferable to the term "effect" because it too leaves more room for choice by those who are being influenced. [. . .]

[. . .]

Many commentators first think of the simplest form of influence, when antagonists react to the *presence of the news media*. [. . .]

[. . .]

There are [. . .] other types of outcomes associated with the news media that are more subtle. Antagonists are just as likely to react to *coverage in the news media*. [. . .] Many important types of adaptations are carried out in *anticipation of media coverage*. [. . .]

It is important to differentiate between those cases where the news media have played a *passive* and *transmissional* role in bringing about change among the antagonists and those in which they have played an *active* and *independent* role [. . .].

[. . .]

Whereas antagonists have every intention of influencing the news media, journalists normally do not have the same goals concerning antagonists. Their goal is to obtain as much information as possible and to produce the best news stories. The influence of the news media on the conflict is *usually unintended* by-products of behavior designed to achieve these goals [. . .].

[. . .]

There are two major classes of political outcomes that can be attributed to the news media. The first set can be placed under the rubric of *antagonist transformations*.

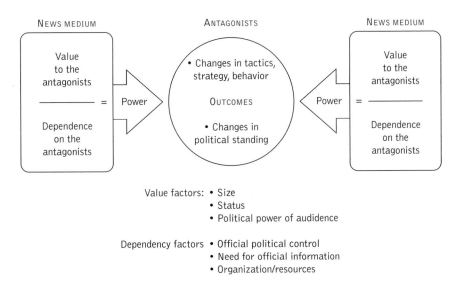

Figure 13.2   The power of the news media over antagonists

Changes in tactics, strategy, group solidarity, and the status of various leaders would all be included in this category. The second [. . .] has to do with *changes in political standing* of the antagonists. The most dramatic cases of such influence are those where the news media serve as equalizers by increasing the political status of challengers or by mobilizing third parties into the conflict. [. . .]

A continuum of media influence

It is useful to think of the role of the news media in political conflicts in terms of a continuum of independence. At one end [. . .] the news media serve as *faithful servants* to the authorities, constantly publicizing official frames of the conflict and ignoring or discrediting challengers. The middle of the continuum [. . .] the news media act as *semi-honest brokers* by offering challengers a significant amount of time and space to air their views against the authorities. The [. . .] end of this continuum [. . .] the news media plays a role of *advocates of the underdog* by amplifying the claims of challengers against authorities. [. . .]

[. . .]

Chapter 14

Oscar Gandy

BEYOND AGENDA SETTING
Information subsidies and public policy

Source: O.H. Gandy, Jr (1982) *Beyond Agenda Setting: Information Subsidies and Public Policy*, Norwood, NJ: Ablex Publishing Company, pp. 61–2, 73–5, 78.

[. . .]

CHAPTER 4 INFORMATION SUBSIDIES

Direct and indirect subsidies

AN **INFORMATION SUBSIDY** is an attempt to produce influence over the actions of others by controlling their access to and use of information relevant to those actions. This information is characterized as a subsidy because the source of that information causes it to be made available at something less than the cost a user would face in the absence of the subsidy.

[. . .] economic considerations enter into our use of information. Information is valued in terms of its expected utility in reducing uncertainty about some future action or decision. That utility estimation may be based on our perception of the credibility or reliability of the information source. Estimates of source credibility may be based in part on our knowledge of that source's personal interest in the information, such that information from interested sources is seen as less credible or less valuable than that from disinterested sources.

Because of the relationship between credibility and source interest, subsidy givers have an incentive to hide or disguise their relationship to the information they provide, in order to maximize its use by the relevant others. Scientific publications, legislative investigations, court testimony, and news reports are generally seen to be relatively objective, unbiased information channels. Subsidy givers have an incentive, therefore, to deliver information through these channels whenever the costs they face do not exceed the expected value, and less costly alternatives are not available.

While the ultimate target of an information subsidy effort may be an elected official or a government bureaucrat, a journalist may also be subsidized in order for that goal to be reached. That is, the delivery of an information subsidy through the news media may involve an effort that reduces the cost of producing news faced by a reporter, journalist, or editor. Faced with time constraints, and the need to produce stories that will win publication, journalists will attend to, and make use of, subsidized information that is of a type and form that will achieve that goal. By reducing the costs faced by journalists in satisfying organizational requirements, the subsidy giver increases the probability that the subsidized information will be used. The journalist receives a *direct* information subsidy, and the target in government receives an *indirect* subsidy when the information is read in the paper or heard on the news. [. . .]

[. . .]

Government information as subsidized news

[. . .] the PR aspect of government information activity is worthy of special attention. Although estimates vary widely, there are at least 3,300 government workers whose principal goal is the generation of public information that produces or reinforces an impression of governmental competence and efficiency, or results in the adoption of a preferred perspective on some policy.[1] At every level of government, in every agency, there are information specialists whose responsibility it is to ensure that the nation's public media carry the desired message forward to the general public, other government officials, and key corporate leaders who have a role to play in the formulation and implementation of public policy.

The flood of information from government agencies has grown so much in recent years that a thriving cottage industry has developed in Washington to digest this material for corporations affected by regulatory policies. Described as the "fourth and a half estate," 400 newsletters report on the day-to-day actions of government agencies and the courts that affect business and industry planning and operations. While they ostensibly perform a news function, their audience is primarily interested in only one side of regulatory issues . . .

[. . .]

At the executive level, the President and the White House staff are constantly aware of the need to influence the public agenda, to define issues, to specify policy options, and to create an impression of active competence. The modern Chief Executive uses a variety of information channels and subsidy techniques to deliver messages to the general public, or to key DMs (Decision Makers) at home or in foreign capitals. Formal channels include the press release, and its pseudo-event, the presidential press conference, or the daily briefings by the presidential press secretary. The press corp is supplied with summaries of speeches by key administration officials before their scheduled delivery, background or position papers on issues under discussion at the cabinet level, and on a somewhat less frequent basis, access to high-level officials for on-the-record interviews.

More frequently, information subsidies from the executive branch are delivered to the press in the form of leaks, off-the-record interviews, or back-grounders, which provide reporters with enough information to construct a news story without identifying its source. Although the press appears to give more attention to the activities of Congress, in that the sources for a greater proportion of newspaper content are congressional rather than executive,[2] the executive branch is said to spend "more on publicity, news, views, publications, and special pleadings than is spent to operate the entirety of the Legislative and Judicial branches."[3] [. . .]

[. . .]

There is every indication that the public information specialists, or "flacks," as they are called by less charitable observers, have gotten considerably more sophisticated in their use of public media channels to deliver an agency's message. The press release, the long-time standby of media sources, is said to be in a state of declining importance, replaced more and more by "more and more sophisticated tools – orchestrated advertising campaigns, television commercials, videotape cassettes, full-color brochures, and glossy magazines."[4] By taking policy matters to the "grass roots," agency information campaigns seek to influence all participants in the policy process. [. . .]

Notes

1   Steinberg, C. (1980) *The Information Establishment*. New York: Hastings House, page 39 in footnote 35.
2   Hess, S. (1981) *The Washington Reporters*. Washington, D.C.: The Brookings Institution.
3   Rivers, William L. (1970) *The Adversaries. Politics and the Press*. Boston, Mass.: Beacon Press, pp. 49–50.
4   Perry, James M. (1981) 'Washington PR staffs dream up ways to get agencies' stories out', *The Wall Street Journal* (May 23), 1.

Chapter 15

Jarol Manheim

STRATEGIC PUBLIC DIPLOMACY AND AMERICAN FOREIGN POLICY
The evolution of influence

Source: J.B. Manheim (1994) *Strategic Public Diplomacy and American Foreign Policy. The Evolution of Influence*, Oxford: Oxford University Press, pp.7, 9–10, 40–41.

Propaganda in the age of strategic communication

[. . .]

THE MOST CONTEMPORARY approach to this set of phenomena, and the one that will frame the balance of this book, is perhaps best described as an emphasis on *"strategic* public diplomacy." Strategic public diplomacy is the international manifestation of a relatively new style of information management that I have characterized elsewhere (1991), drawing on use of the term by some practitioners, as "strategic political communication." In this view, political communication encompasses the creation, distribution, control, use, processing, and effects of information as a political resource, whether by governments, organizations, groups, or individuals. *Strategic* political communication incorporates the use of sophisticated knowledge of such attributes of human behavior as attitude and preference structures, cultural tendencies, and media-use patterns – as well as knowledge of such relevant organizational behaviors as how news organizations make decisions regarding news content and how congressional committees schedule and structure hearings – to shape and target messages so as to maximize their desired impact while minimizing undesired collateral effects. Strategic public diplomacy, then, is public diplomacy practiced less as an art than as an applied transnational science of human behavior. It is, within the limits of available knowledge, the practice of propaganda in the earliest sense of the term, but enlightened by half a century of empirical research into human motivation and behavior.[1] [. . .]

[. . .]

From [these] studies and related literature, when considered in the aggregate, we know that:

- There exists a knowledge base in such disciplines as communication, journalism, political science, and psychology sufficient to guide relatively sophisticated efforts at strategic communication, which efforts can be employed to further the interests of governments in the international system.

- Such strategic approaches to public diplomacy, grounded in social scientific knowledge regarding attitude structures and change, media-use habits, and the like, have been demonstrated to be effective under certain circumstances, and ineffective under other, more or less clearly delineated ones.

- In particular, differential strategies, derived from such notions as cognitive balance theory (e.g., Festinger, 1957) or psychological inoculation (e.g., McGuire, 1964; Pfau and Kenski, 1990), have been identified and evaluated under differing conditions defined by characteristics of extant news portrayals of the image-object in question, and relevant case studies illustrating several such conditions have been developed.

- Increasing numbers of governments are coming to appreciate the potential utility of taking a more strategic view of their external communications. This assertion is supported by both aggregate statistics on such activity and by a small number of case studies of decision making in such countries as Nigeria, the Philippines, Pakistan, and South Korea.

- Specifically, many governments around the world (roughly 160 according to the most recent Department of Justice foreign agent registration records), in addition to their own trained staffs of public diplomatists, engage the services of US lobbyists, public relations consultants, and others to assist them in communicating with the US media and public. Some, but not all, of these efforts could be characterized as having "strategic communication" components.

- Typically, governments with special needs or problems, or with generally negative images, in the United States are the most likely to engage in US-directed strategic communication, but strategies are available for, and employed by, those with positive images as well.

- For a variety of reasons, ranging from the "obtrusiveness" of issues to the economics of newsroom decision making, strategic communication campaigns within the United States can be more effective when directed at issues or actors in foreign affairs than when employed in domestic politics.

- One condition under which the effectiveness of strategic public diplomacy is minimized or eliminated is where the communication strategy itself becomes widely known. In the United States, all such efforts become matters of public record. However, in part because journalists tend to underestimate their effectiveness, these activities are seldom widely publicized.

[. . .]

In formulating this analysis, I will draw upon a communication-based analytical framework that examines the internal decision making of, and the interactions among, the media, the public, and the makers of US foreign policy, all with an eye toward identifying the opportunities each creates for influencing the process by some interested outside party. [. . .] the central idea – that foreign policymaking is an exercise in domestic politics and occurs within a system that is open to purposeful and informed manipulation using basic social scientific knowledge – will illuminate the presentation from the outset.

[. . .]

[. . .] We begin by considering the role of image management in developing a policy environment supportive of US military intervention in the Persian Gulf.

Memories of the event are probably still strong enough – and the impressions of the event sufficiently potent – that each of us can still call to mind a repertoire of images associated with the Persian Gulf Conflict: Saddam Hussein petting a small boy who was a "guest" in Iraq. Former Ambassador April Glaspie under what amounted, nearly, to house arrest in the State Department, lest she comment on her final meeting with the Iraqi leader. George Bush trying to redefine the Gulf crisis as a *golf* crisis. The rockets' red glare over Baghdad, and Peter Arnett hanging out the hotel window to describe it. The "baby formula" factory, and infants being removed from their incubators and left on the floor to die. Bombs that were almost cartoon-like in their ability to select targets. Protective gear for chemical warfare. Adolf Hitler.

There were, as well, images that weren't – images that might have colored popular perceptions of the conflict except that their distribution was impeded, or at the very least, not facilitated, by those in a position to shape the flow of news coverage – principally officials of the various governments involved on the side of the so-called "allies": 80 percent collateral damage from less-than-smart bombing. Individual stories of individual hostages and their families. Body bags being unloaded for burial in the United States. An official US estimate of the Iraqi death toll. And there were those for which the image managers might dearly have hoped: The emir rushing home to the embrace of a grateful people.

As the art of managing conflict evolves, so, too, does the art of managing the images of that conflict that are conveyed to the populations of the principals, and increasingly, to a larger world audience.

The motivations for image management during conflict are manifold, and they are not, for the most part, new. They include, among others, the mobilization of support among one's own population and the demobilization of support in the opposition camp, the legitimation of one's own objectives and the delegitimation of the opposition's, the empowerment of one's own forces and the disempowerment of those on the other side, the contrast of the potency of one's own forces with the impotency of those arrayed in opposition, and the very definition of the circumstances and objectives of the conflict on terms most favorable to one's own needs.

What *is* relatively new are the array of technological, institutional, and psychological tools available to the contemporary image manager and, importantly, the growth of expertise in the practice of strategic political communication. The technology of image management is that of modern electronic communication generally: highly mobile field packs, two-way satellite transmission, instantaneous worldwide distribution, and the like. The institutional tools include, in addition to out-right censorship, the creation and management of media pools, the selective provision of access to sources and events, the selective granting of media credentials, appeals to the patriotism of journalists and news organizations, the conduct of briefings, grass-roots organizing, and other devices intended to govern who is able to report what to whom, under what circumstances, and, most importantly, at whose discretion. And the psychological tools are those typically found in the workbox of the professional persuader. They are, essentially, those devices by which public opinion can be created, shaped, sustained, manipulated, and directed toward defined objectives. [. . .]

[. . .]

Note

1   For a recent compendium of research findings regarding persuasion, many of which underlie the theory and practice of strategic political communication, see O'Keefe, 1990. This perspective also draws on applications of persuasion theory developed in the field of issues management, which focuses on corporate image making and the importance of corporate interests of public opinion. For an overview of developments in this field, see Heath and Nelson, 1986. Finally, for an analysis that applies to techniques of new-product marketing to the management of political images, see Mauser, 1983.

References

Festinger, Leon (1957) *A Theory of Cognitive Dissonance*. Evanston, IL: Row, Peterson.

Heath, Robert L. and Richard A. Nelson (1986). *Issues Management: Corporate Public Policymaking in an Information Society*. Beverly Hills, CA: Sage.

McGuire, William J. (1964) "Inducing Resistance to Persuasion: Some Contemporary Approaches," in L. Berkowitz (ed.) *Advances in Experimental Social Psychology*, Vol. 1. New York: Academic Press, pp. 191–229.

Manheim, J.B. (1991) *All of the People, All the Time: Strategic Communication and American Politics*. Armonk, NY: M.E. Sharpe

Mauser, Gary A. (1983) *Political Marketing: An Approach to Campaign Strategy*. New York: Praeger.

O'Keefe, Daniel J. (1990) *Persuasion: Theory and Research*. Newbury Park, CA: Sage.Mauser, Gary A. (1983) *Political Marketing: An Approach to Campaign Strategy*. New York: Praeger.

Pfau, Michael and Henry Kenski (1990) *Attack Politics: Strategy and Defense*. New York: Praeger.

SECTION 3

Election campaigns

WHAT IS THE PURPOSE of election campaigns and who benefits from them? These are the straightforward, yet perceptive questions that lead this section. By their directness, these questions force us to look at the assumptions (usually taken for granted) about elections and their coverage. **Katz**, in the first extract, suggests that political parties may benefit more from the type of coverage usual in the traditional media (in the 1960s, when he wrote this piece) than do citizens. While this piece reflects the concerns of the day, the themes remain important and should lead us to ask questions about how election coverage could be improved and, indeed, the point behind it all.

Should campaign coverage be less focused on the political parties and their agendas (and more on citizen's agendas)? The second extract, by **Semetko** *et al.*, suggests that although political parties succeed in getting their messages across, there is a larger question about whether the media should simply reflect what the parties want and say, or whether they should question more. (This also underpins some of the themes in Katz's piece.)

Why those questions may need to be asked and dealt with can be seen from **Jamieson**'s piece on American presidential campaigns and the 'spot ads' that so populate those campaigns. Are they the best form of communication? Should they continue? Should they be so 'negative'?

The other four pieces in this section touch of elections and campaigns in different ways. **Scammell** and **Negrine and Papathanassopoulos** look at the development of elections and campaigning in a more global context. Both extracts highlight the interest in 'Americanisation' and the growing similarities becoming evident globally when it comes to election campaigns.

Why there is a trend towards convergence is dealt with in the last two extracts. **Swanson and Mancini** offer some conclusions based on their comparative work.

They suggest why things are converging (e.g. 'modernisation') and why democratic practices have similar appearances, and also question whether such trends can be held back. **Norris**, on the other hand, offers an insight into changing forms of election campaigns – from modern to postmodern, for example – and at the same time touches on the question of why such change is taking place. Taken together, the last two extracts provide a well-considered overview of the nature of modern (or postmodern) electioneering.

All these extracts form a backdrop to the extracts in Section 4, 'Marketing politics', which expand on the themes introduced here.

Chapter 16

Elihu Katz

PLATFORM AND WINDOWS
Broadcasting's role in election campaigns

Source: E. Katz (1972) 'Platform and Windows: Broadcasting's Role in Election Campaigns', in D. McQuail (ed.), *Sociology of Mass Communications*, Middlesex: Penguin Books, pp. 353–71.

[. . .]

IN THE WORDS of Blumler and McQuail (1968), the challenge is to help make broadcasting less of a platform for election rhetoric and more of a window through which the voter can get a true view of the political arena.[1] [. . .]

The use of election campaigning

[. . .]
It is evident [. . .] that even if election propaganda generally influences only an extremely small proportion of the voters (if 'influence' means converting them from one party to another, during the relatively brief period of the campaign), the investment of effort and money may be worthwhile, nevertheless, *from the point of view of the political parties*, for small minorities may make large differences. This is obvious in two-party systems where a single vote may, theoretically, change the result [. . .]
   [. . .]
   The parties, perhaps, have good reason to continue their traditional forms of campaigning to change voting intentions, even if one might expect more imaginative use of the information available to them from opinion polls concerning their most likely target audiences and the ways to approach them. They also have reason to provide their followers, particularly those who may influence others' votes, with reinforcement.

From the point of view of the voters who are actively seeking guidance or reinforcement [. . .] the functions of political campaigning are also clear. But these political motives for exposure to mass communications at election time are less important than other 'uses' which the voter finds for political communications. Thus, in reply to Blumler and McQuail's questions, those who intended to watch a party broadcast during the 1964 campaign (four-fifths of the population surveyed) said they would do so 'to see what some party will do if it comes to power' (55 per cent); 'to keep up with the main issues of the day' (52 per cent); 'to judge what political leaders are like' (51 per cent). The frequency with which these 'surveillance' functions were mentioned far exceeds the functions connected with decision-making.

These expectations of the electorate help to explain the high level of dissatisfaction with political broadcasting in the British elections of 1964 and 1966. While the dissatisfaction surely has a variety of causes – including the feeling of being imposed upon by the monopoly granted to party broadcasts – the politically-relevant reasons for the dissatisfaction of the voter-viewer appear to converge on the inherent inability of party broadcasts to satisfy his need for 'surveillance'. What the voter wants, in return for his investment of time, is the feeling that he has fulfilled his duty as a citizen by orienting and updating himself to the political situation. He wants to be able to identify the candidates and the issues; he wants the issues clearly and interestingly explained; he wants to know where the parties stand with respect to the issues, and how their stands are likely to affect him. If you ask him whether he knows where to get what he wants, he will tell you: in direct confrontation. The voter wants to see the candidates in action under stress, responding to challenge. He wants 'debates.'

This brings up the question of the functions of election campaigns *from the point of view of the society*, a point of view which is not identical either with that of the parties or even with that of the voter. Election campaigns are an integrative institution for the society. They focus all eyes on the center of political power at a time when the political parties are attempting to divide the society as best they can. From this point of view, election campaigns are a socializing institution, educating members of the society to the fundamental rights and obligations of the role 'citizen' at a time when the parties are simply trying to win. Moreover, to optimize their usefulness for society, campaigns must be designed so as to make change seem possible, to make evident that leadership may be replaced in response to the demands of changing situations. From the point of view of the social system, the campaign must underline the legitimacy of opposition and the acceptability of the 'other' candidates and parties even to those who opposed them. In other words, society must combat the individual voter's tendency to selectively expose himself only to his own side.

Perhaps the political parties have reason to be satisfied with the traditional forms of campaigning. The voter, for his part, is less well served. Society – the social system – benefits least of all.

A formula for political broadcasting

The question that must be asked, therefore, is how to employ television, and the other media, in a way which will maximize the unique educational opportunity as well as the societal functions of political campaigns. Even if the parties are out only for themselves, and even if the voter exposes himself to political communications for irrelevant reasons, it is up to the society to devise a system whereby the interested voter will be intelligently served and whereby the political consciousness of the uninterested voter will be aroused and channeled to the central issues which are at stake. [. . .] In other words, the society must strive toward a system of election campaigning which constrains the principal actors – even when it does not coincide with their perceived self-interest – to serve it in the best possible way.[2]

But how? The answer is not a simple or standard one – and it will surely vary from nation to nation – but in so far as public broadcasting is concerned, it involves two dimensions: the method of dividing broadcasting time, and the overall division of labor in the production of political broadcasts.

[. . .]

However, even a completely ideal allocation of time to party broadcasts is not a substitute for a better division of labor in the production and presentation of politically relevant broadcasts. There is no substitute for 'confrontation.' This is accomplished, first of all, by the intervention of journalist-broadcasters who know how to join the issues in documentary and discussion programs. The media themselves – not just the parties – must take an active share in presenting the candidates, introducing the issues, challenging the parties to take clearcut stands on the issues, and in general 'representing' the intelligent voter in trying to make sense of the campaign. And the public must be given what it wants – and almost never gets – direct confrontation among the leading candidates. This need not be an actual debate – as, indeed, the Kennedy–Nixon 'debates' were not debates – but rather the successive replies of each candidate to the same set of questions, one by one, as put to them by a panel of journalists. The better-known candidate – usually the incumbent – runs the greater risk in such a confrontation, hence this much-touted innovation in American politics has remained unused in the two presidential elections since 1960. It has been similarly praised, but avoided, in England – where the problem is additionally complicated by the question of fitting Liberal party leaders into the format of a 'debate'.

One may object that a candidate's 'performance' on television – his showmanship – is not a good predictor of how he will perform in office where administrative skills and effective face-to-face diplomacy are more important requirements than gala appearance; but one may argue the other side with equal cogency. At any rate, observers of American and British elections who are concerned with designing a campaign context in which communications appeals are directed to the intelligence of the interested and rational voter and in which the marginally involved voter is aroused are convinced that the institutionalization of direct televised confrontation is one of the most important answers.

Problems of bias and freedom

[. . .]

All agree, however, that the case for greater freedom for broadcaster initiative during election campaigns rests on the journalist-broadcaster's ability to resist the temptation to overdramatize and oversimplify serious and complex issues. Yet, it is ironic to note, with Jay Blumler, that it is now the politicians who are increasingly guilty of this kind of irrationality and trivialization as they adopt the styles of television advertising and 'drama.' In this context, the case for giving professional journalism a more active role seems strong.

If the role broadcasters should play in issue-setting is controversial, there seems rather less disagreement over how the issues should be debated. The principle of proportional time – the allocation of broadcast time according to the parties' previous strength – seems undesirable; this is all the more evident where one party predominates. More generally, the party-produced broadcasts deserve to be curtailed, because they seem constrained to go to one extreme or the other: either too dry, one-sided talk or too slick dramatization. The citizen appears better served by the intervention of the professional broadcaster. The broadcaster-journalist should be free to explore the issues and to confront party leaders with his questions. He should be a catalyst for the confrontation of members of the public and of various interest groups with party leaders, and of course, of the leaders with each other. These are the things that are 'useful' to the voter and to society.

But the politician is very reluctant to agree, and understandably so, from his point of view. It is not simply that he is still afraid of television, as many writers argue, or that party managers do not trust their clients without a script. It happens to be true that persuasion – which is what the parties are after – is not abetted by 'arguing.'

Again and again, one is led to the conclusion that election campaigns are better designed to serve the political parties, particularly the dominant ones, than to serve society or the voter – if the liberal desiderata of optimizing rationality and participation are accepted. Campaigns can be better designed, but politicians will not do this voluntarily. [. . .]

Notes

1   The metaphors are from Blumler and McQuail (1968).
2   Recent proposals for redesigning election campaigns include Rose (1967), Kelley (1960) and Blumler and McQuail (1968, Part IV). The design of elections in Israel, and the legal basis therefore, is reviewed by Witkon (1970).

Bibliography

Blumler, J.G. and McQuail, D. (1968) *Television and Politics: Its Uses and Influence*. London: Faber & Faber.
Kelley, S. Jr (1960) *Political Campaigning: Problems in Creating An Informed Electorate*. The Brookings Institution: Washington.
Rose, T. (1967) *Influencing Voters: A Study of Campaign Rationality*. London: Faber & Faber.
Witkon, A. (1970) 'Elections in Israel', *Israel Law Review*, vol. 5, pp. 42–52.

Chapter 17

Holli Semetko *et al.*

THE FORMATION OF CAMPAIGN AGENDAS

Source: H.A. Semetko, J. Blumler, M. Gurevitch, D. Weaver, S. Barkin and G.C. Wilhoit (1991) *The Formation of Campaign Agendas: A Comparative Analysis of Party and Media Roles in Recent American and British Elections*, Hillsdale, NJ: Lawrence Erlbaum, pp. 175–80.

[. . .]

In conclusion: what have we learned?

WHAT HAVE WE LEARNED from this two-nation enquiry into the formation of election campaign agendas? What insights does this study give us . . .? . . . In considering here what emerged from this [study], we aim not so much to restate findings. . ., as to reflect on some of their broader implications for political communication scholarship – for conceptual development, future research, and policy.

The notion of agenda setting

It now seems to us that agenda-setting theory and research require attention and development from two main angles. One concerns perspectives on the process itself; the other concerns the sources that feed it in different systemic conditions.

First, academic researchers need to appreciate more fully a basic truth about the formation of campaign agendas, which most practitioners (politicians and journalists alike) have entirely absorbed by now – namely, that the process is a deeply political one, as is the role of the media in it. Agenda-setting terminology is not well placed to alert us to this. It tends to reduce the process to a semi-mechanical practice, connoting a sedate ordering of items for sequential consideration before the real business of debate and decision taking over them begins.

In election communication, however, the reality is quite different. Once a campaign is announced (or approaches), a common element in both the United States and Britain is the unleashing in earnest of an implacably competitive struggle to control the mass media agenda, a struggle that pits, not only candidates and parties in contention for agenda domination, but also campaign managements against news organization teams. [. . .]

[. . .]

The root of this process is the fact of course that (apart from advertisements and party broadcasts) journalists command the gates of access for political messages to reach the electoral audience, including powers not only of selection but also of contextualizing commentary, packaging, and event definition. To would-be wooers of increasingly volatile voters, breaking through those gates with one's preferred message as intact as possible is quite vital. Interpreting the ensuing struggle as "political" is useful in highlighting an advantage that politicians bring to it. They have no difficulty or inhibition about treating message projection as a process of exerting leverage, pressure, and manipulation. After all, they regularly play games of that kind in all their other activities. For media personnel this does present a problem, however, because it highlights their involvement in a political process, despite their claims to outsiders and their protestations that they are merely observing and reporting campaign events through the self-denying norms of objectivity and impartiality.

[. . .]

Agenda setting, then, should be conceived as a dynamic process, not a settled procedure. Regarded as a struggle for control, it will take place differently in different societies, depending on differences of political systems, the positions of media within those systems, and the internal differences of media organizations . . . Because, however, both sides deploy significant resources in the struggle, and because the outcome matters greatly to each, for self-identity as well as for pragmatic reasons, even those who gain an upper hand in one election moment cannot confidently count on retention of their superiority at the next. [. . .]

[. . .]

A second major implication . . . is that future studies should not take mass media agenda setting for granted. . . That is, media agendas should not be regarded as solely determined by journalists and news organizations. Nor should they be regarded as primarily determined by political parties and candidates during election campaigns. Instead there are a number of differentiating influences that affect how much discretion both journalists and politicians have in setting campaign agendas, and how these influences must be considered in drawing conclusions about how much either journalists or politicians contribute to campaign agendas.

At the system level, such influences include:

1. The strength of the political party system – with a stronger party system generally associated with less discretion on the part of journalists to set the campaign agenda and more opportunity for politicians to do so.
2. Public service versus commercial media systems – with commercial systems associated with more desire by journalists to set political agendas and not merely

reflect party and candidate agendas, but with less newshole into which to squeeze their contributions.

3. Differing levels of competition for media audience – with more competition being associated with more attention to perceived audience interests and less attention to politicians' agendas by journalists.

4. Differing degrees of professionalization of the campaign – with more professional management or political campaigns associated with less discretion for journalists to set the agenda and with a growth of cynicism and skepticism about the legitimacy of the election communication process generally.

5. Cultural differences – with more respect for politics being associated with a greater willingness on the part of journalists to let the political parties and candidates have more discretion in setting the campaign agenda and less emphasis on the election as a game or a horse race at the expense of substantive issues.

These system-level or macro influences are not the only ones affecting the agenda-setting process. There are also more specific, or micro-level, conditions that enhance and limit the discretionary power of journalists and politicians to set campaign agendas . . . including:

1. The partisan or ideological leanings of specific media organizations. Even though this influence is more obvious in editorials, feature columns, and commentaries, there is some evidence that it can affect specific subject and theme agendas in news coverage.

2. The status of the candidate. An incumbent president or prime minister is usually in a better position to influence the campaign agenda than a challenger. . . .

3. Journalistic norms of balance and objectivity. [. . .]

4. The size of the newshole. [. . .] More space permits more issues to be covered in greater detail and has the potential to broaden the agenda.

5. Journalists' notions of what roles are most appropriate [. . .] when covering a campaign. [. . .]

Taken together, these influences suggest that the formation of the campaign agenda is a complex process that varies from one culture and one election to another. [. . .]
  [. . .]
  [. . .] future studies of the formation of media and public agendas might wish to conceive of a continuum from "agenda setting" to "agenda reflecting" with "agenda shaping" and "agenda amplifying" falling in between the two extremes. Regardless of the labels applied, future studies of the media agendas need to take into account a variety of macro- and micro-level influences in analyzing how the media agenda is formed before trying to relate that agenda to public concerns. [. . .] Without taking into account the various influences on the formation of the media agenda, there is a tendency to overestimate the power of journalists and news organizations to set campaign or other agendas and thus to oversimplify the influence of journalists, however crucial, on public priorities.

  The preceding discussion should also alert us to the possibility that the agenda-setting approach in its conventional form may miss out on important aspects of the role of the media in election campaigns. Might the media, especially television, indeed play only a relatively marginal "agenda-shaping" or "agenda-amplifying" role in political campaigns? [. . .] In other words, a limitation of agenda-setting research is in its emphasis on the *what* (i.e. what stories are selected and which priorities guide the selection and placement of news items) rather than on the how (the manner in which stories are framed and how close the media's frames are to the frames of the candidates and their campaign managers).

This suggests that [. . .] we may need to supplement the traditional emphases of the agenda-setting approach with insights emanating from a "construction of meanings" approach that looks in more detail at the processes of meaning production that take place within and between media and political organizations. Such a process of framing campaign events may take place somewhat independently of the degree of discretion that media professionals in different societies exercise in reflecting, amplifying, shaping, or setting political news agendas.

Chapter 18

Kathleen Hall Jamieson

PACKAGING THE PRESIDENCY
A history and criticism of presidential campaign advertising

Source: Kathleen Hall Jamieson (1992) *Packaging the Presidency. A History and Criticism of Presidential Campaign Advertising*, Oxford: Oxford University Press, pp. xix, xxii–xxiii, 485–92.

Introduction

NEVER BEFORE in a presidential campaign have televised ads sponsored by a major party candidate lied so blatantly as in the campaign of 1988.

Television ads of previous presidential contenders have, to be sure, seized upon votes cast by the opposition candidate and sundered them from context, resurrected political positions from the distant past and interpreted legislative moves as sweeping endorsements of unpopular positions. [. . .] But in the era of mass visual communication, major party candidates, until 1988, assumed that outright lying in an ad would create an outcry from the press, a devastating counter-assault from the other side, and a backlash from an incensed electorate.

That assumption no longer governs. [. . .]

[. . .] How then, can the electorate be protected? The best available defense seems to be the vigilance of the opposing candidate and party. But. . . a candidate's access to news, counter-advertising and debates protects the public only if the attacked candidate moves quickly and strategically. Moreover, the protection of news and debates presuppose that the attacked candidate is comfortable with personally rebutting untruths and counter attacking. [. . .]

There is also the risk that a counter-attack may simply legitimize false claims and magnify their impact. It can also reduce the campaign to a shouting match in which each candidate calls the other a liar, leaving the electorate disillusioned and confused. That was where the campaign of 1988 wound up. Its also where future campaigns are likely to be headed unless this country can discover among the ranks of its politicians a pair of candidates self-assured enough to campaign on the facts. [. . .]

Conclusion

Political advertising is now the major means by which candidates for the presidency communicate their messages to voters. As a conduit of this advertising, television attracts both more candidate dollars and more audience attention than radio or print. Unsurprisingly, the spot ad is the most used and the most viewed of the available forms of advertising. By 1980 the half hour broadcast speech – the norm in 1952 – had been replaced by the 60 second spot.

Ads enable candidates to build name recognition, frame the questions they view as central to the election, and expose their temperaments, talents, and agendas for the future in a favorable light. In part because more voters attend to spot ads than to network news and in part because reporters are fixated with who's winning and losing instead of what the candidates are proposing, some scholars believe that ads provide the electorate with more information than network news. Still, ads more often successfully reinforce existing dispositions than create new ones.

Ads also argue the relevance of issues to our lives. In the 1950s the public at large did not find political matters salient to it.[1] From the late 1950s to the early 1970s the perception of the relevance of political matters to one's day-to-day life increased[2] at all educational levels. Citizens saw a greater connection between what occurred in the political world and what occurred in their lives.[3]

TV ads' ability to personalize and the tendency of TV news to reduce issues to personal impact have, in my judgment, facilitated that change. [. . .] As the salience of political issues increased so too did the consistency of the beliefs of individual voters. Dissonant views are less likely to be simultaneously held now than before. This tendency is also reinforced by political advertising, for politicians have increasingly argued the interconnection of issues of importance to them. [. . .]

[. . .]

Ads also define the nature of the presidency by stipulating the attributes a president should have. In the process they legitimize certain occupations. [. . .]

[*Packaging the Presidency* was premised on] the assumption that advertising provides an optic through which presidential campaigns can be productively viewed. In the ten campaigns I have focused on we have seen, for example, various styles of leadership reflected in the candidates' treatment of their advertisers and advertising. [. . .] At the same time, ad campaigns that lurched uncertainly from one message form to another, from one set of strategists to another, [. . .] suggested perhaps that the candidate and his advisers were unable to provide a clear sense of the direction in which they wanted to take the country, an observation consistent with the failure of these campaigns to forecast their candidates' visions of the future.

Occasionally, a candidate's response to the requirements of advertising raises troublesome questions about his suitability for the office or, perhaps, about the intensity of his desire to hold it. [. . .]

When the acceptance speech and the election eve telecasts are taken as the brackets bounding advertising, a focus on paid messages can reveal a campaign's fundamental coherence or incoherence. In a coherent campaign, the acceptance speech at the convention synopsizes and polishes the message the candidate has communicated in the primaries as a means of forecasting both the themes of the general election campaign and of this person's presidency. The message is then systematically developed in the advertising of the general election and placed in its final form on election eve where the candidate tries on the presidency by indicating for the country his vision of the next four years under his leadership. When from the first campaign advertising of January through the last on election eve in November, candidates offer consistent, coherent messages about themselves and the future as they envision it, they minimize the likelihood that their record or plans will be distorted effectively by opponents, and create a clear set of expectations to govern their conduct in office, expectations that may haunt them when they seek re-election.

Viewing campaign advertising as an extended message rather than a series of discrete message units also enables us to see how a candidate's response to attacks in the primaries can either strengthen or strangle the candidate's chances in the general election. When attacks are raised in the primaries and effectively neutralized [. . .] the issues can be effectively dispatched in the general election. . . .

Preventing candidates from using advertising to create a sense of themselves discrepant from who they are and what they have done is the vigilant presence of opponents and the potentially vigilant presence of the press. Throughout this book [original publication] we have seen instances in which candidates' words and actions in settings they did not control undermined the crafted images of their ads. [. . .] When ads lie, the vigilance of press and opponents can, but do not necessarily, protect the public.

In many ways televised political advertising is the direct descendant of the advertised messages carried in song and on banners, torches, bandannas, and broadsides. [. . .]

What differentiates the(se) claims [. . .] from those aired today is the role the press has now assumed as monitor of presidential advertising. [. . .] The difficulty in relying on news to correct distortions in advertising is, of course, that comparatively few people consume news while many are exposed to ads.

One of the argumentative ploys born in the political and product advertising of the nineteenth century was refined by politicians in the age of television and then shunted aside by Watergate. By visually associating the favored candidate with pictures of well-fed cattle, happy families, large bundles of grain, and bulging factories, banners and broadsides argued to literate and illiterate alike that this candidate stood for prosperity. The opponent, on the other hand, was visually tied to drawings of starving cattle, poverty-ravished families, empty grain bins, and fireless factories. Some of the associations seemed to have no direct bearing on what sort of president the candidate would make.

Political argument by visual association flowered for the same reason it appeared in product advertising. [. . .] Distinguishing attributes-some real, some fictional-were sought to persuade customers that one product rather than its twin should be purchased. [. . .] Since the advertising of the early nineteenth century relied on drawings rather than photographs the range of possible associations was limited only by the artist's imagination.

The wizardry of videotape and film editing did not change the nature of argument from visual association – it simply increased its subtlety. In the process, the evidentiary burden that candidates should assume dropped. [. . .]

[. . .]

By replacing attack ads that use visual not verbal means to prompt sweeping inferences with attack ads that verbally and visually invite judgments based on verifiable facts, Watergate temporarily transformed a form of presidential attack advertising from an exercise in the prompting of false inferences to an exercise in traditional argument. In 1988, invitations to false inference were back with a vengeance.

[. . .]

As I have noted in each chapter [of the original publication], the convention acceptance speeches are a highly reliable predictor of the content of the candidate's ads in the general election. For those who read the campaign's position papers, examine its brochures, and listen to its stump speeches, the ads function as reinforcement. Those who ignore the other campaign-produced material receive a digest of them in the ads. This is true both of the advertising against the opponent and the advertising supporting the candidate. The cost of reaching voters through broadcast advertising poses other problems. Since spot advertising is both costly and often the most cost efficient means of reaching a mass of voters, the contemporary reliance or spots means that those who cannot afford to purchase them, with rare exceptions, are denied the ability to have their ideas either heard or take seriously in presidential primaries.

For these and related reasons. . . public concern over the nature and influence of political advertising has been rising. [. . .]

Underlying the debate over [. . .] proposals is widening consensus that the electoral process would benefit if the candidates' cost of reaching a mass audience could be reduced; if all bona-fide candidates could be provided with sufficient access to communicate their basic ideas; if politicians made greater use of longer forms of communication and the electorate as a whole attended more readily to such forms; if candidates assumed or could be enticed to assume the obligation of being viewed by the public in forms such as debates that they do not control; if the advantage PACs can bring to a presidential candidate could be countered or muted.

Still, if political advertising did not exist we would have to invent it. Political advertising legitimizes our political institutions by affirming that change is possible within the political system, that the president can effect change, that votes can make a difference. As a result, advertising like campaigns in general channels discontent into the avenues provided by the government and acts as a safety valve for pressures that might otherwise turn against the system to demand its substantial modification or overthrow.

Political advertising does this, in part, by underscoring the power of the ballot. Your vote makes a difference, it says, at the same time as its carefully targeted messages imply that the votes that would go to the opponent are best left uncast.

Political ads affirm that the country is great, has a future, is respected. The contest they reflect is over who should be elected, not over whether there should be an election. The very existence of the contest suggests that there is a choice, that the voters' selection of one candidate over the other will make a difference.

Notes

1   Stouffer, S. (1955) *Communism, Conformity and Civil Liberties*. New York: Wiley.
2   Nie, N.H., S. Verba and J.R. Petrocik (1979) *The Changing American Voter*. Cambridge, Mass.: Harvard University Press, p. 152.
3   Ibid., 153.

Chapter 19

Margaret Scammell

THE WISDOM OF THE WAR ROOM
US campaigning and Americanization

Source: Margaret Scammell (1998) 'The Wisdom of the War Room: US Campaigning and Americanization', *Media, Culture and Society*, 20 (2): 251–75.

Americanization and professionalization

A LL THE DISTINCTIVE features of modern campaigning – political marketing, personalization, escalating levels of technological sophistication – share a common theme, 'professionalization.' Blumler *et al.* (1996) characterize the modern campaign precisely as the professionalized paradigm. This approach may be criticized on historical grounds. Virtually any period of mass democratic electoral history, in the US and Britain at least, will offer good evidence of increasing 'professionalization' compared to earlier campaigns, as politicians adapt to changing media and electoral environments. Present day concerns about the impact of advertising and public relations in politics echo the propaganda debates of the 1920s and 1930s (Sproule, 1989). However, there are two senses in which modern 'professionalization' is claimed to be qualitatively different: specialization and displacement.

Specialization

The explosion of new communication technologies over the last 40 years has fostered a profusion of specialist technical experts, in such matters as polls, computers and software, the internet, television presentation and advertising. Farrell (1996) makes a useful distinction between capital-intensive campaigns and labor-intensive campaigns.

The more capital-intensive the more professional (modern and 'American') the campaign, because the new technologies require new sets of consultants and new batteries of technocrats. Labor-intensive campaigns are essentially 'amateur' run, relying heavily on party workers and volunteers for mass canvassing and public meetings. Thus, specialization is largely driven by technology, and of course, the money needed to hire the expertise. This is partly a quantitative argument, which is saying roughly, that the degree of specialization has accumulated to the point where campaigns qualitatively become altered.

Displacement

This takes specialization a stage further by arguing that party strategists have been replaced by non-party 'professional' strategists. Employed at first for their expertise with the technologies mentioned above, the professionals become increasingly central to campaign strategy and even policy-making. They claim and are perceived to possess expertise essential to the winning of elections. [. . .].

[. . .]

[. . .] we must be content to agree that modern campaigns are characterized by increasing specialization and replacement of party campaign managers by outside expertise. These features alone would not, however, be sufficient to label campaigning 'professional.' More important is the suggestion that the new campaign technocrats possess a body of knowledge increasingly considered essential to electoral success. This takes us to the core of our investigation to examine whether 'modern' campaigners are more professional, not simply in the sense of technical expertise but that they operate on the basis of an increasingly 'scientific' understanding of the political market and voter persuasion.

Professional campaigning in the US

[. . .] Political consulting is clearly a flourishing business, but to what extent might it legitimately be deemed a profession? Our working definition of a profession includes the following elements: control over entry; a self-regulating code of conduct; definable bodies of knowledge, supported by a systematic body of theory; training and certification by recognizable standards that individuals are qualified in that body of knowledge; full-time employment of professionals in the field; and formal organization of professionals into societies which defend professional standards and protect members interests (Jackson, 1970; Norris, 1996; Vollmer and Mills, 1966). Political consulting lacks one of the fundamental criteria of hard-core professions such as medicine or law: control over entry. Anyone may run for elected office in the US, provided they meet relatively few legal requirements, and equally they may choose anyone to campaign on their behalf. [. . .]

[. . .]

In other ways, however, political consulting carries stronger claims to professionalism. It is now a full-time occupation in the USA and there are signs of an emerging common identity, of political consulting with its special sets of skills as distinct from other trades and crafts. [. . .] A second indicator is the proliferation over 30 years of various campaign specialisms. At first these depended almost completely on technical expertise, for example polling advice or advertising production, but now have expanded across a much wider range of campaign activities, which require few or no particular technical skills: e.g., direct mail fund-raising, media buying, conference, event and meeting planning, and political researching.

A third sign is the self-conscious attempt to professionalize the business of campaigning through training and education. [. . .]

[. . .]

A fourth and crucially defining characteristic of professionalization is ethics. [. . .] Contrary to popular myth, the business is not without ethical concerns. [. . .]

[. . .]

As yet [. . .] the emergence of a full-time occupation, a common identity and development of unique sets of skills may be more properly described as commercialization rather than professionalization, despite some fledgling attempts to create consensus around professional norms. Moreover, it would be naïve to underestimate the importance of the money motive in the growth of political consultancy. [. . .]

Conclusion

It is widely accepted that 'professionalization' is the hallmark of modern campaigning and the USA has the world's most professional campaigners. Yet, this investigation found that professionalization is problematic in the US. There are some emerging signs: the growth of a common identity, specialist knowledge, efforts to establish specialist education and training, and even to develop a common code of conduct. In these respects the US is further down the professional road than the rest of the democratic world. However, as yet, US political consultancy is characterized more by commercialism than professionalism. It is less the *professional paradigm* and more the *commercial* paradigm. [. . .]

The point is not merely to suggest that studies of comparative campaigning have over-estimated the degree of professionalism in modern campaigning, but to argue that there are consequences for 'Americanization.' [. . .] Generally, then, this investigation supports the prevailing academic consensus which emphasizes the *limits* of American influence on overseas campaigns. The usefulness of American campaign knowledge is restricted precisely because it is US-specific wisdom, and largely undeveloped on a wider theoretical plane. American-style methods are likely to be most fully incorporated into foreign electioneering in those countries where electoral conditions are most similar to the USA. This again is the consensus view of research into comparative electioneering. [. . .] There are considerable structural constraints on the wholesale import of American methods, to which should be added the *knowledge-base* itself of US campaigning.

Equally, however, the examination of the source of campaigners' ideas can help us identify more precisely those US practices which *might* be successfully imported and adapted elsewhere. [. . .] Most of these come from marketing: the importance of strategy, identifying target voters and of concentrating campaigning resources on those targets. Correspondingly, market research becomes increasingly significant, to establish the target market and the positioning of the candidate/party in relation both to the targets and the opponents. [. . .] One might expect that lessons of US political advertising will also be adopted elsewhere. The first of these is that advertising matters; Second, that judicious repetition does increase the prospects of voter influence (Just *et al.*, 1996). Third, that negative advertising is the most effective. [. . .] In short, the marketing approach, strategy and research tools, and the reliance on advertising, especially negative advertising, are features which promise to flourish abroad, even where structural conditions are vastly different from the US. Britain, for example, with its strong party and parliamentary system, tightly regulated media and ban on paid TV political advertising, is often considered resistant to American methods (Blumler *et al.*, 1996). Yet the last two elections have demonstrated clear evidence of the marketing approach to strategy and communication, and for the Conservatives, especially, of increasing faith in the value of advertising and negative appeals (Scammell and Semetko, 1995).

[. . .] the marketing approach, advertising and campaigning-as-warfare, are by no means a definitive list of the possibilities of American influence, whether by export or by role model. However, they are intended to illustrate the value of an approach which stresses the importance of understanding campaigners' thinking. This does not replace, but it does supplement the existing comparative research emphasis on the manifestly observable features of campaigns, the what rather than the why. It can offer us more precise clues to the direction of modern campaigning, and fresh insight into its commonly-agreed key characteristics: 'professionalization,' 'personal-ization,' increasing importance of image and TV presentation and so on. It can help us separate more clearly changes in campaigning processes from effects of media change. [. . .]

References

Blumler, J.G., D. Kavanagh and T.J. Nossiter (1996) Modern Communication versus Traditional Politics in Britain: Unstable Marriage of Convenience. In D. Swanson and P. Mancini (eds) *Politics, Media and Modern Democracy*. New York: Praeger, pp. 49–72

Farrell, D. (1996) Campaign Strategies and Tactics. In L. LeDuc, R.G. Neimi and P. Norris (eds) *Comparing Democracies: Elections and Voting in Global Perspective*. Thousand Oaks, CA: Sage.

Jackson, J.A. (1970) *Professions and Professionalism*. Cambridge: Cambridge University Press.

Just, M.R., A. Crigler, D. Alger, T. Cook, M. Kern and D. West (1996) *Crosstalk: Citizens, Candidates and the Media in a Presidential Campaign*. Chicago, IL: University of Chicago Press.

Scammell, M. and H. Semetko (1995) Political Advertising on Television: The British Experience. In L.L. Kaid and C. Holtz-Bacha (eds) *Political Advertising in Western Democracies*. Thousand Oaks, CA: Sage.

Sproule, J.M. (1989) Social Responses to Twentieth Century Propaganda. In Ted Smith III (ed.) *Propaganda*. New York: Praeger, pp. 5–22

Vollmer, H. and Mills, D. (1966) *Professionalization*. Englewood Cliffs. NJ: Prentice-Hall.

Chapter 20

Ralph Negrine and Stylianos Papathanassopoulos

THE 'AMERICANIZATION' OF POLITICAL COMMUNICATION
A critique

Source: Ralph Negrine and Stylianos Papathanassopoulos (1996) 'The "Americanization" of Political Communication: A Critique', *Press/Politics*, 1 (2): 45–62.

Campaigning practices and political communication

[. . .]

SUCH PRACTICES AS POLITICAL commercials, the selection of candidates in part for the appealing images they project on television, technical experts advising candidates on strategies, media professionals hired to produce compelling campaign materials, mounting campaign expenses, and the mass media moving to center stage in campaigns are now common characteristics of many elections across the globe.

This raises some fundamental questions. Are these countries copying Western practices wholesale? Are they adapting them to meet local needs? Are these countries becoming more like the Western countries which they are emulating? Are they becoming more like them in their media practices?

It is easier to document the existence of similar practices, e.g. the use of 'experts' or the increased use of television (Swanson, 1991, 15), than to make sense of the significance or meaning of those practices in different political and social settings. Thus, although elections all comprise similar elements – candidates, media practices, voters, etc. – the way these elements are grouped together and their significance varies from one political system to another. In some countries, such as the United States and France, voters have to choose between candidates for President as well as other representatives, whereas in countries like the Netherlands and Greece, the choice is between different political parties. Even where there are apparent similarities, differences of detail may exist: American presidential candidates can appear almost out of nowhere and can make themselves into viable contenders for national office through careful and extensive use of the mass media; in contrast, French or Greek presidential candidates cannot progress far without extensive party political support, and they tend to be well-known figures before they stand for election. Political parties differ so significantly from one political system to another with regards to their organization and ideological make-up, that it is deceptive to discuss them as if they were one and the same thing. (Tunstall, 1977, 264) [. . .]

[. . .]

One reason why such questions [about resemblances and convergence] are difficult to answer can be found in their formulation. They are conceived as if countries lead separate and isolated existences and that what we are presently experiencing is the importing, and the exporting, of practices across clearly defined boundaries. Although it may be true that certain practices may have, in recent years, been imported from powerful nations, such as the United States or Britain, or from powerful neighboring states, this 'transfer' has in fact taken place in a world that has become increasingly internationalised. [. . .] As Blumler and colleagues also argue, 'comparative research [. . .] implies the interpenetration of space and time [. . .] system features and patterns are not eternal but instead are in continual flux, *increasingly brought about these days by influences from a larger world system of communication.*' (1992, 8–9, emphasis supplied) If that is the case, the focus of attention need not necessarily be on the transfer of practices from one specific country to another, but on the broader pattern of practices being adapted from a variety of sources, even a 'common pool' of resources, to meet domestic needs.

In spite of the recommendation for a better understanding of the implications of 'the interpenetration of space and time' for the emergence of similar practices across the globe, a significant part of the literature focuses directly on the importation of American experiences rather than any others. David Butler and Austin Ranney, for instance, identify a range of practices – including the use of computers, fax and direct mailing – that originated in the United States but are currently widely used elsewhere (1992). As they also point out, even phrases like sound-bite, photo-opportunity, and news management, have American origins, yet they are commonly heard today 'in every election strategy conference in Western Europe' (p. 8). The suggestion is, then, that the nature of campaigning in democracies around the world is becoming more and more Americanized as candidates, political parties, and news media take cues from their counterparts in the United States. (See Kaid and Holtz-Bacha 1995 for a sustained attempt at tracing the American influence in 'political advertising' across a range of countries; and Maarek 1995 for a French account of the development of American 'political marketing.')

However [. . .] the use of the word 'Americanization' to describe a complex process is not particularly helpful. Does 'Americanization' simply refer to the adoption of practices first used in the US? Does it refer to the take-up of technological developments? Does it refer to imitation and importation of practices and values? Does it actually contribute to our understanding of the significance of the transfers being alluded to? [. . .] Such comments reveal the lack of specificity of the

Americanization thesis and, at the same, time the need to pin down the term more firmly. They also raise three other issues:

1. Given the 'easy and incessant two-way traffic in fads, fears, music, fiction, poetry, inventions, reforms, theories' between the US and Europe, how does one 'evaluate the effects?' (Cunliffe, 1974, 41) The sense of ideas and practices being constantly adapted, imitated, altered and basically changing as they meet new circumstances does make it difficult to work with the idea of a unilinear process of transfer from the US to other countries.

2. It is almost impossible to refute the 'Americanization' thesis. [. . .] what, would a country not influenced by American (British, French, Portuguese, Spanish, Islamic [. . .]) practices and institutions actually look like, and is it possible to conceive of such a thing in the modern world? The problems inherent in the impossibility of disproving the Americanization thesis, or of making any real meaningful headway with it are in no small way related to the increasing speed and wholesale manner in which modern practices flow across the contemporary world.

3. Although the Americanization thesis strongly implies that it is a one-way flow of influences, in reality we may be observing a more complicated process. Not only do some countries adapt practices from outside the United States – in Greece, for instance, European influences may loom larger than American ones; [. . .] – but the United States may itself import practices (Walker 1992). [. . .]

[. . .]

Under these circumstances, to focus on specific patterns of importation and exchange of practices and to attribute to them a single source undermines the complexity of the modern world and the sorts of inter-connections that the preceding examples make evident. It underplays 'the interpenetration of space and time' in the modern world. Nevertheless, because it is the American experience that has come to dominate thinking in the context of electoral communication practices, it is important to appreciate the ways in which the American influence has spread into other countries. [. . .]

[. . .]

Conclusions

In reviewing some of the literature in this field, it becomes apparent that there are two major interpretations of the processes at work. The first is a fairly straight-forward account of the American influence on electronic electoral practices across the world; given the numerous examples that can be referred to, it is unlikely that this interpretation will cease to have any currency. If anything, it will continue to be in use so long as the latest American practices, such as political communication via the Internet, find a place in other countries (as the use of the Internet has found a use in the United Kingdom). What is regrettable, though, is that the recitation of examples stands in the way of exploring of the possibility that the organization of US social and political life makes it a particularly suitable setting for the use of the practices described above – practices that which may not always travel easily into settings where different features dominate. The intriguing question, though, is whether even these examples actually signal much more than a simple transmutation of practices.

This question is a crucial one in the second interpretation of Americanization, which offers a more theoretically informed account of the way changes in social structures bring about changes in communication practices which are, in turn, shaped in part by the American influence. This interpretation is more difficult to deal with because it combines social analysis with an analysis of communication practices whereas in fact the two may be constitutive of one another. For example, it can be argued that one of the things now commonly experienced is a sense of government ineffectiveness in the face of not dissimilar economic, social and political problems. Although the roots of these problems are many and complex, the media and political actors continue to interact in traditional ways: the former questions whilst the latter assumes the mantle of responsibility and control.

Yet it is abundantly clear that neither of these roles are what they used to be. The media question political actors, but they also put them on the defensive and sometimes force them to act in haste. For their part, political actors respond as if they *can* steer the ship of state. Both sets of actors seek the support and trust of the public. With the electronic media so dominant, it is not surprising that they are used to justify and support political actions. In other words, what we may be seeing is responses to problems that derive from the very nature of modernity, rather than some process that is linked to Americanization per se. [. . .]

References

Blumler, J., McLeod, J.M. and Rosengren, K.E. (1992) (eds) *Comparatively Speaking: Communication and Culture across Space and Time.* London: Sage.

Butler, D. and Ranney, A. (eds) (1992) *Electioneering. A Comparative Study of Continuity and Change.* Oxford: Clarendon Press.

Cunliffe, M. (1974) New world, old world: the historical antithesis. In Rose, R. *Lessons from America.* London: Macmillan, pp. 19–45.

Kaid, L. and Holtz-Bacha, C. (eds) (1995) *Political Advertising in Western Democracies.* London: Sage.

Maarek, Philippe (1995) *Political Marketing and Communication.* London: John Libbey.

Swanson, D. (1991) Theoretical dimensions of the French–US Presidential campaign studies. In Kaid, Lynda *et al.* (eds) (1992) *Mediated Politics in Two Cultures: Presidential Campaigning in the United States and France.* New York: Praeger

Tunstall, Jeremy (1977) *The Media are American.* London: Constable.

Walker, Martin (1992) 'Major says sorry for Tory help to Bush.' London: *The Guardian*,. November 21, 1992, p. 14.

Chapter 21

David Swanson and Paolo Mancini

POLITICS, MEDIA AND MODERN DEMOCRACY

An international study of innovations in electoral campaigning and their consequences

Source: David Swanson and Paolo Mancini (eds) (1996) *Politics, Media and Modern Democracy. An International Study of Innovations in Electoral Campaigning and their Consequences*, Westport, CT: Praeger, pp. 249–53.

The modern model of campaigning

[. . .]

THERE ARE NO DISAGREEMENTS about what constitutes the modern model of campaigning. Its key attributes – including personalization of politics, expanding reliance on technical experts and professional advisers, growing detachment of political parties from citizens, development of autonomous structures of communication, and casting citizens in the role of spectator – figure in one way or another (in nearly every chapter in this volume). There is disagreement, however, about whether the term Americanization is the most appropriate label for these campaign innovations. Some readers may take the term as implying that adoption of modern campaign methods necessarily, results from a desire – to emulate US practices, perhaps with overtones of US superiority and power. [But] [. . .] elements of the modern campaign model have emerged in various countries in response to internal developments in those countries, not out of desire to imitate the United States, which, after all, conducts its political campaigns in ways that more often elicit opprobrium than approval within the United States and around the world.

A number of countries including Germany, France, and the United Kingdom are now "exporters" of consultants and technical experts who provide advice about modern campaign methods. The result is reciprocal influence [. . .] where consultants from other countries have provided advice to US campaigners. More generally, [. . .] we have entered an era in which routine exchanges between countries, at many levels, lead naturally to cross fertilization in the political and other domains. Thus, perhaps the best description of the present situation is an international network of connections through which knowledge about new campaign practices and their uses is disseminated constantly across national borders by independent consultants for economic reasons, by ideologically kindred political parties for political reasons, and by mass media to aspiring political candidates and interested members of the public worldwide.

While we acknowledge that the term Americanization refers more to the origins [of] most of the campaigning techniques we are interested in than to the present system for exchanging technical knowledge about them, it is important not to over-look the fact that each new development in US campaigns is studied with special care by political parties and candidates around the world. As Blumler, Kavanagh, and Nossiter (1996) observe [. . .] the United States continues to be "perceived as on the cutting edge of electioneering innovation." Nevertheless, to best represent the current international network of reciprocal exchange, we shall refer to the "modern model of campaigning" rather than to the Americanized model.

Comparing the experiences of the countries that have been examined, we are struck by two themes that most often are cited [. . .] as the direct and immediate causes of electoral innovations. One theme is a fundamental transformation in the relationship of political parties to their constituents. In the established democracies, we are hard pressed today to find successful, competitive political parties that retain the traditional organic relationship with constituents that is cemented and perpetuated by well-defined, stable commitments to class and group interests. Instead, the parties' links to particular groups and institutions generally have weakened, while at the same time these groups and institutions have lost much of their former ability to influence members' voting choices (such as trade unions and farmers' organizations in Sweden, religion and social class in Germany, and religious affiliations and traditional subcultures in Italy). The point is perhaps put best [. . .] by Waisbord (1996), who describes the transformation of parties in Argentine politics from "sacred" to "secular." In many democracies, voting seems to have been transformed from an expression of solidarity with one's group and its institutions to, today, an expression of one's opinions. Moreover, the opinions which are cited most often as shaping persons' voting choices – such as opinions about the performance of government, the appropriate ideological and pragmatic bases for public policy, and the appeal of a party's leader and other visible spokespersons – cut across class lines and other traditional social cleavages, so that a sharp decline in the relationship between social class and voting has been observed nearly everywhere. [. . .]

No longer able to rely on a secure base of party loyalists, the most competitive political parties in many countries have taken on attributes of "catch-all" confederations that exist more to win elections by appealing to a broad range of voters' opinions than to implementing defined programs, and their electoral fortunes wax and wane with voters' pragmatic assessments of their leaders and the performance of the current government. The evolution to catch-all parties and the adoption of various media-centered campaign techniques often relegate specific ideological commitments to the background of campaigns and blur programmatic differences between parties, except on a few issues where a party believes it holds the more popular view.

A second theme that stands out [. . .] is that when the fortunes of political parties rest on opinion rather than membership and historical allegiances, the means for cultivating and shaping public opinion become crucial to electoral success. In modern society, these means are, of course, the mass media of communication, which have proliferated especially as commercial enterprises while government and party-influence over media has generally declined. The media have become the dominant source of information and entertainment in nearly every society and, in many countries, have assumed a new level of independence from which to interject their own voice into the political dialogue. Among other things, the independent voice of mass media in politics reflects the development and spread of an ideology of journalism as a profession in its own right with an autonomous role to play in the political process. [. . .]

It seems to be the case nearly everywhere that mass media have developed their own "media logic" for covering political campaigns, with news values and interpretive frames that are thought to best serve the need to attract and hold an audience in a competitive media environment (see Altheide and Snow, 1979; Mazzoleni, 1987). Among other consequences, this logic leads to a style of political reporting that prefers personalities to ideas, simplicity to complexity, confrontation to compromise, and heavy emphasis on the "horse race" in electoral campaigns. [. . .]

Recognition of their dependence on mass media has shaped the activities and decision-making processes of political parties in various ways. Many parties have, to greater or lesser degrees, incorporated into their strategies a "marketing" approach to campaigning, relying on experts in public relations, opinion polling, and communications for advice about how to craft an appealing message tailored to the voters' opinions and concerns. The centerpiece of this approach typically consists of focusing attention on the personalities of party leaders, for appealing personalities are currency of high denomination in media logic.

Television appears to be the mass medium of greatest importance to the political process, because of its strategic position as the dominant source of news and entertainment and its ability to reach the mass audience, not just those who have particular interests in politics. Television news and election programs are almost universally regarded as having great influence on the success of candidates and parties. Even in countries where political parties are provided free airtime for political programs (such as Russia, the United Kingdom, Spain, Israel, Italy, and Argentina) or may purchase or receive free airtime for broadcasting political advertisements on television (such as Germany, Italy, Argentina, Russia, and the United States), frequent and favorable coverage in television news is believed by many to be critical to electoral success.

In many countries, the presumed importance of mass media, especially television news, as a conduit to citizens whose voting decisions reflect momentary opinions rather than historical allegiances has led to a struggle between politicians and a more or less independent media establishment over who shall control the agendas of campaigns. For their part, politicians everywhere seem to have become embroiled in what Blumler (1990) has aptly described as "the modern publicity process": tailoring more of their activities and decisions to the demands of media logic, engaging in highly visual events staged for television, scheduling activities to meet media deadlines, pushing telegenic candidates and spokespersons to the forefront, polishing their ability to produce "sound bites," and so on. On the other side, journalists often have sought to assert their neutrality and independence from politicians' manipulation, by such means as concentrating on the campaign horse race rather than candidates' statements, reporting candidates' strategic blunders, adopting a "disdaining" style of reporting that exposes the manipulative intention behind staged campaign events (see Gurevitch and Blumler, 1993; Semetko, Blumler, Gurevitch, and Weaver, 1991), and producing independent coverage of issues to prod the parties to address pressing national concerns (as in the case of the BBC; see Gurevitch and Blumler, 1993). In turn, politicians have responded by becoming even more sophisticated in manipulating journalists and, in the 1992 US presidential campaign, by going around journalists to reach the public directly through "the new news" – popular interview programs, unorthodox venues such as appearances on music television cable channels, and the like (see Rosen and Taylor, 1992). This struggle between journalists and politicians has often been cited as leading to a greater amount of campaign coverage that is negative in tone, reflecting poorly on politicians and occasionally undermining the public standing of the mass media. [. . .]

In sum, the experience of the democracies considered [. . .] provides support for the description of the modern media-centered model of campaigning outlined in our general theoretical framework. The defining elements of that model – including personalization of politics; adapting campaign practices to media logic and priorities; and employing technical experts to advise parties on public relations, opinion polling, and marketing strategies – have emerged to a greater or lesser extent in every country we examined. Most often, these innovations are linked to two related developments: weakening of political parties and the proliferation of an increasingly independent mass media system that pursues an autonomous agenda.

Modernization as the origin of campaign innovations

[. . .]
[. . .] it seems appropriate to define the role of modernization in changing campaign practices in this way: Modernization leads to a weakening of political parties and emergence of a powerful role for mass media. These conditions seem to be the immediate causes of changes in electoral practices, and thus mediate between modernization on the one hand and the modern model of campaigning on the other. To this view of underlying causes (modernization), intermediate facilitating conditions (weakened parties and powerful autonomous media), and results (modern campaign practices) should be added three variations. Sometimes, an additional intermediate condition is present in pragmatic political reforms that also may grow out of the pressures of modernization (such as desire for more efficient civil administrations) and lead to further weakening political parties and ensuing adoption of modern electoral practices. At other times, professional consultants endeavor to persuade candidates and parties to adopt innovative campaigning techniques before the conditions that favor them are in place. In these cases, the techniques are not likely to be widely practiced until the appropriate political and media environment has

developed, at which point the new techniques move to center stage in the political process [. . .] Finally, in the case of new democracies, the modern model of electoral practices may be adopted in order to stimulate more general modernization processes, rather than as an outgrowth of them. Modernization plays a critical role in the emergence of campaigning innovations in all these cases, but the path that leads from the former to the latter can take several different turns that represent important variations. [. . .]

References

Altheide, D.L. and Snow, R.P. (1979) *Media Logic*. Beverly Hills, CA: Sage.

Blumler, J. (1990) Elections, the Media and the Modern Publicity Process. In Ferguson, M. (ed.) *Public Communication. The New Imperatives*. London: Sage, pp. 101–113.

Blumler, J.G., Kavanagh, D. and Nossiter, T.J. (1996) Modern Communication versus Traditional Politics in Britain: Unstable Marriage of Convenience. In D. Swanson and P. Mancini (eds) *Politics, Media and Modern Democracy*. Westport, CT: Praeger, pp. 49–72.

Gurevitch, M. and Blumler, J. (1993) 'Longitudinal Analysis of an Election Communication System: Newsroom Observation at the BBC 1966–1992', *Austrian Journal of Political Science*, 22(4), 427–444.

Mazzoleni, G. (1987) 'Media Logic and Party Logic in Campaign Coverage: The Italian General Election of 1983', *European Journal of Communication*, 2(1), 81–103.

Rosen, J. and Taylor, P. (1992) *The New News v. the Old News: The Press and Politics in the 1990s*. New York: Twentieth Century Fund.

Semetko, H.A. *et al.* (1991) *The Formation of Campaign Agendas: A Comparative Analysis of Party and Media Roles in Recent American and British Elections*. Hillsdale, NJ: Lawrence Erlbaum.

Waisbord, S.R. (1996) Secular Politics: The Modernization of Argentinian Electioneering, in D. Swanson and P. Mancini (eds) *Politics, Media and Modern Democracy. An International study of Innovations in Electoral Campaigning and their Consequences*. Westport, CT: Praeger, Ch. 11.

Chapter 22

Pippa Norris

A VIRTUOUS CIRCLE
Political communications in postindustrial societies

Source: P. Norris (2000) *A Virtuous Circle: Political Communications in Postindustrial Societies*, Cambridge: Cambridge University Press, pp. 137–40, 149–51.

The evolution of campaign communications

MANY ACCOUNTS HAVE NOTED the decline of traditional forms of party campaigning, such as local rallies and door-to-door canvassing, and new developments like the growth of spin-doctors and political consultants. A growing series of case studies has documented these trends in a range of established and newer democracies.[1] Different accounts have interpreted these changes in various ways: as the 'rise of political marketing', if the techniques have been borrowed from the private sector, or as the 'Americanization of campaigning' if these forms of electioneering originated in the United States.[2] Building upon this literature, the core argument of this [source chapter] is that such changes in campaign communications can best be understood as evolutionary processes of *modernization* that simultaneously transform party organizations, the news media, and the electorate. This typology is illustrated schematically in Table 22.1 and Figure 22.1.

In this theoretical framework, *premodern campaigns* are understood as having three basic characteristics: The campaign organization is based upon direct forms of interpersonal communications between candidates and citizens at the local level, with short-term, ad-hoc planning by the party leadership. In the news media, the 'partisan press' acts as core intermediary between parties and the public. During this era, local parties selected the candidates, rang the doorbells, posted the pamphlets, targeted the wards, planned the resources, and generally provided all the machinery linking voters and candidates. For citizens, the model is one that is essentially *local-active*, meaning that most campaigning is concentrated within local communities, conducted through relatively demanding political activities like rallies, doorstep canvassing, and party meetings.

Modern campaigns are defined as those with a party organization coordinated more closely at a central level by political leaders, advised by external professional consultants like opinion pollsters. In the news media, national television has become the principal forum for campaign events, supplementing other media. And the electorate has become increasingly decoupled from party and group loyalties. Politicians and professional advisors conduct polls, design advertisements, schedule the theme du jour, leadership tours, news conferences, and photo opportunities, handle the press, and battle to dominate the nightly television news. For citizens, the typical experience of the election becomes more passive, in the sense that the main focus of the campaign is located within national television studios, so that campaigns have become more distant from most voters, leaving them disengaged spectators outside the process.

Postmodern campaigns are understood as those in which the coteries of professional consultants on advertising, public opinion, marketing, and strategic news management become more coequal actors with politicians, assuming a more influential role within government in a 'permanent' campaign, in which they coordinate local activities more efficiently at the grassroots level. The news media is fragmenting into a more complex and incoherent environment of multiple channels, outlets, and levels. And the electorate becomes more dealigned in their voting choices. For some citizens, the election may represent a return to some of the forms of engagement found in the premodern stage, as the new channels of communication potentially allow greater interactivity between voters and politicians.

The essential features of this model can be expected to vary from one context to another. Rather than claiming that all campaigns are inevitably moving into the postmodern category, this view emphasizes that contests can continue to be arrayed from the premodern to the postmodern, due to the influence of a range of inter-mediary conditions, such as the electoral system, campaign regulations, and organiza-tional resources. And instead of seeing the development of a specifically American pattern, with practices like negative advertising, personalized politics, and high campaign expenditures that are subsequently exported to other countries, it seems more accurate to understand the changes in campaigning as part of the moderniza-tion process rooted in technological and political developments common to many postindustrial societies. [. . .]

[. . .]

[. . .]

Mediating conditions

The way these changes become manifest in different countries, and the pace of change over time, will be heavily dependent on certain mediating conditions. Postmodern campaigns are exemplified most clearly by contests like the US presidential and congressional elections – characterized by two major catch-all parties, with minimal ideological baggage, in winner-take-all elections, involving an army of hired technical consultants, widespread use of capital-intensive TV ads in a fragmented multichannel environment, rapid expansion in the political uses of the Internet, and an electorate

Table 22.1 Typology of the evolution of campaigning

	Premodern Mid-19thC to 1950s	Modern Early 1960s to late 1980s	Postmodern 1990s+
Campaign organization	Local and decentralized party volunteers	Nationally coordinated with greater professionalization	Nationally coordinated but decentralized operations
Preparations	Short-term, ad hoc	Long campaign	Permanent campaign
Central coordination	Party leaders	Central party headquarters, more specialist advisors	Special party campaign units and more professional consultants
Feedback	Local canvassing and party meetings	Occasional opinion polls	Regular opinion polls plus focus groups and interactive Web sites
Media	Partisan press, local posters and pamphlets, radio broadcasts	Television broadcasts through main evening news	Television narrow casting, targeted direct mail, targeted ads
Campaign events	Local public meetings, whistle-stop leadership tours	News management, daily press conferences, controlled photo-ops	Extension of news management to routine politics and government
Costs	Low budget	Moderate	Higher costs for professional consultants
Electorate	Stable social and partisan alignments	Social and partisan dealignment	Social and partisan dealignment

Source: Adapted from Pippa Norris (1997) *Electoral Change since 1945*, Oxford: Blackwell, Figure 9.1.

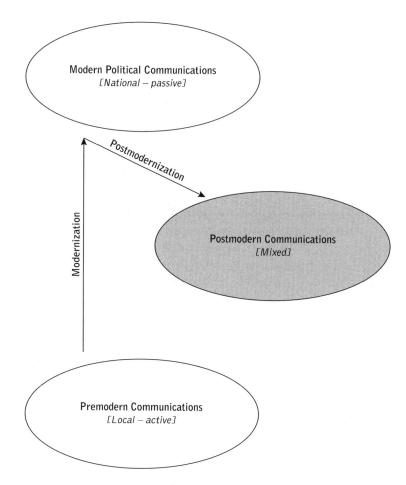

Figure 22.1 The evolution of campaign communications in postindustrial societies

Source: Adapted from Ronald Inglehart (1997) *Modernization and Postmodernization: Cultural, Economic and Political Change in 43 Societies*, Princeton, NJ: Princeton University Press, Figure 3.1.

with weakened party loyalties. Such an open environment is ideal for an entrepreneurial approach designed to maximize electoral support. In contrast, premodern campaigning continues to characterize many other types of contests, such as British local elections, which are second-order, low-salience contests in which the major parties rely primarily on volunteer grassroots members, activists, and candidates in each local constituency to canvass voters and mobilize partisan support. In those campaigns there is minimal national coverage on television or in newspapers, the chief means of publicity remain handbill displays and printed pamphlets, and financial resources are restricted.

Four major factors can be identified as important mediating conditions affecting the modernization process:

- The *regulatory environment*, including the *electoral system* (whether single-member majoritarian or proportional party list), the *type of election* (including the frequency of elections, the type of office, such as presidential or parliamentary, and whether at a subnational, national, or supranational level), and the *laws governing campaigning* (such as rules on party funding and state subsidies, campaign expenditures, the publication of opinion polls, and access to political broadcasts or ads),

- The *party system*, including the organizational structure, membership, and funding of parties (such as whether elite-led, mass-branch, catch-all, or cartel) and the system of *party competition* (such as one party predominant, two-party, moderate or polarized pluralism),
- The *media system*, including the level of development of the *political-consultant industry* (including the availability of professional market researchers, opinion pollsters, advertisers, and campaign, managers) and the *structure and culture of the news media* (such as the contrast . . . between newspaper-centric or television-centric systems, between the partisan leaning or 'objective' models of journalism, and whether broadcasting reflects a public service or commercial ethos),
- The *electorate*, including the patterns of *voting behaviour* (such as whether electors display strong or weak party loyalties, and whether there is limited or extensive electoral volatility).

Notes

1   For recent accounts of campaigning in different nations, see Frederick Fletcher (ed.). 1991. *Media, Elections and Democracy*. Toronto: Dundurn Press; David Butler and Austin Ranney, 1992. *Electioneering*. Oxford: Clarendon Press; Shaun Bowler and David M. Farrell (eds). 1992. *Electoral Strategies and Political Marketing*. London: Macmillan; Richard Gunther and Anthony Mughan (eds). 2000. *Democracy and the Media: A Comparative Perspective*. Cambridge University Press; Bruce I. Newman (ed.). 1999. *The Handbook of Political Marketing*. Thousand Oaks, CA: Sage.

2   For the debate on Americanization, see Dennis Kavanagh, 1995. *Election Campaigning: The New Marketing of Politics*. Oxford: Blackwell; Ralph Negrine and Stylianos Papathanassopoulos. 1996. 'The "Americanization" of Political Communications: A Critique.' *Harvard International Journal of Press/Politics* 1(2): 45–62; David Farrell. 1996. 'Campaign Strategies and Tactics.' In *Comparing Democracies: Elections and Voting in Global Perspective* (eds). Lawrence LeDuc, Richard G. Niemi, and Pippa Norris. Thousand Oaks, CA: Sage; David L. Swanson and Paolo Mancini (eds). 1996. *Politics, Media, and Modern Democracy: An International Study of Innovations in Electoral Campaigning and their Consequences*. New York: Praeger; Margaret Scammell. 1997. 'The Wisdom of the War Room: US Campaigning and Americanization.' *The Joan Shorenstein Center Research Paper* R-17. Cambridge, MA: Harvard University.

SECTION 4

Marketing politics

WHILE SECTION 3 dealt with a set of introductory themes that are familiar in the study of elections and campaigns, this section seeks to deepen our understanding of some of these by exploring how elections and campaigns have changed in recent years. Overall, the theme of this section is that things are different from what they were before, more 'professional' in some ways, and more attuned to politics as an activity that is now 'marketed' differently.

Leon **Mayhew** focuses on the way the growth of knowledge of techniques in public relations and opinion polling has been applied to politics. Developed in the world of commerce, such knowledge has gradually been taken up by political parties – and their advisers – in order to mobilise and persuade the voters. Who those advisers are is the theme of both **Farrell** *et al.* and **Plasser and Plasser**. Based on comparative work, both extracts give us an insight into who those advisers are, what they do and, importantly, how they interact or coexist with traditional party workers. Do they supplement them or do they replace them? This is touched on in the extract from **Mancini** – based on the Italian experience as well as the experiences of other countries – and the piece by **Lilleker and Negrine**.

These five pieces, in other words, focus on the consultants and the 'professionals' who have come to sit alongside traditional party employees and who increasingly run election campaigns on behalf of political parties. But they also ask questions about why such developments have come to the fore.

Whether such involvement by others and outsiders is or is not beneficial is touched on in the extract from Dominic **Wring**'s book on the ways the British Labour Party has come to embrace these new techniques. The party may have won three elections in a row but has this come at a cost? Has it lost (or abandoned) its traditional supporters in its search for the middle ground, or in its search for the key votes (which guarantee wins) in marginal constituencies? Wring has his own view on this topic and his extract connects issues of 'professionalisation', consultants and party politics in the domestic context. It also introduces the subject of 'marketing' which is developed in the final extract by **Scammell**, which seeks to understand how political communication has changed and whether the interest in 'marketing' supersedes more traditional concerns about the political communication process – at least as it relates to elections and campaigning. Has the idea of 'marketing' introduced a new set of issues in the study of political communication and political science? Has it raised the spectre of political marketing as a new development or as a development that can now embrace more traditional understandings of political communication? Can we think about elections, in other words, in ways other than in relation to marketing?

Together, the extracts in Sections 3 and 4 cover the key themes in the study of contemporary electioneering.

Chapter 23

Leon Mayhew

THE NEW PUBLIC

Professional communication and the means of social influence

Source: Leon H. Mayhew (1997) *The New Public. Professional Communication and the Means of Social Influence*, Cambridge: Cambridge University Press, pp. 4–5, 189–91, 212–14.

[. . .]

The New Public

IN THE NEW PUBLIC, communication is dominated by professional specialists. The techniques employed by these specialists are historically rooted in commercial promotion, but beginning in the 1950s, rationalized techniques of persuasion born of advertising, market research, and public relations were systematically applied to political communication. As this movement took flight in the 1970s and exploded in the 1980s and 1990s, political consultants, media specialists, public opinion pollsters, professional grassroots organizers, specialized lobbyists, focus group organizers, specialists in issue research, and demographic researchers burgeoned in numbers and established increasingly specialized roles. Political consultants now specialize in fields as narrow as strategies for countering negative advertising. The experts of the New Public have brought us the often impugned methods of civic persuasion that now dominate public communication: sound-bite journalism, thirty-second political advertising, *one-way* communication, evasive spin control by public figures who refuse to answer questions, and the marketing of ideas and candidates by methods developed in commercial market research.

Some of these roles have become conjoined in new approaches to public influence. Lobbying, though an old profession, now uses new methods that integrate the specialized contributions of market research, pollsters, purchased policy research, partisan studies done in "think tanks," and the efforts of other agents of communication not previously involved in shaping public opinion, such as public accountants. Political consulting has also flourished, integrating a similar array of differentiated contributions. The systematic conjoining of the expertise of varied political specialists has produced professional "grassroots" lobbying, often called astroturf lobbying, for it creates the appearance of support by artificial means, not by grassroots discussion. It has also promoted a process that I refer to as "the certification of facts." Professional political operatives now orchestrate the testimony of experts to create the appearance of factual foundations for political positions.

These new specialized techniques suggest manipulation and furnish evidence for critics who proclaim the decline of the public, and judge democratic institutions, including elections, to be a sham. Political communication, say the critics, merely manufactures consent, rather than allowing discursive formulations of policy in the public interest. When influence is fully paid for and serves a process of reaching compromises among powerful private interests, it is not realistic to call the sphere of influence a guiding "system" or to claim that influence is the currency of a differentiated integrative realm, emancipated from political and economic pressures. Influence cannot be idealized if it is cooked in the back rooms of influence specialists who manipulate behind the scenes rather than in settings designed for truly public discourse. Rhetoric calculated by experts belongs in the category of fraud – a type of coercion. To the critics, this rhetoric is surely not rational argument but the "cookery" of which Plato so disparagingly spoke. [. . .]

The emergence of the New Public: advertising, market research, and public relations

The rise of the New Public could be recounted as a tale of Enlightenment betrayed and rationality perverted by good intentions gone awry. There is some merit in this ironic interpretation. Public opinion polling can be traced to late nineteenth-century British surveys of poverty by researchers motivated by hopes for reform (Abrams, 1951). Market research was promoted by people who sincerely believed that increasing consumption was an essential means for ensuring prosperity in a late capitalist economy. Some of the earliest lobbying in pre-revolutionary America was conducted on behalf of the religious liberties of American left-wing Protestants through friendly, mutually beneficial exchanges between parliamentarians and British dissenters representing their American brethren who, in a colonial situation, were without representation of their own. Later, in the nineteenth century, mass lobbying began in the United States in the name of legislating general rights for groups of people – initially veterans – who had until then been required to pursue redress individually, seeking the personal patronage of legislators powerful enough to secure private bills for them. The electoral reforms of the progressive movement, including the direct primary, were directed against the party bosses. Reforms were designed to promote democratic aims, but they helped undermine political parties and thus contributed to creating the vacuum that was ultimately filled by political consultants.

The rationalization of persuasion

Whatever the immediate aims of the creators of the New Public, the dominant principle governing their means was the rationalization of persuasion. The pioneers of the movement sought effective means of persuasion based on research on audiences and the organization of systematic campaigns. The rationalization of persuasion transforms influence by altering the character of its tokens. When persuasion becomes entirely instrumental, its techniques governed by the criterion of effectiveness, the warrants of sincerity that allow audiences to extend credit to their persuaders are undermined. There is no longer a presumption that persuaders' tokens will be redeemed on demand. On the contrary, the strategies employed by the new breed of expert communicators are designed to avoid confrontations that would require serious elaboration of their claims. In consequence, influence becomes inflated in the sense that it lacks what I have called "relational backing." Influence comes to be based not on conversation but on token appeals to the general predispositions of the audience, which does not build commitment to common cause. Accordingly, the "system backing" of influence is also neglected.

The prehistory of the New Public. Expert communication is not an invention of recent decades, nor is concern over the distorting effects of communication for hire a modern phenomenon. Socrates' critique of the teachers of rhetoric is the prototype of attacks on instrumental approaches to communication that aim to win, not to seek enlightenment through deliberation. Primitive versions of virtually every element of the New Public preceded the full-blown domination of expert communication that burgeoned and matured in the 1970s. For example, in 1903, Rowntree Chocolate began placing sample packets of their Elect brand cocoa in British homes. Influenced by social surveys begun in England by Charles Booth and others in the last decades of the nineteenth century, Joseph Rowntree authorized the deliverers of the samples to administer survey questionnaires to the recipients (Goodall 1986).[1] Market research is the principal historical root and the current core of instrumentally rationalized public communication, but Rowntree's early entree into the genre is an isolated harbinger, not a paradigmatic beginning. Modern market research reached Britain in the 1930s as an import from the United States after new methods for assessing markets and marketing had became prominent on the American scene in the 1920s. Despite Rowntree's early experiments, *systematic* use of marketing strategies guided by *rational research* programs did not follow in the wake of his efforts. Rationalized market research did not begin to take hold until valid sampling techniques for surveys were established, and this development was stimulated less by trends internal to marketing than by pressures to improve the accuracy of public opinion polling following the famous debacle of the Literary Digest poll predicting that Roosevelt would lose the election of 1936 (Abrams, 1951; Lockley, 1974). These events belong to the prehistory of a complex that did not become the New Public as we now know it until marketing research moved beyond selling consumer goods and came to dominate the management of persuasive communication across a broad range of public spheres. Even the export, by professional experts, of rationalized persuasive techniques to political communication, a development that began in California in 1933, when Clem Whitaker and Leone Smith successfully defended the Central Valley Project against a destructive voter initiative sponsored by the Pacific Gas and Electric Company, presaged rather than established the New Public. The employment of political consultants by a limited number of candidates and causes was an important innovation, but it was not until after the 1970s that political consultants were regularly employed in American elections at national, state, and local levels, and later spread to the international scene. [. . .]

Advertising: the roots of the New Public

The New Public did not emerge full blown. It grew in increments as each component built upon and reshaped practices already in place to create the system of rationalized, specialized, and professionalized, public communication that defines and dominates the New Public. Advertising was the first component, the root from which the complex grew.

[. . .]

In the last decade, political consulting has flourished, expanding on the base established in the 1960s, as professional political management became the prevailing norm. [. . .] A summary overview of these services and the number of providers of each type provides impressive evidence of the range, differentiation, and availability of professional political assistance. [. . .]

[. . .]

The role of polling in managed campaigns. I take 1968, [. . .] to be an important turning point. The Nixon–Humphrey presidential contest of that year was chronicled in Joe McGinniss' (1969) well known *The Selling of the President.* McGinniss portrayed Nixon's campaign as a successful commercial marketing job on the part of Nixon's managers. Most observers believe that McGinniss' account somewhat exaggerates the capacity of advertising alone to turn elections. Moreover political marketing through extensive advertising was established long before 1968. In any event, the campaign of 1968 was a watershed in another crucial respect: the unprecedented importance of public opinion polling. Mendelsohn and Crespi (1970, 164) succinctly summarized the place of opinion in that year's presidential contest:

> In the 1968 Presidential election poll data undoubtedly comprised the single type of information used by political leaders to evaluate candidate strength and weakness within different sectors of the public to determine the effectiveness of alternative campaign issues, and to assess the progress (or lack thereof) being made in campaigns. Decisions about over-all strategies and specific techniques (from the type of image to be projected to the selection of advertising media) were all conditioned by information obtained from surveys of public opinion.

The rise of contemporary campaign management is commonly attributed to the influence of television and the large sums of money now required to saturate the airwaves with visual appeals. The impact of television on the current format and dynamic of campaigns – the new electoral public as we know it – cannot be denied.

Nevertheless, if we are to hold to the dictum that causes must precede their effects, the core features of late twentieth-century electronic campaign practice cannot be attributed to television *per se*, or to the powerful effects of visual broadcast images [. . .]

[. . .]

Important as television has become as a means of political communication, the late twentieth-century electoral campaign and the attendant changes in the social organization of the influence system are products of new means of managing political marketing, not television alone. Poll results can be used to persuade potential donors that investment in a candidate has a good probability of success or to encourage the efforts of campaign workers. Polls are used to guide the planning of systematic campaign strategy. Strategic planning typically begins by assessing the climate of opinion within which the campaign must proceed, gauging the views of various subgroups within the electorate on a variety of relevant issues and topics as well as the popularity and images of candidates and their opponents. Using this information, planners can forge strategies for exploiting combinations of issues and target groups that promise possibilities of victory. Tracking polls inform managers regarding the changing intentions of the electorate and its constituent groups, sometimes on a daily basis, allowing tactical adjustments by way of counter attacks, spin control, or new lines of appeal.

The primary purpose of political polls is to provide research-based information for planning and managing the *messages* of the campaign. [. . .]

Note

1   Joseph Rowntree may have been influenced by his son, Seebohm Rowntree, whose work in York included important early English social surveys (Abrams 1951, 41–4).

Bibliography

Abrams, Mark (1951) *Social Surveys and Social Action*. London: William Heinemann.
Goodall, F. (1986) Marketing Consumer Products before 1924, Rowntree and Elect Cocoa. In Davenport-Hines, R.P.T. (ed.) *Markets and Bagmen: Studies in the History of Marketing and British Industrial Performance, 1830–1939*. Aldershot, Hants: Gower Publishing Company, pp. 16–57.
Lockley, L.C. (1974) History and Development of Marketing Research. In Ferber, R. (ed.) *Handbook of Marketing Research*. New York: McGraw Hill, pp. 1–15.
McGinnis, J. (1969) *The Selling of the President*. New York: Random House.
Mendelsohn, H. and Crespi, I. (1970) *Polls, Television, and the New Politics*. Scranton, Penn.: Chandler.

Chapter 24

Paolo Mancini

NEW FRONTIERS IN POLITICAL PROFESSIONALISM

Source: Paolo Mancini (1999) 'New Frontiers in Political Professionalism', *Political Communication*, 16: 231–45.

[. . .]

Changes in party structures

[. . .]

G ENERALLY, IN ACCORDANCE with the original meaning of the term, the special competence and knowledge of political professionals is confined entirely to the field of politics. If they happen to have acquired other specialized skills from a previous career before they entered politics, they do not use those other skills in their political careers.

[. . .] this form of political professionalism was typical of the "mass party." In the second half of this century, however, the mass party began to weaken, especially in the United States, until it almost disappeared, leaving in its place what Kirchheimer (1966) called the "catch-all party," and then introducing several variations on Kirchheimer's hypothesis, what Panebianco (1982) called the "professional-electoral party."

[. . .] [Panebianco's work] [. . .] introduces a notion of political professionalism that differs from that of Weber and that, from many points of view, is more suitable in explaining the transformations of recent years [. . .] [He] states that "in the new [professional-electoral] party a major role is played by professionals [experts with technical skills] who are more useful when the organization moves its center of gravity from members to voters" (Panebianco, 1982, p. 481). For Panebianco, the new political professionals are media experts, public relations experts, pollsters, and political consultants.

In addition to the centrality of the specialists, he enumerates the main characteristics of the new form of party: the weakness of the organization, the reference to an electorate of opinion to which issues and leaders are proposed for discussion rather than ideological identifications, and the essential financial contribution of interest groups. Structured in this way, the new party has one main function: to collect votes at election time. For this reason, Panebianco admits that his professional-electoral party is very similar to Kirchheimer's catch-all party in that both essentially aim at winning elections and not at constructing processes and structures of political socialization or ideological identification as was the practice of the mass party.

There are clear differences between the professional-electoral party and the earlier mass party. The professional-electoral party has a weak organizational structure in which the contribution of the traditional bureaucrats is limited relative to that of external professionals endowed with specific technical skills not belonging exclusively to the political sphere. [. . .] The essence of the party now tends to shift from activists to voters; a large part of its activity revolves around the need to know who the potential voters are in order to reach them and attract their support. [. . .]

From party bureaucrats to new professionals

In Panebianco's (1982) interpretation, the distinction between bureaucrats and political professionals is of particular importance, as he affirms that the new political professionals are "technicians endowed with specialized knowledge." From this vantage point, it is possible to understand why political professionalism today is something completely different from what was foreseen by (Max) Weber in his time.

[As we have seen,] Weber described political professionalism in terms of the source of their economic resources (the party) and the area of their competence (politics). The new political professionalism is profoundly different [. . .] As noted, the technicians [. . .] are mainly advertising and public relations experts, media experts, journalists, and pollsters who not only work for the parties but also apply their expertise in fields such as business communications and commercial advertising. [. . .] Thus, their life does not depend exclusively on politics, and therefore in most cases, politics is not their only area of competence. [. . .]

[. . .]

A further difference between the new professionalism and the Weberian formulation should be noted. In [Weber's] formulation, the political professional was unconditionally dependent on, and motivated by esteem and respect for, the leader and the party. [. . .] The new professionals do not have an exclusive relationship with one party or leader; like all members of modern professions, they offer their technical knowledge to whom-ever needs it and has the resources to pay for it. [. . .]

Professionalism in campaigning

The professionalization of politics, as it has developed in recent years, involves two fundamental fields of political life, campaigning and policy decision making. The first field is certainly the best known and the one that thus far has produced the most evident and macroscopic effects. More particularly, three aspects of campaigning can be distinguished in which the intervention of professionals is very pronounced: definition of the strategies and organization of the campaign, polling, and media production and interaction.[1] [. . .]

[. . .].

In effect, the first aspect is not a temporal phase of the campaign but, rather, an area of intervention that embraces its entire duration. This is the specific field of intervention of the political consultant. [. . .] Political consultants define the lines of campaign strategy as well as their organization and management, functions that in the mass party were performed by the collective organism that supported the leader. In the mass party, decisions about these matters very often emerged from complex processes of discussion and elaboration in which all levels of party organization contributed, often including lower-level party activists. Today, however, political consultants do not limit themselves to executive duties, technical support, or specific skills; rather, in many ways they substitute for what used to be the very essence of the party, at least at election time, namely decision making and organization.

It is not by chance that the figure of the political consultant is most fully developed in countries such as the United States where the party apparatus has been reduced to the bone and the consultant supplies the candidate with the decisional and organizational support that previously were supplied by the party. [. . .]

[. . .]

In most European countries, because of their different cultural and political contexts, the management of the campaign is rarely consigned to outside professionals who are not a part of the party apparatus. The campaigns are strongly centralized, as in the United States, but overall management typically is assigned to someone within or close to the party. [. . .]

[. . .]

Polls are a second area in which political professionalism is highly developed, and not just in the United States. Polls do not concern campaigning only. [. . .] polls are no longer merely a research instrument to inform campaign and policy decision making; they have become campaign and political events in themselves, able not only to inform but also to determine the consensus regarding the candidates, the issues, and the choice among candidates' proposals. [. . .]

[. . .]

Polls and, more recently, focus groups have represented an alternative to that dense network of interpersonal relationships and section meetings that once were the backbone of the mass parties and circulated information, opinions, emotions, and perceptions.

[. . .]

A third area in which political professionalism has advanced is connected with mass media and, more specifically, with media production and interaction. In particular, the development of television required that the parties obtain—by hiring the services of professionals—technical knowledge of the medium and its language, which was absolutely necessary to operate successfully in the new political arena where the mass media are the main instruments of contact with the voters. [. . .]

[. . .]

[. . .] All of this has therefore forced parties and candidates to develop strategies of "news management" that mainly are entrusted to spin doctors and media professionals. In the process, sources of political information have become more and more professionalized. [. . .]

Note

1   Other areas of professional intervention in the electoral campaign can be found in several very specialized fields, such as fund raising. The development of professionalism in campaign fund raising has been based closely on the experience of the United States, where campaign financing comes mostly through voluntary contributions and where the availability of data on possible contributors and the ability to contact them with success can be fundamental ingredients in determining available resources and, therefore, the final result.

Bibliography

Panebianco, A. (1982) *Modelli di partito* [Models of parties]. Bologna, Italy: Il Mulino.
Weber, M. (1977) *Il Lavoro Intellettuale come Professione* [Intellectual work as a profession]. Torino, Italy: Einaudi.

Chapter 25

Darren Lilleker and Ralph Negrine

PROFESSIONALIZATION
Of what? Since when? By whom?

Source: Darren G. Lilleker and Ralph Negrine (2002) 'Professionalization: Of What? Since When? By Whom?', *Press/Politics*, 7 (4): 98–101.

PROFESSIONALIZATION AND RELATED words have become the normative way of describing development in political campaigning and communication in recent year. [. . .] the authors assert that the use of such terms are confusing and provide little detail to the actual change in the nature and conduct of campaigning, when these changes took place, and what force drove the change.
[. . .]

However, the more the literature focuses on the way political campaigning and communication have become professionalized, the broader the definition of the process of professionalization becomes. This brief commentary, [. . .] seeks to question whether the use of the word *professional* and its derivatives – *profession, professionalization, professionalism* – is helpful in explaining the nature of change in processes of political communication and whether different, more specific terms should be employed.

Contemporary literature in the field of political communication introduces readers to recent developments through such phrases as a "professionalization of politics" (Mancini 1999), "source professionalization" (Blumler 1990), "campaign professionalization" (Gibson and Rommele 2001: 40), the "professionalization of media relations" (Schlesinger and Tumber 1994: 67), and even "the smoothness, slickness and all-too-evident professionalism of recent campaigning" (Watts 1997: 142). While there are attempts to define the tools of a professional campaign, of which Gibson and Rommele's (2001) is a highly effective example, these essentially describe a process whereby many tasks, formerly ascribed to party members, are given over to outside agencies. The differing definitions of professionalization illustrated above present the reader with some confusion over the use of the term: Is professionalization a process of making communication more effective through updating and enhancing the modes for delivering a political message? Alternatively, is professionalization related to the employment of professional communicators – public relations experts, image consultants, data analysts, and so forth – to manage the campaign (Mancini 1999)?

Furthermore, should the term also be applied to elected representatives? It is clear that much of the current literature conflates these processes into the catchall term *professionalization*. For example, political marketing models of campaigning introduce the reader to a process that combines specialist roles with effective delivery (Farrell *et al.* 2001; Lees-Marshment 2001; Scammell 1996) These stress the role played by a professional campaign team in analyzing the market, advising on policy, creating effective vehicles for transmitting messages, and training those directly involved in the campaign on style, image, and communication. The marketing literature also ascribes a prominent role to nonprofessionals who, although guided to varying degrees by the campaign team, are responsible for campaign communication. But this account of the process of professionalization differs markedly from the discourse of professionalization, which suggests that as political campaigning becomes professionalized, all those involved in campaigning will be or will become professionals within their ascribed roles. [. . .]

[. . .] This indicates that the term *professionalization* is multifaceted, often highly subjective, and not fully able to describe the nuances in the complex nature of political communication. There are other difficulties with using the term. While political scientists, by and large, link the professionalization of politics, and particularly of members of parliament, to the ways in which politics have now become a full-time paid career (see Rush 1989), writers on political communication [. . .] use the phrase much more loosely. Not only is it used to refer to those individuals employed by political parties for their expertise and skills in dealing with the media, but it can also be used to identify any individual, whether an employee or an elected representative, who has a "basic competence in news management techniques" (Schlesinger and Tumber 1994: 84). To act in a professional way, and to be a professional, is thus to display a range of skills in handling the media and an ability to use modern communication facilities. When used in these ways, the phrase inevitably highlights its direct opposite: amateurism. [. . .]

[. . .]

But in what ways can political actors be said to be professionals, to act in a professional way, or to have become professionalized? One problem in trying to understand these questions is that the use of words such as *professional* often makes sense only in relation to the activities and to the requirements of the media. Does being a professional mean any more than simply systematically providing the media with the sorts of information and in the form that they need? Are such activities and skills both media specific and temporally located? Under what circumstances does the professional and skilful use of the media prove counterproductive and lead to accusations of excessive control and manipulation? Another problem is that these words take on a different meaning and importance when placed within a broader party political context. With the modern political party seeking to centralize and manage all its communication processes, its elected members are inevitably confronted by a set of restrictions and expectations that are almost a requirement of membership: They should not dissent or create controversies, they should toe the party line, and so forth. In this context, is professionalism little more than accepting and acquiescing to the wishes of those at party headquarters? Conversely, is dissent unprofessional?

What emerges quite clearly from the above brief discussion of professionalization is that the word *professional* is perhaps more often used to describe degrees of specialization related to the development of new knowledge or new skills. For example, elected representatives learn how to deal with the media in a professional way; political consultants build up expertise, which they can apply in different circumstances and in different conditions. Pollsters, too, apply basic skills in different environments. In contemporary media-centered democracies, such skills and specialized techniques are undoubtedly invaluable additions to the party machine, particularly when the need to persuade volatile voters is paramount. This goes a long way toward explaining the phenomenon surrounding the growth and deployment of political marketing techniques as well as the emergence of associations that seek to legitimate the role of the political consultant as that of a professional (see Plasser 2001). Interestingly, both the creation of associations between politics and the world of the communication specialist and the certification of consultants in the field of public relations and related professions are characteristics of occupations seeking to exercise professional authority. [. . .]

[. . .] elected politicians, who are by the very nature of their occupation generalists, can nevertheless acquire levels of expertise in their media-handling skills that could permit them to be described as professional. This, however, is not addressed effectively in the literature on professionalization. In fact, judgments about professionalization and professionalism are being made in the abstract and without an appreciation for the evolutionary process that has taken place in respect of the conduct of political campaigns and the way in which that change is related to specific technologies, practices, and knowledge. In other words, the process of professionalization should be examined in its historical context. [. . .]

[. . .]

The use of terms such as *professionalization* and *professionalism* often hinders attempts to explain how the political campaign and the nature of communication have changed in recent decades. What is needed is a multilayered approach, which explains not only how the campaign has become more centralized but also how this process has affected the campaign at the local and the individual level. One can then talk about the specialization of key roles within the campaign and the increased use of modes of delivery that require skills that traditional party employees and volunteers may not have. Furthermore, one can also then discuss the ways in which political communication has become more slick, media-friendly, and tailored for media coverage. But can all of these be attributed solely to the introduction of specialists or "professionals" into the campaign?

Clearly there have been technological advances and changes in the way in which politics is covered by the media that have forced a response from political parties and individuals who seek election to office. This pattern of technological change has always been a feature of political life and predates the introduction of electronic communication. [. . .] In many ways, political campaigning has, therefore, always been in a state of constant evolution. We need to be able, therefore, to place these sorts of changes accurately within their proper historical context, and to assess more precisely what changes have taken place, their causes and the responses to them.

The real problem with discussing all of these changes beneath the umbrella term of professionalization is that much of the nuanced and multi-faceted nature of change is lost; consequently, the term fails to stand up to the task ascribed to it. We would wish to argue, and our present research lends support to this assertion, that the term professionalization needs to be more carefully defined and, when explaining certain aspects of a process of evolution, abandoned in favor of more specific and more accurate phrases such as *specialization of tasks, the increased use of experts,* and the *management of centralization of the campaign.*

Otherwise, we are only left with the normative conclusion that political campaigns have become "more professional," which still begs the questions: more professional than what, since when, and on whose part? [. . .]

Bibliography

Blumler, J. (1990) Elections, the Media and the Modern Publicity Process. In Ferguson, M. (ed.) *Public Communication: The New Imperatives.* London: Sage.

Farrell, D.M., R. Kolodny, and S. Medvic (2001) 'Parties and Campaign Professionals in a Digital Age', *Press/Politics*, 6(4): 11–30.

Gibson, R., and A. Rommele. (2001) 'A Party-Centred Theory of Professional Campaigning', *Press/Politics*, 6(4): 31–43.

Lees-Marshment, J. (2001) *Political Marketing and British Political Parties: The Party's Just Begun.* Manchester: MUP.

Mancini, P. (1999) 'New Frontiers in Political Professionalism', *Political Communication*, 16: 231–45.

Plasser, F. (2001) 'Parties Diminishing Relevance for Campaign Professionals', *Press/Politics*, 6(4): 44–59.

Rush, M. (1989) *The Professionalisation of the British Member of Parliament.* Papers in Political Science: 1.

Scammell, M. (1996) *Designer Politics.* Basingstoke: Macmillan.

Schlesinger, P. and H. Tumber (1994) *Reporting Crime: The Media Politics of Criminal Justice.* Oxford: Oxford University Press.

Watts, D. (1997) *Political Communication Today.* Manchester: MUP.

Chapter 26

David Farrell, Robin Kolodny and Stephen Medvic

PARTIES AND CAMPAIGN PROFESSIONALS IN A DIGITAL AGE
Political consultants in the United States and their counterparts overseas

Source: David M. Farrell, Robin Kolodny and Stephen Medvic (2001) 'Parties and Campaign Professionals in a Digital Age. Political Consultants in the United States and Their Counterparts Overseas', *Press/Politics*, 6 (4): 11–30.

Consultants, parties, and campaign discourse in the United States

A CENTRAL QUESTION scholars ask concerns the relationship of political consultants to political parties (Agranoff 1976; Luntz 1988; Sabato 1981; Thurber and Nelson 2000). Arguably, this is a fundamental issue in the study of political consultants, for if candidates and issue groups believed that their electoral needs could be entirely served by political parties, there would be no market for this bevy of outside vendors. Certainly, there is good reason to argue that modern campaigns demand specialized, technical services that are simply beyond the political parties' institutional capacity to deliver. If we consider that political parties were formed to make mass mobilization of voters occur efficiently for several levels of officeholders (Aldrich 1995), then who is to say that parties still do not deliver on these promises? In short, can parties be reasonably expected to respond fully to the demands of campaigning in a Digital Age? Have the techniques of modern campaigning really been so significant as to force parties to redefine their roles and call for the services of the consulting industry? We suggest below that technology-dependent modern campaigning has indeed exceeded the institutional capacity of political parties in the United States (and, by implication, may be doing the same in other democracies as well). When campaigning in the Digital Age, parties had two options: either to provide the services candidates needed (and become very different organizations than they currently are, or have historically been) (Troy 1996), or to rely on others to help them fulfill their mission. [. . .] Inevitably, political consultants must have an important role here, and one that we would suggest has plenty of capacity for being cooperative and constructive vis-à-vis the parties.

[. . .]

We can construct a fourfold typology of consultants at work in the United States based on [. . .] two dimensions (background and client type). This helps sort out the conflicting conclusions that consultants are at once a danger to and an ally of political parties (see Figure 26.1). Marketers (type IV in our scheme) are consultants who come from nongovernmental training and take on mostly nongovernmental clients. Early US consultants were of this type, and it seems many contemporary European consultants belong in this category. Vendors (type III) also do not have political backgrounds, but provide technical services to predominantly political clients. In the United States, these include specialty software firms, Web page designers, and voter file compilers. Traditional politicos (type II) are the predominant form of consultant in the United States today and refer to individuals who have begun by working for the parties or government, left their employment to form independent firms, and take on predominantly political clients. More than half of political consultants in the United States follow this career path (Kolodny and Logan 1998; Thurber *et al.* 2000). Finally, strategic consultants are a new breed of politically bred specialists who take on (by outsourcing) commercial clients for

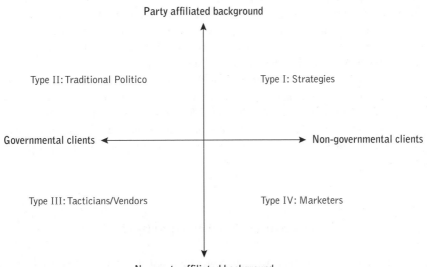

Figure 26.1 Distinguishing different types of political consultants

governmental affairs work (e.g., lobbying) or broad public interest campaigns designed to change public opinion and policy (a good example today is the British anti-fox hunt campaign, which has received some professional advice from US consultants).[1]

Our typology has the principal merit of indicating variations in the individual and institutional links between the campaign consultancy industry and political parties. It also provides a useful means of comparing different scenarios under which such relationships may occur. For instance, there are clear signs of a temporal dimension, especially regarding generational cohorts of political consultants. In the early era of political consulting (1930s to 1960s), consultants were more likely to have nonpolitical backgrounds but applied their trades to political settings. As campaigning became more technologically sophisticated (1970s to 1980s), we find more traditional politicos emerging. More recently, as these consultants begin to age and move farther away from political work and business firms are recognizing the need for more political savvy, strategist consultants are becoming more prominent. In short, our typology should not be viewed as a static diagram, but rather, a typology consisting of several significant stages in which consulting appears to be developing a particular life cycle.

Much has been written on the decline, resurgence, and general role of political parties in US elections. Whatever may have been the cause for the initial usurpation of the parties' dominance in electoral politics, it is now generally believed that professional consultants and parties have important roles to play in campaigns (Herrnson 1988; Sabato 1988). Indeed, the relationship between parties and consultants has even been called "cooperative" (Herrnson 1994: 55). But exactly which tasks are carried out by the individual candidates or parties, and which are best devolved to the political consultants? [. . .]

Whether in the United States or elsewhere, certain elements of campaigns are thought necessary at even the most basic level. These include: headquarters and staff organization, polling, message and strategy creation, day-to-day campaign management, fund-raising, message dissemination, issue and opposition research, speech writing, scheduling and advance work, media production and placement, canvassing and voter contact by phone (both of which require data-base and file management), volunteer coordination, direct mail production and printing, press relations, get-out-the-vote efforts, and (increasingly) Web site creation and maintenance.[2] Obviously, not every campaign undertakes each of these activities in a well-thought-out, coordinated fashion, though in the US context, individual candidates are expected to create this separately from the party organization. As we move toward higher offices we find more and more of these functions carried out in a professional manner.[3] [. . .]

[. . .]

Consultants versus parties?

Do consultants add something to campaigns that had never before existed, or are they now responsible for some functions that had previously been the purview of parties? The answer may very well be both. It would appear that much of what traditional politico consultants offer campaigns—tapping voter sentiment, developing and disseminating a message, and mobilizing voters—are those things that have always been done, albeit now in a more sophisticated fashion. Consultants and parties seem to agree that some of these functions are better left to parties, while others are more effectively (if not efficiently) conducted by consultants. Thus, on one hand, consultants have risen to prominence as surrogates for parties.

On the other hand, consultants do appear to be providing at least some new services. [. . .] Most of the unique services that consultants provide are the result of rapid technological developments that consultants (who on the whole focus on a relatively narrow area of campaigning) were better positioned than parties to learn and provide. Thus, parties never had the opportunity to offer Web site maintenance, for instance, because when the Internet came along vendors were already in place to offer their wares.

[. . .]

[. . .] Indeed, the consultants/party relationship has simultaneously witnessed consultants offering a unique product as well as replacing the parties in providing traditional services (though mostly on the cutting edge of technology), just as parties have been maintaining responsibility for those things they do best.

In general, our review of the evidence would suggest a healthier relationship than has previously been assumed between US parties and consultants. The majority of today's consultants are traditional politicos who start life as party operatives (or, at least, with some kind of party-affiliated background), and the bulk of whose clients are in some ways linked to government. With few (if any) exceptions, they remain loyal to their ideological roots: The Dick Morrises of this world (i.e., consultants who will work for any candidate regardless of party or ideology) are few and far between. There are even some consultants with political parties as clients who go so far as to describe themselves as part of the party, almost like extensions of the party staff.[4] Quite apart from the degree of linkage between parties and (most) consultants, it is also apparent that the consultants fill an important skills gap for the parties. New technologies require new technicians, and, as we have seen, as the demands and specializations of the modern professional campaign have grown, so also has the need for consultants. [. . .]

[. . .]

Party staff changes and the role of agencies

[. . .]

[. . .] Campaign professionalization has gone through a number of phases of change, arguably the most recent of which has only begun in the past decade. Coinciding with and in large part caused by the emergence of new information technologies, the parties have been gearing up for campaigning in the new Information Age (Farrell 1996). The latest technologies are being brought to bear on the campaign process; the focus of the campaign is shifting, with even more attention focused on the presidentialized leadership and campaign imagery; and new technicians are being employed to facilitate this process of campaign transformation. There is plenty of anecdotal evidence of how parties are employing new types of staff: people from the marketing and public relations world, "bright young things" who are not afraid to bury the party philosophy where necessary so long as the number-one objective of keeping the campaign "on message" is achieved (Norris *et al.* 1999).

This suggests that not only are the contemporary West European parties' staff members continuing to become ever more professional—with old-fashioned party bureaucrats being replaced by new-fashioned marketing, public relations, and media professionals—there may also be important internal shifts taking place in terms of the balance of loyalties of a lot of these new staff. For instance, the phenomenon of the "leader's office" has achieved a certain prominence in recent years in a number of countries. [. . .] Clearly it would be going too far to argue that these developments presage a move toward candidate-centered politics, because the party leader remains just that—the leader of a party. However, they are indicative of a further peeling off of the parliamentary party from the other parts of the party (Katz and Mair 1995).

It is also the case that party staffing is far less permanent, not simply because talented and ambitious people are more likely to be mobile anyway, but also because the parties are moving toward more of a "revolving-door" philosophy toward their staff. Specialists are employed for particular services, and once the task is complete the employee is (and should be) dispensable. [. . .]

[. . .]

Given these trends—different staff working for different bosses within the same party, a far greater fluidity in the nature of party employment, and the movement of party staff in and out of political work and commercial work—the West European picture starts to look quite familiar to a North American audience. We appear to have a lot of the ingredients for a description of the US campaign process (at least in terms of the role and flow of campaign personnel). Indeed, in many respects what we are looking at in terms of the profile of the contemporary party staffer in Western Europe bears increasing resemblance to the traditional politico political consultant described previously. The principal remaining difference is nominal; rather than referring to these staff specialists as political consultants, they may instead be given such titles as spin doctors (in the United Kingdom) or handlers (in Ireland).

Of course, in the new campaign environment of Western Europe, the personnel changes are not only internal to the parties. For the past twenty years or more, parties right across Western Europe have been making increased use of specialist agencies (Bowler and Farrell 1992). Work that in the past would have been handled in-house (advertising design, public relations, campaign feedback, etc.) is increasingly being farmed out to agencies and specialist individuals.[5] Indeed, in many respects the major determinant of just how much of this kind of work is farmed out is related to the extent of in-house expertise among the party employees and the willingness of the party leadership to make use of outside agencies. [. . .]

Notes

1   Kolodny/Farrell interviews with US consultants, Washington DC, 1998.
2   In fact, *Campaigns & Elections'* most recent "Political Pages" lists at least thirty-eight activities for which professional consultants can be hired.

3   What distinguishes professionalism from amateurism is the extent to which a campaign or a campaign function is handled by someone who works on campaigns for a living; or, more formally, someone who derives at least part of his or her income from providing campaign services to multiple political clients.

4   Kolodny/Farrell interviews with US consultants, Washington DC, 1998.

5   These agencies lie somewhere between US type III (tacticians/vendors) and type IV (marketers) consultants. Their origin is most definitely non-party, but they tend to have a mix of political and commercial work.

References

Agranoff, R. (1976) *The New Style in Election Campaigning*. Boston, MA: Halbrook.

Aldritch, J. (1995) *Why Parties: The Origin and Transformation of Political Parties in America*. Chicago, IL: University of Chicago Press.

Bowler, S. and Farrell, D. (1992) *Electoral Strategies and Political Marketing*. London: Macmillan.

Herrnson, P.S. (1988) *Party Campaigning in the 1980s*. Cambridge, MA: Harvard University Press.

Herrnson, Paul S. (1994) The Revitalization of National Party Organizations. In Maisel, S.L. (ed.) *The Parties Respond: Changes in American Parties and Campaigns*. Boulder, CO: Westview.

Katz, R. and Mair, P. (1995) 'Changing Models of Party Organization and Party Democracy: The Emergence of the Cartel Party', *Party Politics*, 1: 5–28.

Luntz, F. (1988) *Candidates, Consultants and Campaigns: The Style and Substance of American Electioneering*. New York: Basil Blackwell.

Norris, P., Curtice, J., Sanders, D., Scammell, M. and Semetko, H. (1999) *On Message: Communicating the Campaign*. London: Sage.

Sabato, L.J. (1988) *The Party's Just Begun: Shaping Political Parties for America's Future*. Glenview, IL: Scott, Foresman.

Sabato, L.J. (1981) *The Rise of Political Consultants: New Ways of Winning Elections*. New York: Basic Books.

Thurber, J.A. and Nelson, C. (eds). (2000) *Campaign Warriors: Political Consultants in Elections*. Washington, DC: Brookings Institution.

Chapter 27

Fritz Plasser with Gunda Plasser

GLOBAL POLITICAL CAMPAIGNING
A worldwide analysis of campaigning professionals and their practices

Source: Plasser, F. with Plasser, G. (2000) *Global Political Campaigning.
A Worldwide Analysis of Campaigning Professionals and their Practices*,
Westport, CT: Praeger, pp. 15–20, 350–1.

[. . .]

The worldwide proliferation of American campaign techniques

THE CENTRAL TOPIC of this chapter is the ongoing process of professionalization and internationalization of electioneering and campaign practices in media-centered democracies.[1] [. . .] Prominent figures of the American political consultancy business have worked as overseas consultants outside the United States since the 1970s. In the 1980s they concentrated on Latin America and Western Europe. Since 1989 the former communist countries of East Central Europe, and since 1993 the Commonwealth of Independent States (CIS) and also the newly democratized countries in Asia and Africa, have become competitive marketplaces for American overseas consultants and a market-driven proliferation of American campaign techniques (Plasser 2000a). Since the 1980s, observers of Australian, Canadian, Western European and Latin American election campaigns have stated that there is a universal process of Americanization, though this concept is defined in many different ways (Kavanagh 1995, 1996; O'Shaughnessy 1990; Irwin 1997; Scammell 1995, 1998). The global diffusion of a common "Americanized" model has been explained, stressing "imitation, desire to implement new technologies and practices thought to be effective and the influence of American consultants selling their wares in other countries" (Swanson 1999: 206). But can we speak of an Americanization of election communications if we observe that in Italy, the United Kingdom, Brazil, Russia and Taiwan election campaigns are at present also primarily run on television? Is the advanced degree of professionalization in the planning of election campaigns enlisting the services of external communications and advertising experts proof enough to speak of an Americanization? Does the dramaturgy of media coverage, and the tendency of journalists to define election campaigns as sporting events and to speculate about the chances of winning or the success of individual parties, justify warnings against an Americanization of the media coverage of election campaigns? Obviously, the listed indicators of Americanization of international election communications are *singular* observations, which at best reflect the continuing modernization and professionalization of the actors of political communications, but do not furnish any proof for a *directional* convergence and diffusion process, which the concept of Americanization claims to include.

In simplified terms, we can differentiate between two contrary points of view (see Figure 27.1). From the point of view of *diffusion theory*, Americanization is a directional (one-way) convergence process (Gurevitch 1999: 283). Seen from this angle, central parameters of the actions of Australian, Canadian, European, Latin American and East Asian actors of political communication become similar to the communication process in the United States. This results in *a directional (one-way)* convergence between US-American and European, Latin American or Asian election communications, where – independent of institutional restrictions on the political competitive situation – foreign actors of communication adopt central axioms and strategic parameters of the behavior of US-American actors. Examples for a unilateral adoption of American actions of political communication are, for instance, the orientation of planning strategies of political communication similar to the ways of political marketing (Bowler and Farrell 1992; Butler and Ranney 1992; Swanson and Mancini 1996; Scammell 1998), or the adoption of US-American forms of political coverage and their underlying news values.

However, the advocates of *modernization theory* argue differently. They consider the Americanization of election communication to be the consequence of an ongoing structural change in politics, society and the media system (Negrine and Papathanassopoulos 1996; Kavanagh 1996; Caspi 1996; Norris 2000a, b). The fragmentation of the public sphere linked to these changes leads to a higher degree of specialization and professionalization among the actors of political communications (Blumler and Kavanagh 1999). From this point of view, similarities in the practice of election communication such as excessive personalization, a political star system, mass media impression management and an increasing negativity of campaigns, and the coverage thereof, are the consequences of an endogenous change. The supporters of this theory admit that some campaign practices are borrowed from the far more professionalized competition of the United States; the characteristic components of political communication in Europe, Latin America or East Asia, however, are basically retained, they say (Mazzoleni and Schulz 1999). Thus, Americanization is seen as a synonym for *modernization* and *professionalization* (Mancini 1999). Accordingly, what is happening between the United States and Western Europe or Latin America, is a process of *nondirectional* convergence, which results in an increased similarity between the political communication process in media-centered democracies (Negrine and Papathanassopoulos 1996; Plasser 2000c; Swanson and

Modernization approach	Diffusion approach
Americanization as a consequence of the **Modernization** of media systems and voter-party relationship	Americanization as a consequence of the **Transnational diffusion** and implementation of US concepts and strategies of electoral campaigning

Figure 27.1 Two approaches to the elusive concept of Americanization

Mancini 1996; Axford and Huggins 2001; Bennett and Entman 2001; Norris 2000b; Gunther and Mughan 2000).

From the viewpoint of modernization theories, structural changes on the macro-level (media, technologies, social structures) lead to an adaptive behavior on the micro-level (parties, candidates and journalists), resulting in gradual modifications of traditional styles and strategies of political communications. The outcome of these modifications might at first glance be seen as a transnational pattern of uniformity, but after taking into consideration the cultural and historical *path-dependency* of modernization processes it can be assumed that culture- and context-specific factors determine the reaction to changing technological and environmental conditions. On the contrary, the diffusion approach to the phenomenon of Americanization concentrates on a voluntary proliferation of US-campaign styles. The focus is primarily on the micro-level of entrepreneurial actors, exporting their strategic know-how to foreign contexts by supply- or demand-driven consultancy activities, thus changing and modifying the campaign practice in the respective countries. [. . .] Explaining the ongoing modernization of campaign practices worldwide as partly caused by an elite-driven diffusion of US-campaign styles, it is therefore necessary to take a closer look at the most advanced campaign professionals worldwide: the influential role of American overseas consultants shaping and changing campaign practices on the global political market-place.

The practice of political communication in the United States is regarded as "the cutting edge of electioneering innovation" (Blumler, Kavanagh and Nossiter 1996: 59) by international experts. Therefore, it is no exaggeration to say that the American campaign expertise is an international "role model of campaigning" (Scammell 1998). The transnational diffusion of US-American campaign and marketing techniques is fostered by the internationalization of the campaign consulting business (Bowler and Farrell 2000; Farrell 1998; Plasser 2000b; Johnson 2000). It is effected via a complex "international network of connections through which knowledge about new campaign practices and their uses is disseminated constantly across national borders by independent consultants for economic reasons, by ideologically kindred political parties for political reasons and by the mass media to aspiring political candidates and interested members of the public worldwide" (Swanson and Mancini 1996: 250). However, the diffusion of US American campaign and marketing techniques is not a linear process resulting in a uniform standardization of international campaign practices (Caspi 1996: 174–176). The most widespread model of adopting selected innovations and techniques of American election campaigns might be the *shopping model*, whereby certain techniques and organizational routines of professional campaigning practice are imported from the United States and are modified and implemented taking the national context of political competition into account (Plasser, Scheucher and Senft 1999: 105; see Figure 27.2). The shopping model primarily focuses on down-to-earth techniques that can easily be implemented in the national context while maintaining the country- and culture-specific campaign styles and philosophies (Farrell 2002).[2]

A model that will probably have more far-reaching effects on the political competition in Europe, Latin America and Asia is the *adoption model*. In this case, the foreign observers tend to adopt the strategic axioms of US-American consultants and campaigning experts, which are regarded as more promising than the traditional local campaign approach. The adoption of American axioms of political election communication is characterized by the disregard for conventional organizational election campaigns and programmatic-ideological continuity. Another attribute of this adoption is a fixation on the candidate's image, strategic product development, target-group marketing, news management, spin control, permanent campaigning and negative advertising. The shopping model accelerates the transition from amateur campaigning to capital-intensive campaigning, while the adoption model stands for a break with the distinct styles of European, Latin American and Asian campaigning.

While the shopping model concentrates on the implementation of select American campaign techniques as a supplement to country- and context-specific campaign practices, the adoption model is stressing the transformational consequences of winning on-air, research-driven message development and targeted message delivery. Whereas the shopping model leads to a *hybridization* of various campaign styles defined as "the ways in which forms become separated from existing practices and recombine with new forms in new practices" (Pieterse 2000: 101–102), the adoption model points to a *standardization* of campaign practices. As a consequence, traditional campaign styles may be withering away or fading out in the long run and might be replaced by advanced standards of media- and message-driven campaigning, following the US role model of electioneering in media-centered democracies. Hence, the elusive concept of Americanization is implying at least three distinct forms of diffusion. According to Blumler and Gurevitch (2001), it can imply "direct *imitation* of American styles and practices; it can be based on a selective *importation* and *adoption* of such practices or it can involve *adaptation* of American practices to an existing set of practices, assimilating new modes of operation into older ones. But what all this omits is the role of *indigenous conditions* both in sustaining unique features of national systems and in precipitating changes in such systems" (400). [. . .]

[. . .]

Conclusion: the hybridization of campaign practices in media-centered democracies

[. . .]

Summing up our worldwide analysis of campaign professionals and campaign practices, we found plenty of evidence for an advanced degree of professionalization

Shopping model	Adoption model
Implementation of select US-campaign techniques and practices	Adoption of US-stratagems of successful campaigning
Professionalization of political campaigns outside the US	Transformation of political campaigns outside the US
Hybridization Country-specific supplementation of traditional campaign practices with select features of the American style of campaigning	**Standardization** gradual phase-out of country-specific traditional campaign styles and their substitution by capital-intensive media- and consultant-driven campaign practices

Figure 27.2 Two models of the global diffusion of American campaign and marketing techniques

among campaign managers and consultants, and complex paths of diffusion of modern campaign techniques; but at the same time there are also a variety of regulatory frameworks, restrictions regarding access to political television and a viability of country-specific campaign cultures, far from supporting one global style or one standard model of campaigning. Obviously, the variety of institutional and cultural features leads to a multitude of reactions and responses of campaign actors to changing media environments and electoral markets, resulting in some similarities but also in differences regarding core practices and styles of democratic electioneering. A reflection of the patterns found both on the basis of the *modernization* as well as the *diffusion* hypothesis supplies strong evidence for a *hybridization* – or a merger of traditional country – and culture-specific campaign practices – with select transnational features of modern campaigning. Thus globalization of campaigning does not lead to a uniform standardization of campaign practices.[3] Despite some ubiquitous trends in media-centered democracies, campaign practices still reflect system – and culture-specific characteristics. We come to this conclusion in spite of some evidence that core features slowly become weaker as a consequence of changing electoral markets, more fragile voter-party relations, more adversarial styles of news reporting and the progressive fragmentation of the public sphere.

Notes

1   The chapter is a substantially revised, enlarged and updated version of an article first published in the *Harvard International Journal of Press/Politics* (2000) 5(4) on "American Campaign Techniques Worldwide."

2　Norris (2001) refers in this connection to "an 'import-export' shopping model with campaigners borrowing whatever techniques are believed to work" (163).

[. . .]

3　Summarizing their comparative in-depth analysis of campaign practices in 11 countries, Swanson and Mancini (1996) reached a similar conclusion and noted, "it would be wrong to conclude that campaign practices in each country have followed paths which are completely unique" (269). (pp. 350–1)

References

Axford, B. and R. Huggins (eds) (2001) *New Media and Politics*, London: Sage.

Bennett, W. Lance, and Robert M. Entman (eds) (2001). *Mediated Politics: Communication in the Future of Democracy*. New York: Cambridge University Press.

Blumler, J. and Gurevitch, M. (2001) Americanization Reconsidered: UK-US-Campaign Communication Comparisons Across Time. In W.L. Bennett and R.M. Entman (eds) *Mediated Politics: Communications in the Future of Democracy*. New York: Cambridge University Press, pp. 380–403.

Blumler, J.G. and Kavanagh, D. (1999) 'The Third Age of Political Communication: Influences and Features', *Political Communication*, 16: 209–230.

Blumler, J.G., D. Kavanagh and T.J. Nossiter (1996) 'Modern Communication versus Traditional Politics in Britain: Unstable Marriage of Convenience', pp. 49–72 in D. Swanson and P. Mancini (eds) *Politics, Media and Modern Democracy*. New York: Praeger.

Bowler, S., and D. Farrell (1992) *Electoral Strategies and Political Marketing*. London: Macmillan.

Bowler, S. and D.M. Farrell (2000) The Internationalization of Election Campaign Consultancy. In J.A. Thurber and C. Nelson (eds) *Campaign Warriors: Political Consultants in Elections*. Washington, DC: Brookings Institution.

Butler, D. and A. Ranney (eds) (1992) *Electioneering: A Comparative Study of Continuity and Change*. Oxford: Clarendon.

Caspi, D. (1996) American-Style Electioneering in Israel: Americanization versus Modernization. In D.L. Swanson and Paolo Mancini (eds) *Politics, Media, and Modern Democracy: An International Study of Innovations in Electoral Campaigning and Their Consequences*. Westport, CT: Praeger.

Farrell, D. (1998) 'Political Consultancy Overseas: The Internationalization of Campaign Consultancy', *Political Science & Politics*, 31 (2), 171–175.

Farrell, D. (2002) Campaign Modernization and the West European party: Shopping in the US Political Market? In K.R. Luther and F. Muller-Rommel (eds) *Political Parties and Democracy in Western Europe*. Oxford: Oxford University Press.

Gunther, R. and Mughan, A. (eds) (2000) *Democracy and the Media: A Comparative Perspective*. New York: Cambridge University Press.

Gurevitch, M. (1999) 'Whither the Furture? Some Afterthoughts', *Political Communication* 16(3), 281–284.

Irwin, G. (1997) Americanization: Infiltration or Imitation? Paper delivered at the International Conference, 'Images of Politics', Amsterdam, October 23–25.

Johnson, D.W. (2000) *American Consultants Abroad*. Chapter 9 (mimeo).

Kavanagh, D. (1995) *Election Campaigning: The New Marketing of Politics*. Oxford: Blackwell.

Kavanagh, D. (1996) 'New Campaign Communications: Consequences for British Political Parties', *Press/Politics*, 1 (3), 60–76.

Mancini, P. (1999) 'New Frontiers in Political Professionalism', *Political Communication*, 16(3): 231–246.

Gianpietro Mazzoleni and Winfried Schulz (1999) '"Mediatization" of Politics: A Challenge for Democracy?', *Political Communication*, 16: 247–261.

Negrine, R. and Papathanassopoulos, S.(1996) 'The "Americanization" of Political Communication: A Critique', *Harvard International Journal of Press/Politics*, 1(2), 45–62.

Norris, P. (2000a) The Impact of Party Organization and the News Media on Civic Engagement in Post-Modern Campaigns. Paper presented at the ECPR workshop, 'Do Campaigns Matter?' Copenhagen, April 14–19.

Norris, P. (2000b) *A Virtuous Circle: Political Communication in Post-Industrial Democracies*. New York: Cambridge University Press.

Norris, P. (2001) Political Communications and Democratic Politics. In John Bartle and Dylan Griffiths (eds) *Political Communications Transformed*. Basingstoke: Palgrave, pp. 163–180.

O'Shaughnessy, N. (1990) *The Phenomenon of Political Marketing*. London: Macmillan.

Pieterse, J.N. (2000) Globalization as Hybridization. In F.J. Lechner and J. Boli (eds) *The Globalization Reader*. Malden, MA: Blackwell, pp. 99–108.

Plasser, F. (2000a) 'American Campaign Techniques Worldwide', *Harvard International Journal of Press/Politics*, 5 (4), 33–54.

Plasser, F. (2000b) 'Amerikanisierung' des Politischen Wettberts in Osterreich. In A. Pelinka, F. Plasser and W. Meixner (eds) *Die Zukunft der osterreichischen Demokratie*. Vienna: Signum, pp. 203–230.

Plasser, F. (2000c) Americanization of Campaign Communications in Western Europe. In H. Bohrmann, H. Jarren *et al.* (eds) *Wahlen und Politikvermittlung durch Massenmedien*. Wiesbaden: Westdeutscher Verlag, pp. 49–65.

Plasser, F., Scheucher, C. and Christian Senft, C. (1999) Is There a European Style of Political Marketing? A Survey of Political Managers and Consultants. In B.L. Newman (ed.) *The Handbook of Political Marketing*. Thousand Oaks, CA: Sage.

Scammell, M. (1995) *Designer Politics*. Basingstoke: Macmillan.

Scammell, M. (1998) 'The Wisdom of the War Room: US Campaigning and Americanization', *Media, Culture and Society*, 20(2), 251–275.

Swanson, D.L. (1999) 'About This Issue', *Political Communication*, 16(3), 203–207.

Swanson, D.L. and Mancini, P. (eds) (1996) *Politics, Media, and Modern Democracy: An International Study of Innovations in Electoral Campaigning and Their Consequences*. Westport, CT: Praeger.

Chapter 28

Dominic Wring

THE POLITICS OF MARKETING
THE LABOUR PARTY

Source: D. Wring (2005) *The Politics of Marketing the Labour Party*,
Basingstoke: Palgrave Macmillan, pp. 174–9.

[. . .]

FOLLOWING THE 1979 [BRITISH] ELECTION several commentators argued the [Labour] party lost because of its poor reputation and described it as having a cloth cap image, being old fashioned, extremist and beholden to 'minorities'. [. . .] From his earlier work for the party in 1985 onwards, Philip Gould promoted a broadly similar analysis to that offered by a dissenting minority after 1979; the difference was that his would soon become received wisdom. Despite its emancipatory pretensions, the reality of opinion research was that it encouraged a secretive, hierarchical culture within the party and an ideological conservatism anti-pathetic to spontaneity and transparency. The resulting caution was hardly surprising given marketing is a capitally intense function of strategic management rather than a participatory form of democratic dialogue. Labour's electoral professionals, like corporate executives working on commercial projects, determined who counted (and who did not) in their calculations and, by extension, the political public sphere. This trend was if anything exacerbated by focus groups because they, more than quantitative forms of polling, promoted the demographic as well as psychological characteristics of those voters increasingly seen as crucial in the pursuit of power. Yet here there was scope for misperception arising from widespread ignorance among the media and political elite as to the methodology, purpose and role of qualitative research. . . . The consequence of the widespread ignorance about focus grouping could be seen in the way selected findings were inappropriately used to analyse the popularity or not of certain politicians, policies or proposals.

The aspirations of most of the voluntary party and core vote became increasingly marginal to a strategy that sought to align Labour with popular opinion on a range of salient domestic issues including tax, crime and the Euro. Blair's discourse of progressive politics was anything but on occasions and some policy initiatives appeared reactive if not downright reactionary in responding to populist right-wing press concerns over benefit claimants and asylum seekers. Strategic memos to the prime minister based on focus group analysis suggested media campaigns were having an impact on key voters who were interpreted as desiring what was euphemistically termed 'economic' and 'cultural stability'.[1] Blair's sensitivity to public opinion, particularly through feedback from qualitative research, became a recurrent theme in the reporting about his motives and actions. Underlying this type of commentary was a failure to appreciate how this kind of study was more concerned with the depth rather than breadth of public opinion on a given subject [. . .]

[. . .]

The Blair leadership's interest in pandering to broader public opinion has always been secondary to its preoccupation with the discreet targets within the electorate who have disproportionately populated the focus groups disclosed in journalistic reports. These are invariably the voters who have moved between the two major parties and whose loss to a rival is in effect worth double the value of any other defector or abstentionist. [. . .] More fundamentally the real effect of political market research and analysis is not felt in relation to specific policies, no matter how important, nor from week to week or month to month. Rather the influence can be felt in the focus group evidence amassed and accumulated *over decades* and which has conditioned the Labour elite's thinking about voters' perceived prejudices and convinced them to jettison social democracy. [. . .]

[. . .]

The perils of stratified electioneering

The theory and practice of political marketing raises important questions about the nature of modern elections, participation and democratic accountability. Although it is claimed that opinion research represents the views of a silent majority who otherwise might be ignored this laudable ambition conflicts with the primary motives of those commissioning private polling: the desire to cultivate support, win votes and/or get elected.[2] The healthy functioning of democracy is a secondary consideration and, at most, something to be addressed once politicians are safely in office given: 'marketing tends to focus upon satisfying short-term customer wishes rather than long-term individual or group needs'. There is then no paradox, as has been suggested, between a political elite using unprecedented amounts of research to gauge the opinions of an increasingly disillusioned citizenry.[3] Where there is an irony it is in the way polling has placed a barrier between politicians and the wider electorate with discernible consequences for more complex matters of long-term public concern involving everything from civil rights and justice to health, education, transport or (not) joining the Euro.

At the core of Labour's politics of support is an approach preoccupied with the 'aspirational', owner occupiers, certain women, first time voters and those living in the English marginals of the South East, North West and West Midlands. This is because the modern application of stratified electioneering is devoted to understanding the groups seen as being 'key' to future electoral success, namely the 'new middle-class'.[4] The strategy has persistently disregarded those traditionally associated with the party such as the public sector workforce, committed partisans, blue-collar workers, ethnic minority communities, trade union members and the poor. By contrast the preoccupation with the security and aspirations of the new middle-class is reminiscent of the motivating factor behind *Must Labour Lose?* There is, however, a major difference between now and then in that whereas the 'revisionists had an ideological compass to steer by, (Neil) Kinnock has opinion surveys'.[5] As Rita Hinden warned in her prescient conclusion to *Must Labour Lose?*, the party ought not to embark on an 'extreme' polling conscious strategy:

> [. . .] the more (Labour) could fashion itself on the lines of the present-day Conservatives the more successful it would presumably be – for what the Conservatives are giving is, it seems, what the people want. This may be an inglorious path but – so it is claimed – it is the path to power . . . (This meant) destroying the socialist inspiration of the Labour Party and the source of its vitality. The Labour Party has always been something more than a class party . . . the philosophy of socialism gave it its ideals and won for it the devotion of people of all classes. If it reduces itself now to an imitation of its rivals, its emotional strength will be disastrously undermined.[6]

Hinden's fears were realised decades later with the rise of what Galbraith termed a culture of contentment in which the increasingly vocal 'haves' threatened to limit the ability of social democrats to represent the 'have nots'. Shortly before becoming leader Tony Blair rejected Galbraith's thesis in a televised encounter between them in which the former argued the overriding goal for the left was winning office. The Policy Review ensured Blair's view had already become party orthodoxy and its image reinvented in a 'modern, managerial, middle-class guise' before he succeeded to the leadership.[7] Despite its professed desire to fashion a more 'inclusive' society, the Labour government would repeatedly alienate or ignore those who had traditionally formed its most loyal supporters. [. . .] Labour's preoccupation with the least committed (or uncommitted) elements of its electoral base resulted in the leadership complaining about unrealistic demands from left partisans including a trade union movement that was told to expect 'fairness not favours'. Blair dismissed the unions as 'vested' interests, yet this is arguably a more fitting description for the various corporate bodies that continue to exert considerable influence over the political system. [. . .]

The increasing marketisation of the political system and its evocation of the 'citizen-consumer' have subsequently placed greater emphasis on the value of economic activity as a form of public participation.[8] Despite some claims made of it, this process is not about democratisation, not least because those who form the core Conservative and Labour votes come from different social strata and resource backgrounds. The latter have been historically more dependent on their party and the public realm to safeguard and advance their material interest and is why the neo-liberal inspired promotion of 'depoliticisation' has had such a stark impact.[9] This registered most profoundly in 2001 with the director of the British Election Study describing the record near 40 per cent of voters abstaining as 'a crisis of democratic politics in Britain'. Previously Barry Cox, one of Blair's closest allies, had ventured to suggest a lack of political activity might actually be a sign of democratic stability and maturity. The 2001 turnout undermined this facile notion:

> Elections confer equal citizenship on all adults, as a counterweight to the inequalities of the market and natural endowment. In 2001 turnout fell to an exceptionally low level in the most deprived areas of Britain's cities. In 67 constituencies, all in such areas, the majority of the registered electorate failed to vote; in a few, under 40 per cent did so. The majority of the poor, the unemployed, the unqualified, single mothers on benefit and blacks disengaged from the election. The socially excluded felt politically excluded and so excluded themselves from the electoral process.[10]

Disquiet has rightly been expressed over the way the packaging of politics has led to debate being manipulated by spin doctoring and image making.[11] But marketing's colonisation of campaigning raises other, more fundamental concerns about the ends as well as the means of the democratic process and, more specifically, the way stratified electioneering devalues the importance and influence of the predominantly stable sections of the voting population. The logic of Dick Morris and Philip Gould's position is that it is actually counter-productive to have a fixed principled stance. This is 'political' marketing. . . . Blair, the supposed enemy of electoral complacency when it concerned floating voters, revealed the professionally sanctioned cynicism that had long informed party strategy when he calculated a section of his core vote would stay Labour because they had 'nowhere else to go'. The dramatic fall in turnout at the 2001 general election suggested otherwise. [. . .]

Notes

1   *The Sun*, 19th July 2000.

2   Those broadly sympathetic to the role of marketing in politics include: Harrop, M. (1990) 'Political Marketing', *Parliamentary Affairs*, 43 277–91; Scammell, M. (1995) *Designer Politics*. Basingstoke, UK: Macmillan; and Lees-Marshment, J. (2001) *Political Marketing and British Political Parties*. Manchester: MUP.

3   Mauser, G. (1989) Marketing and Political Campaigning: Strategies and Limits. In Margolis, M. and Mauser, G. (eds) *Manipulating Public Opinion*. Pacific Grove, California: Brooks Cole, p. 44; Tyrell R. and Goodhart, D. (1998) 'Opinion Poll Democracy', *Prospect*, October, pp. 50–54.

4   Gould, P. (1998) *The Unfinished Revolution*, London: Little Brown, p. 397

5   Marquand, D. (1999) *The Progressive Dilemma: from Lloyd George to Blair*. London: Phoenix, Second Edition, p. 219.

6   Abrams, M. and Rose, R. with Hinton, R. (1960) *Must Labour Lose?* Harmondsworth: Penguin, pp. 101–2.

7   *New Statesman and Society*, 18 March 1994. The editorial was a response to the rise of anti-system politics of the far right.

8   Crouch, D. (2003) *Commercialisation or Citizenship*. London: Fabian Society Tract 606; Needham, C. (2003) *Citizen-Consumer*. London: Catalyst Forum; Marquand, D. (2004) *The Decline of the Public*. Cambridge: Polity.

9   Whiteley P. *et al.* (2001) 'Turnout', *Parliamentary Affairs*, 54: 4, pp. 775–788.

10   Crewe, I. (2002) A New Political Hegemony. In King, A. (ed.) *Britain at the Polls 2001*. London: Chatham House, p. 224; Cox, B. (2000) 'Defending Apathy', *Prospect*, August/September.

11   Qualter, T. (1991) *Advertising and Democracy in the Mass Age*. London: Macmillan; Franklin, B. (1994) *Packaging Politics*. London: Edward Arnold.

Chapter 29

Margaret Scammell

POLITICAL MARKETING
Issues for political science

Source: Margaret Scammell (1999) 'Political Marketing: Issues for Political Science', *Political Studies*, XLVII: 718–26, 739.

Introduction

WHAT IS POLITICAL MARKETING? There is no single un-ambiguous answer from the field. There is a broad and rapidly expanding international literature connected by a focus on electioneering and political communications. However, as yet, there is no consensus about a definition of political marketing, nor even that it is the most appropriate label for the common focus of study. Various titles compete to describe the common object, sometimes 'political marketing' or 'political management',[1] 'packaged politics',[2] 'promotional politics'[3] or more broadly 'modern political communications'.[4] They reflect the diverse perspectives and youthfulness of the field. Less than 10 years ago, 'political marketing' was a phrase seldom found in academic journals outside the USA. Even there, the study of role of political consultants and political campaigning styles was in its infancy.[5]

However, the last few years have seen the emergence of a coherent subset of the broad field. A group of scholars, based in Britain, Germany and the USA, accepts the label 'political marketing' and is attempting to establish it as a distinctive subdiscipline, generating regular conferences and a specific literature.[6] It is developing cross-disciplinary political/marketing/communication perspectives not simply to explain the promotional features of modern politics but as tools of analysis of party and voter behaviour. . . .

Political marketing claims to offer new ways of understanding modern politics. It says that 'political marketing' is increasingly what democratic parties and candidates actually do to get elected and that this is different from earlier forms of political salesmanship. It claims that marketing is a specific form of economic rationality that offers insights into the strategic options and behaviour of parties. It shares with history a desire to investigate and explain the behaviour of leading political actors, and thus its focus extends from campaigning into the high politics of government and party management. It shares with political science a desire to understand underlying processes, and therefore to create explanatory models of party and voter behaviour. It shares with political communications the key continuing interest in persuasion. Above all, it claims that political marketing is important. The use of marketing changes relationships between leaders, parties and voters. It has consequences for democratic practice and citizen engagement. Its influence cannot be confined to the limits of the formal election campaign periods, nor can it be reduced to the details of appearance, packaging and spin doctoring, the common trivia of much media attention.

[. . .] First, however, it is helpful to situate the emerging self-conscious sub-discipline of political marketing in relation to the broader field. We will offer a brief summary of the various multi-disciplinary perspectives before moving to look at the origins of the study of political marketing.

Political marketing: research perspectives

Campaign studies and political marketing

Researchers from predominantly political science backgrounds generally locate marketing within *'campaign studies'*.[7] Harrop and Miller identified the study of campaigns, as opposed to elections,[8] as a major gap in the political science literature, notwithstanding accounts of individual elections, exemplified by the Nuffield series and more recently the *Political Communications* series.[9] Electioneering is the starting point and the central concern is with a particular type of modern campaigning, evident across much of the democratic world, which is 'largely [. . .] a response to new technology and the importation of skills of professional communicators'.[10] Campaign studies, as opposed to the study of individual campaigns, originated in the USA where researchers traced the change in campaigns from a relatively amateur craft towards a profession.[11] Similar developments were observable in Europe. In the pre-television era, campaigns were characterized by great land armies of volunteers, canvassing, leafleting, organizing meetings, and cajoling the faithful to turn out at elections. They were labour-intensive, low technology affairs with decision-making centres dispersed across the network of full-time regional and constituency agents. By contrast the modern campaign is capital intensive, relying on a much smaller base of volunteers, much tighter central direction of campaign operations, increased reliance on non-party experts from media and marketing, far less face-to-face communication with voters and increased targeting of floating voters.[12] There is agreement that marketing is significant in modern campaigns, as evidenced by the increasing use of marketing and public relations consultants and agencies, but disagreement that marketing is adequate as a general theoretical framework within which to understand campaign processes. Bowler and Farrell, for example, agree that marketing lends vocabulary and a typology of actions to the study of campaigns. However, they criticize the marketing literature for being 'more an exercise in rationalizing success or failure in hindsight' that in offering theoretical tools.[13] 'Political marketing' here then, to the extent that it is used at all, is effectively reduced to a subset of campaign studies.

Political communications and political marketing

The political communications literature also tends to treat political marketing as only one *aspect* of broader processes.[14] Here too, political marketing is seen primarily as a response to developments in media and communication technologies. There are similar justifications also for the study of campaigning: the increasing importance of elections in the context of partisan dealignment, increasingly volatile electorates, and increasing importance of media, especially television, in setting the agenda for public debate and ultimately influencing voter choices. There are differences, though, in emphasis. While 'campaign studies' stress the increasing significance of campaigns for *election results*, political communications accent consequences for *citizen engagement* with the democratic process as a whole. The manner in which campaigns are conducted is considered as important as the result,[15] with the capacity to silence or empower sections of society, foster support or alienate citizens from governments. Political communication scholars tend to see modern politics and media as inextricably entwined, the activities, intentions and processes of the one inevitably affecting the other.[16] The core questions concern the quality of communications, and are set, often implicitly, within a framework of anxiety about the stability of democratic systems.

[. . .]

The political communications approach occupies a pivotal position for virtually all campaign-related research. To a significant degree, it is leading the agenda. Typically, the political science response is to attempt to quantify and measure campaign and media effects: how is the media agenda set, how does the campaign in the media influence the knowledge, attitude and partisanship of voters.[17] Typically, the political marketing response is to address the normative issues raised through a discussion of marketing ethics.

Marketing management and politics

The third main research perspective on political marketing comes from management and marketing disciplines. The seminal author is Philip Kotler, who argues that election campaigning has an inherently marketing character and that the similarities of salesmanship in business and politics far outweigh the differences.[18] The thrust of much of Kotler's work has been to expand the practical applicability of marketing disciplines from profit-driven commercial enterprises to non-profit organizations.[19] The political market, as the commercial market, contains sellers and customers who exchange 'something of value': the parties/candidates offer representation to customers who in turn offer support (votes). Kotler and like-minded scholars from management disciplines[20] sought not simply to apply marketing frameworks for analysis of campaigns but to proselytize its key concepts as a way of improving campaigning efficiency. As Kotler put it: 'Marketing strategy is at the heart of electoral success because it forces a campaign to put together, in a very short period of time, a winning relatively stable coalition of diverse and sometimes irreconcilable groups'.[21]

The emphasis on strategy is the prime distinctive contribution of the marketing literature, a point highlighted by Harrop in his early article on political marketing in Britain.[22] It shifts the focus from the techniques of promotion to the overall strategic objectives of the party/organization. Thus it effectively *reverses* the perspective offered by campaign studies/political communications approaches. Political marketing is no longer a subset of broader processes: political communications becomes a subset of political marketing, tools of promotion within the overall marketing mix. This is a key premise of the emerging sub-discipline of political marketing. The prime drivers of change in campaigning practice and communications are not the media, nor American influence (important as these are), but campaigners' strategic understanding of the political market.[23] [. . .]

The study of political marketing

[. . .]
The initial interest then in 'political marketing' was in the possibility that it offered an increasingly scientific armoury of persuasive weapons to political leaders. This was encouraged by the claims of some marketers themselves. Mauser, for example, introduced his book on political marketing with the claim that it was the science of influencing mass behaviour in competitive situations.[24] This strand of attention to persuasion fits smoothly in the line of scholars studying the engineering of consent opinion this century.[25]

However, since the early 1980s there began to develop two other influential strands of investigation into political marketing. One comes from marketing scholars, their debate over the marketing concept and its applicability to noncommercial organizations. The other, influenced by propaganda studies, asked whether marketing brought something genuinely new to politics or whether it was simply a version of age-old propaganda activities allied to modern technology?[26] Did the term political marketing denote any unique properties or contain any analytic value, or was it simply a convenient shorthand description of modern persuasive techniques? In a nutshell 'why all the fuss about political marketing'? Both strands looked to the development of marketing theory for answers.

[. . .]
The development of appropriate political marketing models is one of the prime areas of current research. However, the fundamental question remains, not about the specifics of descriptive or theoretical models but of the influence within politics of the marketing concept. Have parties and candidates adopted a customer-focus, putting voters at the beginning rather than the end of the policy-production process? To what extent is this possible in strong party systems with traditions of active memberships? The 'marketing concept' is the key to understanding political marketing. Without it, we are still talking about essentially a modern form of propaganda. With it, we are dealing with a transformation of political organizations and fundamental relationships between leaders, parties, members and voters.

There is room for debate about how genuinely new the marketing concept is to politics. One can find evidence of it in Britain at various times throughout this century,[27] notably in Labour's 1964 victory which Rose called the first 'rational' campaign.[28] It is neither surprise nor new that parties interested in maximizing votes should shift policies in search of support. However, the general pattern of change over this century, as described for business, may be valuable also for politics: from production (propaganda) to sales (media/advertising) to marketing (customer focus).[29] The drivers of change are similar in both politics and business, intensity of competition. Kirchheimer describes precisely as a 'competitive phenomenon' the process of conversion of European parties into 'catch-all'[30] parties. Parties in secular, welfare states were decreasingly able to rely on appeals to class, religion and ideology and increasingly forced to broaden their bases of support among diverse interest groups. In marketing terms, this general trend of weakening party allegiances represents a shift in market power from producers to consumers, precisely the change that transformed business philosophy from production to marketing. Marketing models, political marketing scholars argue, may prove to be more precise and useful analytical tools than Kirchheimer's 'catch-all party'. [. . .]

Conclusion

[. . .] Marketing offers a rational economic theoretical basis for explaining party and voter behaviour that is more broad and inclusive than either the conventional political science campaign studies or political communications approaches. Its tools of strategic analysis offer generic explanations of party behaviour, which are sensitive to but not restricted by the specifics of particular campaigns, political systems, media systems, or left-right ideological typologies. It offers a systematic way of arranging and explaining the various key features of modern campaigning highlighted by the other research perspectives. Thus, the techniques of promotion, advertising, news management and image development all have a logical and clear place within the marketing model. However, the use of promotional instruments *follows* the establishment of party/candidate objectives and strategy development. It does not lead the way. Marketing therefore disputes accounts of political change that attempt to explain modern campaigning largely as a response to media developments. The 'packaging of politics' is, of course, increasingly obvious and well-documented. However, to focus overwhelmingly on the packaging is effectively to do what critics claim to despise in modern politics: to elevate style over substance.

Notes

1   'Political management' is the most common descriptive label in the US trade literature of political consultants. See R. Faucheux (ed.), *The Road to Victory: The Complete Guide to Winning in Politics* (Washington DC, Campaigns and Elections, 1995).

2   See B. Franklin, *Packaging Politics* (London, Edward Arnold, 1995).

3   See A. Wernick, *Promotional Culture* (London, Sage, 1991).

4   See P. Maarek, *Political Marketing and Communication* (London, John Libbey, 1995).

5   The 1980s were the significant years for the growth of the US academic study of political consultants and campaigns. See R. Agranoff (ed.), *The New Style in Election Campaigns* (Boston, Halbrook, 2nd ed., 1976); S. Blumethal, *The Permanent Campaign* (New York, Simon Schuster, 1982); K.H. Jamieson, *Packaging the Presidency* (Oxford, Oxford University Press, 1984); F. Luntz, *Candidates, Consultants and Campaigns* (Oxford, Blackwell, 1988); L. Sabato, *The Rise of Political Consultants* (New York,

Basic, 1981). Before then accounts were dominated by journalists and practitioners, with the exception of two seminal texts: S. Kelley, *Professional Public Relations and Political Power* (Baltimore, John Hopkins, 1956); and D. Nimmo, *The Political Persuaders: the Techniques of Modern Election Campaigns* (Englewood Cliffs, NJ, 1970).

6   See *European Journal of Marketing*, 30, 10/11 (1996), 1–188; S. Henneberg and N. O'Shaughnessy (eds), *Readings in Political Marketing* (New Jersey, Praeger, 2002); B. Newman, *Handbook of Political Marketing* (Thousand Oaks, CA, Sage, 1999).

7   See S. Bowler and D. Farrell (eds), *Electoral Strategies and Political Marketing* (Basingstoke, Macmillan, 1992), pp. 1–2.

8   M. Harrop and W. Miller, *Elections and Voters: a Comparative Introduction* (Basingstoke, Macmillan, 1987), p. 240.

9   D. Butler and D. Kavanagh have collaborated for the Nuffield series *The British General Election of . . .* for every election from February 1974 onwards. Butler with various co-authors has written for the series since 1951 (published in each case by London/ Basingstoke, Macmillan). The series *Political Communications: the General Election Campaign of . . .* has been running since the first publication in 1982 under various editors, starting with R. Worcester and M. Harrop, then I. Crewe and M. Harrop and most recently I. Crewe, B. Gosschalk and J. Bartle, *Political Communications: Why Labour Won the General Election of 1997* (London, Frank Cass, 1998).

10   D. Kavanagh, *Election Campaigning: The New Marketing of Politics* (Oxford, Blackwell, 1995), p. 1. See also D. Butler and A. Ranney (eds), *Electioneering* (Oxford, Oxford University Press, 1992).

11   Nimmo *(The Political Persuaders)* is considered the first scholar to make this substantial point. Subsequent studies of US campaigning trace the rise of professional political consultants and the consequences for campaigning, selection of candidates and party organization. See K. Johnson Cartee and G. Copeland, *Inside Political Campaigns* (1997); J. Trent and R. Friedenberg, *Political Campaign Communication: Principles and Practices* (New Jersey, Praeger, 1995); J. Thurber and C. Nelson, *Campaigns and Elections American Style* (Boulder, CO, Westview, 1995).

12   For a typology of modern versus pre-modern campaigns see D. Farrell, 'Campaign Strategies and Tactics', in L. LeDuc, R. Niemi and P. Norris (eds), *Comparing Democracies: Elections and Voting in Global Perspective* (Thousand Oaks, CA, Sage, 1996).

13   Bowler and Farrell, *Electoral Strategies and Political Marketing*, p. 6.

14   See J.G. Blumler, D. Kavanagh and T.J. Nossiter 'Modern Communications versus Traditional Politics in Britain: Unstable Marriage of Convenience', in D. Swanson and P. Mancini (eds), *Politics, Media and Modern Democracy* (Westport, CT, Praeger, 1996), pp. 49–72.

15   P. Mancini and D. Swanson 'Introduction', in D. Swanson and P. Mancini (eds), *Politics, Media and Modern Democracy* (Westport, CT, Praeger, 1996), p. 1.

16   Political communications as a discrete and consciously cross-disciplinary field of study began to emerge in the late 1950s in the USA predominantly. See D. Swanson and D. Nimmo (eds), *New Directions in Political Communications* (Beverly Hills, CA, Sage, 1990). It is premised on the belief in the prime importance of communication above all other fields of inquiry, and, following Aristotle, the natural affiliation of politics and communication.

[. . .]

17   Important recent studies of media/campaign effects include: M. Just, A. Criegler, D. Alger, M. Kern, W. Darrell and T. Cook, *Crosstalk: Citizens, Candidates and the Media in a Presidential Campaign* (Chicago, University of Chicago Press, 1996); W. Miller, *Media and Voters* (Oxford, Clarendon, 1991); P. Norris, J. Curtice, D. Sanders, M. Scanmell and H. Semetko, *On Message* (London, Sage, 1999); S. Popkin, *The Reasoning Voter* (Chicago, University of Chicago Press, 1994).

18   P. Kotler, 'Business marketing for political candidates', *Campaigns & Elections*, 2 (1981), 24–33.

19   P. Kotler, *Marketing for Non-profit Organisations* (Prentice Hall, 2nd ed., 1982); P. Kotler and S. Levy, 'Broadening the concept of marketing', *Journal of Marketing*, 33 (1969), 10–15.

12   See, e.g. G. Mauser, *Political Marketing* (New York, Praeger, 1983); A. Shama 'The marketing of political candidates', *Journal of the Academy of Marketing Sciences*, 4 (1976), 764–77; A. Steinberg, *Political Campaign Management: A Systems Approach* (Lexington MA, D.C. Heath, 1976).

21   Kotler, 'Business marketing for political candidates', p. 25.

22   M. Harrop, 'Political marketing', *Parliamentary Affairs*, 43 (1990) 277–91.

23   A fourth key perspective on political marketing comes from the 'inside' accounts of practitioners, politicians and journalists. These are valuable resources for students of political campaigning. There is no space here to list more than a few of most significant works. For the USA: R. Faucheux, *The Road to Victory*; M. Matalin and J. Carville, *All's Fair* (New York, Random House, 1994); J. McGuinness, *The Selling of the President* (New York, Trident, 1969); D. Morris, *Behind the Oval Office* (New York, Random House, 1997); J. Napolitan and M. Fitzwater, *Call the Briefing*; T. White, *The Making of the President 1960* (London, Jonathon Cape, 1962). For Britain: B. Bruce, *Images of Power* (London, Kogan Page, 1992); M. Cockerell, *Live from Number 10* (London, Faber & Faber, 1988); P. Gould, *The Unfinished Revolution*; J. Haines, *The Politics of Power* (London, Hodder & Stoughton, 1977); C. Hughes and P. Wintour, *Labour Rebuilt: The New Model Party* (London, Fourth Estate, 1990); S. Hogg and J. Hill, *Too Close to Call: Power and Politics – John Major in No. 10* (London, Little, Brown, 1995); M. Hollingsworth, *The Ultimate Spin Doctor: The Life and Fast Times of Tim Bell* (London, Hodder & Stoughton, 1997); N. Jones, *Soundbites and Spin Doctors* (London, Cassell, 1995); N. Jones, *Campaign 1997* (London, Indigo, 1997); R. Tyler, *Campaign* (London, Grafton, 1987); D. Wilson, *Battle for Power* (London, Sphere, 1987); Lord Windlesham, *Communication and Political Power* (London, Jonathon Cape, 1966).

[. . .]

24   Mauser, *Political Marketing*, p. 5.

25   W. Lippmann, *Public Opinion* (New York, Macmillan, 1922); H. Lasswell, *Propaganda Technique in the World War* (New York, Knopf, 1927).

26   See N. O'Shaughnessy, *The Phenomenon of Political Marketing* (Basingstoke, Macmillan, 1990); M. Scammell, *Designer Politics* (Basingstoke, Macmillan, 1995), pp. 5–23.

[. . .]

27   See Scammell, *Designer Politics*; and D. Wring, 'Political marketing and party development in Britain: a "secret' history"', *European Journal of Marketing*, 30 (1996), 100–111.

28   R. Rose, *Influencing Voters* (London, Faber & Faber, 1967).

29   See G. Smith and J. Saunders, 'The application of marketing to British politics', *Journal of Marketing Management*, 5 (1990).

30   O. Kirchheimer, 'The Transformation of Western European Party Systems', in J. LaPalombara and M. Weiner (eds) *Political Parties and Political Development* (Princeton, NJ, Princeton University Press) pp. 177–200.

SECTION 5

Media effects

THIS SECTION FOCUSES on the effects of the mass media on audiences. The pieces selected serve to remind the reader of the essentially contested nature of media effects in the field of political communication, with studies producing often contradictory findings.

The section starts with an extract from Lazarsfeld *et al.*'s classic study *The People's Choice*. In this excerpt, Lazarsfeld and his colleagues spell out what became the dominant view of the impact of the media for much of the post-war period – namely that the media reinforced voters' existing intentions and did not change them. This same conclusion is reached nearly sixty years later in research by Norris *et al.*, albeit in a different democracy. This research, on whether a switch in party allegiance by the press affected voting, concludes that the press had little ability to change the voting behaviour of British voters in 1997.

Other studies interested in effects have sought to move beyond the limited focus on voting behaviour which characterises much of effects research. Perhaps one of the first attempts to rethink the impact of the media is McCombs and Shaw's work on agenda setting. They started from the premise that if the media were not successful in telling voters what to think during a campaign, they might be successful in telling them what to think about. Their research was the first study of the power of the media to set the public agenda; their conclusion being that, even if campaign messages have no behavioural impact, they might well have a cognitive one. A similar interest in the cognitive impact of campaigns can be seen in the work of Lewis *et al.*, although their concern is with what voters learn from the media about candidates. Through comparing heavy and light television viewers, their research (based on the 1992 US presidential campaign) found that campaign coverage misleads viewers, especially heavy viewers, about the importance of certain issues.

Some of the most interesting effects research has been on 'framing'. Frames are, in simple terms, interpretive frameworks used by the news media to make sense of the world they report. By their very nature, these frames present a partial view of the world. So, unlike agenda-setting research, it is not merely the presence of an issue in the news that is important, but the way that issue is framed. **Capella and Jamieson** note that news frames invite the audiences to make certain inferences, and not others. Their extract argues that strategic news frames employed in covering politics, such as the focus on party strategy or winning and losing, 'activate cynical attributions' within the audience. In an experimental study on framing, **Iyengar** seeks to discover whether news frames shape the way the public attributes blame. He argues that the allocation of responsibility for particular problems in society, such as crime and terrorism, is determined in part by the way the news media frame particular societal problems.

In the final extract in this section, **Katz and Dayan** (2003) move beyond the confines of the campaign and party messages in an effort to comprehend the long-term impact of the media. They re-examine one of the earliest studies about the 'effects' of television, a study by Kurt and Gladys Lang of MacArthur Day in Chicago. In this study, the Langs sought to compare the experiences of the people on the street, who took part in the welcoming ceremonies, with those of the people who watched the event on television. They concluded that television brought a 'unique perspective' to the event and that this had a number of effects, including political ones. The importance of the study is highlighted in this extract, which broadens the discussion to include comments on the extent to which the Langs' work heralded an interest in 'media events', namely, a totally different genre of television that is highly constructed and highly politicised.

Chapter 30

Paul F. Lazarsfeld, Bernard Berelson and Hazel Gaudet

THE REINFORCEMENT EFFECT

Source: Paul F. Lazarsfeld, Bernard Berelson, and Hazel Gaudet (1944 [1969])
*The People's Choice: How the Voter Makes Up His Mind in a Presidential
Campaign* (3rd edn), New York and London: Columbia University Press,
pp. 87–93.

PARADOXICALLY ENOUGH, campaign propaganda exerted one major effect by producing no overt effect on vote behavior at all – if by the latter "effect" we naively mean a *change* in vote. Half the people knew in May, before the campaign got underway, how they would vote in November, and actually voted that way. But does that mean that campaign propaganda had no effect upon them? Not at all. For them, political communications served the important purpose of preserving prior decisions instead of initiating new decisions. It kept the partisans "in line" by reassuring them in their vote decision; it reduced defections from the ranks. It had the effect of reinforcing the original vote decision.

The importance of reinforcement can be appreciated by conjecturing what might have happened if the political content of the major media of communications had been monopolized, or nearly monopolized, by one of the parties. European experience with totalitarian control of communications suggests that under some conditions the opposition may be whittled down until only the firmly convinced die-hards remain. In many parts of this country, there are probably relatively few people who would tenaciously maintain their political views in the face of a continuous flow of hostile arguments. Most people want – and need – to be told that they are right and to know that other people agree with them. Thus, the parties could forego their propagandizing only at considerable risk, and never on a unilateral basis. So far as numbers of voters are concerned, campaign propaganda results not so much in gaining new adherents as in preventing the loss of voters already favorably inclined.

Wherever the parties stand in substantial competition – as they do throughout most of the country and as they did in Erie County in 1940 – party loyalties are constantly open to the danger of corrosion. Party propaganda – from his own party – provides an arsenal of political arguments which serve to allay the partisan's doubts and to refute the opposition arguments which he encounters in his exposure to media and friends – in short, to secure and stabilize and solidify his vote intention and finally to translate it into an actual vote. A continuing flow of partisan arguments enables him to reinterpret otherwise unsettling events and counter-arguments so that they do not leave him in an uncomfortable state of mental indecision or inconsistency. For example, Republicans who might be disturbed by Willkie's relationship to utility interests were equipped with the notion that his experience in business would make him a better administrator of the national government than Roosevelt. Similarly, Democrats uneasy about the third term as a break with American tradition were able to justify it by reference to the President's indispensable experience in foreign affairs at such a time of world crisis. (In fact, this latter argument was the answer to the disturbing third-term argument for many loyal Democrats.)

The provision of new arguments and the reiteration of old arguments in behalf of his candidate reassure the partisan and strengthen his vote decision. Should he be tempted to vacillate, should he come to question the rightness of his decision, the reinforcing arguments are there to curb such tendencies toward defection. The partisan is assured that he is right; he is told why he is right; and he is reminded that other people agree with him, always a gratification and especially so during times of doubt. In short, political propaganda in the media of communication, by providing them with good partisan arguments, at the same time provides orientation, reassurance, integration for the already partisan. Such satisfactions tend to keep people "in line" by reinforcing their initial decision. To a large extent, stability of political opinion is a function of exposure to reinforcing communications.

Partisanship, partisan exposure, reinforced partisanship

The availability of partisan propaganda in Erie County in 1940 was somewhat out of balance. There was much more Republican material available [. . .] but it was still reasonably easy to read or listen to the Democratic side. If the exposure of the partisans paralleled the partisan distribution of available communications, they would always be running up against the case of the opposition, especially the Democrats. Thus reinforcement would take a step forward and then a step back, and its effect would be halting and lame at best.

But, of course, actual exposure does *not* parallel availability. Availability *plus* predispositions determines exposure – and predispositions lead people to select communications which are congenial, which support their previous position. More Republicans than Democrats listened to Willkie and more Democrats than Republicans listened to Roosevelt. The universe of campaign communications – political speeches, newspaper stories, newscasts, editorials, columns, magazine articles – was open to virtually everyone. But exposure was consistently partisan, and such partisan exposure resulted in reinforcement.[1]

By and large about two-thirds of the constant partisans – the people who were either Republican or Democratic from May right through to Election Day – managed

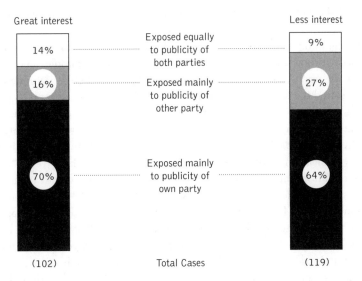

Figure 30.1 The more interested people are in the election, the more they tend to expose themselves to propaganda of their own party. This chart deals only with those with constant vote intention from May to November.

to see and hear more of their own side's propaganda than the opposition's.[2] About one-fifth of them happened to expose more frequently to the other side, and the rest were neutral in their exposure (Figure 30.1). But – and this is important – the more strongly partisan the person, the more likely he is to insulate himself from contrary points of view. The constants with great interest and with most concern in the election of their own candidate were *more* partisan in exposure than the constants with less interest and less concern. Such partisan exposure can only serve to reinforce the partisan's previous attitudes. In short, the most partisan people distance themselves from the disturbing experience presented by opposition arguments by paying little attention to them. Instead, they turn to that propaganda which reaffirms the validity and wisdom of their original decision – which is then reinforced.

One of the assumptions of a two-party democratic system is that considerable inter-communication goes on between the supporters of the opposing sides. This evidence indicates that such inter-communication may go on in public – in the media of communication – without reaching very far into the ranks of the strongly partisan, on either side. In recent years, there has been a good deal of talk by men of good will about the desirability and necessity of guaranteeing the free exchange of ideas in the market-place of public opinion. Such talk has centered upon the problem of keeping free the channels of expression and communication. Now we find that the consumers of ideas, if they have made a decision on the issue, themselves erect high tariff walls against alien notions.

Reinforcement described by the reinforced

Partisans need reasons for being partisan, and the formal media supply them and thus reinforce their partisanship. At one point during the interviews, the respondents who maintained a constant voting preference were asked why they favored the candidate of their choice. Their answers sometimes showed the effect of reinforcement.

Faint beginnings of doubt about the wisdom of their decision were counteracted by appropriate propaganda, and corrosion is thus halted. For example, a young married woman, a Democrat with low income, reported: "In FDR's Wednesday night speech, he stated the facts of his administration. He mentioned several facts of which I had been unaware – for example, that there have been fewer bank failures in his administration than in previous ones. I cannot recall any others at present, but *I had no idea FDR had accomplished so much.*" The final phrase clearly expresses this partisan's relief and gratification in the apparent validity of her decision.

Similar reinforcement – the other side of the coin – is evident in the case of a young salesman on a low SES level who was for Willkie in 1940 just as he had been for Landon in 1936. His actual economic position conflicted with his appraisal of himself as belonging to small business. He granted that "Roosevelt's policies were good but we don't need them now," and then continued: "I have been reading various articles about Roosevelt lately and he didn't do as much as I thought . . . . Read in *Nation's Business* about the NLRB. The basic idea was all right but they didn't push it far enough. *It just sounds like he has done a lot but he really didn't.*" This man's wife disagreed with him on politics. Under all these cross-pressures, perhaps insecure in his Republican vote intention, he turned to business publications to reassure himself, to convince himself that he was right, and to get good ideas for purposes of argument. Without such reinforcement, this man might have swung away from the Republicans.

But some respondents had more than the faint beginnings of doubt; they had enough doubts actually to leave their original choice for indecision or even the other party, after which they returned to their first decision. Such people are the waverers we have discussed in earlier chapters. The influence exerted upon them by the media of communication to return to their original decision is no less a reinforcement effect than that exerted upon someone who doubted but never actually left his party. It is just that they needed *more* reinforcement.

Consider the case of a young unemployed laborer on a low SES level – a "natural" Democrat. Originally Democratic, he favored Roosevelt because "he gave us work" and because he is "damned if he knows" who will benefit from Willkie's election. And yet he decided in August to vote Republican because of the third term issue: "Two times is enough. The rest of 'em didn't take it." But then he heard an argument which served to reinforce his Democratic predispositions: "I heard a Lowell Thomas broadcast yesterday saying that *Hitler and Mussolini wanted Willkie elected.* I don't want to vote for any Bund." And so this respondent returned to his Democratic vote intention because "FDR has the experience we need at this time and I don't have the confidence in Willkie, without experience in this crisis." And once again, he cited his favorite commentator, Lowell Thomas, as the source of this reason for change.

Another illustration of the effect of reinforcement upon a waverer involves the vice-president of a bank, with strong Republican predispositions. In May he was Republican, but by June – after Germany's conquest of Western Europe – he was not sure: "My decision will depend upon who will keep us out of war. That is paramount in my mind." But all his attitudes and values, and probably associates, were so firmly Republican that his indecision was short-lived. By August he was back doing business at the same old stand: "For one thing, FDR's running for a third term made me very disgusted . . . *Any man (Willkie) who has made such a success of himself in such a big business* as Commonwealth and Southern will do a lot for this country in a business way. I've read articles about him in the *Cleveland Plain Dealer* and also the *Chicago Tribune*. I have also read a book, 'The Smoke Screen,' which woke me up to just how badly FDR is spending the taxpayers' money."

It is in comments of this kind that we find indications of the reinforcement functions of partisan arguments. They reinforce by validating, orienting, and strengthening the original decision, by minimizing tendencies toward an internal conflict of opinions, by buttressing some opinions at the expense of others, and by countering possible or actual corrosion of partisan attitudes.

Notes

1   Such partisan exposure is not confined to politics. Its application to other areas of communication has also been established. For example, educational broadcasts reach primarily those people who need them least; in a recent series of programs on the contributions of various national minorities to American life, the audience for each program was primarily composed of the members of the particular minority group being extolled. Such exposure even extends to commercial communications; people tend to read advertisements of the things they already own and listen to the radio programs sponsored by the company which manufactures their most important possessions.

2   This represents only an extension of what we saw in operation in the case of activation, where people undecided in vote selected communications. which fit their political predispositions. Here, however, this is intensified because not only predispositions (in most cases) but also vote preference makes for the selection of partisan communications.

Chapter 31

Pippa Norris, John Curtice, David Sanders, Margaret Scammell and Holli A. Semetko

THE EFFECTS OF NEWSPAPERS

Source: Pippa Norris, John Curtice, David Sanders, Margaret Scammell and Holli A. Semetko (1999) *On Message: Communicating the Campaign*, London, Thousand Oaks, CA, New Delhi: Sage, pp. 152–69.

O N 17 M A R C H 1997, John Major, the incumbent Conservative Prime Minister, announced that the general election would be held on 1 May. [. . .] The next morning, *The Sun*, Britain's best-selling national daily paper, announced that it was backing Labour.

[. . .] The Sun's change of allegiance was simply the most dramatic of a number of changes of allegiance amongst Britain's newspapers in 1997. [. . .] Overall, during the 1997 campaign more than twice as many people were reading a newspaper that backed Labour as were reading one that supported the Conservatives. The traditional Tory advantage amongst the press was dramatically broken for the first time in post-war British politics.

[. . .]

Britain's highly partisan press (Dalton *et al.* 1998) has meant that it has always been worth asking the question, 'do newspapers influence votes?' (Curtice, 1997). But the difficulty in answering the question, as in other research on the impact of the media, is that any association between newspaper read and vote choice could reflect the outcome of one or other or both of two different social processes. One possibility is indeed that newspapers influence the way that people vote. The other, however, is that people choose to read a newspaper that chimes with their own views. Unfortunately, much previous writing on the alleged influence of the British press has failed to take sufficient account of this difficulty (see, for example, Dunleavy and Husbands 1985; Newton 1991).

The changed partisanship of the press in 1997, and not least the switch by *The Sun*, gives us, however, an unusually powerful opportunity to try and untangle the two processes.

[. . .]

Newspaper readership and vote switching during the 1997 campaign

[. . .]

Although the BES [British Election Campaign Study] campaign panel survey did interview its respondents before polling day, that interview took place as much as twelve months before the campaign started. [. . .] The survey did, however, contact its respondents in the first fortnight of April 1997, [. . .]. Respondents were asked on that occasion both which newspaper they had read the previous day and a number of questions about their vote intentions. By comparing these reports with voters' accounts in the final wave of the survey of how they actually voted we can therefore see whether those who actually reported reading *The Sun* or any other newspaper were more likely than other voters to switch towards Labour during the most intense part of the campaign. [. . .]

A simple summary of some of the relevant data is provided in Table 31.1. In this table we compare, for each group of newspaper readers, the level of Conservative and Labour support on polling day with the equivalent levels in early April when respondents were asked whether they had decided which way they were going to vote, and if so for whom.

[. . .] We should note first that both parties secured a higher share of the actual vote than they did of vote intentions a fortnight earlier even though we have included non-voters in our denominator. This reflects the fact that no less than two in five of our respondents said that they had not decided for whom they would vote when they were first interviewed during the campaign while, in contrast, only one in six said they did not vote on polling day. But it will be noted that, overall, Labour was

Table 31.1 Change in Conservative and Labour support during 1997 campaign by readership

	% Voted	—	% Saying had decided to vote early April
	Con	Lab	
Paper read:			
Tory faithful	+12	+7	(221)
The Sun	+ 3	+2	(139)
Other ex-Tory	+ 3	+5	(68)
Labour faithful	+ 0	+8	(166)
Other	+ 5	+4	(64)
None	+ 5	+7	(723)

Note: Paper read yesterday, early April 1997.

Source: British Election Campaign Study 1997.

no more successful at gathering votes during the campaign itself than were the Conservatives. [. . .] However, if we compare what happened amongst readers of different kinds of newspaper we do have some counterfactual evidence upon which to rest claims about the influence or otherwise of newspapers. And we can see that there are some differences between the various newspaper groups in Table 31.1. Most striking is the fact that Conservative support rose by 12 points amongst readers of the Tory faithful press but not at all amongst readers of the equivalent Labour press. And while Labour was not particularly successful at winning over votes amongst *Sun* readers, such readers together with readers of other ex-Tory newspapers were not particularly likely to return to the Tory fold either.

In short, we do appear to have here some evidence that which newspaper people read did make some difference to the likelihood that they would decide during the course of the campaign to opt for one party rather than another. But there are, of course, some important limitations to this analysis. Not only have we not examined whether any of our differences are statistically significant, but we also have to bear in mind the possibility of floor and ceiling effects in our measures of changes in party support. For example, with no less than 58 per cent of readers of Labour faithful papers having already decided to back Labour by early April, and with just 23 per cent unsure about what they would do, the scope for further increases in Labour support in this group was less than it was, for example, amongst those who were not reading a newspaper, only 30 per cent of whom backed Labour and 43 per cent of whom were undecided.

[. . .]

Our results are relatively straightforward. As we might have expected from Table 31.1, we find that readers of a Tory-faithful paper were significantly more likely to decide during the campaign to opt for the Conservatives while readers of a Labour-faithful paper were less likely to do so. Meanwhile, as we suspected might be the case once we take into account floor and ceiling effects, the rise in Labour

Table 31.2 Logistic model of vote switching in 1997 campaign by readership

	Dependent variable vote 1997			
	Con v. non-Con		Lab v. non-Lab	
Probability of voting Con	+.63	(.04)		
Probability of voting Lab			− +.51	(.03)
Newspaper read:				
Tory faithful	+.80	(.27)*	−.39	(.25)
The Sun	−.12	(.37)	−.04	(.28)
Other ex-Tory	+.09	(.48)	−.08	(.05)
Labour faithful	−1.24	(.59)*	+.86	(.25)*
Other	+.93	(.58)	−.45	(.36)

Note: Main entries are logistic parameter coefficients. In the case of newspaper read they are contrast coefficients which show the difference between the behaviour of the relevant group and those who reported reading a newspaper. Entries in brackets are standard errors. *Coefficient is significant at the 5 per cent level or less. The period is early April 1997.

Source: British Election Campaign Study 1997.

support amongst readers of the Labour-faithful papers was rather greater than we might have anticipated. In short we once again appear to have evidence that at the margins at least newspapers can help shore up the loyalty of their readers to the party the newspaper favours. [. . .] At the same time, however, we find little evidence that the defection of *The Sun* or any other ex-Tory newspaper had much impact on their readers, who behaved little differently from those who did not read a newspaper at all. Over the relatively short period of a campaign, at least, it seems that newspapers trumpeting a relatively new tune are unlikely to receive an echo from their readers. *The Sun's* defection may have been of symbolic significance, but whether it was of any practical significance seems open to doubt. There is, however, one important caveat to this argument. For we might ask ourselves what might have happened amongst their readers during the campaign if *The Sun* and the other ex-Tory papers had in fact decided to continue to back the Conservatives. On the evidence of Table 31.2 it might be suggested that they would have been more likely to have switched to the Conservatives just as the readers of the Tory faithful press did. Labour may not have gained any advantage for themselves in winning over *The Sun*, but they may well have helped neutralize what otherwise would have been a benefit for the Conservatives.

Newspaper readership and vote switching between 1992 and 1997

Of course, one argument against what we have done so far is that no matter how intense an election campaign might be, in the British context at least it is simply too short a period in which to anticipate much in the way of evidence of media influence. It is not the few dramatic headlines or pictures that might be produced during a campaign that matter, but rather the constant and consistent diet of partisan-coloured news that readers might receive over months or even years. If so, no sudden switch of partisanship can be expected to make a difference. In practice, as we have already noted, none of the newspapers that failed to back the Conservatives in 1997 after having done so in 1992 underwent a sudden conversion. The tone of their coverage over much of the previous Parliament had been unfavourable to the Conservatives too. So perhaps we might see clearer evidence of newspaper influence if we look at vote switching across the whole of the 1992–7 Parliament. This we can do by looking at the evidence of the 1992–7 British Election Panel Study.

[. . .]

Despite the fact that we are looking at a much longer time period, many of the results do not immediately suggest that the partisanship of newspapers influenced their readers. Support for the Conservatives might have dropped more amongst *Sun* readers than those consistently not exposed to a partisan newspaper, but the same is also true of those consistently reading a Tory-faithful newspaper. And support amongst the latter fell as much as it did amongst those who stopped reading a proConservative newspaper. Meanwhile, Labour's gains amongst *Sun* readers are no greater than they were amongst those consistently not reading a partisan paper.

But some results are consistent with the expectations we would have if the partisanship of newspapers matters. Labour's support rose most amongst those who started to read a Labour-faithful newspaper between 1992 and 1997, while its support barely rose amongst those who stopped reading such a newspaper. *The Sun* may not have made much difference to Labour's apparent support, but *The Mirror* evidently could (see also Curtice and Semetko 1994; Curtice 1997). Equally Labour does not do well amongst those who consistently read a Tory-faithful paper.

[. . .]

Politics and newspaper switching 1992–1997

So, if the partisanship of newspapers has only a marginal impact on readers' voting behaviour, and cannot be held responsible for the outcome of the 1997 election, why might this be so? One possibility, of course, is that voters choose newspapers so that the political message they receive chimes in with their dispositions. True, as we have already seen, patterns of newspaper readership may be relatively stable over the short period of an election campaign, but we have also seen that in the five years between 1992 and 1997, well over one in three of the respondents to BEPS changed the newspaper they read. But what evidence is there that their politics might have influenced their decision?

[. . .]

The period between 1992 and 1997 was one which saw a dramatic shift in the fortunes of the Conservative and Labour parties. We might thus anticipate that one reason why people wanted to change the kind of newspaper they read was because they were looking for a paper that was more in tune with their current political views. [. . .] We have therefore also included in our model the difference between how the respondent felt towards the Conservative (in the Labour model, Labour) Party in 1994 and how they felt in 1992. [. . .]

The results partly confirm our expectations. Those who were less favourably disposed towards the Conservative Party in 1992 were less likely to switch to a Conservative paper between 1992 and 1997. Equally, those who were less favourably disposed towards Labour in 1992 were less likely to take up the habit of reading a pro-Labour paper. However, in neither model were changes in respondents' feelings towards the relevant party between 1992 and 1994 statistically significant. In short, it would seem from this evidence that voters' choice of paper may well be influenced by long-held political affinities, but not by relatively recent changes of attitude. [. . .]

Conclusion

The 1997 election provided a clear opportunity for the power of the press, and of Britain's top-selling newspaper in particular, to reveal itself. In practice on the evidence of this chapter it still tended to prefer to remain in hiding. *The Sun's* conversion did not evidently bring the Labour Party new recruits. Equally Labour's new recruits did not prove particularly keen to switch to *The Sun*. At best we have found, in line with our previous research, that newspapers have but a limited influence on the voting behaviour of their readers. Where they can make a difference is in mobilizing their more faithful readers by playing them a familiar tune, readers who indeed may well have chosen that paper precisely because it plays a tune they have long considered an old favourite. Like social class, the partisanship of British newspapers is clearly part of the structure of British voting behaviour, but whether they can explain the flux is very much open to doubt.

References

Curtice, J. (1997) 'Is the Sun Shining On Tony Blair?', *Harvard International Journal of Press/Politics* (2) 2: 9–26.

Curtice, J. and Semetko, H. (1994) Does it Matter What the Papers Say? In Anthony Heath, Roger Jowell and John Curtice (eds) *Labours Last Chance?* Aldershot: Dartmouth.

Dalton, R J., Kawakami, K., Semetko, H., Suzuki, H. and Voltmer, K. (1998) 'Partisan Cues in the Media: Cross National Comparisons of the Media'. Paper presented at the Annual Meeting of the Mid-West Political Science Association, Chicago.

Dunleavy, P. and Husbands, C. (1985) *Democracy at the Crossroads*. London: Allen & Unwin.

Newton, K. (1991) Do People Believe Everything They Read in the Papers? Newspapers in the 1983 and 1987 General Elections. In Crewe, I., Norris, P., Denver, D. and Broughton, D. (eds) *British Elections and Parties Handbook 1991*. Hemel Hempsted: Harvester Wheatsheaf.

Chapter 32

Maxwell E. McCombs and Donald L. Shaw

THE AGENDA-SETTING FUNCTION OF MASS MEDIA*

Source: Maxwell E. McCombs and Donald L. Shaw (1972) 'The Agenda-Setting Function of Mass Media', *Public Opinion Quarterly*, 36 (2): 176–87.

[. . .]

I N O U R D A Y , more than ever before, candidates go before the people through the mass media rather than in person.[1] The information in the mass media becomes the only contact many have with politics. [. . .]

Although the evidence that mass media deeply change attitudes in a campaign is far from conclusive,[2] the evidence is much stronger that voters learn from the immense quantity of information available during each campaign.[3] People, of course, vary greatly in their attention to mass media political information. Some, normally the better educated and most politically interested (and those least likely to change political beliefs), actively seek information; but most seem to acquire it, if at all, without much effort. It just comes in. [. . .] Voters do learn.

They apparently learn, furthermore, in direct proportion to the emphasis placed on the campaign issues by the mass media. [. . .]

Perhaps this hypothesized agenda-setting function of the mass media is most succinctly stated by Cohen, who noted that the press "may not be successful much of the time in telling people what to think, but it is stunningly successful in telling its readers what to think *about*."[4] While the mass media may have little influence on the direction or intensity of attitudes, it is hypothesized that *the mass media set the agenda for each political campaign, influencing the salience of attitudes toward the political issues.*

Method

To investigate the agenda-setting capacity of the mass media in the 1968 presidential campaign, this study attempted to match what Chapel Hill voters *said* were key issues of the campaign with the *actual content* of the mass media used by them during the campaign. Respondents were selected randomly from lists of registered voters in five Chapel Hill precincts economically, socially, and racially representative of the community. [. . .]

Between September 18 and October 6, 100 interviews were completed. To select these 100 respondents a filter question was used to identify those who had not yet definitely decided how to vote – presumably those most open or susceptible to campaign information. Only those not yet fully committed to a particular candidate were interviewed. [. . .] Concurrently with the voter interviews, the mass media serving these voters were collected and content analyzed. [. . .]

The answers of respondents regarding major problems as they saw them and the news and editorial comment appearing between September 12 and October 6 in the sampled newspapers, magazines, and news broadcasts were coded into 15 categories representing the key issues and other kinds of campaign news. Media news content also was divided into "major" and "minor" levels to see whether there was any substantial difference in mass media emphasis across topics.[5] For the print media, this major/minor division was in terms of space and position; for television, it was made in terms of position and time allowed.

[. . .]

Findings

The over-all *major* item emphasis of the selected mass media on different topics and candidates during the campaign is displayed in Table 31.1. It indicates that a considerable amount of campaign news was *not* devoted to discussion of the major political issues but rather to *analysis of the campaign itself.* [. . .] Thirty-five percent of the major news coverage of Wallace was composed of this analysis ("Has he a chance to win or not?"). For Humphrey and Nixon the figures were, respectively, 30 percent and 25 percent. At the same time, the table also shows the relative emphasis of candidates speaking about each other. For example, Agnew apparently spent more time attacking Humphrey (22 percent of the major news items about Agnew) than did Nixon (11 percent of the major news about Nixon). The over-all *minor* item emphasis of the mass media on these political issues and topics closely paralleled that of major item emphasis.

[. . .]

The media appear to have exerted a considerable impact on voters' judgments of what they considered the major issues of the campaign (even though the questionnaire specifically asked them to make judgments without regard to what politicians might be saying at the moment). The correlation between the major item emphasis on the main campaign issues carried by the media and voters' independent judgments of what were the important issues was +.967. Between minor item emphasis on the main campaign issues and voters' judgments, the correlation was

Table 32.1 Major mass media reports on candidates and issues, by candidates

	Quoted source						
	Nixon	Agnew	Humphrey	Muskie	Wallace	Lemay[a]	Total
The issues							
Foreign policy	7%	9%	13%	15%	2%	—	10%
Law and order	5	13	4	—	12	—	6
Fiscal policy	3	4	2	—	—	—	2
Public welfare	3	4	(*)[b]	5	2	—	2
Civil rights	3	9	(*)[b]	0	4	—	2
Other	19	13	14	25	11	—	15
The campaign							
Polls	1	—	—	—	1	—	(*)[b]
Campaign events	18	9	21	10	25	—	19
Campaign analysis	25	17	30	30	35	—	28
Other candidates							
Humphrey	11	22	—	5	1		5
Muskie	—	—	—	—	—	—	—
Nixon	—	—	11	5	3	—	5
Agnew	—	—	(*)[b]	—	—	—	(*)[b]
Wallace	5	—	3	5	—	—	3
Lemay	1	—	1	—	4	—	1
Total percent	101%[c]	100%	99%[c]	100%	100%	—	98%[c]
Total number	188	23	221	20	95	11	558

a Coverage of Lemay amounted to only 11 major items during the September 12–October 6 period and are not individually included in the percentages; they are included in the total column.

b Less that .05 per cent.

c Does not sum to 100% because of rounding.

+.979. In short, the data suggest a very strong relationship between the emphasis placed on different campaign issues by the media (reflecting to a considerable degree the emphasis by candidates) and the judgments of voters as to the salience and importance of various campaign topics.

[. . .]

If one expected voters to pay more attention to the major and minor issues oriented to their own party – that is, to read or view *selectively* – the correlations between the voters and news/opinion about their own party should be strongest. This would be evidence of selective perception.[6] If, on the other hand, the voters attend reasonably well to *all* the news, *regardless* of which candidate or party issue is stressed, the correlations between the voter and total media content would be strongest. This would be evidence of the agenda-setting function. The crucial question is which set of correlations is stronger.

In general, Table 32.2 shows that voters who were not firmly committed early in the campaign attended well to *all* the news. For major news items, correlations were more often higher between voter judgments of important issues and the issues

Table 32.2 Intercorrelations of major and minor issue emphasis by selected media with voter issue emphasis

Selected media	Major items		Minor items	
	All news	News own party	All news	News own party
New York *Times*				
Voters (D)	.89	.79	.97	.85
Voters (R)	.80	.40	.88	.98
Voters (W)	.89	.25	.78	−.53
Durham *Morning Herald*				
Voters (D)	.84	.74	.95	.83
Voters (R)	.59	.88	.84	.69
Voters (W)	.82	.76	.79	.00
CBS				
Voters (D)	.83	.83	.81	.71
Voters (R)	.50	.00	.57	.40
Voters (W)	.78	.80	.86	.76
NBC				
Voters (D)	.57	.76	.64	.73
Voters (R)	.27	.13	.66	.63
Voters (W)	.84	.21	.48	−.33

reflected in all the news (including of course news about their favored candidate/party) than were voter judgments of issues reflected in news *only* about their candidate/party. For minor news items, again voters more often correlated highest with the emphasis reflected in all the news than with the emphasis reflected in news about a favored candidate. Considering both major and minor item coverage, 18 of 24 possible comparisons show voters more in agreement with all the news rather than

Table 32.3 Correlations of voter emphasis on issues with media coverage

	Newsweek	Time	New York Times	Raleigh Times	Raleigh News and Observer
Major items	.30	.30	.96	.80	.91
Minor items	.53	.78	.97	.73	.93

	Durham Sun	Durham Morning Herald	NBC News	CBS News	
Major items	.82	.94	.89	.63	
Minor items	.96	.93	.91	.81	

with news only about their own party/candidate preference. This finding is better explained by the agenda-setting function of the mass media than by selective perception.

Although the data reported in Table 32.2 generally show high agreement between voter and media evaluations of what the important issues were in 1968, the correlations are not uniform across the various media and all groups of voters. The variations across media are more clearly reflected in Table 32.3, which includes all survey respondents, not just those predisposed toward a candidate at the time of the survey. There also is a high degree of consensus among the news media about the significant issues of the campaign, but again there is not perfect agreement. [. . .]

Discussion

The existence of an agenda-setting function of the mass media is not *proved* by the correlations reported here, of course, but the evidence is in line with the conditions that must exist if agenda-setting by the mass media does occur. This study has compared aggregate units – Chapel Hill voters as a group compared to the aggregate performance of several mass media. This is satisfactory as a first test of the agenda-setting hypothesis, but subsequent research must move from a broad societal level to the social psychological level, matching individual attitudes with individual use of the mass media. Yet even the present study refines the evidence in several respects. Efforts were made to match respondent attitudes only with media actually used by Chapel Hill voters. Further, the analysis includes a juxtaposition of the agenda-setting and selective perception hypotheses. Comparison of these correlations too supports the agenda-setting hypothesis.

Interpreting the evidence from this study as indicating mass media influence seems more plausible than alternative explanations. Any argument that the correlations between media and voter emphasis are spurious – that they are simply responding to the same events and not influencing each other one way or the other – assumes that voters have alternative means of observing the day-to-day changes in the political arena. This assumption is not plausible; since few directly participate in presidential election campaigns, and fewer still see presidential candidates in person, the information flowing in interpersonal communication channels is primarily relayed from, and based upon, mass media news coverage. The media are the major primary sources of national political information; for most, mass media provide the best – and only – easily available approximation of ever-changing political realities.

It might also be argued that the high correlations indicate that the media simply were successful in matching their messages to audience interests. Yet since numerous studies indicate a sharp divergence between the news values of professional journalists and their audiences, it would be remarkable to find a near perfect fit in this one case.[6] It seems more likely that the media have prevailed in this area of major coverage.

[. . .]

Notes

* This study was partially supported by a grant from the National Association of Broadcasters. Additional support was provided by the UNC Institute for Research in Social Science and the School of Journalism Foundation of North Carolina.

1   See Bernard R. Berelson, Paul F. Lazarsfeld, and William N. McPhee, *Voting*, Chicago, University of Chicago Press, 1954, p. 234. Of course to some degree candidates have always depended upon the mass media, but radio and television brought a new intimacy into politics.

2   See Berelson *et al.*, op. cit., p.223; Paul F. Lazarsfeld, Bernard Berelson, and Hazel Gaudet, *The People's Choice*, New York, Columbia University Press, 1948, p. xx; Joseph Trenaman and Dennis McQuail, *Television and the Political Image*, London, Methuen and Co., 1961, pp. 147, 191.

3   See Bernard C. Cohen, *The Press and Foreign Policy*, Princeton, Princeton University Press, 1963, p.120.

4   Cohen, op. cit., p. 13.

5   Intercoder reliability was above .90 for content analysis of both "major" and "minor" items. Details of categorization are described in the full report of this project.

6   While recent reviews of the literature and new experiments have questioned the validity of the selective perception hypothesis, this has nevertheless been the focus of much communication research. For example, see Richard F. Carter, Ronald H. Pyszka, and Jose L. Guerrero, "Dissonance and Exposure to Arousive Information," *Journalism Quarterly*, Vol. 46, 1969, pp. 37–42; and David O. Sears and Jonathan L. Freedman, "Selective Exposure to Information: A Critical Review", *Public Opinion Quarterly*, Vol. 31, 1967, pp. 194–213.

7   Furthermore, five of the nine media studied here are national media and none of the remaining four originate in Chapel Hill. It is easier to argue that Chapel Hill voters fit their judgments of issue salience to the mass media than the reverse. An interesting study which discusses the problems of trying to fit day-to-day news judgments to reader interest is Guido H. Stempel III, "A Factor Analytic Study of Reader Interest in News", *Journalism Quarterly*, Vol. 44, 1967, pp. 326–330. An older study is Philip F. Griffin, "Reader Comprehension of News Stories: A Preliminary Study", *Journalism Quarterly*, Vol. 26, 1949, pp. 389–396.

Chapter 33

Justin Lewis, Michael Morgan and Andy Ruddock

IMAGES/ISSUES/IMPACT
The media and campaign '92

Source: Justin Lewis, Michael Morgan and Andy Ruddock (1992)
Images/Issues/Impact: The Media and Campaign '92. A Report by the
Center for the Study of Communication, University of Massachusetts at
Amherst.*

[. . .]

IN THIS STUDY, [. . .] we have tried to provide a more three-dimensional picture of the American electorate during the 1992 Presidential Election campaign. In an important departure from most polls, we are concerned not only with what people think, but with the information and knowledge that lies behind those attitudes and the factors that have shaped them.

We begin with the acknowledgment that democracy in the United States depends increasingly upon the news media. The media are, for most citizens, the principle source of information about politics and political candidates. Of the myriad news outlets available, the most important is network television, which is the place (to quote ABC News) where most Americans get their news. Our study focuses on the role played by the news media (and TV news in particular), in order to ask the following questions:

- Have the news media successfully communicated enough information for voters to understand the political issues?
- Do some forms of media (say, print as opposed to TV) succeed better than others in communicating such information?

- How does people's knowledge of hard issues compare with more trivial knowledge and images, and how do these, in turn, relate to media exposure?
- Does the information people receive suggest any bias toward or against any of the major candidate? Have, for example, the media effectively communicated more "negative" or "positive" facts with regard to either Bush or Clinton?

[. . .]

At the heart of the study are more fundamental questions about the state of American democracy. Is the public well informed, only partially informed or ill-informed about the issues that influence their voting decisions? What will be most likely to influence people's decisions: hard facts about the issues or the "softer" facts that constitute campaign PR? Are the news media politically impartial, or do they incline voters toward certain political attitudes?

The study is based on two kinds of data: first, a nationwide telephone survey of 601 randomly selected Americans, conducted during the first week of October; second, a series of six focus groups conducted in Springfield, Massachusetts in August and September. Since this is a study of the electorate, the nationwide survey is made up of people who said that they would "probably" or "definitely" vote (the survey is thus made up of a slightly better educated cross section than the US population as a whole). [. . .]

[. . .]

1: What people know about the candidates: Millie, Murphy and the issues

Why do people vote for one candidate rather than another? This question is never as simple as it looks, and the many possible answers to it are enough to stimulate the thriving industry of political punditry. What we can say with some degree of certainty is that people make their decisions to vote based on what they know (or believe they know) about the candidates. This assumption led us, in this survey, to ask people not so much what they think of the candidates, but what they know about them. The answers make for depressing reading.

[. . .]

Despite voters' proclaimed desire to base their votes on the issues rather than on more trivial information about the candidates, most people, we discovered, know very little about the former and a great deal about the latter. When asked facts about the candidates' policies and backgrounds, the only questions that a majority knew the answers to were: "Which candidate's family has a dog called Millie?" and "Do you recall which TV character Dan Quayle criticized for setting a poor example of family values?"

86% knew that Millie belonged to the Bush family, and 89% correctly identified Murphy Brown. This compares this with 19% who could name the Reagan/Bush cabinet member recently indicted for his role in the ongoing issue of Iran/Contra, Caspar Weinberger. Perhaps the only surprise, in this respect, is that only 23% could correctly recall the name of the bete noir of the early Clinton campaign, Gennifer Flowers.

Even an issue that was topical in the week the survey took place had a majority confused. At the beginning of the week in which the survey was conducted, President Bush vetoed an attempt by Congress to impose sanctions on China for its human rights abuses, a position the President has publicly adopted since the Tiananmen Square crackdown. Despite this, when asked what position Bush had taken on China since Tiananmen Square, when given a choice, only 44% knew that Bush was against sanctions, while nearly as many (43%) stated that Bush had actually imposed trade sanctions. In other words, people were as likely to associate Bush with a policy he steadfastly opposed as they were to link him with the one he actually pursued.

When it comes to Governor Clinton's record, perceptions of the candidate bear even less resemblance to reality. Independent testimony on Clinton's record in Arkansas has revealed that his record on taxes has been "good" (Arkansas state taxes being among the lowest in the nation) while his record on the environment has been "bad" (an independent monitoring group putting Arkansas near the bottom in most areas of environmental policy). Despite this, when asked:

"To your knowledge, how high were Arkansas state taxes while Clinton has been governor?" Only 21% responded (correctly) that they were "among the lowest in the nation", while more – 32% – reported that they were, in fact, "among the highest in the nation". Similarly, when asked: "How has Governor Clinton's record on the environment been rated by an independent monitoring group?", only 19% correctly stated "among the worst in the nation" (52% said "about average" and 7% said "among the best").

We asked, in total, 21 factual questions about the candidates and the issues. The average percentage of correct responses was 32%, a figure that drops to 27% if the more trivial, less "issue-oriented" questions are excluded. While there were no enormous differences, we did find that, overall, some groups were more knowledgeable than others. Not surprisingly, those with a college education tended to score higher than those without.

What is particularly surprising, in this respect, is that while Clinton supporters are more likely to be drawn from less educated groups (his lead among those with no college education stretches to 25%), they are, overall, the best informed group of voters, followed by Perot supporters, with Bush supporters scoring the lowest.

[. . .]

More predictably, we find far more undecided voters among the least knowledgeable (22% of this group are undecided) than among the most knowledgeable, only 10% of whom are undecided.

It is also notable that exposure to the main information source in our culture, television, did not increase knowledge. Heavy TV viewers knew, on the whole, slightly less than light TV viewers. Similarly, those who relied on TV as their main source of news scored significantly lower than those who relied on other sources, such as newspapers.

The success of the Republican campaign

Many in the Bush campaign have lamented (in public, at least) about Bush's failure to get his message across – often blaming the "liberal media" for this failure. Our survey suggests that in a number of respects, the opposite is true. This relates not simply to Clinton's record on taxes and the environment, but other areas where Republican attacks appear to have hit home. Take for, example, a question about the candidates and Vietnam: "Of the 4 candidates for President and Vice President, who has been accused of using family influence to avoid being sent to Vietnam?"

This statement could be seen to apply to both Bill Clinton and (especially to) Dan Quayle, yet only 23% named both, while those choosing one of the two were almost three times more likely to pick Clinton (41%) as Quayle (15%). To put it another way, we could say that in a competition between a Republican campaign answer, a Democratic campaign answer and the correct answer, the Republican answer wins.

[. . .]

The Democratic attacks on the Bush record, on the other hand, have a more mixed success rate. Democrats have complained, for example, that despite Bush's account of the "tax and spend" Congress, the President proposed a bigger budget last year than the one Congress finally appropriated. This may be true, but most people do not know it: in fact most believe the opposite is true. When asked the question: "Last year, which do you think was greater: the amount of money President Bush proposed spending on the Federal Budget, or the amount Congress actually passed?" 73% said Congress, and only 24% correctly identified Bush. Even Clinton supporters held Congress more responsible than Bush for high spending, by a margin of over two to one.

[. . .]

Despite the apparent success of the GOP in getting its message across, the fact remains that people who state a preference tend to choose Clinton over Bush. This suggests that the general level of antipathy toward Bush is so deep-rooted that voters can see Clinton as a draft-dodging big spending liberal and still vote for him: as one of our focus group members put it, "I think anybody would do a better job than Bush is doing right now". Many voters, in other words, have absorbed Republican criticisms of Clinton but intend to vote for him anyway. It is not surprising, then that some members of our focus groups express mixed degrees of enthusiasm about their preference for Clinton, as one respondent put it: "Yeah, I'll give this guy a shot. You know, hoping he's not going to botch it too badly, not like Bush botched things."

[. . .]

There is also a more profound problem highlighted by these results. Regardless of which side is more successful in getting the media to report its version of events, the voting public is ill-served by the entire process. The news media's emphasis on reporting campaign rhetoric rather than the facts, their reluctance to focus on the record rather than on "claims" about the record, seem to make it difficult for voters to distinguish between truth and propaganda. In the stress on claims and counter claims, the facts become elusive and, in the end, unimportant. It would appear that the news media, the message carrier in a modern democracy, have allowed the impoverishment of the political process whereby most voters know little about what is really going on.

[. . .]

Clinton the imaginary liberal

Perhaps the most conspicuous aspect of the Bush campaign's success lies in its somewhat disingenuous attempt to portray Clinton as an unreconstructed liberal. When asked about the candidates' policy positions, voters consistently attribute Clinton with positions that are more liberal than those he has endorsed, while a majority are ignorant of his more conservative stances.

So, for example, only 33% know that Clinton supports cuts in capital gains taxes (and less than 5% know that both Bush and Clinton endorse versions of such a policy). Only 38% know Clinton supports the death penalty (12% know that Bush does too), and only 37% know that Clinton supports "right to work" laws opposed by organized labor. While it is true that Clinton has proposed reducing military spending by more than Bush, 73% think that he wants significantly more substantial cuts — 50% over the next 5 years — than those he has proposed.

Perhaps the most glaring misconception concerns the source of the Democrat's campaign money. Independent assessments (from groups such as the Center for Responsive Politics) indicate that both Republicans and Democrats rely, indirectly, on corporate and business interests for much of their campaign money. It is certainly true that in other countries (such as Britain), the main parties to the left of the political spectrum may rely on contributions from labor organizations: in the United States, however, both main parties are financed by corporate and business interests. Yet, when asked whether labor or business contributes more to the Democratic Presidential campaign, people overwhelmingly say labor (69%) rather than business (16%). Again, while it is true that Democrats tend to get more support from organized labor than do Republicans, the differences between the parties are far smaller than most people imagine.

While it desirable for the GOP (and easier for the media) to portray the election as a straightforward battle between liberal and conservative ideologies, our survey would suggest that such a framework is, on a number of issues, misleading the public. Similarly, the media's tendency to emphasize the differences between the candidates may be understandable, but it does seem, in this election, to create a distorted impression.

[. . .]

Note

*The Center for the Study of Communication would like to thank Fairness and Accuracy in Reporting (FAIR) and the Foundation for Media Education for helping to fund the surveys analyzed in this report. We would also like to thank Standage Accureach, who conducted the fieldwork, for their promptness and efficiency. Thanks also to Karen Schoenberger for all her assistance and patience.

Chapter 34

Joseph N. Capella and Kathleen Hall Jamieson

COGNITIVE BASES FOR FRAMING EFFECTS

Source: Joseph N. Capella and Kathleen Hall Jamieson (1997) *Spiral of Cynicism: The Press and the Public Good,* New York and Oxford: Oxford University Press, pp. 58–86.

[. . .]

A model of framing effects

OUR GOAL HAS NOT BEEN to lay the groundwork for a general cognitive model for the processing of political information but to make explicit the necessary cognitive assumptions for a model of media-framing effects. A schematic version of that model is presented in Figure 34.1. The model aims to account for the relationship between news frames generally and two categories of outcomes – learning and judgments.

News frames include strategic, conflict, personality, issue, and episodic frames. They are always about a topic and usually carry substantive information within their particular frame. News frames highlight certain aspects of news and downplay others through selection, emphasis, exclusion, and elaboration.[1] News frames activate constructs, invite inferences (trait as well as other types), and cue stories in receivers as a function of the content and style of the news story.

The processes of spreading activation and priming increase the accessibility of nodes associated with those directly activated by the story itself. News frames that describe behavior will tend to activate trait inferences easily and even automatically. Constructs in the associative network that are semantically related to those activated

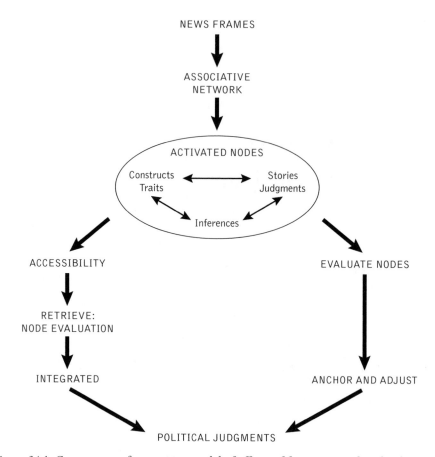

Figure 34.1 Components of a cognitive model of effects of framing on political judgment

directly will also tend to be made more accessible, allowing them to be more retrievable in the short run. Stories stored as associations among constructs and personal episodes may also be activated by the stories presented in the news (as well as other cues), especially under conditions where stories in the news are similar to those stored in memory.

The model of Figure 34.1 hides a great deal of information in the notation that inferences and traits are activated by political news frames. When the texts direct attention to behaviors implying personal characteristics, traits can be inferred automatically from texts. Even political issues have an effect on character evaluations.

Once information has been activated, it becomes available for use. Political judgment in the form of affective evaluation or choice occurs through two processes: memory-based and on-line. The first presumes that information is retrieved from memory along with its affective implications[2] and integrated into a summary judgment.[3] What is retrieved is the basis (or reasons) for the summary judgment. The online process presumes that the message is evaluated sequentially. These evaluations are integrated with the existing evaluative node (the anchor) and an adjusted evaluation is made and stored.[4] We think that the currently available evidence supports our assumption that online and memory-based components of judgment together account for evaluative outcomes.

Retrieval of information depends on what is accessible; that in turn depends on the recency and frequency of activation and chronic accessibility levels. What is accessible depends in turn on the spread of activation, priming, trait, and other types of inferences drawn within the associative network and cued initially by the message.

Retrieval and evaluative judgments give feedback to the associative network. They strengthen (and weaken) existing association, add new associations, modify existing evaluative tags, and, in general, alter the patterns of association tying the network together.

The basic assumption of our research and of the model of Figure 34.1 is that people learn from news. What they learn is both explicit and implicit, substantive and evaluative. And what they learn depends in large measure on how information about the political world is framed. In these senses, our model is consistent with current cognitive models of political information processing.[5] It differs from other models primarily in emphasis. Price and Tewksbury specifically take up the effects of news, reducing them to changes in accessibility and failing to give serious consideration to rules for integrating information in the judgment process. Lodge's model seems to minimize the role of memory-based judgment, implying that most of what has passed for a correlation between memory and judgment is an artefact. The model of Figure 34.1 finds a place for both memory-based and on-line judgment and assumes that stories play a significant role in the information retrieved about politics and in the judgments people make about political events.

[. . .]

Agenda setting, media priming, and framing

[. . .]

Episodic news frames

Framing effects are more subtle than media priming and agenda setting. Framing is not simply concerned with the presence of the topics but with how topics are treated in the news. The implication is that how the news frames issues will invite certain inferences and suppress others, cognitively priming some information in the network of knowledge while bypassing other nodes. These inferences and associations become a part of what is made accessible by the framed message. Framing may alter the interpretation of the events described through these inferences and associations.

Shanto Iyengar's research examined the effects of episodic and thematic news frames.[6] Episodic frames focus "on specific episodes, individual perpetrators, victims, or other actors at the expense of more general, thematic information" and depict "concrete events that illustrate issues while thematic framing presents collective or general evidence".

Iyengar finds that episodic frames tend to elicit attributions of responsibility for the cause and the treatment of problems that are directed at individuals rather than society or situations. The reasons for this effect may be found in what has been called the fundamental attribution error and actor-observer differences.[7] When viewing the behavior of others, there is a consistent tendency to explain actions in terms of a person's characteristics rather than the surrounding situation. This bias is stronger for explaining other's behaviors than explaining one's own. Creating situational explanations requires more cognitive energy than person-based explanation does.[8] When television portrays the news in personal terms, psychological biases attributing responsibility to individuals are activated and require the least cognitive work.

Iyengar explains episodic framing in terms of the accessibility bias, indicating that "[e]pisodic reporting tends to make particular acts or characteristics of particular individuals more accessible, while thematic reporting helps viewers to think about political issues in terms of societal or political outcomes."[9] Our model suggests an alternative.[10] Viewers do not perform heavy cognitive work remembering details of individual events. Instead, viewers exposed to episodic frames make relatively automatic trait inferences to the individuals portrayed and in so doing orient their attributions toward persons rather than situations. These same trait inferences may be made accessible in later recall or may contribute to an on-line judgment of the situation portrayed through the process of trait evaluation, and anchoring and adjustment.

In our view, the effects of episodic framing on attributions of responsibility occur through a process of automatic trait attribution implying personal rather than situational responsibility and not a process of retrieval of concrete, specific behaviors portrayed in the news. Whether the inferred traits are retrieved or evaluated on-line in subsequent judgments depends on the various task, goal, and motivational factors favoring on-line and memory-based judgments. But what is activated in episodic news is personal trait information rather than situational considerations.

Strategic news frames

Like episodic news, strategic news draws the audience's attention to the motivations of the people depicted. In doing so, personal traits are automatically activated. With the focus of strategic coverage squarely on winning and losing and the self-interest implied by this orientation, the traits activated are likely to be negative ones indicative of artifice, pandering, deceit, staging, and positioning for advantage – in general, mistrustfulness.

Our model suggests that both memory-based and on-line processes will explain the effects of strategic news coverage. People will learn about candidates' strategic activities recalling the basis for their judgments of cynicism and will evaluate candidates and their campaigns in more cynical ways. The stories they tell also will reflect cynicism about political life. In short, strategic news will encourage learning of strategic information, activate cynical attributions, and reinforce cynical political narratives.

Over the long haul, as patterns of association are activated and reactivated and strategic stories told and told again, cynicism about a candidate will be cultivated to become cynicism about candidates and campaigns generally and, perhaps, policy debates and governance as well.

Summary

Our model of how people process news provides an organizational frame for the studies of the effects of news frames on learning and cynicism that follow. We have argued that framing is a way of inducing a particular kind of understanding about events in the news. This understanding comes about through processes of activation, association, and inference. The inferences people make when they read or watch news depend on what the news activates and what patterns of association already exist in the audience's mind. Activation and association will make certain concepts and their semantic neighbors more readily accessible in future encounters and, in this sense, news reception should have a direct effect on learning what is read and watched. It may also have an indirect effect by readying news consumers to learn related ideas because they too are activated, although to a lesser extent, when news is fully received.

Our model recognizes that how the news is covered is as important as what it covers. People are especially sensitive to making inferences about others' personal traits. When strategic news implicates the self-interested motivations of political actors, it invites negative political judgments. It may do so through memory-based learning or automatically through a process of on-line tallying of inferred negative traits or both.

[. . .]

In addition to learning and judging, people are interpreters of political reality, trying to make sense of it. We have argued that personal stories are an important device allowing people to organize, recall, and make sense of the political world they encounter. Strategic news tells a particular kind of story – focusing on winning and losing, positioning for advantage, and implicating self-interested motivation. These news stories may invite a parallel set of personal stories reflecting the cynicism of news.

[. . .]

Notes

1   James Tankard, Laura Henderson, Jackie Silberman, Kriss Bliss, and Salma Ghanem (1991) "Media Frames: Approaches to Conceptualization and Measurement," paper presented to the Communication Theory and Methodology Division, Association for Education in Journalism and Mass Communication, Boston, 1991.

2   Susan Fiske and M.A. Pavelchak (1986) "Category-based Versus Piecemeal-based Affective Responses: Developments in Schema-triggered Affect." In R.M. Sorrentino and E.T. Higgins (eds), *Handbook of Motivation and Cognition: Foundations of Social Behavior*. New York: Guilford, pp. 167–203.

3   Norman H. Anderson (1981) *Foundations of Information Integration Theory*. New York: Academic Press.

4   Lola Lopes (1985) *Towards a Procedural Theory of Judgment*. (Technical Report #17, pp. 1–49). Information processing program, University of Wisconsin, Madison, 1982; H.J. Einhorn and R.M. Hogarth, "Ambiguity and Uncertainty in Probabilistic Inference," *Psychological Review*, 92 (1985), pp. 433–61.

5   Milton Lodge (1995) "Toward a Procedural Model of Candidate Evaluation." In Milton Lodge and Kathleen M. McGraw (eds) *Political Judgment: Structure, and Process*. Ann Arbor, MI: University of Michigan Press; [. . .] Robert S. Wyer and Victor C. Ottati

(1993) "Political Information Processing." In Shanto Iyengar and William J. McGuire (eds) *Explorations in Political Psychology*. Durham, NC: Duke University Press; Victor C. Ottati and Robert S. Wyer, in John A. Ferejohn and James H. Kuklinski (eds) *Information and Democratic Processes*. Urbana, IL: University of Illinois Press, pp. 186–216.

6   [. . .] Shanto Iyengar (1990) "Shortcuts to Political Knowledge: The Role of Selective Attention and Accessibility." In John A. Ferejohn and James H. Kuklinski (eds) *Information and Democratic Processes*. Urbana, IL: University of Illinois Press.

7   Lee Ross, "The Intuitive Psychologist and His Shortcomings: Distortions in the Attribution Process," in Berkowitz, op. cit., Vol. 10, pp. 174–221. For a review see Susan T. Fiske and Shelley E. Taylor (1991) *Social Cognition* (2nd ed.) New York: McGraw Hill.

8   D.T. Gilbert, B.W. Pelham, and D.S. Krull (1988) "On Cognitive Busyness: When Person Perceivers Meet Persons Perceived," *Journal of Personality and Social Psychology*, 54 (1988), pp. 733–39; D.T. Gilbert, and D.S. Krull (1988) Seeing Less and Knowing More: The Benefits of Perceptual Ignorance," *Journal of Personality*, 54, pp. 593–615.

9   Shanto Iyengar (1990) Shortcuts to Political Knowledge: The Role of Selective Attention and Accessibility. In Ferejohn and Kuklinski (1990), op. cit., p. 134.

10   Robert S. Wyer and Thomas K. Srull [*Memory and Cognition in Its Social Context* (Hillsdale, NJ: Lawrence Erlbaum, 1989)] argue that the evidence for the priority of processing tasks in impression formation has the encoding of traits and their evaluation at the top of the list and encoding of behaviors – which confirm the traits – at the bottom of the list [. . .].

Chapter 35

Shanto Iyengar

EFFECTS OF FRAMING ON ATTRIBUTIONS OF RESPONSIBILITY FOR CRIME AND TERRORISM

Source: Shanto Iyengar (1991) *Is Anyone Responsible? How Television Frames Political Issues*, Chicago, IL and London: University of Chicago Press, pp. 27–46.

O**N THE SURFACE, CRIME AND TERRORISM,** appear to be similar political issues because both entail threats to public security. Crime, however, is the more immediate danger and, for many, is a matter of intense personal experience, providing a dramatic connection between everyday life and the affairs of society at large. The threat posed by terrorism is generally distant and remote. Indeed, terrorism is the prototypical mediated issue, public awareness is limited to scenes of aircraft hijackings, hostage situations, bombings, and similar dramas played out in the mass media. Though spectacular, these events are of little direct personal relevance.

Differences in the relative obtrusiveness of the two issues has important implications for the framing hypothesis. Because crime is a real personal threat, citizens were expected to have more intimate familiarity with the issue, and attributions of responsibility for crime were expected to be less responsive to contextual cues such as framing. In contrast, because terrorism is associated with poorly understood disputes in distant locales and with ideological conflicts, attributions of responsibility for terrorism were expected to be highly responsive to framing. In short, media influence on attribution was expected to be more powerful for terrorism than for crime.

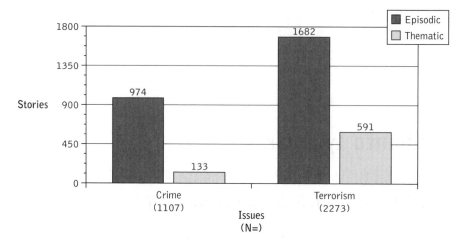

Figure 35.1 Episodic and thematic coverage of crime and terrorism, 1981–86

How television news frames crime and terrorism

Crime and terrorism, especially the latter, were at the forefront of the networks' reports on crime and more than 2,000 reports on terrorism were aired by ABC, CBS, and NBC between 1981 and 1986. The average of eleven stories on terrorism per month for each network represented an unusually intense degree of coverage. Between 1981 and 1986, more stories were broadcast on terrorism than on poverty, unemployment, racial inequality, and crime combined. Hijackings, hostage situations, and similar events have been emblazoned on the public consciousness.

The networks framed crime and terrorism almost exclusively in episodic terms (see Figure 35.1). Eight-nine percent of all news stories on crime fell into this "police-blotter" format.[1] Within both the thematic and episodic categories, the news tended to focus on violent crime. Thus, the focus of the typical news report was a specific individual (perpetrator or victim) and a violent criminal act.

Although news coverage of terrorism was slightly more thematic than coverage for crime, episodic reports still outnumbered thematic reports by a ratio of three to one: 74 percent of all news stories on terrorism consisted of live reports of some specific terrorist act, group, victim, or event, while 26 percent consisted of reports that discussed terrorism as a general political problem [. . .]. These results are consistent with prior content analyses performed by others, which identified a strong "event" bias in network treatment of terrorism. [. . .] These researchers have speculated that the event bias and the concomitant inattention to general, background information occurs because of the dramatic qualities of news stories on terrorist acts.

[. . .]

Episodic and thematic treatments of terrorism were examined within specific subject matter categories. Episodic reports were classified by the nationality of the subject individual(s), group(s), or organization(s). Third-world nationals accounted for 51 percent of episodic stories; within this group, Middle Easterners received the most attention, followed by Central Americans. Western terrorists were also the subject of extensive coverage, accounting for 34 percent of episodic stories.

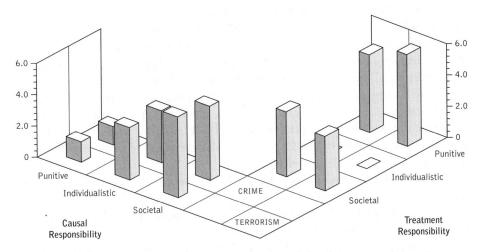

Figure 35.2 Causal and treatment attribution of responsibility for crime and terrorism

Thirty-three percent of the thematic news reports focused on the US government's counter-terrorist efforts. The remaining thematic stories were widely scattered in subject matter focus.

Who is responsible?

Crime elicited the highest average number of causal and treatment attributions of responsibility (2.7 and 2.1 per respondent, respectively) of any of the issues examined (see Figure 35.2). Presumably, people had more to say about crime because crime is more of a "doorstep" issue than terrorism, poverty, unemployment, or racial inequality.

Causal responsibility for both crime and terrorism was assigned to the individuals who commit criminal or terrorist acts, to a variety of societal conditions, and to a lack of adequate punitive policies. [. . .] Individualistic attributions for crime consisted of two causal themes: character deficiencies (such as greed, personality disorders, and the desire to avoid working) and, inadequate education and employment skills. Individualistic attributions for terrorism consisted exclusively of character references, primarily political fanaticism and associated personality traits, such as lack of concern for human life and a craving for power. The level of individualistic attributions of causal responsibility was virtually identical for crime and terrorism (38 and 34 percent, respectively).

References to society in causal attributions for crime and terrorism consisted of two opposing themes. Participants either referred to a variety of social, economic, or political conditions that fostered crime and terrorism or to society's failure to punish adequately those who engage in criminal or terrorist acts. The former category was labelled societal causal responsibility, and the latter punitive causal responsibility.

Attributions of societal causal responsibility for crime included references to economic conditions, discrimination, racial inequality, poverty, and cultural institutions

institutions. The category of cultural institutions was reserved for responses that cited the role of the mass media and the entertainment industry in glamorizing crime and legitimizing the use of violence. Societal causes of terrorism included economic and political oppression, the actions and policies of the US government (including support for Israel, insufficient economic aid to underprivileged nations, siding with repressive leaders, and realpolitik), global politics (such as meddling by the super-powers and other nations, most notably, Libya), and local political turmoil (including breakdown of institutions, political strife, and lack of strong leadership). Societal attributions represented 48 and 52 percent of all attributions of causal responsibility for crime and terrorism, respectively.

Punitive causal responsibility – the argument that people engage in crime and terrorism because they are able to avoid severe punishment – was infrequently mentioned. Approximately 10 percent of all causal responses for both issues referred to the lack of adequate punitive measures.

Respondents assigned treatment responsibility for both crime and terrorism almost exclusively to society in general. Very few responses implied that self-improvement was an appropriate treatment, indicating that apparently individuals do not view criminals and terrorists as able or willing to mend their ways. Thus, the prescription for crime and terrorism was almost exclusively improvements in the underlying socioeconomic and political order (societal treatment responsibility), or the imposition of stricter and more certain punishment (punitive treatment responsibility).

Societal treatments suggested for crime included reductions in poverty and inequality, rehabilitative and educational programs, and an improved economy. Respondents also cited heightened public awareness ("form neighborhood crime-prevention groups"; "educate people on ways to avoid being a victim") as a potential treatment. These four categories made up 42 percent of all crime treatments mentioned. In the case of terrorism, suggested societal treatments included resolution of terrorists' political grievances, putting an end to oppression, the use of more responsive methods of negotiating with terrorists, and greater public awareness (for example, "provide tourists with information regarding political conditions"). Societal responsibility accounted for 35 percent of the treatment responses directed at terrorism.

The dominant prescription for both issues (both in terms of content and frequency) called for the imposition of more severe retaliation or punishment against terrorists and criminals (punitive treatment responsibility). This category accounted for nearly 66 percent of all treatment responses for terrorism and 50 percent of all treatment responses directed at crime.

The degree to which causal and treatment responses corresponded within each issue was also examined by constructing dichotomized "net" causal and treatment responsibility scores. In the case of causal responsibility, low scores indicate a tendency to cite individual characteristics or inadequate punishment as causes; high scores indicate a tendency to assign causal responsibility to prevailing societal conditions. In the case of treatment responsibility, low scores represent a preference for attributions of punitive responsibility, while high scores represent a preference for attributions of societal responsibility [. . .].

By combining the causal and treatment responsibility scores, a four-fold typology was identified, as follows:

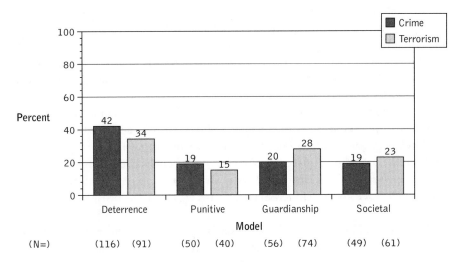

Figure 35.3 Models of responsibility: crime and terrorism

1   Deterrence model: individual tendencies and insufficient punishment cause crime and terrorism; stronger punishment of criminals and terrorists is the treatment.
2   Societal model: inadequate societal conditions cause crime and terrorism; improvements in societal conditions are the treatment.
3   Guardianship model: individual tendencies and insufficient punishment are the primary causal factors; improvements in societal conditions are the treatment.
4   Punitive model: inadequate societal conditions cause crime and terrorism; stronger punishment is the appropriate treatment.

Figure 35.3 shows the number and percentage of participants falling within each of the above models. For both issues, the deterrence model was applied most frequently and, in the case of crime, attracted close to 50 percent of the sample. The societal and guardianship models were applied to terrorism more frequently (by small margins) than to crime. The punitive model of responsibility attracted less than 20 percent of the sample for both issues. Overall, the pattern of causal and treatment responsibility for crime and terrorism was similar.[2]

Experimental tests of framing

Terrorism experiment 1

This study was essentially an exploratory probe of individuals' causal attributions. The experimental manipulation focused on a specific terrorist event – the hijacking of TWA Flight 847 and the ensuing hostage situation in Beirut.[3] Following the release of the hostages, all three networks broadcast detailed recapitulations of the crisis. The ABC report was edited into three very different versions. Two of the reports embodied a thematic frame, while the third represented the more frequently encountered episodic frame.

The first thematic-framing condition, "US Foreign Policy," interpreted the hijacking incident as an act of political protest against US foreign policy. The report commented on the role of the United States as a traditional ally of Israel and the hijackers' demands that Israel release Lebanese citizens held as political prisoners. President Reagan was then shown declaring that the United States would never negotiate with terrorists.

The second thematic-framing condition, "Local Turmoil," examined the incident exclusively within the context of Lebanese political strife. The report discussed the breakdown of governmental authority and the rise of various Lebanese paramilitary organizations, including Amal, the Shiite organization holding the hostages. The group's ideology was described, and its growing influence noted. This condition made no reference to the United States, to Israel, or to the broader Middle East conflict.

The third condition was designed as a noninterpretive, episodic frame – "Hostages Released." The report merely announced the release of the hostages. Individual hostages were seen greeting each other prior to departing from Beirut. Some of the former hostages commented on their health and their treatment in captivity. This condition provided no particular perspective on the hijacking incident beyond describing the eventual outcome.

Finally, a fourth, "control" condition was added to the design. Individuals assigned to this condition saw no news of the TWA hijacking. In place of the hijacking, they watched a story describing recent developments in the US space program.

The major objective of this study was to examine the possibility that alternative news frames for the identical act of terrorism might induce shifts in attributions of responsibility. First, it was expected that thematic framing would induce viewers to attribute responsibility for terrorism to societal factors while episodic framing was expected to contribute to higher levels of individual or punitive responsibility. In addition, it was anticipated that viewers in the control condition would seize upon individual responsibility in their explanations of terrorism – the terrorist's fanaticism, evil intent, amorality, and other related traits. This prediction was derived from attribution theory, which suggests that people typically exaggerate the role of individuals' motives and intentions and simultaneously discount the role of contextual factors when attributing responsibility for individuals' actions, a tendency that psychologists have dubbed "the fundamental attribution error."[4]

In order to examine framing effects on attributions of causal responsibility for terrorism, indices of societal, punitive, and individualistic responsibility were computed corresponding to the number of responses that referred to these themes divided by the total number of responses (Figure. 35.4). In the case of societal causal responsibility, for example, the index was the percentage of causal attributions citing political oppression or other societal factors. The use of such a standardized indicator of attribution served to neutralize possible differences in respondents' writing ability, locquacity, political interest, and related skills.

The degree to which attributions of causal responsibility for terrorism were affected by the particular news frame is shown in Figure 35.4. As expected, societal attributions were least prominent when the hijacking was framed in episodic terms, and the episodic condition differed significantly from the thematic Local Turmoil condition.

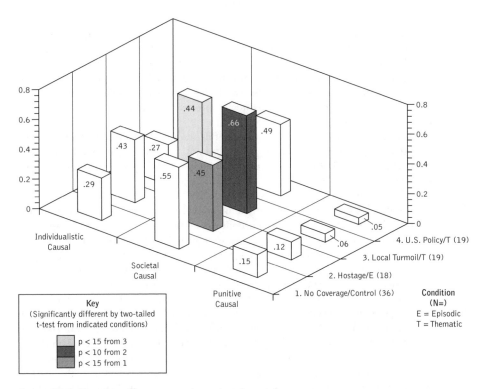

Figure 35.4 Framing effects: terrorism experiment 1

Contrary to expectations, however, the two thematic conditions did not elicit an equivalent pattern of responses. The frequency of individualistic attributions was highest in the thematic US Foreign Policy condition and lowest in the thematic Local Turmoil condition. As a result, the two thematic conditions differed significantly in the level of individualistic attributions.[5]

Another surprising result was that individuals in the control condition attributed causal responsibility to society rather than to the individual terrorist. Rather than making the "fundamental attribution error," individuals who were given no information about terrorism tended to think of the issue as a product of social or political problems.

Finally, there were no differences between the four conditions in the proportion of viewers citing punitive responsibility. The level of punitive treatment responsibility did not exceed 15 percent in any of the experimental conditions.

Thus the results from the initial study are at least suggestive of network framing. Thematic framing of terrorism that placed an airplane hijacking in the context of local political upheaval raised the prominence of societal causal attributions. When the same hijacking was framed in episodic terms, characteristics of individual terrorists were at the forefront of viewers' attributions.

[. . .]

Notes

1   For similar findings based on a content analysis of newspapers, see Graber 1980. The extent to which the networks presented episodic reports on crime fluctuated, but episodic framing accounted for at least 75 percent of coverage of crime in every year.

2   This aggregate-level similarity should not, however, be taken to imply that any given individual assigned responsibility for the two issues consistently. As the results in chapter 9 demonstrate, individual-level consistency in causal and treatment attributions for both issues was weak.

3   In every methodological respect except one this study was identical to all others. The exception was the use of a control group that watched no news report dealing with terrorism. This study was carried out in September 1985, shortly after the hijacking occurred.

4   See, for instance, Ross 1977; Jones 1979.

5   A plausible post hoc explanation for the high level of individualistic attributions for terrorism in the thematic US Foreign Policy condition concerns affect. Because this report presented the hijacking as an expression of political opposition to the United States, and because President Reagan angrily condemned the terrorists, the story may have prompted a stronger "outgroup" stereotype (i.e., higher negative affect toward the hijackers) thus strengthening participants' inclination to cite terrorists' personal deficiencies as causal factors. The post-test questionnaire included a set of questions asking viewers whether the story on the hijacking had "made them feel" a variety of emotions, including "disgust," "anger," and "fear." These responses were summed to form a summary measure of negative affect. Participants in the US Foreign Policy condition were significantly ($p < .05$) more aroused by the news report than were subjects in all remaining conditions. Moreover, across all conditions, the greater the arousal of negative affect, the greater the proportion of individual causes cited. In short, the presentation in the US Foreign Policy condition unintentionally raised viewers' hostility toward the hijackers, thereby inducing individualistic attributions.

References

Graber, D. (1980) *Crime News and the Public*. New York: Praeger.

Jones, E.E. (1979) "The Rocky Road from Acts to Dispositions." *American Psychologist*, 34: 107–117.

Ross, L. (1977) The Intuitive Psycholo|gist and His Shortcomings. In Berkowitz, L. (ed.) *Advances in Experimental Social Psychology Vol. 10*. New York: Academic Press.

Chapter 36

Elihu Katz and Daniel Dayan

THE 'LANDSLIDE EFFECT'

E. Katz and D. Dayan (2003) 'The Audience is a Crowd, the Crowd is a Public: Latter-Day Thoughts on Lang and Lang's "MacArthur Day in Chicago"', in E. Katz, J.D. Peters, T. Liebes and A. Orloff (eds), *Canonic Texts in Media Research*, Cambridge: Polity Press, pp. 121–36.

[. . .]

MacArthur Day as collective behaviour

IN 1951, [. . .] President Truman recalled General Douglas MacArthur for having overstepped his postwar authority in the Pacific [. . .] The news media followed the general's return very closely, and reported in detail on the widespread indignation over Truman's *chutzpa* and the enthusiastic welcome he was receiving. After a reception in San Francisco, MacArthur flew to Washington to address both houses of Congress and went on to a "triumphal homecoming" in New York and, a week later, in Chicago.

The itinerary of the Chicago visit called for a festive welcome at the airport, a motorcade through the city, with a stop to dedicate a bridge in memory of the fallen at Bataan and Corregidor, and an evening rally at Soldier Field. [. . .]

[. . .]

Television scheduled three hours of live coverage, giving Chicagoans a first taste of the dilemma of having to choose between going out to an event and viewing it at home. Two observers were assigned to view the television coverage (videotape was not yet available). Nobody was assigned to observe the viewers at home. [Researchers Kurt and Gladys Lang] were focused on what would happen in the streets, and did not think to compare audiences at home and those on the streets. Later, however, as they begun to reconceptualize the event, they set about analyzing the broadcast in order to infer some of the ways in which television must have been implicated, first, in "the 'landslide effect' of national indignation over MacArthur's abrupt dismissal" that constituted the prologue to the event, and then, in the live coverage of the event itself, which gave "the impression of enthusiastic support, bordering on 'mass hysteria'" (1953, p. 4). [. . .]

What the Langs saw

When the day was over, the researchers were surprised to learn that the *televised* event, not the "real" event, lived up to the excitement that had been anticipated. There were very large crowds – apparently the largest turnout since war's end – but these crowds were disappointed on the whole. At the airport, along the route of the motorcade, at the Bataan Bridge and at Soldier Field, would-be spectators were misinformed about the vantage points, were left to wait and wait for the brief moment when the motorcade would pass by, and were jostled at the bridge ceremony, which they could neither see nor hear. They missed the pomp they had anticipated – no parade, no music, no patriotic gore – and there was very little tension. Some felt pride, they said, at being present at a historic event; some felt the thrill of the spectacle, however flawed; some had a glimpse of the general. Others began to perform themselves – for the TV cameras. Observers overheard remarks to the effect that it might have been better to stay home and watch the event on television.

Meanwhile, say the Langs, television was telling a better story, though not the whole of it. Let us review what they saw.

1   First, they were struck by the fact that television was giving live to an amorphous, episodic, somewhat dull event. They noted that the television narrator could provide continuity and the cameras could play with "foreground and background." While the spectators were rubbing their hands and stomping their feet, television was producing drama.

2   They were surprised at how television distorted the "real" event. It portrayed the crowd as high-pitched and enthused; it exaggerated the size of the turnout and the extent to which the city had shut down to celebrate; it created the illusion of continuous cheering by combining the fragmented cheers of separate clusters of spectators. In their effort to understand, the Langs managed to infer and catalogue some of the major elements of media "selectivity," which guide us still today. These include (a) technological bias, whereby the production team selectively arranges the camera shots; (b) the bias of the commentary which provides verbal structure and meaning; (c) the rearrangement of the "real" world to match the timing and demands of the medium; and (d) the attempt to satisfy viewer expectations.

3   The Langs were distressed that television made no mention of the event's context. Even if spectators on the spot seemed uninterested in what had occasioned MacArthur's return, the Langs expected that a television news service would supply the missing information. They noticed that television limited its role to one of acclamation, and wondered whether the medium had been co-opted. They realized that television was catering to the celebratory register that public

opinion had been led to expect, but also wondered whether the media weren't taking the hawkish side of the American debate over the Cold War. In other words, the Langs noted that television events might have political effects, wisely anticipating a situation in which the "imagery of momentary opinion" represented by live television "may goad [politicians] into action which . . . may objectively be detrimental" (cf. Liebes, 1998).

4   The Langs also speculated that the TV audience, sitting alone at home, might be particularly vulnerable to TV's uncritical message. Spectators on the scene had recourse to each other; they could "test" reality by sensing and consulting their neighbours' thoughts and feelings. Television viewers had only themselves, and could be misled much more easily. Developed more fully in the 1968 version of their paper, this is an anticipation of the social psychology underlying "pluralistic ignorance," "spiral of silence," "bandwagon," and "brainwashing."

The Langs concluded that the event was poorly planned on the ground, and speculate that its schedule might have been more attuned to the dictates of the "air" than to the satisfaction of onlookers. This is an early insight into the ways in which the media privilege their viewers (and advertisers) at the expense of real-life spectators. Nowadays we take for granted that events are tailored and time-shifted to meet the requirements of the medium.

Within the limits of one early event in the history of television, the Langs saw very far. We certainly cannot fault them for having backed into the study of media events: we too began our work serendipitously, when we realized that the live broadcast of Anwar Sadat's visit to Jerusalem was of a piece with the moon landings and the Pope's visit to Poland, and was therefore better studied as a subtype of a genre of "media events" than as an example of "media diplomacy," as we had planned. Indeed, the Langs' later work includes studies of the Kennedy–Nixon debates, as well as a theory of reputation and renown (Lang and Lang, 1983, 1990) that led ultimately to the realization that a latent genre underlay all these public representations.

What the Langs didn't see

The Langs, however, did not see the genre of media events looming. They were first to identify many of its component elements, but they did not – could not, perhaps – recognize that the MacArthur broadcast was the harbinger of a new form of live television that would frame some of the most memorable moments of the second half of the twentieth century, for the Langs – at least in this essay – ceremonial media events are not yet clearly distinguished from the news, or from the then generic category "News and Special Event Features." "Unlike other television programs," they say, "news and special events features constitute part of that basic information about 'reality' which we require in order to act in concert with anonymous and like-minded persons in the political process" (1953, pp. 10–11). So far, so good. But where we differ, given the wisdom of hindsight, is in claiming that media events of this sort – openly constructed, clearly performative, and obeying specific sets of rules – are not tainted news events or shady practices of the sort that Boorstin (1964), some ten years later, would (also) describe as "pseudo events."[1]

Nor are they documentaries. They are a different genre of public affairs broadcasting, to which different rules apply. This is not just a quibble. The Langs accept the self-definition of "news and special events" as being bound by the classic norms of objective journalism, while we argue that the events genre in full bloom calls for a new theoretical perspective that asks different questions, makes different observations, and comes to different conclusions.

Our main difference with the Langs stems from their demand that television faithfully reproduce the "reality" they attribute to the crowd on the streets and to the politics of the Cold War. We ask: Is the street more "real?" If so, how do we access its "reality?" The Langs' observers represented the street as consisting of very large crowds – but the statistics of the transit system, the Langs discovered, diminished this claim. The observers represented the street as disappointed, based on titbits of observation – but those who were formally interviewed by the same observers said that they were enthralled (as they said when interviewed on TV). There also seems to have been a different reality at the beginning, when enthusiasm was still high, and at the end, when the poor arrangements apparently dampened enthusiasm. As we know by now, street reality, too, needs to be represented (Peters, 1993).

A better answer, as far as the portrait of the street is concerned, is that television provided a different representation of reality. At each point the motorcade passed, there was loud cheering. Very interesting, too, is that there was cheering and miming when spectators saw the cameras. Television, then, both represented reality and changed the reality it was representing. In short, "reality" can be constructed in street fashion and in the fashion of ceremonial television, and the debate is no longer between reality and the lack of it, but between different constructions.

[. . .]

Media events research also knows a thing or two about politics. While giving the ceremonial its due, it is continually aware of the political function of such events, where the establishment – not its rivals – is almost always the beneficiary. In a word, media events are hegemonic, almost without exception. [. . .]

[. . .]

But the originality of the Langs' essay, in comparison with the many it has inspired, is to combine the study of the public sphere with that of public space. The Langs are perfectly aware that when the media became custodians of the public sphere, they surrendered the roles of observer and watchdog; they became judges of their own power. While the public sphere is theoretically restricted to the circulation of issues, the presence of the media is a public space raises Goffmanian questions about the meaning of cheers; about the difference between being there, being an onlooker, being committed. It raises Noelle-Neumann's (1984) question of when to speak, when to listen, and when to remain silent. [. . .]

[. . .] As sociologists of public opinion, as well as of collective behaviour, [the Langs] are *not* claiming that each member of the television audience was directly infected by the reported hysteria of the crowd. They say, rather, that

> The most important single media effect . . . was the dissemination of an image of overwhelming public sentiment in favour of the General. This effect gathered force as it was incorporated into political strategy, picked up by other media, entered into gossip, and thus came to overshadow

immediate reality as it might have been recorded by an observer on the scene. We have labelled this the 'landslide effect' because in view of a particular public welcoming ceremony the imputed unanimity gathered tremendous force. This 'landslide effect' can, in large measure, be attributed to television. (1953, p. 11)

Note

1   Boorstin (1964) would discredit any ceremonial performance, including televised press conferences, as "pseudo," going far beyond the Langs' displeasure with the media's fictionalizing of the "real" event.

References

Boorstin, D.J. (1964) *The Image: A Guide to Pseudo-Events in America*. New York: Harper & Row.

Lang, G.E. and Lang, K. (1983) *The Battle for Public Opinion*. New York: Columbia University Press.

Lang, K. and Lang, G.E. (1953) 'The Unique Perspective of Television and its Effects: A Pilot Study', *American Sociological Review*, 18, 3–12.

Lang, K. and Lang, G.E. (1990) *Etched in Memory: The Building and Survival of Aesthetic Reputation*. Chapel Hill, NC: University of North Carolina Press.

Liebes, T. (1998) Television's Disaster Marathons: A Danger for Democratic Processes. In T. Liebes and J. Curran (eds) *Media Ritual and Identity*. London: Routledge, 71–84.

Noelle-Neumann, E. (1984) *The Spiral of Silence: Public Opinion – Our Social Skin*. Chicago, IL: University of Chicago Press.

SECTION 6

The media and political engagement

THERE HAS BEEN CONSIDERABLE discussion recently about whether the media cause and/or amplify political disenagagement among the citizens of advanced industrial democracies, or whether in fact they offer new opportunities for citizens to become engaged in political life. The first extract in this section, from **Putnam**, argues that television in effect squeezes out forms of civic engagement. The emergence of television, its spread, and the increase in time spent watching it, has meant a 'privatisation of leisure time'. Time expended on watching television means less time spent in civic involvment. Drawing on a wide variety of data sources, Putnam's piece shows that television actually dampens political activism.

Putnam is not alone in his concerns about the impact of the media on civic and political engagement. In his extract, **Patterson** explores the American public's engagement with the presidential election process. He observes that fewer citizens are tuning-in to key events in the presidential campaigns, as they once did, now finding the whole process boring. The cause of such apathy is not just the extensive coverage, but the increasingly drawn-out nature of modern presidential election campaigns, which last over a year.

However these pessimistic assessments about the impact of the media and the electoral process are not unproblematic. **Buckingham**'s extract examines the relationship of young people with conventional politics through the news media. He shows that the process of engagement is complex, and it is difficult to generalise about society-wide impacts. The study finds that young people tend to see conventional politics as distant and removed from their daily lives – but this does not mean that they are apolitical, in fact the opposite is true.

Instead of seeing television as crowding-out engagement, **Jones** focuses on viewer engagement with political output. He looks in particular at viewer engagement with political-entertainment output, in the form of the US cult TV show, *Politically*

Incorrect. He observes that TV entertainment formats (such as *Politically Incorrect*), rather than 'squeezing out' political engagement, form a basis for discussion. The show's viewers use the show as a means to talk about politics.

McNair *et al.* remind us that media organisations increasingly attempt to facilitate public participation in politics, and that the number of public access programmes has grown in the post-war period. They explore the history of public access programmes in the UK, arguing that, since the 1960s, the predominantly 'one-way' political output has been supplemented by a growing number of shows that invite citizen input and encourage interaction. These shows, many based on a phone-in format, help initiate political discussion.

Bucy and Gregson, in their extract, argue that the abundance of media outlets, especially with the emergence of the Internet, provides new opportunities for citizens to particpate in discussions, interact with politicians, donate money to political causes, or sign petitions. They refer to these activities as media participation. Far from dampening political and civic involvement, the media empower citizens in a variety of ways.

Chapter 37

Robert D. Putnam

TECHNOLOGY AND MASS MEDIA

Source: Robert D. Putnam (2000) *Bowling Alone: The Collapse and Revival of American Community*, New York: Simon and Schuster, pp. 216–46.

[. . .]

I N 1950 BARELY 10 percent of American homes had television sets, but by 1959, 90 percent did, probably the fastest diffusion of a technological innovation ever recorded. (The spread of Internet access will rival TV's record but probably not surpass it.) [. . .] In the early years TV watching was concentrated among the less educated sectors of the population, but during the 1970s the viewing time of the more educated sectors of the population began to converge upward. Television viewing increases with age, particularly upon retirement, but each generation since the introduction of television has begun its life cycle at a higher starting point. Partly because of these generational differences, the fraction of American adults who watch "whatever's on" – that is, those of us who turn on the TV with no particular program in mind – jumped from 29 percent in 1979 to 43 percent by the end of the 1980s. By 1995 viewing per TV household was more than 50 percent higher than it had been in the 1950s.[1]

[. . .]

The single most important consequence of the television revolution has been to bring us home. As early as 1982, a survey by Scripps-Howard reported that eight out of the ten most popular leisure activities were typically based at home. Amid all the declining graphs for social and community involvement traced in the DDB Needham Life Style surveys from 1975 to 1999, one line stands out: The number of Americans who reported a preference for "spending a quiet evening at home" rose steadily. Not surprisingly, those who said so were heavily dependent on televised entertainment.[2] While early enthusiasts for this new medium spoke eagerly of television as an "electronic hearth" that would foster family togetherness, the experience of the last half century is cautionary.

[. . .]

Television viewing has steadily become a more habitual, less intentional part of our lives. Four times between 1979 and 1993 the Roper polling organization posed a revealing pair of questions to Americans:

> When you turn the television set on, do you usually turn it on first and then look for something you want to watch, or do you usually turn it on only if you know there's a certain program you want to see?

> Some people like to have a TV set on, sort of in the background, even when they're not actually watching it. Do you find you frequently will just have the set on even though you're not really watching it, or [do you either watch it or turn it off]?

Selective viewers (that is, those who turn on the television only to see a specific program and turn it off when they're not watching) are significantly more involved in community life than habitual viewers (those who turn the TV on without regard to what's on and leave it on in the background), even controlling for education and other demographic factors. For example, selective viewers are 23 percent more active in grassroots organizations and 33 percent more likely to attend public meetings than other demographically matched Americans. Habitual viewing is especially detrimental to civic engagement. Indeed, the effect of habitual viewing on civic disengagement is as great as the effect of simply watching more TV.[3]

Year by year we have become more likely to flick on the tube without knowing what we want to see and more likely to leave it on in the background even when we're no longer watching [. . .]. As recently as the late 1970s selective viewers outnumbered habitual viewers by more than three to two, but by the mid-1990s the proportions were reversed. In 1962, only a few years after television had become nearly ubiquitous, the leading character in *The Manchurian Candidate* could say, "There are two kinds of people in the world – those who walk into a room and turn the TV on, and those who walk into a room and turn the TV off."[4] Four decades later the first kind of people have become more common and the second kind ever rarer.

[. . .]

This massive change in the way Americans spend our days and nights occurred precisely during the years of generational civic disengagement. How is television viewing related to civic engagement? In a correlational sense, the answer is simple: More television watching means less of virtually every form of civic participation and social involvement. Television viewing is also correlated with other factors that depress civic involvement, including poverty, old age, low education, and so on. Thus in order to isolate the specific connection between television and social participation, we need to hold those other factors constant, statistically speaking. Other things being equal, such analysis suggests, each additional hour of television viewing per day means roughly a 10 percent reduction in most forms of civic activism – fewer public meetings, fewer local committee members, fewer letters to Congress, and so on.[5]

If the time diary estimates are correct that Americans spent nearly an hour more per day in front of the tube in 1995 than in 1965, then that factor alone might account for perhaps one-quarter of the entire drop in civic engagement over this period.[6] I must, however, add two qualifications to this estimate, one that might bias it upward and one that might bias it downward. On the one hand, I have as yet offered no evidence that the causal arrow runs from TV watching to civic disengagement rather than the reverse. On the other hand, this estimate presumes that the only effect of TV on civic engagement comes from the number of hours watched, rather than something about the character of the watching, the watcher, and the watched.

Before we turn to these important subtleties, Figure 37.1 presents some of the evidence linking TV watching and civic disengagement. In order to screen out the effects of life cycle and education, we confine our attention here to working-age, college-educated Americans. (The pattern is even more marked within other, more TV dependent segments of the population, such as retired people or the less well educated.) In this group those who watch an hour or less of television per day are half again as active civically as those who watch three hours or more a day. For example, 39 percent of the light viewers attended some public meeting on town or school affairs last year, as compared with only 25 percent of the demographically matched heavy viewers. Of the light viewers, 28 percent wrote Congress last year, compared with 21 percent of the heavy viewers. Of light viewers, 29 percent played a leadership role in some local organization, as contrasted with only 18 percent of heavy viewers. Light viewers were nearly three times more likely to have made a speech last year than were equally well-educated heavy viewers (14 percent to 5 percent).

The significance of these differences between heavy and light viewers is magnified by the fact that even among this select group of well-educated, working-age Americans, heavy viewers outnumber light viewers by nearly two to one. A major commitment to television viewing – such as most of us have come to have – is incompatible with a major commitment to community life.

In chapter 2 [of the original] we noticed that collective forms of engagement, such as attending meetings, serving on committees, or working for a political party, had diminished much more rapidly over the last several decades than individual forms of engagement, such as writing to Congress or signing a petition. Both types of engagement can have political consequences, but only the former helps to foster and reinforce social connections. Television, it turns out, is bad for both individualized and collective civic engagement, but it is particularly toxic for activities that we do together. Whereas (controlling as always for demographic factors) watching lots of TV cuts individual activities, like letter writing, by roughly 10–15 percent, the same amount of additional TV viewing cuts collective activities, like attending public meetings or taking a leadership role in local organizations, by as much as 40 percent. In short, just as television privatizes our leisure time, it also privatizes our civic activity, dampening our interactions with one another even more than it dampens individual political activities.[7]

[. . .]

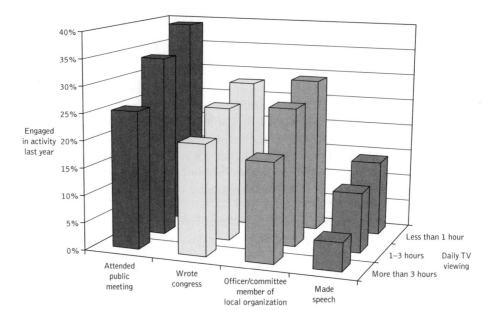

Figure 37.1 More TV means less civic engagement (among college-educated, working-age adults)

[. . .] But most of us watch television for entertainment, not news. Of all Americans 7 percent say that they watch primarily for information, as compared with 41 percent who say they watch primarily for entertainment. [. . .]

One way to detect the effects of television entertainment on social participation is to focus on those people – half of all Americans – who say that "television is my primary form of entertainment." Not surprisingly, these people watch much more TV than other Americans, and they are much more likely to concede that "I'm what you would call a couch potato."[8] In terms of civic engagement these people who are most heavily dependent on televised entertainment turn out to differ most remarkably from the other half of the American population.

Considered in combination with a score of other factors that predict social participation (including education, generation, gender, region, size of hometown, work obligations, marriage, children, income, financial worries, religiosity, race, geographic (mobility, commuting time, homeownership, and more), dependence on television for entertainment is not merely a significant predictor of civic disengagement. It is *the single most consistent* predictor that I have discovered.

People who say that TV is their "primary form of entertainment" volunteer and work on community projects less often, attend fewer dinner parties and fewer club meetings, spend less time visiting friends, entertain at home less, picnic less, are less interested in politics, give blood less often, write friends less regularly, make fewer long-distance calls, send fewer greeting cards and less e-mail, and express more road rage than demographically matched people who differ only in saying that TV is *not* their primary form of entertainment. TV dependence is associated not merely with less involvement in community life, but with less social communication in all its forms – written, oral, or electronic. This simple question turns out to distinguish those Americans who are most socially isolated from those most involved in their communities, [. . .]. Nothing – not low education, not full-time work, not long commutes in urban agglomerations, not poverty or financial distress – is more broadly associated with civic disengagement and social disconnection than is dependence on television for entertainment. [. . .]

Notes

1   *Statistical Abstract of the United States* (various years); Veronis, Solder & Associates, *Communications Industry Report: Five-Year Historical Report* (1991–95) (New York: Veronis, Suhler & Associates, 1996); Cobbett S. Steinberg, *TV Facts* (New York: Facts on File, 1980); Russell, Master, *Trend*, 59; 'People, Opinion, and Polls: American Popular Culture', *Public Perspective*, August/September 1995: 47; Bower, R.T. (1985) *The Changing Television Audience in America*. New York: Columbia University Press, esp. pp. 33, 46; George Comstock *et al.* (1978) *Television and Human Behavior*. New York: Columbia University Press; Comstock, G. (1989) *Evolution of American Television*. Newbury Park, Calif.: Sage Publications; and Graber, D.A. (1993) *Mass Media and American Politics*. Washington, D.C.: CQ Press.

2   *Where Does the Time Go? The United Media Enterprises Report on Leisure in America* (New York: Newspaper Enterprise Association, 1983), 10; author's analysis of DDB Needham Life Style archive. Preference for a quiet evening at home rose from 68 percent in 1975 to 77 percent in 1999. Those who agreed were also more likely to agree that "TV is my primary form of entertainment."

3   Authors analysis of Roper Social and Political Trends surveys in 1979, 1985, 1989, and 1993; David E. Campbell, Steven Yonish, and Robert D. Putnam, "Tuning In, Tuning Out Revisited: A Closer Look at the Causal Links between Television and Social Capital." Paper presented at the Annual Meeting of the American Political Science Association (Atlanta, Ga., September 1999). Thanks to the co-authors for their many insights into this topic. They are, however, not responsible for my conclusions here.

4   Thanks to Steve Yonish for spotting this line as part of his research duties watching late-night movies.

5   All estimates in this and the following two paragraphs are based on multivariate logistic regression analyses of Roper surveys front 1973, 1974, 1977, 1983, 1988, 1991, and 1993, controlling for education, income, marital, parental, and work status, sex, age, race, region, and city size. Only social class (as measured by education and income) rivals television viewing as a predictor of all twelve forms of civic participation in the Roper archive. Figure 37.1 is limited to working-age, college-educated respondents and to four common measures of participation to illustrate that the negative correlation is strong even within the most civically engaged segment of the population, but the pattern is found across all subsets of the population and all measures of participation. Of working-age, college-educated Americans, 17 percent reported watching less than an hour of TV per day, 54 percent one to three hours, and 29 percent more than three hours. For the population as a whole, the equivalent figures were 12 percent, 43 percent, and 45 percent

6   This estimate is intended only to indicate the potential order of magnitude of the effect of television on civic engagement. civic engagement declined roughly 40 percent over the last third of the century, and additional TV viewing over those years might account for a 10 percent decline.

7   This pattern appears in both the Roper Social and Political Trends data and the DDB Needham Life Style data; see Campbell, Yonish, and Putnam, "Tuning In, Tuning Out Revisited."

8   All generalizations in this and the following six paragraphs are based on the author's analysis of the DDB Needham life Style survey archive. The fraction of respondents who agree that "television is my primary form of entertainment" has tended to rise from about 47 percent in tire 1970s to about 53 percent in the 1990s. (Inexplicably, the fraction surged sharply to 60–65 percent in 1987–88 and then declined somewhat, but the secular trend is upward.) Of those who rely on TV for entertainment, 47 percent also concede that "I'm what you'd call a couch potato," as compared with 17 percent of other Americans. Based on the time slots per day in which they report watching TV, those who say that TV is their primary form of entertainment watch about 40 percent more TV than other Americans. This question effectively singles out the one American in every two who is most dependent upon television entertainment.

Chapter 38

Thomas E. Patterson

THE LONG CAMPAIGN
The politics of tedium

Source: Thomas E. Patterson (2002) *The Vanishing Voter: Public Involvement in an Age of Uncertainty*, New York: Alfred A. Knopf, pp. 99–127.

T̲HE LONG PRESIDENTIAL CAMPAIGN has been criticized for disrupting the policy process – every four years, Washington slows to a crawl awaiting the election of the next president. But the long campaign has been praised for its capacity to inform the voters' judgment. "That year-long test of endurance . . . reduces the risk that voters will make a rash decision they will come to regret not too much later," says the journalist Robert Friedman.[1]

The long campaign would seem to offer everything that a citizen would need to cast an informed vote. Unlike European national elections, which are crammed into a few weeks, the US presidential contest spans a full year and includes a score of televised events, including the primary debates, the October debates, and the national party conventions. Moreover, unlike Europeans, Americans get two chances – once in the primaries and again in the general election – to cast a vote.

But time by itself does not create an informed electorate. Having the time and taking the time are two different things, as students who put off their homework until the last minute know only too well. [. . .]

The long campaign dulls citizens' interest and taxes their attention. Although the campaign is filled with events, many of them are so devoid of meaning or so remote from Election Day that they get little attention. Rather than stimulating interest, the long campaign blunts it. [. . .]

[. . .] By Christmas 1999, the candidates had been on the hustings every day for three months. Nine televised debates had been held. Several candidates, including

Elizabeth Dole, Dan Quayle, and Lamar Alexander, had already quit the race. More than $50 million had been spent, and hundreds of news stories had been filed.

Few cared. During the average week only one in seven was following the election with any degree of regularity. The average citizen didn't say anything at all about the campaign to anyone more than once a week.[2] [. . .] When asked in our Vanishing Voter survey in late 1999 why they were not following the campaign more closely, more than half the respondents indicated "it's simply too early in the campaign."

Before the first primaries are held, candidate debates are the main attraction. They do not get as much fanfare as the October election debates, but they are the biggest challenge that the candidates face until actual votes are cast, and they get reporters' attention.[3] [. . .]

The two dozen primary debates in 2000 drew 36 million viewers, less than the number who watch a single October debate.

Even for the interested few, the primary debates gradually lost their appeal. Cable networks carried fourteen prior to the Iowa caucuses. The first seven attracted 1.7 million viewers on average. The last seven averaged only 675,000. Only 200,000 saw a January debate in Iowa that was carried on MSNBC and C-SPAN. "I'm tired of hearing the same answers over and over again," said one citizen in explaining why she quit watching after only a few minutes.

Debate audiences would have been larger if the major broadcast networks had participated more fully. They carried only two debates, neither in prime time. Even so, these debates had the biggest audiences. A December encounter on ABC's *Nightline* attracted 4.5 million viewers. A week later, 4.7 million tuned in a debate on NBC's *Meet the Press*. Of the twenty-odd debates carried exclusively on cable, the Bush–McCain–Keyes encounter on CNN's *Larry King Live* just before South Carolina's GOP primary was the biggest draw: 3 million viewers. [. . .]

Nevertheless, a lack of interest more than anything else explains the small debate audiences. Half who came across a primary debate while watching television quickly switched to another channel. "I had little interest, so I turned it off," said one such viewer.

[. . .]

Today's conventions are akin to coronation events, a fact that riles the press to no end. Midway through the 1996 GOP convention in San Diego, Ted Koppel of ABC's *Nightline* left in a huff, saying that he was returning to New York in search of real news. Koppel's departure prompted one commentator to remark: "The smoke-filled rooms are gone, but the spectacle that remains is as barren as a pond hit by acid rain: crystal clear, utterly beautiful, and utterly dead."[4]

In earlier times, the press could hardly get its fill of the conventions. [. . .] Today, with the outcome known in advance, the convention is no longer eagerly anticipated by the press, or by the voters. A week before the 2000 Republican national convention, only 19 percent of the public knew it was only days away. Seventy-five percent said they had no idea when it was scheduled and 6 percent placed it a month or more in the future.[5]

Convention audiences have fallen sharply. Even as late as 1976, 28 percent of American households at the average moment had their TV sets on and tuned to the convention. By 1988, convention ratings had slipped to 19 percent. In 2000, only 13 percent of TV households were tuned in during the average prime-time minute, which was below even that of 1996, when the race was one-sided and the nominees better known.[6]

When our survey respondents were asked in 2000 why the conventions were getting so little of their attention, the leading response – aside from the customary ones, "I'm too busy" or "I don't care for politics" – was that the nominees had already been selected.[7]

Cutbacks in broadcast coverage have also contributed to the declining convention audience. In 1976, each of the major networks – ABC, CBS, and NBC – broadcast 25 hours of coverage of each convention. By 1984, that average had fallen to 12 hours. It was a mere 5 hours in 2000.

Although cable outlets provide gavel-to-gavel coverage, they are no substitute for the networks. A fourth of US households do not have satellite or cable service. Moreover, most TV viewers routinely monitor only selected channels, which usually include the major networks. An event that appears simultaneously on the three networks is more likely to attract viewers' attention. Fully half the audience for the 2000 conventions consisted of inadvertent viewers – those who sat down in front of their television sets, discovered the convention was on, and decided to watch some of it. Three times as many of these viewers were captured through a broadcast channel as through a cable channel. But they cannot be corraled if ABC, CBS, and NBC are all televising something else.[8]

The eclipse of the convention as a deliberative forum and television sensation has reduced campaign involvement. In the heyday of the televised conventions – the 1950s through the 1970s – the average American household watched ten to twenty hours of coverage. Voters learned more about the candidates and issues during the conventions than at any other single period in the campaign. The convention was quite an education, even for children and adolescents. Just as the World Series served to awaken them to major league baseball, the summer conventions introduced them to party politics.

Conventions still do all this, only on a smaller scale. They remain a key moment in terms of their ability to draw people into the campaign. Their audience, though diminished, is not minuscule. In our Vanishing Voter surveys, roughly a fourth of the respondents said they had watched "all" or "most" of the previous night's coverage. Nearly 15 million were tuned in during the average prime-time minute. Four of five who watched said they liked what they saw.[9]

[. . .]

Labor Day speeches are the traditional kickoff to the fall campaign. They once served as coming-out parties for the newly chosen party nominees. The candidates were fresh news and so were their pronouncements. Today, the candidates are such old news by Labor Day that, as far as most people are concerned, it might as well be Groundhog Day. During Labor Day week in 2000, Americans were actually less attentive to the presidential campaign than in the preceding or the following week.[10]

September was once a highlight of the campaign. As the candidates toured the nation, speaking in city squares, they packed in the crowds and laid out their positions. [. . .] But September is now just another month on the long road to November. [. . .]

The voters, too, are worn out. In 2000, public involvement dropped during September. Unlike the post-Super Tuesday period, Americans did not flee the

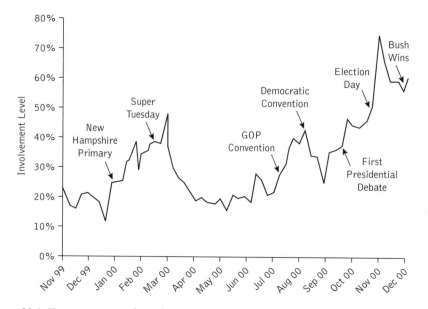

Figure 38.1 Key moments and involvement in the 2000 presidential campaign

During most weeks of the 2000 campaign, the majority of Americans were paying almost no attention. Interest was high only around key moments – the contested primaries, the conventions, the October debates, and Election Day. Involvement rose dramatically during the post-election period when the election's outcome was at issue. [. . .]

campaign. But they talked and thought about it less often and followed it less closely than they had during the convention period. As they pulled back, they forgot some of the information acquired earlier.[11] Issue awareness dropped by 22 percent during the month after the convention period. The optimism of that period had also dissipated. A majority now claimed that the campaign was boring and uninformative.[12]

Presidential elections might seem interminable if the October televised debates had not been resurrected in 1976. [. . .]

[. . .]

However, the malaise that has depressed other election activities has also affected the debates. More than half of television households had their sets on and tuned to debates in 1976 and again in 1980.[13] The number fell to 46 percent in 1984, 36 percent in 1988, and 29 percent in 1996. Although the 2000 Gore–Bush debate ratings were expected to top the 1996 figure because of the tight race, they did not rise, and the rating for the third debate was the lowest ever (26 percent).

[. . .]

[. . .] Soon after the last debate in 2000, interest increased as the campaign moved toward Election Day. During the final week, involvement reached one of its highest levels of the entire campaign 34 percent said they were paying close attention.[14] Citizens were more involved in other ways, too. On the average day, 49 percent reported having talked about the election – the highest level at any time during the campaign.[15] Intense news coverage in the campaign's closing days contributed to the rise in interest. Although the news media have cut back on their election coverage in recent elections, the final days are still heavily reported. In the last week of the 2000 campaign, roughly half of Americans each day reported having read, seen, or heard an election story. This level, too, was a campaign high.[16]

Although interest peaked at the end, its full potential had not been tapped, as the post-election period revealed. During the five weeks that the outcome of the 2000 election rested on the results of the Florida recount, citizen involvement – as measured by people's thoughts, conversations, and news exposure – averaged 61 percent, far higher than was registered at any time during the campaign. The Florida wrangling captured public attention in a way the campaign itself did not.

[. . .]

Notes

1   Robert Friedman, "Perot: Co-Opting Legitimate Issues," *St. Petersburg Times*, Nov. 21, 1993, p. 4.
2   Vanishing Voter survey, Feb. 6, 2000.
3   The Vanishing Voter Project's media tracking found that election coverage in major news outlets increased by 60 percent in response to the first primary debate.
4   *New Standard*, Aug. 16, 1996, Internet copy.
5   Vanishing Voter survey, July 26–30 and Aug. 18–22, 2000.
6   Ratings and viewing hours from Nielsen Media Research.
7   Thomas E. Patterson, "Lessons from the Last Convention," p. 3. Paper presented at Shorenstein Center panel at the the Democratic National Convention, Los Angeles, August 2000.
8   This rough estimate is based on Vanishing Voter surveys. That the size of the inadvertent audience is a function of the hours of broadcast coverage is apparent from the increase in this audience as network convention coverage increases. It might be thought that, as a convention unfolds, inadvertent viewers would decline as a proportion of the total audience because people are more aware that the convention is under way. In fact, however, the inadvertent audience peaked on the fourth, and final, convention night. It was the night when ABC, CBS, and NBC provided the most hours of coverage.
9   Vanishing Voter surveys, Aug. 1–2, 2–6,15–16,16–17, 2000.
10   Vanishing Voter national surveys, 2000.
11   Vanishing Voter national surveys, Aug. 18–22, Sept. 13–17, 2000.
12   Vanishing Voter national surveys, September 2000.
13   Nielsen Media Research data, for all debate audience references.
14   Average of Vanishing Voter national surveys, Nov. 5 and 7, 2000.
15   Ibid.
16   Ibid.

Chapter 39

David Buckingham

TALKING NEWS, TALKING POLITICS

Source: David Buckingham (2000) *The Making of Citizens: Young People, News and Politics,* London: Routledge, pp. 59–99.

[. . .]

Talking news

DESPITE THE DIFFERENCES between the various groups of students whom I interviewed, few expressed great enthusiasm for television news. The programmes nominated as favourites in our warm-up discussions were almost exclusively comedies, soaps, movies and sport. Some students appeared to believe that news might be a required answer here, and claimed that it was among their favourites, although when asked to recall news stories they had seen recently, they were often unable to do so. With a few exceptions, expressions of even moderate interest in news were only to be found among the oldest age group. More frequently, news was rejected as simply 'boring', and in several cases exaggerated groans greeted my introduction of the topic.

In fact, it was clear from their subsequent discussions that most of the students did watch news, in several cases on a regular basis, but that in itself does not suggest that they necessarily enjoyed it. In some instances, they argued, they had no option but to do so, simply because there was 'nothing else on', or because their parents insisted on watching it. Nevertheless, this rejection of news also seemed to be a kind of expected ritual, which was partly to do with the students' collective construction of themselves as 'young people'. From this perspective, anything associated with 'adults' is automatically condemned as boring and irrelevant, unless it has the kudos of being explicitly forbidden to children.

The more working-class students in the Philadelphia pilot school were most explicit – or perhaps least polite – about this. Tom (13), for example, repeatedly assured me that 'news sucks': 'it's all the same thing . . . it comes on, like, six times a day." Dana (14) and Rosa (13) likewise claimed that the news was boring and that it 'put them to sleep'. Nevertheless, similar 'complaints were made in both the other schools, in Philadelphia and in London'. In general, news was perceived as repetitive and lacking in entertainment value. [. . .]

Somewhat facetiously perhaps, several students suggested that news might be made more entertaining, not only by incorporating more entertainment news in the content, but also by changing the format. Candace (12) argued that '[news] should be made into a TV show'; while Diana and Walida (14) suggested that they should incorporate stories that were not real, and call it 'Fakes' instead.

On the other hand, there were several students, particularly among the older age group, who rejected what they saw as a drift towards sensationalism and triviality in news. [. . .] The UK students were highly critical of the publicity stunts being used in the 1997 election campaign, and argued that the media played a part in encouraging this. In general, however, these charges of sensationalism and triviality were mainly directed at the tabloid press, and at the local news programme London Tonight, which was comprehensively demolished by one group. These students were also well aware of the political bias of the popular press. By contrast, the main evening news seemed to possess greater authority. [. . .] Perhaps surprisingly, such complaints were less prevalent in the Philadelphia schools, although (as we shall see below) some students did criticize what they saw as the media's preoccupation with trivial political scandals.

These criticisms were to some extent supported by the evidence of what the students were able to recall from recent news broadcasts. Crime, entertainment and sport were far and away the leading categories here. In the Philadelphia schools, the kinds of stories most frequently mentioned included local murders and fires, as well as national stories such as the Unabomber and (inevitably) the O.J. Simpson case. In the London school, sport and entertainment were even more prominent, along with several bizarre 'human interest' stories. On the other hand, most students had seen coverage of the forthcoming elections – even if they typically dismissed such material as boring or trivial. Furthermore, many of the apparently 'non-political' stories that were recalled had implicit 'political' dimensions – and these were directly referred to by some of the students themselves. Thus, for example, some UK students recalled stories about Tiger Woods' victory in the US Open, noting that he was the first Black player to win, while others referred to the racially-motivated murder of the London teenager Stephen Lawrence.

However, several students rejected the news on the grounds that it was emotionally upsetting. This was more strongly the case in the US, where local news in particular is much more graphic in its coverage of crimes and disasters than in the UK. Noah (11, US), for example, said he was 'disgusted' by much of what he saw on the news: 'like murder and child abuse and fire and stuff . . . sometimes I don't watch the news because some days it can be just plain depressing.' Likewise, Suzanna (17, UK) said that she was inclined to avoid news stories like those about the Dunblane primary school massacre on the grounds that 'it just makes you upset'. [. . .]

On the other hand, there were some who saw this kind of material as interesting and as necessary to know about (cf. Buckingham, 1996: Chapter 6). One UK group of 14-year-old girls complained that the news was sometimes 'too horrible to watch', citing the coverage of wars in Rwanda; although they also acknowledged that, as Nisha put it, 'if you watch it right, it gives the idea of other people, the way they live, their feelings, it makes our feelings stronger towards them'.

[. . .]

These general discussions of news thus revealed some typically contradictory and ambivalent responses. On the one hand, the large majority of students asserted that news was 'boring'; and much of what they remembered having seen of it might broadly be described as 'entertainment' rather than 'hard news'. Yet on the other hand, many of them condemned attempts to make the news more entertaining: if the news was bad, it seemed that 'light news' was even worse. There was equal ambivalence about the serious content of news – for example, its coverage of crime and disasters. On the one hand, it was argued that such material was often too upsetting to watch; yet on the other, it was argued that viewers (including young people) had a right to know about it.

In general, the older students displayed greater interest in news, although they were also more inclined to criticize it, on the grounds of its sensationalism or its potential bias. As I shall indicate, these differences can partly be understood in developmental terms; yet they also reflect the ways in which speakers actively position themselves in talk, and thereby claim particular social identities. Critical judgements about bias or sensationalism in the news, assertions of one's need to know, ritualized rejections of news as 'boring' – all need to be understood as social acts, not merely as reflections of how individuals really think and behave.

Talking politics

Given the fact that the interviews in both countries were conducted in the run-up to an election (in 1996 in the US, 1997 in the UK), one might have expected the students to be more aware of politics – and perhaps to be more interested in it – than they might have been at any other time. Yet of all the issues covered in news, politics was the one most consistently singled out for rejection and condemnation. The picture of young people's alienation from politics described in Chapter 1 [of the original publication] was, on one level, very much confirmed in these discussions. Politics was seen by the large majority as simply irrelevant to their lives.

> *Michael* (14, *US*): If it affects me particularly, like my family, then I will pay attention to it. But if it's like something that's not really all that important, but they just did to make it look like they are doing something in Congress, I don't really watch that, 'cause that's really boring.

As Michael's comment illustrates, 'politics' was defined here primarily in terms of the actions of politicians and elected representatives. As I have noted, several of the news stories that were discussed – from the O.J. Simpson case to Tiger Woods –

clearly had broader 'political' dimensions and resonances, even if these were not always made explicit by the students themselves. But only a small minority of students expressed any interest in 'politics' as conventionally defined, and those who did appeared to do so more out of politeness towards the interviewer than from any great enthusiasm. For most, politics was simply 'boring', not least because it was 'hard to understand'.

This sense of the irrelevance of politics was partly seen as a structural consequence of the students' position as 'children'. Many argued that political changes did not directly affect them as much as they did adults; but they also pointed out that they did not have any stake in bringing about those changes. They did not pay taxes and they were not allowed to vote, so what difference did it make what they thought? As Liam (14) argued, 'I'd rather take an interest when I can change [things], but not when I can't.'

However, this sense of alienation was also fuelled by a profound – albeit quite generalized – cynicism about the motivations of politicians. For many students, the word 'politician' was effectively a term of abuse. Politicians were routinely condemned as untrustworthy, insincere, inconsistent and incompetent. They were simply 'playing games', trying to maintain their own popularity at any cost, and they could be counted upon to break their own promises or otherwise 'mess things up'. While some students claimed to be interested in keeping up with the electoral race, there was considerable criticism of the tactics used in the campaigns, and particularly of the emphasis on negative campaigning. As we shall see, politicians were also criticized for their neglect of issues specifically relating to children and for what were seen as authoritarian policies in areas such as education and youth crime.

Here again, there were differences in terms of age and social class. While the older children were generally more aware of politics, they were also the ones who condemned politicians most strongly. Even among the older middle-class children, some of whose parents were active in party politics, there was considerable cynicism and disaffection. Significantly, this also extended to the minority of students who were more enthusiastic about news: the desire to 'know what's going on in the world' rarely seemed to encompass the desire to know about politics. One group of 17-year-old girls in the London school debated this issue at some length:

> *Siobhan:* [Politics] doesn't really affect our lives that much, so you don't notice it.
> *Nandi:* I don't think people realize that it will affect their lives, and so there's no point [being interested in it] . . . I think it has a lot to do with class and school, so it's not just young people . . . the more middle-class people are more interested in it than working-class people . . . I just think that most people don't care, because even though they're more likely to be affected by it than us, they just don't care, they're not aware, they don't have the information that would say this could really . . . who wins this election could change my job or my education or what have you.
> *Suzanna:* We've had a Conservative Party for so long, nothing's gonna change. It's like, what's the point voting if nothing's gonna change . . .

> *Siobhan:* We've all had Conservative for our entire lives, so we can't
> think back and think 'oh yeah, Labour did that then'. And now,
> because Labour have switched, it makes it even less important.

These students provide some very cogent reasons for their own alienation from politics. These are partly to do with their position as young people, and partly with what they perceive as a lack of information. Class and education are also seen as important, although it is difficult to identify how Nandi classifies herself in these terms. Interestingly, they also situate this historically, effectively defining themselves as 'Thatcher's children'. Siobhan clearly knows enough about contemporary politics to assert that 'Labour have switched'; although this also confirms the view that voting – and, by extension, informing oneself about politics – is fairly pointless. This extract makes particularly interesting reading in the light of Labour's subsequent election victory – although of course these students were just too young to be first-time voters. It might perhaps qualify the triumphalist assertion that this victory reflected a more fundamental change of political mood or orientation.

Despite this general alienation from the world of national politics, many students clearly had very strong feelings about more 'local' political issues. In this, I am not referring to the rather generalized 'politics of everyday life' identified by Fiske (1989: see Chapter 3), as much as to issues that arose in the students' experiences of *institutions* – not least school itself – and in their experiences of their local *neighbourhood* and *community*. Thus, for example, one group of Philadelphia students engaged in an extended discussion of proposals to introduce school uniform. This is an issue that might be seen by some as merely a matter of personal preference, but the students' discussion explicitly drew out the broader political dimensions. For example, they pointed out that uniforms were being promoted as a solution to the problem of violence, and argued that this was a distraction from its real causes; they also saw it as a civil rights issue, which applied specifically to students in public rather than private schools.

This dimension was very apparent in the UK students' discussions of *Wise Up*. At the end of the second interview, I asked them if they would like to make their own report for the programme, and if so what topic they would choose. Some of the topics suggested here were more obviously 'political', at least in a somewhat broader sense, such as racism in the police or environmental pollution. Others were seemingly 'non-political', although on further discussion it became apparent that the students perceived them to have a clear political dimension. Thus, for example, one group suggested a report about the poor quality of school dinners, and they went on to blame this on the fact that the school meals service had been privatized. Likewise, another group said they would like to produce an item about sport on TV, but here again, their concerns were motivated by the fact that major sporting events have been bought up by subscription channels, thus preventing the students from watching them. Several of the issues identified here could be seen to derive from a kind of 'youth politics', which was most explicit in the case of the group who proposed an item about the contradictions in the laws relating to the age of majority. In almost every case, these suggestions were based on the students' direct personal experiences, yet they displayed a striking ability to think through the implications of those experiences in broader social and political terms. In some respects, this supports the more general need for 'relevance', [. . .]; although it also implies that relevance is not so much inherent in a given topic as a matter of how the connections between the 'personal' and the 'political' are forged.

Here again, it is important not to take these observations at face value. Expressions of distrust in politicians have become almost ritualistic conversational cliches, not just among the young. As I shall argue, they may reflect little more than a superficial form of cynicism, which derives from a sense of individual powerlessness – although ultimately they may also serve to reinforce it. In this respect, perhaps, the students were merely saying what they thought they were expected to say. Yet when it came to political issues that were closer to their own experience, which they might have some power to influence, and they were much more engaged. To this extent, their sense of alienation from politics, as conventionally defined, cannot be seen to derive simply from a kind of laziness or ignorance. On the contrary, it could be seen as a logical response to the constraints of their own social position.

[. . .]

References

Buckingham, D. (1996) *Moving Images: Understanding Children's Emotional Responses to Television*. Manchester: Manchester University Press.
Fiske, J. (1989) *Reading the Popular*. London: Unwin Hyman.

Chapter 40

Jeffery P. Jones

AUDIENCE ENGAGEMENT WITH
POLITICALLY INCORRECT

Source: Jeffery P. Jones (2005) *Entertaining Politics: New Political Television and Civic Culture*, Lanham, MD: Rowman & Littlefield, pp. 161–86.

[. . .]

I **HAVE SET OUT,** then, to examine audience reception of NPTV [(new political television)] through the program *Politically Incorrect*. As noted previously, this program offered several distinctive avenues for studying audiences, including the unique feature of audience auditions to be a "Citizen Panelist" on the program in several major US cities. Another aspect of audience activity that is more pronounced for P.I. than for other shows is an active on-line discussion forum that has operated since 1997 (when P.I. moved from cable to network television) and continues to this day. Finally, my access to the show's producers also allowed me to examine viewer mail to the program. [. . .] I therefore analyzed viewers who themselves had chosen to engage the program in some way: by writing a letter to the program, auditioning to be a participant on the show, being a studio audience member, or talking on-line with other viewers about the show. I was interested in learning what type of relationship they had with the program. That is, how did they engage it and why? What did the programming do for them, or why did they watch? How did they conceive of the programming in ways like or unlike other political talk programming?

[. . .]

Viewer mail

On average, *Politically Incorrect* received about seven pieces of correspondence a day (plus an additional thirty e-mails), [. . .]. [. . .] In reviewing correspondence to the show from February 1997 to March 2000, I too am struck by the burning desire of citizens, transformed from simply being viewers, to engage in political conversation with Maher. [. . .] In fact, a vast majority of the mail I reviewed contained a politically discursive focus.

[. . .]

[. . .] Here are a few examples.

> "Thank you for expressing some of my views. . . . We concur on women, population explosion, personal responsibility, and reprehensible Republicans." "Here are a few comments on subjects discussed on PI in recent days. The subjects are the free classical music CD's and the protesters at abortion clinics." "I am very excited finally to have the opportunity to contribute something to the lively discussions which have kept me fascinated and entertained these past few years."

[. . .] The one belief or value that viewers felt compelled to write about was freedom of speech, not because it was being challenged, but because the show exemplified it so well (as is discussed below). The other value was religion, which many viewers believe Maher often denigrates. Overall, the dominant reason most viewers made the effort to write a letter to the show was to continue the conversation that Maher and his guests had begun.

Part of that conversation was the need to criticize Maher and/or his guests. [. . .] Other writers were offended more by the guests, [. . .]. In both instances, the writers were generally intent on connecting the issues espoused with the personal characteristics of the person espousing them. [. . .] The politics and the personal, the person and the idea are not so easily separated – at least not in the form of political conversation this show creates or by the people who enjoy/dislike watching it.

[. . .]

Audience interviews

Over the course of nine months in 1999–2000, I interviewed approximately sixty-five people in four major US cities. In three of those cities – Houston, Baltimore, and Atlanta – these individuals had shown up early on a Saturday morning at their local ABC affiliate to audition for a guest spot as "Citizen Panelist" on *Politically Incorrect*. In the fourth case, I interviewed people outside the studios of CBS Television City in Los Angeles as they waited in line to serve as the studio audience for two tapings of P.I. [. . .]

[. . .]

The responses I received for why they watched the program and what they enjoyed about it were similar to the reasons offered in the viewer mail. That is, their responses tended to coalesce around the distinctive and unusual qualities that the show offered. As with the letter writers, these viewers also appreciated the mix of entertainment and information they felt the show delivered [. . .].

[. . .]

[. . .] The viewers of P.I. that I interviewed generally had no problem with the mixture of entertainment and information that the show presented. Instead, they recognized the enjoyment of such a coupling, while suggesting that perhaps these features would also bring less politically engaged and astute citizens into the fold. The show is seen as being accessible because it includes people with whom the viewing public is familiar, because it discusses issues that people are concerned about, and because it does it in a way that is not intimidating. On the other hand, many viewers expressed their dislike of traditional political talk on television, seeing it as scripted, predictable, and unaffecting. Furthermore, because such talk is somewhat inaccessible for many viewers, it tends to leave people feeling inadequate and uninformed. The irony, then, is that rather than leading people to be informed about politics, pundit shows repulse some citizens by reminding them of all that they do not (though perhaps should) know. Finally, the public also wonders why they should care about pundit talk (and by association, the issues covered there) because they don't really know who is doing the talking and why. [. . .] Who or what many of these viewers do "know" or care about are celebrities. The celebrity guests seen on P.I. are familiar because of the affective relationship that viewers maintain with these characters who comprise popular culture. The political opinions celebrities state are seen as more real, more heartfelt, and pronounced in a language that is more easily understood than pundit talk. These celebrities, for the most part, are not politicized persons. Therefore, audiences don't feel they must endure the entrenched positions or the predictable and scripted lines that typically accompany televised political talk. Celebrity political talk emanates from the same sources as the audience, and it is stated in the same raw and unrefined ways as one would find in a bar or at work (and as a result, enhances its validity). Therefore, the audience appreciates the means and manner in which the program and its celebrity guests have articulated the public with the private. [. . .]

[. . .]

Online discussion groups

[. . .]

Of all political talk shows on television, the discussion forum dedicated to *Politically Incorrect* – alt.tv.pol-incorrect (henceforth referred to as ATPI) has been the most frequented on Usenet, with over 98,000 postings since the group's inception in February 1997 through February 2004. [. . .] I studied the postings made to alt.tv.pol-incorrect for the month of February for every year between 1997 and 2003, as well as for August 1998 [. . .] and September 2001 [. . .]. [. . .]

Usenet discussion groups are strange yet interesting places, with norms, ritual behaviors, patterns of interaction, and a culture all their own. A useful analogy in understanding these forums is to a neighborhood bar (although for ATPI, one with a higher IQ). Like a bar, the discussion group is frequented by regulars, those who drop by occasionally, and those who just happen to wander by and decide to "have a drink (e.g., make a posting) and check out the joint." As such, the regulars are the most frequent posters, and therefore come to know each other quite well. They develop levels of trust, fondness, and support for each others' ideas, as well as general disdain for some of the more annoying regulars. They set the tone for how discussion will generally occur, become de facto experts on the program, perhaps create longer discussion threads by responding more frequently to each other, and take the liberty to be either generous or rude to those just passing by (although rudeness is generally not the dominant motif here). Also like a bar, the talk is a combination of seriousness and irreverence, reflection and playfulness, bluntness and cleverness. Although the myriad activities that go on in a bar also can occur here (i.e., petty fights, drunken banter, cattiness, etc.), it is the focus on the show, Maher as host, and politics in general that remain central to the larger flow of discursive activity and overall purpose people have for coming to this forum.[1]

In some ways, discussions on ATPI are similar to those that occur in other on-line forums where television programming is discussed. For instance, Nancy Baym's study of on-line soap opera discussions reports four primary fan practices that occur there: *informing* others of what occurred in missed episodes; *speculating* about where the show's content will or should go; *criticizing* the show, its narratives, its actors, or other postings; and reworking the show's text in various ways.[2] All of these activities occur in ATPI as well. [. . .]

ATPIers also speculate about Maher or guests on the show, debating, for instance, whether John McCain is a racist for anti-Vietnamese remarks (2/22/00) or whether the comedian Carrot Top is Jewish (3/11/98). The act of criticizing – Maher, the program, and the guests that appear – is one of the most frequent activities that occur in the forum. Indeed, Maher and his guests, from my observations, are more frequently criticized than celebrated.[3] [. . .]

Finally, as is similar with on-line viewer discussions in other television dedicated forums, the participants in ATPI rework the program in various ways. As with letter writers, one popular form of reworking is the (re)construction of favorite past panelist lineups or assemblages the audience should see. [. . .]

[. . .]
Perhaps the most important component of ATPI yet to be discussed is the way in which an entertainment television program has been the base from which quite extensive and substantive discussions of politics regularly occur. Like the letter writers and my interview subjects, participants in ATPI really want to talk about political issues, and as one might imagine, these discussions occur on numerous topics: welfare, gun control, immigration, environmental regulations, taxation, animal rights, free speech, education, race, violence, health care, law enforcement, and so on. The discussants bring with them their own personal characteristics and experiences from different parts of the nation (and Canada). [. . .]

P.I., then, becomes the jumping-off point for political discussion. Someone will comment on a recent show, and a political discussion that can be very specific or wide-ranging will typically occur. [. . .] Again, although the actual program may not have been the best forum for the wide exchange of ideas in certain instances, ATPI allowed viewers to hold a much more extensive, dispassionate, and reasoned argument than that hosted on the program. [. . .]

One might wonder, however, whether these viewers should go to another forum to talk politics – say, for instance, alt.talk.politics. What is significant, however, is that they don't (or if they do, they still come to ATPI). They link their pleasure in watching a television program that features wide-ranging discussions of politics to then activate their interests in participating in their own wide-ranging discussions of politics. They desire to share information (news articles, hyperlinks, experiences) and engage in knowledge formation. [. . .] And they do so in a rather civilized manner (for I find participants in this forum are less likely to engage in ad hominem attacks and are much less ideologically polarized than the participants in some political discussion forums, such as alt.fan.rush-limbaugh).[4] [. . .]

   [. . .]

Notes

1   See Oldenburg's argument for how certain "third places" (as opposed to work and home) are central to community life, social conversation, and grassroots democracy. Oldenburg, R. (1989) *The Great Good Place. Cafes, Coffeeshops, Community Centers, Beauty Parlors, General Stores, Bars, Hangouts, and How They Get You through the Day*. New York: Paragon House.

2   Nancy K. Baym (1998) Talking about Soaps: Communicative Practices in a Computer-Mediated Fan Culture. In Harris, C. and Alexander, A. (eds) *Theorizing Fandom. Fans, Subculture and Identity*. Cresskill, NJ.: Hampton Press.

3   That may simply be the product of this forum's participants portraying themselves as hip and slightly cynical toward popular culture. Comments of praise, though they do appear, are less often made public.

4   Of course, for the Limbaugh forum, consider the source for where those discussions began. Jones, "The Aetherial Rush."

Chapter 41

Brian McNair, Matthew Hibberd and Philip Schlesinger

PUBLIC ACCESS BROADCASTING IN THE UK
A history

Source: Brian McNair, Matthew Hibberd and Philip Schlesinger (2003) *Mediated Access: Broadcasting and Democratic Participation*, Luton: University of Luton Press, pp. 19–30.

O VER THE PAST THREE DECADES there has been a rapid rise in the number of radio and television programmes to which ordinary members of the public contribute in a participatory capacity. Whether as participants in a radio phone-in or guests in a daytime talk show, their contributions have become a regular part of the UK's programming diet. Appearing on television or radio is no longer restricted to the small group of privileged professionals who once dominated the medium. But the phenomenon of public participation broadcasting is not a new one, and indeed goes back to the earliest days of radio.

[. . .]

Public participation broadcasting: the early years

Until the 1960s the relationship between the BBC and its audience was largely one-way, especially in the provision of news and political programming. The broadcasting of politics was a one-sided affair, with the public receiving news of political developments and events. There was little, if any, chance for the public to interrogate political elites. Neither the BBC nor the political parties encouraged such inter-action. In the early years of the BBC, therefore, public contributions to programming remained limited. [. . .] This was due, in part, to the growth and development of national and regional output and the closure of local stations. But antipathy towards public involvement in broadcasting was also due to class and professional biases among BBC staff, beginning with Reith himself:

> In some stations, I see, periodically, men down to speak whose status either socially or professionally, and whose qualifications to speak, seem doubtful. It should be an honour, in every sense of the word, for a man to speak from any broadcasting station. And only those who have a claim to be heard above their fellows on any particular subject in the locality should be put on these programmes.[1]

[. . .]

Public participation in political programmes was thus prevented in the early years of broadcasting by a formidable alliance of the BBC and political elites. The BBC only began to reverse this policy in the post-1945 period, when tentative moves were made to encourage greater public participation in radio programming, including political formats. It took some politicians even longer to accept the idea that the public could play an important part in mediated political discussion. [. . .].

Public participation broadcasting in postwar Britain

[. . .]

[. . .] In 1952 the government introduced proposals to establish commercial television. The news of these proposals provoked intense political debate on behalf of supporters of both sides of the argument. [. . .] The legislation for commercial television was formally introduced in Parliament in 1953 and became law in 1954.

Against this background the BBC undertook to develop and strengthen its political coverage, although until ITV started broadcasting in 1955 the BBC dragged its feet in introducing new and innovative ways of presenting politics on TV and radio. [. . .] The opportunities afforded to the public to participate in broadcast debates remained limited.

The BBC restricted active public involvement to a limited number of programmes, including the political access programme, *Any Questions?*, which began in the Western region in 1948. The programme was eventually given a nationwide transmission slot, and continues broadcasting today as the longest running political access programme on radio. [. . .] [T]he programme's format reflected the political and social values of 1940s Britain. Public participation was strictly limited only to asking questions, with limited possibility of entering into dialogue with politicians. And political parties signalled their resistance to the programme by refusing for many years to allow senior politicians of Cabinet level to take part in the programme (Day, 1989, p. 276). Only later was this rule relaxed and greater public participation also encouraged in the form of *Any Answers?*, a phone-in programme that today follows the Saturday repeat of *Any Questions?*

This situation remained broadly unchanged until the first half of the 1960s, when television and radio broadcasters, led by the BBC, began to develop styles and formats of programming where members of the public gained a higher degree of visibility. This increase was due in part to the overall expansion in the BBC's radio and television political coverage. But it was also due, as Sylvia Harvey argues, to 'a new spirit of democratisation' that developed in the 1960s and which saw the erosion of deference and Reithian paternalism, and 'the emergence of more egalitarian patterns of thought'. (2000, p. 161). [. . .]

[. . .]

While it is true that ITV had introduced more populist programme formats, Pilkington's pessimistic warning was clearly flawed and, with hindsight, an early example of the rhetoric of 'dumbing down' which accompanies almost every effort to reform and innovate political broadcasting to this day (see below [in the original]). In fact, the emergence of ITV as a competitor to the BBC incentivised the latter to be more adventurous, if still as a public service broadcaster. [. . .] And, indeed, it was the BBC not ITV which introduced many of the access formats that, from the 1960s onwards would seek, albeit imperfectly to represent the new spirit of democratisation. The first of these programmes, *Election Forum*, was a television programme where viewers' questions were put to senior politicians immediately prior to the 1964 election campaign. But while this programme introduced a limited form of audience participation, it still had major shortcomings. [. . .]

The 1960s also saw the emergence of a new programme format that soon became a firm favourite with broadcasters: the radio phone-in programme. The first radio phone-in shows were developed in United States in the 1950s. With the development of phone-in programmes members of the public were on a routine basis actively encouraged to contribute to issues under discussion in the studio, including political and social debates. [. . .] The British public were still largely unaccustomed to requests for their views and, unsurprisingly, the quality of debate was often poor. The advent of commercial local radio in 1973 led to a further expansion of phone-in programmes. For these stations, the phone-in was seen as an ideal programme format, combining as it did genuine popular appeal with relatively low production costs.

Local phone-in programmes were soon adapted into national radio formats, including, in 1970, the start of a new political show, *It's Your Line* with Robin Day. This was followed in 1974 by the start of *Election Call* where leading political figures were questioned on a range of issues during the (two) election campaigns that year. In his book on the February 1974 election, David Butler argued,

> It attracted over a million listeners, and up to 9000 calls. It was chaired with exemplary skill and fairness by Robin Day. The public's questions were often penetrating and sometimes blunter than any professional questioner would dare to be . . . Clearly a campaign tradition has been born (Quoted in Day, 1989, p. 184).

The breakdown in negotiations between the BBC and popular presenter Michael Parkinson to host a new late night chat show left a gap in its schedule for autumn 1979. To help fill that gap, the BBC adapted the popular radio programme, *Any Questions?*, to a weekly television programme, *Question Time*, originally hosted by the ever-present Robin Day, and presented as of this writing by David Dimbleby. From the outset, *Question Time* producers sought to differentiate the programme from its radio cousin. While the number of panel members remained the same (four), producers encouraged greater audience participation and the programme was made longer (60 minutes, as against the original length of 45). *Question Time* soon proved a popular addition to the late-night schedule, although few anticipated this at the outset [. . .].

The programme has subsequently been developed and refined, with the addition of a fifth panelist and an enhanced role for audience members [. . .].

In commercial television, too, public access forms have increased in popularity in the past three decades, albeit largely in non-peak time slots. ITV's traditional Sunday lunchtime political slot, which started with *Weekend World* in the 1970s, has now become a public access programme (*Jonathan Dimbleby*).

New TV channels have also developed access formats as part of their political coverage. Channel 4 (which began transmission in 1982) has experimented with a number of access programmes, including its *On Trial* . . . series and *The People's Parliament*, presented by Sheena MacDonald in the 1990s. More recently Channel 4 has staged broadcast debates chaired by *C4 News* presenter Jon Snow on single issue topics such as the health service and the conflict in the Middle East. In the latter, broadcast in October 2002, viewers were invited to contribute opinions as to whether a possible war with Iraq was, (a) inevitable, and (b) desirable (BBC 1 also organised a debate on this topic, broadcast around the same time – both provided access to views which were highly critical of UK government policy on Iraq).

Since its launch in 1997 (and despite having a less rigorous public service remit than the other four terrestrial channels) Channel 5 has broadcast a number of public participation programmes, including one strand presented by Kirsty Young addressing issues such as the legalisation of soft drugs. Channel 5 also launched a morning audience and phone-in programme, *The Wright Stuff*, which frequently addresses political themes. SkyNews has *Your Call* and other access programmes presented by its political editor, Adam Boulton.[2]

On radio, there has been a rise in the numbers of political access programmes on air, associated with the dramatic growth in speech radio (although there have been signs in the past few years that demand has peaked, at least in the commercial sector). As the number of national and local radio channels has increased in the last two decades, so has the space available for talk radio. Indeed, as was noted earlier, talk radio is a particularly cost effective way of filling the countless hours of airtime which now comprise the UK radio sector. For the BBC a key moment in this process was the launch of Radio Five Live in March 1994, a station wholly devoted to news and sport. Five Live has weekday morning and late evening phone-in programmes tackling major political and social issues such as the Nicky Campbell show, but all its news programmes encourage listener participation via email or text messaging. The station has also developed new sports discussion programmes in the mould of political access formats, including *Any Sporting Questions?*, based on *Any Questions?*, and *606*, the sports phone-in programme. The first (national) commercial radio station devoted wholly to speech, Talk Radio, increased the amount of political access programming with phone-ins presented by such as Brian Hayes (its demise in 1999, to become Talk Sport, highlights the growing popularity of sports discussion programmes in recent years).[3]

Broadcasters have also increased the amount of public participation in conventional news and current affairs programmes, by inviting audiences to comment on the major political issues. Today, many radio and television news programmes include regular slots to read out audience letters, faxes and phone. Such feedback has been further encouraged with the development of new technologies such as e-mails and message boards [. . .]. Some programmes have sought to encourage public participation at election times by broadcasting special editions with live audiences.

Conclusion

Since the late 1940s, though not without some resistance, as we have seen, public participation in political programming has been one of the strategies by which broadcasters have sought to persuade and reassure the listening or viewing audience that their services are relevant to the lives and concerns of ordinary people. Phone-in shows and audience discussion programmes have become a permanent feature of radio and TV schedules in the UK, offering viewers the opportunity to see themselves, or others like them, apparently holding their own in the company of resident presenters and guests. As noted in chapter one [of the original], recent studies into the 'crisis' of political broadcasting suggest that they remain an important tool for mobilising and engaging audiences (Kevill, 2002; Hargreaves and Thomas, 2002). [. . .]

Notes

1   Quoted in 'You're on the Air', broadcast by BBC Radio 4, February 2001.
2   Channel 4 was set up as a direct response to the 1977 report of the government-appointed Annan Committee. While the committee was somewhat sceptical about the potential of access programming in general, it did argue for 'the open expression of a wide range of views from many different groups', while endorsing the view that 'the basic principle of access programming is freedom to state opinions' (Home Office, 1977: 296, quoted from Harvey, 2000: 162).
3   According to John Lloyd, Head of News and Current Affairs, the popularity of political access programmes might have peaked in the early 1990s, and there is now less appetite among some commercial broadcasters for political access programmes (Interview with authors, 2001). The build up to war with Iraq in late 2002/2003, however, showed that access broadcasting remains an important element in the construction of national public debate on key political issues.

References

Day, R. (1989) *Grand Inquisitor*. London: Butler & Tanner.
Hargreaves, I. and Thomas, J. (2002) *New News, Old News*, London: Independent Television Council/Broadcasting Standards Commission
Harvey, S. (2000) Access, Authorship and the Voice: The Emergence of Community Programming at the BBC. In Izod, J., Kilborn, R., and Hibberd, M. (eds) *From Grierson to Docu Soap: Breaking the Boundaries*. Luton: University of Luton Press.
Kevill, S. (2002) *Beyond the Soundbite*. London: BBC.

Chapter 42

Erik P. Bucy and
Kimberly S. Gregson

MEDIA PARTICIPATION
A legitimizing mechanism of
mass democracy

Source: Erik P. Bucy and Kimberly S. Gregson (2001) 'Media Participation:
A Legitimizing Mechanism of Mass Democracy', *New Media & Society*, 3 (3):
357–80.

[. . .]

A PREVIOUS INVESTIGATION found that political audiences regarded
certain new media formats, especially call-in shows and the internet, as useful
and valuable to civic life (Bucy *et al.*, 1999). This article builds on the 'new media
use as political participation' argument by specifying that this emergent form of
electronic democracy (a type of political participation through media) involves not
just net activism [. . .], but also a broader range of citizen actions that can take
place online, over the airwaves and through exposure to political messages – actions
which invite involvement. These actions include, but are not limited to, direct
leader/legislator contact, public opinion formation, participating in civic discussions
and agenda building, mediated interactions with candidates and other political actors,
donating to political causes, and joining mobilizing efforts – each of which may
contribute to the psychological feeling of being engaged with the political system.[1]
Collectively, we refer to this class of activity as *media participation*. [. . .]
   [. . .]

Interactivity and the new media

New media formats that came to national prominence during the 1992 election,
and which have been a staple of campaigns since, popularized the concept of

interactivity in politics and have given audience researchers and political communication scholars a new perspective from which to work. A principal component of the new media is the notion of political interactivity, or mediated real-time feedback between political actors and citizens (Hacker, 1996). A primary feature setting interactive media apart from traditional campaign news coverage or political advertising is the potential for spontaneous interaction between political figures, journalists and citizens (Newhagen, 1994). Rather than being proscribed a passive role in the political process, the electorate is symbolically or materially empowered (as discussed later) through the two-way communication architecture to interact directly with candidates. Although constrained by such structural factors as available airtime, social conventions that inhibit extended conversations between people of high and low social status, and the sheer number of audience members (both in studio and at home) relative to political guests, interactive formats provide the appearance at least of an unscripted, unrehearsed civic discussion. If nothing else, new media formats may cultivate the perception of system responsiveness, offering citizens the opportunity to engage in corrective communication with power holders. This form of mediated talk has the capacity to adjust elite impressions of mass opinion to better reflect actual public sentiment.

Given the time and role constraints on audiences, not to mention status and political knowledge differentials, full interactivity between public figures and private citizens is clearly not achievable even through new media formats. However, a semblance or subjective sense of it might be. Some election research has found, for instance, that political television audiences may perceive new media formats to allow for feedback, even if true interactivity is only partially realized, via the mechanism of perceived interactivity (Bucy and Newhagen, 1999; Newhagen, 1994). From this perspective, whether a communication event is regarded as interactive by an outside observer may be irrelevant if the experience of participation leads to a heightened sense of self-efficacy and system responsiveness in the individual.

Table 42.1 illustrates the distinguishing features of new media formats and arrays them according to the number of communication modalities they possess, from most (the internet/world wide web) to least (entertainment television).[2] Entertainment television shows are shown with the fewest modalities because they generally lack direct audience participation mechanisms and a real-time feedback loop that facilitates

Table 42.1 Distinguishing features of new media formats

Modality	New media format				
	Web	Townhalls	Call-in TV	Talk radio	TV
Multimedia	•				
Audience participation	•	•			
Caller feedback	•	•	•	•	
Visuals	•	•	•		•
Audio	•	•	•	•	•

Note: Audience participation incorporates caller feedback, which both the web and electronic townhall forums may accommodate to varying degrees depending on the particular program.

viewer interaction. Call-in television formats are considered more featureful than talk radio on account of visuals. Electronic townhall forums are distinguished from televised call-in shows by the presence of both a studio and remote viewing audience, either of which may interact with the elite guest depending on the format. Finally, the internet/world wide web features the most choices and options, including all of the previous features as well as multimedia, or communication channel choice, which allows the user to select the message delivery method. The civic relevance of each new media format is briefly reviewed later.

Civic relevance of new media formats

Political entertainment television: Set in the casual atmosphere of an informal conversation or comedy skit, political entertainment television relies on interpersonal humor, insider gossip and banter with celebrities and other high-status guests – frequently politicians – to foster a sense of parasocial involvement or illusion of intimacy with media personae (Horton and Wohl, 1956). Through the host's interaction with the show's guests and staff, or through the cast's acting in a bit, members of the audience are invited to feel that this sense of fellowship and social intimacy extends to them, fostering the perception of a face-to-face exchange about a political topic. Shows that feature political entertainment, such as *Politically Incorrect*, *Saturday Night Live*, and *The Late Show with David Letterman*, benefit from their parasocial character and accessibility but their interactivity is limited by the lack of a real-time feedback mechanism (other than applause from the studio audience). Recent surveys by the Pew Research Center (2000) have documented the information value of political entertainment shows, especially for young viewers, and during the 2000 campaign CBS broadcast a weekly round-up of political humor from the late-night television talk shows. [. . .]

Political talk radio: Perhaps more than any of the other new media formats, political talk radio gives voice to the average citizen through its 'open mike' character (Crittenden, 1971). Talk radio provides verbal proximity to media and political elites, as well as access to a mass audience of fellow listeners, via the direct feedback of listener calls. By extending the voice, radio facilitates a sort of amplified conversation that may shape public sentiments and crystallize opinion on certain issues. Moreover, talk radio programs often deliberately attempt to mobilize the public to participate in civic affairs or contact officials (Hollander, 1995–6), serving as a vehicle for political socialization. For reception to be meaningful, talk radio listening requires dedicated attention with the intent of comprehending the discussion (Tankel, 1998). Listening, in turn, may teach the important civic skill of heeding and tolerating opposing arguments. Indeed, Tankel (1998) asserts that a major attraction of talk radio is the multiplicity of voices heard on the air. Research on the talk radio audience has shown listeners to be significantly more civic-minded and participatory than nonlisteners (Hollander, 1995–6). Callers, in particular, are more likely to participate in other political activities. Talk radio can be best understood, Tankel (1998) suggests, 'as a behavior in which the listener is an active participant rather than as a process that constructs a passive recipient' (p. 45).

Political call-in television: Combining the strengths of talk radio with the power of visuals, political call-in television places the viewer in the front row, if not of the political action, at least of the political discussion. Because of television's visual nature, this format invites close scrutiny of the political guest's physical appearance and nonverbal demeanor (Bucy and Newhagen, 1999), perhaps at the expense of what's said. Importantly, call-in television endows the audience member with more sensory modalities – sight as well as sound – than the guest, who can only hear the audio of the caller. The disembodied voice of the caller is awkward for the elite guest and host but in some way empowers the caller because the transparency, though at a distance, is unidirectional. The guest is visually impaired, the caller visually enabled. Call-in formats thus provide visual and verbal proximity to elites, as well as open-mike access to a wide audience (although small by television standards). Public affairs cable channels such as C-SPAN and CNN, which feature daily call-in segments, 'may well stimulate increased levels of political involvement or create new vehicles for political participation' (Frantzich and Sullivan, 1996: 246). Such participation has the potential for changing the climate of opinion and influencing the behavior of decision makers, while enhancing the political efficacy of citizens.

Electronic townhall forums: Electronic townhall forums that feature a participatory studio audience, and sometimes an interactive viewing audience, offer a form of vicarious participation unrivaled by other media. For the home audience, the surrogate experience of viewing a townhall forum is intensified by the ability to witness the active involvement of fellow citizens, whose presence reminds viewers of their own democratic role and civic identity. In response to a citizen question during the second presidential debate of 1996 (which was conducted as a townhall forum) about opening the political process to more grassroots involvement, [. . .]. Through the airing of issues and questions that represent citizen interests rather than journalistic fixations – the two diverge considerably – the public debate is recast so voters come to know their own minds, as it were, before facing a critical choice and thereby have the opportunity to build 'a more conscious democracy' (Elgin, 1993: 9). The visibility of citizen stand-ins who vocalize collective sentiment and concerns creates a sense of civic relevance that consultant-controlled campaigning all but obliterates.

Internet/world wide web: Through convergence and remediation – the repurposing or refashioning of old media with new media, not just in turns of content but by incorporating old media forms into new media venues (Bolter and Grusin, 1999) – the internet/world wide web introduces myriad ways to engage voters and facilitate participation in politics. As a civic medium, the internet fulfills at least four political functions (Davis and Owen, 1998). First, it provides access to news and political information, frequently faster and more in-depth than traditional media. Second, the internet links candidates and office holders with citizens through political web sites and email. Third, the internet provides a space for political discussion, especially through usenet groups organized around various topics. And fourth, the internet can serve as a barometer of public opinion with the capacity of offering reaction to events and decisions in real-time – although, as Wu and Weaver (1997) caution, the validity of online polling is dubious. Quite possibly, the internet/world wide web presents more political information and opportunities for civic engagement than has ever existed. The web is a complex symbolic environment, however, and users spend a considerable amount of time just orienting to the medium. Before it becomes a true medium of the masses, questions of *social access* – the mix of technical knowledge, psychological skills, and economic resources required for effectual use of information and communication technologies – will have to be addressed (Bucy, 2000).

A question inevitably arises as to whether new media formats allow citizens to influence the actual substance and outcome of politics. According to net activists (Schwartz, 1996) and some early confirmatory research (Bucy *et al.*, 1999; Newhagen, 1994), interactive political experiences that occur in cyberspace, via cable channels and over the airwaves are deemed every bit as 'real', useful and important as their nonmediated corollaries – such traditional measures of political activity as attending meetings and rallies, volunteering, writing to legislators, and contacting community leaders. In addition, citizen action through new media formats has already had direct political influence in certain instances, as the talk radio furor over congressional pay raises and Zoe Baird's 1993 ill-fated nomination to US Attorney General demonstrated (Hollander, 1995–6; Page and Tannenbaum, 1996). Yet an over-emphasis on the traditional, political value of media participation risks losing sight of the more important individual consequence of daily citizen involvement with new media – the psychological rewards and personal empowerment derived from civic media use.

[. . .]

Notes

1   The activities enumerated here roughly correspond to the four key transactions of democracy identified by Tambini (1999): information provision/access to information; preference measurement (referenda, polls, and representation); deliberation; and will formation/organization.

2   Although they are arrayed by modality, new media formats don't necessarily vary by level of interactivity because the perception of interactive communication is unique to the individual. Technology can set the upper bounds of message reciprocality, but the experience of interactivity ultimately resides in the user (Laurel, 1991).

References

Bolter, J.N and Grusin, R. (1999) *Remediation: Understanding New Media*. Cambridge, MA: MIT Press.

Bucy, E.P. (2000) 'Social Access to the Internet', *Press/Politics* 5(1): 50–61.

Bucy, E.P. and Newhagen, J.E. (1999) 'The Micro- and Macro-drama of Politics on Television: Effects of Media Format on Candidate Evaluations', *Journal of Broadcasting & Electronic Media* 43(2): 193–210.

Bucy, E.P., D'Angelo, P. and Newhagen, J.E. (1999) 'Engaging the Electorate: New Media Use as Political Participation'. In L.L. Kaid and O. Bystrom (eds) *The Electronic Election: Perspectives on the 1996 Campaign Communication*, pp. 335–47. Mahwah, NJ: Erlbaum.

Crittenden, J. (1971) 'Democratic Functions of the Open Mike Radio Forum', *Public Opinion Quarterly* 35(1): 200–10.

Davis, R. and Owen, D. (1998) *New Media and American Politics*. New York: Oxford University Press.

Elgin, D. (1993) 'Revitalizing Democracy Through Electronic Town Meetings', *Spectrum* 66(2): 6–13.

Frantzich, S. and Sullivan, J. (1996) *The C-SPAN Revolution*. Norman: University of Oklahoma Press.

Hacker, K.L. (1996) 'Missing Links in the Evolution of Electronic Democratization', *Media, Culture & Society* 18(2): 213–32.

Hollander, B.A. (1995/96) 'The Influence of Talk Radio on Political Efficacy and Participation', *Journal of Radio Studies*, 3: 23–31.

Horton, D. and Wohl, R.R. (1956) 'Mass Communication and Para-Social Interaction: Observations on Intimacy at a Distance', *Psychiatry* 19(3): 215–29.

Laurel, B. (1991) *Computers as Theatre*. Reading, MA: Addison-Wesley.

Newhagen, J.E. (1994) 'Self Efficacy and Call-in Political Television Show Use', *Communication Research* 21(3): 366–79.

Page, B.L. and Tannenbaum, J. (1996) 'Populistic Deliberation and Talk Radio', *Journal of Communication* 46(2): 33–54.

Pew Research Center for the People and the Press (2000) 'The Tough Job of Communicating with Voters: Audiences Fragmented and Skeptical', URL, January (consulted July 2000): http://www.people-press.org/jan00rpt2.htm

Schwartz, E. (1996) *Net Activism: How Citizens Use the Internet*. Sebastopol, CA: Songline Studios.

Tambini, D. (1999) 'New Media and Democracy: The Civic Networking Movement', *New Media & Society* 1(3): 305–29.

Tankel, J.D. (1998) 'Reconceptualizing Call-in Talk Radio as Listening', *Journal of Radio Studies* 5(1): 36–47.

Wu, W. and Weaver, D. (1997) 'On-line Democracy or On-line Demagoguery? Public Opinion "Polls" on the Internet', *Press/Politics* 2(4): 71–87.

SECTION 7

Personalisation

PERSONALISATION CAN BE understood, in simple terms, as the process by which both personalities and the issue of personality come to dominate political communication. The extracts in this section deal with those two interconnected aspects of personalisation: examining the rise of celebrity politicians and the increasingly intimate nature of mediated politics.

In many democracies leading politicians have arguably attained celebrity status. They have achieved a level of public visibility that makes them instantly familiar to citizens. In addition, celebrities from other fields, such as sport or entertainment, have entered politics. In the first extract in this section, **West and Orman** seek to categorise this emerging class of celebrity politicians. Based on the US, though applicable to other countries, they develop a typology that distinguishes five different types of political celebrity. One class is the 'famed non-politico': many celebrities in the fields of entertainment or sport, for example, have used their public personas to gain elected office. One example, presented in **Glynn**'s extract, is that of professional wrestler and radio talk-show host, Jesse 'the Body' Ventura. Ventura, although no longer in office, mounted a successful campaign to become governor of the state of Minnesota in 1998, building mass appeal based on his irreverent anti-establishment image.

Celebrity politicians are keen to generate a positive impression among voters. They can do this by carefully revealing aspects of their persona via the media. **Parry-Giles and Parry-Giles** look at the way former US president Bill Clinton utilised the media to project a particular image of himself. Their study examines the auto-biographical campaign film, *A Man from Hope*, showing that Clinton drew on a series of personal reflections and insights from those who knew him to generate an intimate portrait of himself.

Increasingly the private lives of prominent politicians have become the subject of media scrutiny. **Sabato** *et al.*'s extract shows that the contemporary news media in the US focus excessively on the personal aspects of politicians' lives. As in other democracies, they report unsourced allegations as fact, refer to the personal conduct of politicians out of context, and 'mine' politicians' past lives for scandal. Indeed, as **Thompson** observes, scandals in political life have become more prevalent since the 1960s. This, he argues, is due to a combination of factors, not least the growing visibility of politicians, as well as changes in journalistic culture. **Summers** is also interested in trying to understand why the reporting of politician's personal transgressions are more prevalent today. He argues that the exposure politicians receive today can be seen in terms of the rise and fall of 'reticence'. He observes that the character of politicians was central to nineteenth-century political culture, with private transgressions exposed as part of the demand for the highest standards. However, from the late nineteenth century to the Bill Clinton era, stories about indiscretions retreated from view and the search for impropriety lessened. In the early twenty-first century, character is once again central to political culture and journalists are eager to expose politicians' transgressions.

Chapter 43

Darrell M. West and John Orman

THE EVOLUTION OF CELEBRITYHOOD

Source: Darrell M. West and John Orman (2003) *Celebrity Politics*, Upper Saddle River, NJ: Prentice Hall, pp. 1–16.

[. . .]

A S SHOWN IN Table 43.1, there are five different types of celebrities: political newsworthies (politicians and handlers skilled at public relations and selfpromotion), legacies (children or spouses of former politicians), famed nonpoliticos known in fields outside of politics who run for elective office, famed nonpoliticos who act as lobbyists or issue spokespersons (such as actors, singers, business people, athletes, and astronauts), and event celebrities (individuals such as crime victims who gain notoriety overnight due to some tragedy, event, or life situation). Each differs in important respects from the others in terms of how fame originates and the consequences for our society and culture. Some, such as legacies, present deeper challenges for democratic political systems than do event celebrities.

Political newsworthies are the classic celebrities, individuals such as James Carville, Mary Matalin, Jesse Jackson, Sr, and George Stephanopoulos who are skilled at appearing on television and communicating with the general public. In a society that values punchy and entertaining commentary, pundits and leaders earn extensive airtime and become famous for their espousal of particular issues. Carville, for example, guided Clinton to victory in 1992, and then spent the next decade serving as a Democratic attack dog against Republicans. Mary Matalin carved out a visible niche for herself as a GOP advocate for party causes. [. . .]

Legacies include descendants of prominent political families, such as the Kennedys, Rockefellers, Gores, and Bushes. Purely by dint of the family name, these individuals are famous owing to their connection to former politicians. The

Table 43.1 Types of celebrity politicos

POLITICAL NEWSWORTHIES	
James Carville	Mary Matalin
George Stephanopoulos	Jesse Jackson, Sr
John McCain	Barney Frank

LEGACIES	
Patrick and Joe Kennedy	Kathleen Kennedy Townsend
George W. and Jeb Bush	Al Gore
Jay Rockefeller	Jesse Jackson, Jr
Harold Ford, Jr	Evan Bayh

FAMED NONPOLITICOS (Elected officials)	
Ronald Reagan	John Glenn
Jim Bunning	Sonny Bono
Jim Ryun	Steve Largent
Jesse Ventura	Jack Kemp
Bill Bradley	J.C. Watts

FAMED NONPOLITICOS (Lobbyists and spokespersons)	
Charlton Heston	Barbara Streisand
Jane Fonda	Paul Newman/Joanne Woodward
Marlon Brando	Warren Beatty
Robert Redford	Martin Sheen
Willie Nelson	

EVENT CELEBRITIES	
Denise Brown	Carolyn McCarthy
Anita Hill	Sarah Brady
Marisleysis Gonzalez	Ryan White

Bush dynasty now extends over three generations and includes one Senator (Prescott Bush), two presidents (George Herbert Walker Bush and George W. Bush), a vice president (George Herbert Walker Bush), and two governors (George W. and Jeb Bush). With a legacy of public service, famous descendants piggyback on the high name identification and reputation for serving the community of their ancestors.

[. . .]

In contrast, famed nonpoliticos are responsible for their own prominence. These are people such as John Glenn, Jim Bunning, Ronald Reagan, Jesse Ventura, and Jack Kemp who run for office after becoming famous in another area or individuals such as Charlton Heston, Barbra Streisand, or Jane Fonda who lobby on behalf of social causes. Nonpoliticos piggyback fame in one sector onto political life. In a society that elevates sports stars, entertainers, and astronauts, nonpoliticos are seen as political "white knights." Since their prominence comes from outside the political world, these individuals have a high degree of public trustworthiness and star power to boot.

Unlike legacies, who must deal with a fame that is not of their own doing, famed nonpoliticos generally are confident regarding their own fame and fortune. Because they gained acclaim outside of the political realm, they are used to being in the public spotlight and dealing with the accoutrements of celebrityhood – media coverage, adoring fans, gossip columnists, and intrusions into their private lives. This experience makes their entry into a regime based on celebrity politics easier to handle.

Event celebrities are overnight sensations who arise on the local or national scene due to some tragedy or predicament. Generally, these are individuals who were not politically active or socially prominent. Simply by dint of special circumstances, they generate news coverage and become prominent for their high credibility in speaking out about a particular subject. In a very short period of time, their visibility skyrockets.

Crime victims, relatives of crime victims, or parties to a scandal are prominent examples of this genre. Owing to the tendency of the media to highlight these kinds of stories, crime and scandal (or its allegations) have created a number of famous personalities. Owing to saturation media coverage, people such as Denise Brown (the sister of murder victim Nicole Brown Simpson), Carolyn McCarthy (wife of a man slain during the Long Island Railroad shooting spree who went on to win a New York House seat), Sarah Brady (wife of wounded Reagan Press Secretary James Brady and a prominent gun control spokesperson), and Anita Hill (a witness against the Supreme Court confirmation of Clarence Thomas) have become prominent and are put in a position where they subsequently are able to influence the policy process.

[. . .]

Despite clear differences in how star power is gained, each fame category is part of the emerging pattern of celebrity politics that has transformed American politics. Prominent individuals use fame either to run for elective office or influence those who do. They are able to draw on their platform to raise money for themselves and other politicians. In a media-centered political system, celebrities are adept at attracting press attention. They make great copy, and reporters love to build stories around glamorous celebrities.

In a variety of ways, celebrities have become integrally involved in activities such as electioneering, campaigning, fund-raising, endorsing, and lobbying. Their centrality in the mobilization of interests and recruitment of candidates gives them special power. They are able to position themselves in ways that enhance their overall influence. Taken together, these components of celebrity politics make for an eye-grabbing and entertaining American political culture, one that raises a host of important issues for democratic political systems.

In many respects, this trend toward celebrity politics is not new in the United States. Our system has always produced presidents, such as George Washington, Andrew Jackson, and U.S. Grant, who were famous before they entered public service. [. . .]

[. . .]

But several trends over recent decades have converged to accelerate this historical tendency toward celebrity politics. The emergence of radio and television, the democratization of fame, and shifts in how journalists perform their craft have altered the dynamics of our culture, and made it possible for celebrities of many different stripes to move into the political system in large numbers. In these respects, then, the contemporary situation is different from past eras and poses greater challenges to a democratic political system.

Radio and then television were perfect media for a celebrity-oriented political system. For the first time in American history, radio offered famous individuals an opportunity to communicate with the general public in ways that were both personal and intimate. [. . .]

[. . .]

Television elevated the political fortunes of John F. Kennedy by joining the communications power of the electronic medium with the myth-making power of the "Camelot" years. The media coverage of his extended family and personality made Kennedy a video legend even before his tragic assassination on November 22, 1963. [. . .]

Another trend that encouraged celebrity politics has been the "democratization" of fame. As discussed by commentator Leo Braudy, previous epochs in which fame was restricted to royalty, the aristocracy, and those in formal leadership roles gave way to a flowering of celebrityhood in many walks of life.[1] No longer was fame restricted to legacies or individuals holding privileged positions, such as kings and popes, but it was possible for ordinary people to be elevated to social and political prominence.

[. . .]

The celebrity political system has been reinforced by the establishment of "gossip" journalism in which reporters cover the personal lives of politicians. Journalists moved from reporting the "who, what, and where" of civic life to looking at leaders' backgrounds, integrity, and personal foibles. Drinking, womanizing, and drug use became fair game for reporters who sought to determine whether leaders held sufficient character for public office.

[. . .]

It was not long before the celebrity-star system became institutionalized with politicians becoming interchangeable with other guest celebrities on television talk shows. Politicians emerged as the central dramatic figures on the nightly news drama. American citizens quickly became used to watching politics rather than participating in the system. Voter turnout plummeted during this period, while citizen mistrust rose.

In addition to expressing their views about civic life, celebrities from the Hollywood entertainment industry became elected officials.[2] Actors like Helen Douglas and George Murphy crossed over into the political arena in the late 1940s and early 1950s. A successful Hollywood actress, Douglas ran for the US House in 1944 and won. [. . .]

[. . .]

In 1966, a Hollywood actor and corporate television spokesperson named Ronald Reagan became the Governor of California. Suddenly, a glut of celebrity politicos began to emerge in the political system. Former Buffalo Bills quarterback Jack Kemp was elected to the House and former New York Knicks basketball immortal Bill Bradley was elevated to the US Senate from the state of New Jersey. Astronaut John Glenn became a US Senator from Ohio, Clint Eastwood was chosen mayor of Carmel, California, and to demonstrate the power of celebrity politics, Fred Grandy, "Gopher" from the television show *Love Boat*, became an Iowa congressman in 1986.

The "Age of Celebrity," as Kirk Scharfenberg dubbed it, began to flourish.[3] Film and television gave us political activists Paul Newman, Joanne Woodward, Robert Redford, and Ed Asner. The sports industry delivered Jack Kemp, Bill Bradley, Roger Staubach, and Tom McMillan to the political process.[4] Comedy and satire generated names such as Robin Williams, Steve Martin, Billy Crystal, Eddie Murphy, and Gilda Radner who had a particular political view within their comedy. Rock music gave us Bruce Springsteen, Jackson Browne, and John Mellencamp. Legacy politicians included George W. Bush, Al Gore, Jesse Jackson, Jr, Harold Ford, Jr, Patrick Kennedy, Evan Bayh, Hillary Clinton, and Hubert Humphrey, III. Finally, there were all purpose celebrities like Lee Iacocca, Donald Trump, Jerry Falwell, Jesse Jackson, Geraldine Ferraro, and Oliver North, each skilled at the art of television and image-creation.

[. . .]

It is not so much that Americans have not had heroes, but during the past few decades, American heroes came to be replaced by "mere celebrities."[5] Politicians no longer are heroes, but are treated and reported on like celebrities. [. . .]

[. . .]

This trend toward politicians using celebrities and celebrities becoming politicians has been encouraged by structural changes in the American media. Media came to be dominated by "infotainment" shows such as *People Magazine*, *US Today*, *Inside Edition*, and *Entertainment Tonight*. Such episodes reported that celebrities were really interesting political people and that politicians had many hidden stories just like other famous people in celebrity gossip. [. . .]

The media report the comings and goings of American celebrities as they are tied into the political parties. Both parties have celebrity coordinators and press people who try to coordinate celebrities so that publications like *USA Today* and *People Magazine*, along with the television media, will report celebrity movements at the convention or along the campaign trail.

With the entry of celebrities into American politics, politicians and celebrities become indistinguishable. Politicians regularly appear on American talk shows and in situation comedies, dramas, and variety shows. Among the politicos to have appeared on *Saturday Night Live* are Jesse Jackson, George McGovern, Ed Koch, Daniel Moynihan, and Jesse Ventura. Nancy Reagan did an episode of *Different Strokes* and Gerald Ford and Betty Ford showed up on *Dynasty*. Even the staid Henry Kissinger appeared on *Dynasty* and television news people like Connie Chung and Kathleen Sullivan showed up on *Murphy Brown*.

As Barbara Goldsmith has observed, "Today we are faced with a vast confusing jumble of celebrities: the talented and the untalented, heroes and villains, people of accomplishment and those who have accomplished nothing at all."[6] We are not very discerning as a society when it comes to making qualifications for those to be celebrated. We celebrate almost anyone for any reason. Anyone can be a celebrity if the right breaks happen and, hence, anyone can become a celebrity politico. The problem that this influx of celebrities has on the system is that according to Victoria Sackett, "The public has learned to take politics less seriously and stars more seriously. Politics is the perfect meeting ground. Once a field that was restricted to the able and trained, it is now open to anyone with an opinion and a presence."[7]

[. . .]

Notes

1   Leo Brandy, The *Frenzy of Renown: Fame and its History* (New York: Vintage Books, 1986).

2   Ronald Brownstein, The *Power and the Glitter: The Hollywood–Washington Connection* (New York: Pantheon Books, 1990).

3   Kirk Scharfenberg, "Populism in the Age of Celebrity," *Atlantic Monthly*, June 1990, p. 117.

4   David Canon, *Actors, Athletes, and Astronauts* (Chicago: University of Chicago Press, 1990).

5   Dan Hurley, "The End of Celebrity," *Psychology Today*, December 1988, p. 50.

6   Barbara Goldsmith, "The Meaning of Celebrity," *New York Times Magazine*, 4 December 1983, p. 75.

7   Victoria Sackett, "Stage Craft as Statecraft: Actors' and Politicians' New Roles," *Public Opinion* (May/June 1987), p. 16.

Chapter 44

Kevin Glynn

CULTURAL STRUGGLE, THE NEW NEWS, AND THE POLITICS OF POPULARITY IN THE AGE OF JESSE "THE BODY" VENTURA

Source: Kevin Glynn (2000) *Tabloid Culture: Trash Taste, Popular Power, and the Transformation of American Television*. Durham, NC, and London: Duke University Press, pp. 225–45.

[. . .]

JESSE "THE BODY" VENTURA, a former professional wrestler and radio talk show "shock jock" [. . .] became "the nation's first governor to have his own action figure doll" when he was elected by Minnesotans in November 1998.[1] Ventura defeated a liberal Democrat and a conservative Republican, both of whom were vastly better funded than he, by appealing to a broad coalition organized around young people, union members, women, gays, and a heavy concentration of people who typically don't vote. Indeed, many of his supporters reported to exit pollsters that they wouldn't have bothered to vote in 1998 if not for Ventura's candidacy.[2]

In mounting his unconventional campaign, Ventura refused all money from PACs [Political Action Committees] and special interest groups and declined to accept any contribution of more than fifty dollars. Consequently, while his opponents spent $4.3 million on their election efforts, Ventura managed just $250,000. (He is, moreover, refunding all unspent campaign contribution money.) The election result thus flies in the face of conventional wisdom, which says that such contests can be won only through the mobilization of immense fortunes. For his campaign's theme music, Ventura chose a song that reflects the power and resource imbalance between himself and his opponents: the title track from the blaxploitation classic *Shaft* (Gordon Parks, 1971) [. . .]. In addition to tackling the major political parties, Ventura has also, as favorite Minnesota son Garrison Keillor notes, "knocked the struts out from under the religious right."[3] This is not surprising, as Ventura opposes school prayer, school vouchers, and public displays of the Ten Commandments. Ventura has countercultural sympathies as well: "He praises the liberating Sixties, opposes laws against burning the flag, loves rock and roll, and condemns the Vietnam War."[4] (He also opposed Bush's Gulf War.) During campaign appearances Ventura frequently quoted such iconic iconoclasts as Jim Morrison of the Doors and the Grateful Dead's Jerry Garcia, both now dead albeit still resonant in the memories of generations of popular and countercultural mavens. Although in Ventura's incarnation as a popular professional wrestler he wore a gender-bending pink feather boa and sequined tights, his campaign Web site announced that the prototype for the gubernatorial version of his action figure would be a pared-down model with "no strings attached," to match his political philosophy. Among promised additions to the Jesse "the Body" line of accessories were companion dolls of "two-faced career politicians."[5]

Ventura campaigned for abortion rights, gay rights and gun rights, and he "mused publicly about legalizing prostitution and drugs."[6] He supports women in the military and opposes capital punishment. During Minnesota's campaign debates, Ventura was, according to commentator Garry Wills, the only candidate to aggressively denounce a recently passed state law that bans gay marriage. When asked about the law, Ventura replied, "I have two friends that have been together forty-one years. If one of them becomes sick, the other one is not even allowed to be at the bedside. I don't believe government should be so hostile, so mean-spirited. . . . Love is bigger than government."[7] When conservative senator Trent Lott once claimed that sexual preference is determined by individual choice, Ventura responded by asking the senator, "So when did you make yours?"[8] Ventura's iconoclasm extends to the corporate Right as well as the religious one. In one of his most popular campaign commercials, children stage a fight between the Jesse Ventura action figure and a business-suited "Evil Special Interest Man." Once in office, Ventura swiftly alienated Republicans who wanted to turn revenues from a successful Minnesota civil suit against tobacco companies into a tax rebate for the rich; the governor argued that any such refund should be skewed toward the economically dispossessed. Finally, "the Body," who is widely noted for his off-the-cuff wit, his fractured and color-fully blusterous oratorical style, and his penchant for gobbling down half-pound cheeseburgers on the campaign trail, sometimes embraces self-parody as well as iconoclasm, as when he posed as Rodin's The Thinker in the last commercial for his candidacy.[9] After the election he also summoned an air of self-parody uncharac-teristic of politicians when at a public appearance he remarked, "I've never held a job for long, so I may not have a long future in politics."[10]

Significantly, the Minnesota state election that produced "Governor Body" (the Bakhtinian appellation by which Ventura referred to himself at a victory rally) boasted the highest voter turnout in the country [. . .]. [. . .] That more than 60 percent of the Minnesota electorate participated suggests at once both how successfully the election engaged the interests of that state's voters compared with those in other parts of the country and how poorly the US political process manages to do so in general.[11]

Voters for Ventura, whose campaign was laughingly dismissed as a joke by both serious politicians and the pundits of establishment journalism, identified with his marginalization as a candidate and thus expressed with their votes their resentment over their own marginalization by the political system. [. . .] In comments to the media at his victory party, Ventura spoke to the anger that his supporters feel toward conventional politicians: "They're never going to take the people lightly again," he opined (no doubt far too optimistically).[12] "They said a vote for me was a wasted vote," he added. "Well guess what? Those 'wasted' votes wasted *them*."[13] Ventura's campaign had indeed powerfully mobilized the sentiments of the disaffected. According to the pastor of a working-class church in suburban Minneapolis, Ventura's appeal reached deeply into the lowest social strata, beyond the "winners with good jobs" and the "respectables who may not have good jobs but compensate by seeking respect in their community and church." Ventura found a way to connect with the survivors who just get by and the hard-living, rootless folks who have completely given up on trying to be successful or live by conventional norms."[14]

Ventura's ability to speak to the disaffected and the nonconforming can usefully be read against the backdrop of his personal history. Wills observes that Ventura's "hold on employment" has long been tenuous, and that he has been unemployed as recently as 1995 and 1996.[15] His campaign's resonance among the ranks of disenfranchised and dispossessed Minnesotans can also be traced partly to the popular persona Ventura constructed in the World Wrestling Federation (WWF) and on Minnesota talk radio. [. . .]

[. . .]

[. . .] He has also made use of other alternatives to the mainstream political media more recently, for when the establishment politicians and pundits sought to dismiss and marginalize Ventura's gubernatorial campaign, he deployed a cyber-savvy Internet strategy to mobilize popular support. Since his election Ventura has advocated an expanded role for the Internet in Minnesota government to facilitate greater public access to official documents, to cultivate more alternative political candidacies, to enable Minnesotans to more easily hold him and his lieutenant governor "accountable for what they said on the campaign trail," and to "put citizens on an equal footing with lobbyists. "[16] He states that one of his aims as governor is to "keep opening the arms of government and make it citizen friendly."[17]

Ventura made overtures in this direction at his inclusive and unconventional inaugural party (which was perhaps the only such event ever to feature a mosh pit). Billed as "the People's Celebration," the event included musical acts such as folkish alternarockers Soul Asylum, seventies pop icons America, rock legend Warren Zevon, blues prodigy Jonny Lang, and the Sounds of Blackness, a thirty-member ensemble whose work spans the entire gamut of African American music, from R&B to blues, gospel, hiphop, jazz, reggae, spirituals, and field hollers. Still, entry to the event cost not much more than an urban movie ticket and vastly less than the major political parties' more exclusive soirees (all attendees, including journalists and political contributors, paid a twenty-dollar admission fee). Ventura, wearing earrings, a Jimi Hendrix T-shirt, and a buckskin motorcycle jacket with fringes, joined Zevon onstage and, at a key moment in the performance, tore off his bandanna to reveal the same bare skull that was inscribed with the slogan "Head of State" on T-shirts worn by many of the event's capacity crowd of more than seventeen thousand revelers. In this way, "the Body" upturns the ritualized spectacles of the political process, substituting raucous humor and the signs of countercultural disaffection for the traditional pomp and circumstance of the state. Appropriately enough, a large group of celebrants at the inauguration sported mockingly parodic T-shirts boasting that "our governor can beat up your governor."[18] Like *A Current Affair*'s mode of address

[. . .] the movement for "Governor Body" combines playfully irreverent humor directed against the self-seriousness of the political system (which parallels the tabloid program's lampooning of the serious news) with plainspoken populist indignation. It boisterously expresses resentment over the people's alienation from the power structure and mobilizes political skepticism toward fat cats, bureaucracies, and establishment politicos.

[. . .] Against those who would distinguish neatly between the "puffery" of style and the "meat" of substance, I want to claim that Ventura's political substance lies partly though significantly in his style – a style that is as tabloidized as any: sensationally populist, ironically playful, laughingly skeptical, wildly outrageous, sometimes self-mocking and sometimes self-satisfied, inclusive and participatory, blusterous and averse to euphemism, scandalous, offensive, and often in your face. Ventura is to "respectable" politicians what tabloids are to "respectable" journalism. His success should teach us about some of the failures of the current configuration of US electoral politics, which typically works to exclude the very people with whom Ventura has learned to converse. [. . .]

Ventura should also teach us about articulation and rearticulation. These are the cultural processes whereby diverse elements from a variety of discursive, ideological, and representational formations are forged into a new unity that thereby gives rise to the formation of an active social movement that did not previously exist but comes into being around, and is attached to, the newly unified expressive practices.[19] Jesse Ventura succeeded by fusing or articulating together certain images and ideological elements that thereby expressed or articulated certain meanings that could be linked or articulated to the newly emergent social movement to which his activities gave rise. The ideological and representational elements that he astutely fused together (gay rights, the 1960s, and pro wrestling, to name a few) were not in themselves novel. It is Ventura's particular arrangement of those diverse elements that was at once unique and powerful in its capacity to both catalyze and forge an expressive connection with an emergent social formation. [. . .]

Like the tabloid media, Ventura collapses distinctions between politics and entertainment – something I don't believe we should necessarily condemn (as so many have) for reasons that the case of Jesse "the Body" makes clear. Ventura has brought at least some measure of disruption to an all too tight political order that secures the privileges of the few and the exclusion of many. Indeed, the Ventura campaign (and the myriad of dismissive reactions to it) should teach us about the class-cultural basis (and increasing permeability) of the very boundaries between "politics," "news," and "entertainment." Rather than view this permeability as an excuse for further lamentation over the "decline of civilization," we should instead try to identify the opportunities it creates for unsettling and democratizing energies to spill over from the all too often trivialized realms of "entertainment" and popular culture.

[. . .]

Notes

1   Marc Fisher, "Minnesota's Surprise 'Governor Body': Populist Ex-Wrestler Ventura Appears to Have Pinned 2 Rivals," *Washington Post*, 4 November 1998, A1.

2   Andrew Stern, "Minnesota's Governor-Elect Says He's No Rebel," *Excite News*, 4 November 1998, http://nt.excite.com; Garry Wills, "The People's Choice," *New York Review of Books* 46, no. 13 (12 August 1999), http://www.nybooks.com.

3   Quoted in Wills, "The People's Choice."

4   Wills, "The People's Choice."

5   Fisher, "Minnesota's Surprise," A1.

6   Pam Belluck, "A 'Bad Boy' Wrestler Ignores the Script," *New York Times*, 5 November 1998, http://www.nytimes.com.

7   Quoted in Wills, "The People's Choice."

8   This is a paraphrase of the line ascribed to Ventura in stories reported by Wills in "The People's Choice."

9   Fisher, "Minnesota's Surprise"; Benno Groeneveld, "Ex-Wrestler Ventura Sworn in as Minnesota Governor," *Excite News*, 4 January 1999, http://nt.excite.com.

10   Jesse Ventura, quoted in Wills, "The People's Choice."

11   This statistic comes from Groeneveld, "Ex-Wrestler Ventura Sworn in as Minnesota Governor."

12   Jesse Ventura, quoted in Fisher, "Minnesota's Surprise," A1.

13   Jesse Ventura, quoted in Belluck, "A 'Bad Boy' Wrestler Ignores the Script."

14   Rev. Jerry O'Neill, quoted in Miach L. Sifry, "Working Class Hero?", *Salon*, 11 January 1999, www.salonmagazine.com

15   Wills, "The People's Choice."

16   "Interim Page," *Official Site of the Jesse Ventura Volunteer Committee*, http://www.jesseventura.org/interim.htm; Jesse Ventura, "How I Will Use the Internet," 28 December 1998, http://www.jesseventura.org/internet/howuse.htm; Dane Smith, "Ventura Creates Web Site to Influence 2000 Presidential Race," *Minneapolis Star-Tribune*, 9 February 1999, http://www.startribune.com.

17   Jesse Ventura, quoted in Groeneveld, "Ex-Wrestler Ventura Sworn in as Minnesota Governor."

18   This account of Ventura's inauguration is drawn from Jim Derogatis, "Politics as Usual in Minnesota," *Chicago Sun-Times*, 18 January 1999, http://www.suntimes.com.

19   Lawrence Grossberg, ed., "On Postmodernism and Articulation: An Interview with Stuart Hall," in David Morley and Kusan-Hsing Chen, (eds), (1996) *Stuart Hall: Critical Dialogues in Cultural Studies*, Routledge, London, 141–45.

Chapter 45

Shawn J. Parry-Giles and Trevor Parry-Giles

THE MAN FOM HOPE
Hyperreal intimacy and the invention of Bill Clinton

Source: Shawn J. Parry-Giles and Trevor Parry-Giles (2002) *Constructing Clinton Hyperreality and Presidential Image-Making in Postmodern Politics*, New York: Peter Lang Publishing, pp. 24–51.

[. . .]

NOWHERE IS THE OVERT hyperreal construction of "image" more powerfully on display than in the presidential campaign film – the introductory, biographical media event that usually debuts immediately prior to a candidate's acceptance speech at the national party conventions. Beginning with Ronald Reagan's 1984 film, presidential campaign films have served as "centerpiece[s] of the presidential election campaign."[1] These image rhetorics play a central role in the rituals of presidential campaigning,[2] and they are used for campaign commercials, shown to countless audiences, mailed to contributors, and otherwise distributed widely to voters nationwide. Campaign films are, in this way, meaningful texts of presidentiality, defining the nature of presidential qualification and character and putting forth a vision of the office and the institution to justify a particular candidacy.

[. . .]

In this chapter, we examine the 1992 Clinton campaign film entitled *The Man from Hope*. Our analysis of the film's verbal and visual elements exposes a text that is both intimate and mythic,[3] both feminine and masculine, manifesting the tensions and paradoxes of hyperreal politics. But before turning to the text itself, we consider more fully the reordered and restructured nature of political image construction in the postmodern era.

Political scopophilia and gendered politics
in postmodernity

[. . .]

[. . .] Freud theorized that human beings, from early childhood, possess a need to gaze at others, which produces a feeling of pleasure.[4] This impulse is scopophilia. Freud observed that the scopophiliac instinct to gaze represented a phenomenon of infantile sexuality that develops into a normal part of adult sexual behavior. For Freud, looking and displaying are both instinctual and potentially aberrant. He concluded, therefore, that these impulses are present in everyone, but are controlled by social norms, taboos, and rules that prevent their manifestation as perversions. [. . .]

   [. . .]

Television and cinema both encourage and invite the scopophiliac impulse (as opposed to the voyeuristic perversion) in audiences, not only because of technology, but also because of curiosity and possibility. It is this impulsive need to gaze that most adequately accounts for the intimacy demands of contemporary hyperreal politics. An audience's scopophilia is aroused because television and cinema allow for the possibility of gazing, without guilt, into the private affairs of others. As Freud suggests, there is an epistemophiliac impulse, of which scopophilia is a prime component.[5] Pleasure is derived from knowing (as opposed to the controlling/dominating pleasure emergent from voyeurism), which looking and gazing make possible. Television and cinema technologize that pleasure and extend the scopophilia of the viewers beyond their immediate context.

The visuality of postmodern presidentialities, thus, involves not just the frequently mentioned spectacles of political imaging. There is a visually epistemological sense of politics as well.[6] Because politics is so heavily mediated by technologies dependent upon visual cues and images for their impact, voters come to know and experience politics in profoundly visual ways. They expect to see their candidates in increasingly intimate contexts and the visual evidence presented via the mass media validates their political knowledge and understanding. As television and news proliferate endlessly, voters encounter greater opportunities to gaze at political candidates, both literally and figuratively. Television, as a medium, recognizes and capitalizes on the scopophilia present in its audience. To be successful in the world of "electronic electioneering",[7] the politician must willingly accommodate this impulse in an audience of voters accustomed to a televisual diet of intimacy and personal display.

Personal revelation and intimacy on the part of presidential candidates, though, is strategically risky. It was Freud who observed that leaders are powerful when they are substitutes for the ego-ideal and distant from their subjects.[8] This distance is part of a powerful presidentiality that is central to the political and moral leadership of the office and the institution.[9]

Candidates for the presidency must negotiate their image construction carefully within this more complicated and perilous scopophiliac environment. They still must strive for a presidential image, and they must utilize and associate the myths and images of the presidency with their candidacy. However, because of the presence of television and the intimate gazing that this medium invites, candidates must exhibit their private and intimate selves to voters in order to appear credible and forthcoming.

In addition, political intimacy often occurs within the context of "feminine" symbolism because television requires that political speakers assume a more womanly, or feminine, style of communication.[10]

[. . .]

Candidate Bill Clinton and the discourse of hyperreal hope

[. . .]

The Man from Hope featured many personal reflections and revelations from a variety of individuals close to Bill Clinton as well as from the candidate himself. Where previous presidential campaign films offered mostly direct address from relatively few people (usually the candidate and one or two other people), the Clinton film presented the ruminations of the entire Clinton family, from his mother to his daughter. Their stories were almost entirely about Bill Clinton's upbringing, his personal family life, and his character. The film did not discuss any of the offices held by the candidate or any accomplishments achieved by Clinton as Arkansas' governor. In addition to the film's self-disclosive narratives, the visual production techniques of *The Man from Hope* fostered its intimate appeal, inviting the gaze of spectators and appealing to their scopophiliac impulse in the process. As such, the entire structure and content of the film was consistent with the campaign's goal of (re)inventing Bill Clinton for the voting public.

Visualizing Clinton in The Man from Hope

Three production strategies that amplify the intimacy of mediated texts are the use of direct address by a candidate, the reliance on closeup images, and the structure of spectator positioning prompted by camera placement. [. . .]

These three production practices elevated the intimacy of *The Man from Hope*. The film interviewed Clinton in a dimly lit room at the Arkansas Governor's Mansion, where his eye gaze is directed just to the left of camera. The filmmakers positioned Clinton in an interview style; the camera zoomed in and out, vacillating from a talking head shot to a full-body image. The use of direct address and close-ups presumed to offer insight into his character and personality, addressing image issues that Clinton confronted in the aftermath of Gennifer Flowers, alleged draft evasion, and Whitewater allegations. These close-up shots of Clinton were often accompanied by self-disclosive comments about his family. The spectator positioning combined with the close-up and eye gaze to create a sense of intimacy, especially when interfaced with self-disclosive messages.

As Clinton narrated his intimate autobiography, he offered what appeared to be a revealing look into his life and past both visually and verbally. When talking about his childhood, for example, Clinton referenced his early separations from his mother. As Clinton's face filled the screen, he related how his mother cried "because she felt so bad that I was leaving" so she could go to nursing school.[11] The extreme nature of the close-up was attention-grabbing; Clinton's invitational gaze elevated the aura of self-revelation and intimacy. In a similarly self-disclosive moment,

Clinton recalled vivid memories of an incident when he, at only fourteen years old, confronted his alcoholic stepfather about the domestic violence present in the home. [. . .]

Once again, the close-up of Clinton was extreme, which invited a reciprocal gaze, and called forth an assessment of "personality," especially given the character-based exigencies that plagued Clinton's primary campaign. The audience, conditioned by television, instinctively needed to see and to know this candidate, and the film fulfilled that need by the direct address of the candidate concerning personal matters.

As the film's narrative progressed to Clinton's adult family life, it featured his memories of Chelsea – the candidate's daughter – which once again intersected personal revelation and intimate camera angles. [. . .]

[. . .]

While the camera close-ups helped reify Clinton's narrative, the candidate's first person narrative was naturalized further by the use of photographic and filmed images of the Clintons that functioned to elevate the realism of the text's image-making aims. Throughout the film, the Clinton family interviews were enveloped by black and white photographic images of small town life, young Bill Clinton, or significant events in US history. Of course, the use of black and white images heightened the mythology of the past as depicted in the video. So, during the film's opening and conclusion, a black and white photograph of a train station appeared with the sign "HOPE" displayed. Bill Clinton narrated this segment: "I was born in a little town called Hope, Arkansas, three months after my father died." The candidate then appeared on screen talking about growing up in Hope and going to his "grandfather's grocery store." A black and white photograph of two men standing by a grocery counter and a black and white photograph of a marching band in a parade followed Clinton's image. Clinton thus was encased by the historical images of small town life, which helped naturalize and mythologize the candidate's campaign image.

[. . .]

By surrounding Clinton's narration with these archival and historical images, the candidate's persona came to embody the small town myths, the purity and innocence of childhood, the good father and husband personas, and the visions of hope that are symbolized by JFK and by Clinton's birthplace. [. . .]

[. . .] Thus, as Bill Clinton sought to (re)image himself for the general election in the aftermath of the difficult primary campaign, he centered his image on issues of character extracted from his childhood and his personal life. The visual images that enveloped his intimate narration, the sequencing of those visuals, as well as the camera positioning helped reify his message and encourage a scopophiliac response from the voter.

The intimacy of *The Man from Hope* thus emerged from the character and persona of the candidate, and this film represented a significant departure from previous presidential campaign films.[12] The entire Clinton campaign, Bennett suggests, provided a "daily intimacy" that began with the convention film, and offered voters a "fantasy of renewal and hope."[13] That fantasy was made real by the exhibitionist nature of the campaign film that appealed to the scopophilia at work in the viewing, voting public. Seemingly, the Clinton family secrets were revealed and the viewer was asked to "feel his pain" as Clinton demonstrated his strength of character in conquering that pain. The film allowed the viewer the epistemophiliac pleasure of *knowing* the candidate and invited the viewer through both its narrative and its visual components into his personal life and private matters. Clinton represented, fundamentally, the American Dream of conquering adversity and achieving success. *The Man from Hope* let the viewer see that dream's enactment in Clinton's life and gain pleasure from the knowledge that Bill Clinton personified that dream for all of America, a vision that was essentialized by the visual production techniques and the gendered ideologies upon which the film was based.

    [. . .]

Notes

1   Morreale, J. (1991) *A New Beginning: A Textual Frame Analysis of the Political Campaign Film*. Albany, NY: State University of New York Press, p. 3.

2   Morreale, J. (1993) *The Presidential Campaign Film: A Critical History*. Westport, CT: Praeger, p. 178.

3   The mythic and characterological dimensions of *The Man from Hope* are discussed in Bruce E. Gronbeck, "Characterological Argument in Bush's and Clinton's Convention Films," in *Argument and the Postmodern Challenge*: Proceedings of the Eighth SCAIAFA Conference on Argumentation, edited by Raymie E. McKerrow (Annandale, VA: Speech Communication Association, 1993), 392–7.

4   Sigmund Freud, "Three Essays on the Theory of Sexuality, in *The Standard Edition of the Complete Psychological Works of Sigmund Freud*, Vol. 7, edited and translated by James Strachey (London: The Hogarth Press, 1905/1957), 123–246; and Sigmund Freud, "Instincts and Their Vicissitudes" in *The Standard Edition of the Complete Psychological Works of Sigmund Freud*, Vol. 14, edited and translated by James Strachey (London: The Hogarth Press, 1915/1957), 109–40.

5   See Sigmund Freud, "Notes Upon a Case of Obsessional Neurosis," in *The Standard Edition of the Complete Psychological Works of Sigmund Freud*, Vol. 10, edited and translated by James Strachey (London: The Hogarth Press, 1905/1955), 155–318; and Rabinowitz, P. (1992) "Voyeurism and Class Consciousness: James Agee and Walter Evans, 'Let Us Now Praise Famous Men'," *Cultural Critique* 21: 143–170.

6   For further discussions of visual epistemology, see Jay, M. (1993) *Downcast Eyes: The Denigration of Vision in Twentieth-Century French Thought*. Berkeley, CA: University of California Press; and David Michael Levin (ed.) (1993) *Modernity and the Hegemony of Vision*. Berkeley, CA: University of California Press.

7   Sanford F. Schram, (1991) "The Post-Modern Presidency and the Grammar of Electronic Electioneering," *Critical Studies of Mass Communication*, 8: 210–16.

8   In his analysis of group psychology, Freud examines the power of leaders in primitive societies and links that power to the influence of hypnotists. As he reveals, "it is precisely the sight of the chieftain that is dangerous and unbearable for primitive people, just as later that of the Godhead is for mortals." Leaders are successful when they are "of a masterful nature, absolutely narcissistic, selfconfident and independent." See Sigmund Freud, "Group Psychology and the Analysis of the Ego," in *The Standard Edition of the Complete Psychological Works of Sigmund Freud*, Vol. 18, edited and translated by James Strachey (London: The Hogarth Press, 1921/1955), 124–5. See also Borch-Jacobsen (1990) *The Emotional Tie*; and Ian Craib, (1990) *Psychoanalysis and Social Theory*. Amherst, MA: University of Massachusetts Press.

9   Barbara Hinckley (1990), *The Symbolic Presidency: How Presidents Portray Themselves*. New York: Routledge.

10   Kathleen Hall Jamieson (1988) *Eloquence in an Electronic Age: The Transformation of Political Speechmaking*. New York: Oxford University Press, 84. For more on the nature of the postmodern political spectacle, see Barilleaux, R. (1988) *The Post-Modern Presidency: The Office After Ronald Reagan*. New York: Praeger; Gurevitch, M. and Kavooris, A.P. (1992) "Television Spectacles as Politics," *Communication Monographs* 59 (1992): 415–20; Kellner, D. (1990) *Television and the Crisis of Democracy*. Boulder, CO: Westview; Stagecraft, S. and Stagecraft, S. (1992) "The Grammar of Electronic Electioneering"; David L. Swanson, 1992) "The Political-Media Complex," *Communication Monographs* 59 (1992): 397–400; and David Zarefsky, D. (1992) "Spectator Politics and the Revival of Public Argument," *Communication Monographs* 59: 411–14.

11   Harry Thomason and Linda Bloodworth-Thomason (producers), *The Man from Hope* (West Lafayette, IN: Public Affairs Video Archives, 1992). All citations of the text are from this source.

12   For a comparison of intimate appeals and scopophilia in recent presidential campaign films, see Parry-Giles, T. and Parry-Giles, S. (1996) "Political Scopophilia, Presidential Campaigning, and the Intimacy of American Politics," *Communication Studies* 47: 191–205.

13   W. Lance Bennett (1995) "The Clueless Public: Bill Clinton Meets the New American Voter in Campaign '92." In Renshon, S.A. (ed.) *The Clinton Presidency: Campaigning, Governing, and the Psychology of Leadership*. Boulder, CO: Westview Press.

Chapter 46

Larry J. Sabato, Mark Stencel and S. Robert Lichter

OUT OF ORDER

Source: Larry J. Sabato, Mark Stencel and S. Robert Lichter (2000)
Peepshow: Media and Politics in an Age of Scandal, Lanham, MD: Rowman
& Littlefield, pp. 71–86.

A MONG THE MANY JOURNALISTIC offenses detailed in this volume [in the original], one pattern of press behavior stands out: the obsessive focus on personal foibles that distorts traditional news standards, especially during a political scandal. Smears and gossip that are usually the topic of off-the-record banter suddenly appear in print and on the air. Old rumors are dusted off and reexamined, and allegations of misconduct are resurrected, even if they've already been addressed publicly. Everything a politician now says and everything he or she has ever done are viewed through the distorting prism of the controversy at hand.

Numerous forces contribute to this self-destructive media process. They include professional adrenaline, deadline pressure, peer pressure, accelerated news cycles, a fear of being scooped, and a desire to move the story forward, to name several. Collectively they produce reporting that violates journalists' own sensibilities, distorts the political process, and diminishes public confidence in the fourth estate. Several manifestations of this press behavior deserve special scrutiny: out-of-context references to a political figure's personal conduct, the mining of politicians' pasts for questionable behavior of dubious relevance to his or her public responsibilities, and the increasingly frequent publication and broadcast of unsourced and unsubstantiated political rumors.

[. . .]

Old news

Some stories about political figures are like zombies – old news reanimated from newspaper clipping files and electronic morgues. Others are like mummies – long-forgotten or long-hidden episodes unearthed and put on display many years later. Both kinds of stories can be monstrously unfair. As noted earlier, Arizona senator John McCain exorcised his demons by discussing his past "dalliances" in interviews with journalist Robert Timberg for the 1995 book *The Nightingale's Song*. Timberg's book documents the impact of Vietnam on the lives of several prominent Naval Academy graduates who served in the war. In one passage, paraphrased in numerous interviews and early campaign profiles of the Republican presidential candidate, Timberg describes the failure of McCain's first marriage in 1980 and the womanizing that preceded it, after McCain returned from a Vietnamese prison camp and took up a post in Jacksonville, Florida, in 1974:

> Off-duty, usually on routine cross-country flights to Yuma and El Centro, John started carousing and running around with women. To make matters worse, some of the women with whom he was linked by rumor were his subordinates. In some ways, the rumors were an extension of the John McCain stories that had swirled in his wake since Academy days – some true, some with an element of truth, others patently absurd. Asked about them, he admitted to having a series of dalliances during this period, but flatly denied any with females, officer or enlisted, under his command.[1]

Timberg also spoke to McCain's first wife, Carol, about the breakup, which she said had less to do with the war and her disfiguring car accident while he was a prisoner of war in Vietnam than it did with other factors. "I attribute it more to John turning forty and wanting to be twenty-five again than I do to anything else," she said.[2]

Timberg's account of the McCain breakup, with all its embarrassing revelations, should have been more than enough detail for any reporter profiling the senator. But the conventions of journalism do not work that way. Each reporter feels personally obliged to ask the tough question, even if the subject refuses to discuss the matter any further. During the first months of McCain's White House bid, interviewers from CNN, CBS, ABC, and other media outlets all asked for more details about McCain's divorce and womanizing, which the candidate rightly refused to provide. On ABC's *20/20*, Sam Donaldson asked McCain to comment on "widely written" accounts that "when you got back from prison, you resumed the womanizing habits you had as a young man." On CBS's *60 Minutes*, Mike Wallace phrased the adultery question as a statement: "After Vietnam, you come back, you're married. You begin to carouse again. You're not the most faithful of husbands. So your marriage to Carol unravels." On CBS's *Sunday Morning*, Rita Braver added a new angle to the question: "You admitted to infidelity in your first marriage. Are you worried about the scrutiny that you and your family will have to undergo in this campaign?" McCain's answer to each question was roughly the same: He took responsibility for the divorce and refused to discuss the matter in any greater detail.[3]

[. . .]

Rumors

Political lore holds that Gary Hart lit the match that set his presidential candidacy ablaze in 1987 by challenging reporters to stake him out to test gossip about his womanizing. "Follow me around," Hart had said. "If anyone wants to put a tail on me, go ahead." In reality, though, the *Miami Herald* published its story revealing Hart's relationship with a Florida model on the same day the *New York Times* first published Hart's famous challenge to reporter E.J. Dionne Jr. Hart's reckless personal behavior suggests that his campaign for the White House may well have self-destructed on its own, if not at the hands of a rival. In a 1990 interview with two of the authors, then Republican Party chairman Lee Atwater denied rumors that he had somehow masterminded the Donna Rice incident to help the candidacy of then-vice president George Bush. "I wasn't behind it," Atwater said, "but if I had been, I would have waited until the son of a bitch got the nomination and I'd have broken it then!"

Hart was as much the victim of unfair media rumor-mongering as he was of his own weaknesses. Ironically, the tip that led to Hart's downfall was not just a byproduct of media-circulated rumors, but a press account denouncing media-circulated rumors. As he was setting out on his second bid for the Democratic presidential nomination, news reports often mentioned his suspected womanizing. Some stories described supporters and fund-raisers as being nervous about the gossip. Other articles suggested that Hart's opponents were quietly spreading stories about the front-runner. When Tom Fiedler, then politics editor of the *Miami Herald*, wrote a column denouncing the media scandal-mongering, a reader called to comment – and to offer a tip. The caller's friend, Donna Rice, was involved with Hart and headed to Washington from Florida for a weekend rendezvous. The *Herald*'s subsequent stakeout of Hart and reporting about his weekend with Rice doomed Hart's candidacy.[4]

Although many news stories begin as gossip or rumor, printing or broadcasting unsubstantiated rumors tarnishes journalism's reputation. Published rumors also push a news story along unfairly – accelerating Hart's destruction, for instance. As in Hart's case, many political rumors turn out to be true. Other rumors reporters know – or at least suspect – are true, but the information is not sourced reliably enough to print or broadcast. With increasing frequency, however, unsubstantiated and destructive personal rumors are finding their way into American political journalism.

[. . .]

There is even a growing attitude that circulating rumors is permissible because it is somehow antidemocratic for journalists to withhold information. "Even for traditional media journalists, furtive rumors of dalliance are enough – at least to gossip about among themselves, if not to share with their readers or viewers," wrote Michael Kinsley, editor of the Microsoft-owned online publication *Slate*, in a February 1998 essay for *Time* magazine. "There is something slightly elitist about the attitude that we journalists can be trusted to evaluate such rumors appropriately but that our readers and viewers cannot. Actually, though, almost everybody has the same standards that is, almost none – in passing along juicy rumors to friends and colleagues."[5]

No such "elitism" hampered the early presidential campaign coverage of Texas governor George W. Bush. Rumors about the Republican candidate's partying in his college years and bachelor days were so widespread that many mainstream news organizations appeared to give little thought to repeating the latest gossip, regardless of the source. In March 1999, the supermarket tabloid the *Star* quoted an anonymous source who described a nude photograph of the Republican candidate "cavorting atop a bar in a drunken stupor" during a college party. Millions of Americans learned about the rumored photograph from Jay Leno's monologues on NBC's *Tonight Show*. ("These Republican spin doctors, they're working hard to discredit this story." Leno said one night. "They said today that even if George Bush Jr were dancing naked on a bar, no one got stained."[6]) Two days earlier, a "Page Six" gossip item in the *New York Post* had summarized the *Star*'s story and its sourcing. But as the story quickly worked its way into more conventional journalistic outlets, its source and veracity became increasingly blurry.

The *Post*'s more reserved cross-town cousin, the *New York Times*, mentioned the tabloid report about the photo in a snide column about Bush's "frat boy" image by Pulitzer Prize-winning commentator Maureen Dowd. Asked to respond to the *Star*'s story, Bush spokeswoman Karen Hughes told Dowd, "Yeah, and green aliens have landed on the lawn of the governor's mansion." Dowd repeated the rumor again – this time without attribution – in a humorous June 1999 column, in which she wrote about the Republican Party's infatuation with Bush. Dowd said, "Republicans should remain besotted as long as their crush can pass a few simple tests," one of which was that "if a nude picture of W. dancing on a bar does show up, it will be flattering and have good lighting."[7]

Some news accounts about the rumors noted that the *Star*'s story had not "panned out," as Steve Chapman put it in the *Chicago Tribune*.[8] In a front-page story in May 1999, the *Wall Street Journal* detailed its unsuccessful efforts to track down the sources of various rumors about Bush – including the nude photo story.

> The photo has been written about in the *Star* tabloid, and its existence has been hinted at on the Internet. The gossip is so prevalent that Dorothy Koch, the governor's sister, even raised the possibility with their mother, former first lady Barbara Bush, of releasing naked-baby pictures of her brother, Ms. Koch says. "We all think it's hilarious," says Ms. Koch.[9]

Bush himself discussed the alleged photograph in an interview for the June 1999 issue of *Texas Monthly* magazine, which included a multipart cover story on him. "I don't think there is one," Bush said of the picture. "I'm too modest to have danced on a bar naked."[10] Some news organizations repeated Bush's denial, but his statement did not make the rumor disappear. A profile of the governor in the *Washington Post* the following month also made reference to the photograph in the context of Bush's intentional strategy of inoculating himself against public backlash to press reports about his "irresponsible" youth. "Bush seems to realize that he has created something of a political monster through this approach, spawning countless rumors that have him doing everything from dancing naked on a bar to copping cocaine on a Washington street," the *Post* reported.[11] At the time of this writing, no source has produced a copy of the much-discussed photograph, and no credible source has provided any public evidence that it even exists. Nonetheless, this rumor has received a significant public airing.

Even when unsubstantiated, rumors can be serious news, as when Ronald Reagan joined a Republican whispering campaign by suggesting that 1988 Democratic presidential nominee Michael Dukakis had mental health problems, or when allies of House Speaker Jim Wright tried to delay his ouster in 1989 by smearing his possible successors. In both cases, however, the sources of the rumors and the veracity of the gossip were essential details, without which journalists would have been reporting unfair information out of context. Not repeating the source of a published or broadcast rumor clouds its significance and confuses readers and viewers, blurring the line between fact and innuendo. Salacious gossip repeated in print or on the air without sources or any effort to verify facts is not journalism. It is smut.

Notes

1   Timberg, R. (1996) *The Nightingale's Song.* New York: Touchstone, p. 239.
2   Timberg, The Nightingale's Song, 240.
3   CNN *Late Edition*, CNN, March 2, 1999; *Sunday Morning*, CBS, April 18, 1999; *60 Minutes*, CBS, June 6, 1999; *20/20*, ABC, September 8, 1999.
4   Larry J. Sabato (1991) *Feeding Frenzy: How Attack Journalism Has Transformed American Politics.* New York: Free Press, pp. 77–79, 97–98, 109–110.
5   Michael Kinsley, 'In Defense of Matt Drudge', *Time* (February 2, 1998): from the magazine's online archive, http://www.pathfinder.com/time/magazine/1998/dom/980202/kinsley.html.
6   *The Tonight Show*, NBC, March 31, 1999.
7   Maureen Dowd, 'President Frat Boy?', *New York Times*, April 7, 1999 (from the newspaper's online archive); Maureen Dowd, 'Puppy Love Politics', *New York Times*, June 9, 1999 (from the newspaper's online archive).
8   Steve Chapman, 'The Real Problem With Bush's Past', *Chicago Tribune*, April 11, 1999, 19.
9   Ellen Joan Pollock, 'Empty Chatter: Behind the Rumors About George Bush', *Wall Street Journal*, May 14, 1999, A1.
10   Helen Thorpe, 'Go East, Young Man', *Texas Monthly*, June 1999 (from the magazine's online archive).
11   Lois Romano and George Lardner Jr, '1986: A Life Changing Year', *Washington Post*, July 25, 1999, p. A1.

Chapter 47

John B. Thompson

THE NATURE OF POLITICAL SCANDAL

Source: John B. Thompson (2000) *Political Scandal: Power and Visibility in the Media Age*, Cambridge: Polity Press, pp. 90–118.

[. . .]

Why is political scandal more prevalent today?

[. . .]

POLITICAL SCANDAL HAS a long history, as we have seen, and there were earlier historical periods (such as the postbellum period in the United States – we shall return to this later) when political scandals flourished. But it seems clear that in recent decades, and especially since the early 1960s, scandals have become an increasingly prevalent feature of political life in many Western societies, including Britain and the United States. Why? How can we explain the growing prevalence of political scandal in some modern liberal democracies?

Let us begin by considering two possible answers to this question, both of which have some *prima facie* plausibility but neither of which provides a convincing explanation. One possible answer is this: it might be argued that the growing prevalence of political scandal is due to a decline in the moral standards of political leaders, both with regard to their personal behaviour and with regard to their general probity in the conduct of office. [. . .]

There is another way of answering this question which, like the first answer, emphasizes changing moral standards, but which focuses on the standards *applied to* politics rather than the standards of politicians themselves. It could be argued that the growing prevalence of political scandal is due, not so much to a decline in the moral standards of politicians, but rather to a change in the moral codes and conventions that are used to assess the behaviour of politicians and to the growing salience of these codes in the conduct of political life. [. . .]

I shall try to show that there are several important changes which underlie the growing prevalence of political scandal. I shall focus on five: (1) the increased visibility of political leaders, (2) the changing technologies of communication and surveillance, (3) the changing culture of journalism, (4) the changing political culture, and (5) the growing legalization of political life. I shall argue that these factors, taken together, enable us to understand why, since the early 1960s, political scandal has become an increasingly prevalent feature of Western liberal democracies such as Britain and the United States.

(1) The increased visibility of political leaders is rooted in the broad social trans-formations that I outlined in an earlier chapter [of the original]. The development of communica-tion media created a new kind of visibility which was no longer tied to the sharing of a common locale, a visibility which enabled political leaders – and increasingly *required* them – to appear before others who were situated in contexts that were distant in space (and perhaps also in time). The political field was increasingly constituted as a mediated field – that is, a field in which the mediated visibility of political leaders became increasingly important and in which the relations between polit-ical leaders and ordinary citizens were increasingly shaped by mediated forms of communication.

The increasing visibility of political leaders creates conditions which increase the likelihood of political scandal. The more the lives of political leaders are made visible to others (and the more that political leaders accentuate their traits as individuals by disclosing aspects of self through the media), the more likely it is that previously hidden activities which conflict with the images that leaders wish to project will emerge in the public domain, triggering off a series of events which may spin out of control. To some extent, the growing prevalence of political scandal is the other side – the dark side, as it were – of the increasing visibility of political leaders. In this age of mediated visibility, political leaders (and aspiring leaders) know that they must use the media as a way of achieving visibility in the political field – without it, they will go nowhere. But mediated visibility can be a trap. The more visible you are, the more vulnerable you may be, because more visibility will generate more interest from the media and, however much you may wish to manage your self-presentation through the media, you cannot completely control it. [. . .]

(2) One reason why mediated visibility is so difficult to control is that it depends on technologies of communication and surveillance which are becoming increasingly sophisticated and more widely available. The twentieth century has witnessed a veritable revolution in the technologies available for recording, processing and transmitting information and communication. These new and rapidly changing technologies make it more and more difficult to throw a veil of secrecy around the back-region behaviour of political leaders and other public figures. [. . .]

It would be too strong to say that these new technologies of communication and surveillance herald 'the end of privacy', as some commentators have suggested.[1] But it is undoubtedly the case that, due in part to the growing availability of these technologies, the social conditions of privacy are changing in fundamental ways. [. . .]

(3) The existence of new technologies does not by itself explain how and why they are used. [. . .] While the tradition of investigative journalism stretches back to the late nineteenth century, it was given fresh impetus by the tumultuous political events of the 1960s. [. . .] A number of newspapers in the United States set up special teams of investigative reporters in the course of the 1960s and early 1970s – *Newsday* established a special team in 1967, the *Chicago Tribune* followed suit in 1968, the *Boston Globe* in 1970.[2] *The New York Times* devoted more resources to investigative reporting throughout the 1960s. [. . .]

[. . .]

The renewed emphasis on investigative reporting in the 1960s and 1970s helped to alter the culture of journalism and to create a context in which the search for hidden secrets, and the disclosure of these secrets if and when they were found, were increasingly regarded within media circles as an accepted part of journalistic activity. In the context of this broad shift in the culture of journalism, the distinction between different kinds of secrets became blurred and increasingly difficult to draw. Once it was accepted that the curtains which shrouded the upper regions of power could be drawn back, it would be very difficult to maintain a sharp distinction between secrets bearing on the exercise of power and secrets concerning the conduct of private life. Investigative reporting would easily shade into a kind of prurient reporting in which hidden aspects of the exercise of power would be mixed together with hidden aspects of the lives of the powerful.[3] [. . .]

(4) But it is not only changes in the culture of journalism which have contributed to the growing prevalence of political scandal: it is also changes in the broader political culture. [. . .]

[. . .] The traditional class-based party politics, with its sharply opposed belief systems and its strong contrast between left and right, has not disappeared, but it has been significantly weakened by the social transformations of the postwar period. And in its place has emerged a kind of politics which is based increasingly on the specific policy packages offered by political parties. These policy packages can no longer be backed up by appealing primarily to the class interests of voters, and voters themselves can no longer count on politicians to follow through with their promises by virtue of the long-standing social affiliations of their parties. Moreover, with the decline of the old ideological politics, many people feel increasingly uncertain about how best to tackle the enormously complex problems of the modern world; the world appears increasingly as a bewildering place where there are no simple solutions, and where we have to place more and more faith in our political leaders to make sound judgements and to protect our interests. It is in this context that the question of the credibility and trustworthiness of political leaders becomes an increasingly important issue. People become more concerned with the *character* of the individuals who are (or might become) their leaders and more concerned about their trustworthiness, because increasingly this becomes the principal means of guaranteeing that political promises will be kept and that difficult decisions in the face of complexity and uncertainty will be made on the basis of sound judgement. [. . .]

This changing political culture has helped to give scandal a greater significance in political life today. Part of the reason why political scandal has become so important today is that it has become a kind of *credibility test* for the politics of trust. The more our political life becomes orientated towards questions of character and trust, the more significance we give to those occasions when the trustworthiness of political leaders is called into question. The more we have to rely on the integrity of politicians to follow through with their promises and on their ability to exercise sound judgement, the more significance we give to those occasions when weaknesses of character and lapses of judgement are brought to the fore. Viewed in this light, we can understand why a scandal concerning the private life of a politician is seen by many people to have broader political significance: it is not so much because they believe that politicians should adhere to strict moral codes in their private life, but because they are worried about what this behaviour tells them about the integrity and credibility of the individual concerned. [. . .]

[. . .]

(5) There is a further factor which helps to explain the increasing prevalence of political scandal: what we could describe as the growing legalization of political life. This factor is particularly important in the American context, but its relevance is not restricted to the United States. In the American context, the Ethics in Government Act (1978), passed in the aftermath of Watergate, was a landmark in the legal regulation of political life. The Act required high-ranking officials to disclose details of their financial affairs and tightened the rules on conflicts of interest. Perhaps more significantly, it established a new office, the special prosecutor, who could be called upon to investigate cases of possible law-breaking. [. . .] By creating this office, the Act helped to set in motion a new dynamic which would raise the profile of cases of suspected wrongdoing and endow the investigative process with greatly increased powers and resources – a dynamic that was vividly illustrated by the Iran-Contra affair and by the long-running investigations of Bill Clinton that were carried out by Independent Counsel Kenneth Starr. [. . .]

While the growing legalization of political life is particularly marked in the American context, a somewhat similar trend can be discerned elsewhere. In British law there is no equivalent of the special prosecutor, but a government official suspected of criminal wrongdoing can be subjected to the normal procedures of criminal investigation. Moreover, prime ministers can set up committees of inquiry to investigate matters of public interest and to make recommendations which can be enacted in law. [. . .]

More recent committees of inquiry – including those set up in the wake of the Poulson affair in the early 1970s and the cash-for-questions scandal of the early 1990s – have led to a higher degree of regulation of the private financial interests of MPs and to the establishment of explicit codes of conduct.

The various changes that I have described help us to understand the growing prevalence of scandal in the political life of many Western societies since the early

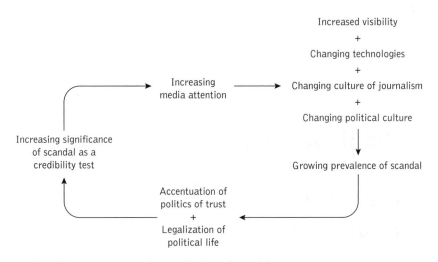

Figure 47.1 The growing prevalence of political scandal

1960s. None of these changes is sufficient by itself to explain this trend, but taken together they form the basis of a plausible explanation. Figure 47.1 summarizes the main elements of this explanation. The increased visibility of political leaders, the changing technologies of communication and surveillance, the changing culture of journalism and the changing political culture have all contributed to the growing prevalence of political scandal. This in turn has led to the accentuation of the politics of trust and to the growing legalization of political life. In these conditions, scandal assumes more and more significance as a credibility test, a factor which fuels media attention and increases still further the likelihood of scandal. In the context of a political field characterized by a competitive party system and an array of relatively independent media organizations which play a key role in shaping the relations between political professionals and ordinary citizens, and in circumstances marked by the growing significance of the politics of trust, political scandal is likely to have a cumulative effect. The more political scandals occur, the more likely it is that new scandals will arise and will be amplified by increasing media attention. The dynamic of scandal, media attention and the politics of trust produces a racheting effect which constantly increases the political stakes.

Notes

1   See Whitaker, R. (1999) *The End of Privacy: How Total Surveillance is Becoming a Reality*. New York: New Press.
2   See Schudson, M. (1978) *Discovering the News: A Social History of American Newspapers*. New York: Basic Books, pp. 189–90; (1992) *Watergate in American Memory: How We Remember, Forget, and Reconstruct the Past*. New York: Basic Books, pp. 118–19.
3   On the rise of prurient reporting, see Schudson, *Watergate in American Memory*, pp. 117–19

Chapter 48

John H. Summers

WHAT HAPPENED TO SEX SCANDALS?

Politics and peccadilloes, Jefferson to Kennedy

Source: John H. Summers (2000) 'What Happened to Sex Scandals? Politics and Peccadilloes, Jefferson to Kennedy', *The Journal of American History*, 87 (3): 825–54.

"**A**NY MAN FAMILIAR** with public life realizes the foul gossip which ripples just under the surface about almost every public man, and especially about every President," observed Theodore Roosevelt in 1913. Varieties of "foul gossip" have plagued officeholders from the founding of the Republic to the present day, as Roosevelt suggested. Yet the nature, effects, and reach of gossip have undergone curious and sometimes striking transformations over the years. Think of one especially common topic of discussion: a politician's reputation for sexual rectitude. In the early Republic and throughout the nineteenth century, American political culture subjected the sexual character of officeholders to close, steady, and often unflattering scrutiny, [. . .] By the beginning of the twentieth century, by contrast, revelations of sexual turpitude among the most prominent elected officials had begun to disappear from public life. Whereas Thomas Jefferson, Andrew Jackson, Grover Cleveland, and other members of the nineteenth-century political elite negotiated their reputations among a broad array of publics, in the new era men such as Warren G. Harding, Franklin D. Roosevelt, and John F. Kennedy benefited from this more circumspect pattern in political speech. [. . .]

What explains this transformation? Historians regularly observe that during the first decades of the century, gossip, confession, and exposure arose as distinctive attributes of mass communication, corroding Victorian modesty in virtually every arena of American life. Indeed, a "repeal of reticence" helps define this era and its aftermath. So why could the leading figures in American politics increasingly expect political culture to spare their sexual transgressions from the popular scrutiny endured by their predecessors? In examining this, the guiding problem of the essay, I consider and reject a number of possible explanations and finally settle on two key developments: changes in the ideology and practice of professional journalism and the psychology of insulation that accompanied the emergence of a newly nationalized political elite at the dawn of the last century.[1] Criticism of the sexual rectitude of politicians first surfaced as a regular part of American public life in the acrimonious milieu of the 1780s and 1790s. [. . .]

[. . .] American politics relentlessly scrutinized the personal morality of politicians for much of the next century, and sexual misbehavior became a favorite topic. A well orchestrated campaign of defamation marked the election of 1800 – the first modern presidential contest – as Federalists furiously circulated tales of "Mr. Jefferson's Congo Harem." Opponents of Andrew Jackson in 1828 and Grover Cleveland in 1884 likewise undertook to question the fidelity and chastity, respectively, of the candidates. Few influential figures of the nineteenth century escaped such imputations. [. . .]

What explains this close attention to the personal character of politicians? [. . .]

Like so many other habits of American political culture, this impetus to demand virtue in leaders derived from multiple traditions. [. . .] Repudiating older, hierarchical notions of authority and service, republicans made personal virtue a foundation of representation and insisted that only persons of exemplary rectitude should occupy positions of power. For without personal integrity, leaders could hardly withstand the temptation of corruption and the pursuit of narrow self-interest. Virtue facilitated tasks widely considered vital to the protection of freedom in consent-based regimes: warding off corruption, checking tyranny, ensuring an enlightened citizenry, and thereby promoting the general welfare. Thus republicans in the antebellum independent press, reflecting the outlook of many of the Founders, forcefully articulated concerns about public morality. [. . .] Evangelical Protestantism also persuaded nineteenth-century voters to seek for public service men of esteemed character. [. . .]

Politicians of both parties heeded such admonitions and presented themselves to voters as men of sexual virtue, honor, integrity, and good judgment [. . .]. The growth of political society, however, soon introduced an awkward problem: If good character conferred legitimacy upon governmental authority, as evangelicals and republicans each contended, what prevented officeholders from wearing virtue as a disguise? By the antebellum period, after all, America's increasingly anonymous society had made "reputation" an unstable concept, easy to counterfeit. [. . .]

Voters, then, relieved trepidation over the specter of the politician as dissembling confidence man by calling upon a vigorous democratic political culture. Nineteenth-century Americans, that is, filtered republican and Protestant world views through a lens of popular democracy that required all claims, public and private, to confront "the broad light of day," as Tocqueville witnessed. [. . .] The repudiation of secrecy by popular democrats also explains why alarms about hypocrisy nearly always accompanied allegations of immoral conduct, and why charges of illegitimacy and adultery (by definition sins of deceit and seduction) occupied pride of place in this era. Republicanism and evangelical Protestantism demanded virtue among leaders, but the active, intensely public search for sullied sexual character derived from the democratic incarnations of these traditions.[2]

[. . .]

Like Republicans, the Democrats did not hesitate to attack rivals, internal and external, for iniquity. Nor did they fail to trumpet the personal integrity of deserving candidates, as the 1884 presidential election indicates. That campaign, in fact, amply demonstrates the convergence of partisan, republican, religious, and democratic exigencies around the notion of sexual virtue. Throughout his brief career in politics, the Democrats' nominee, Grover Cleveland, had deliberately projected moral uprightness and unassailable honesty. [. . .] In late July 1884, however, a minister from Buffalo imputed to Cleveland "habitual immoralities with women." Writing in the *Buffalo Evening Telegraph*, the Reverend George Ball claimed that Cleveland had once made the acquaintance of a "beautiful, virtuous, and intelligent young lady" named Maria Halpin, who worked in the cloak department of a Buffalo department store. Swiftly Cleveland "won her confidence and finally seduced her." Halpin became pregnant, but Cleveland withdrew his promise to marry her, then "employed two detectives and a doctor of bad repute to spirit the woman away and dispose of the child."[3]

These sensational charges, quickly transmitted throughout the nation, generated a tempest of debate, eliciting heated commentary from ministers, partisans, and independents alike. [. . .] Democratic party operatives retaliated by circulating a claim that Blaine's wife had given birth to her son only three months after the couple's marriage. Already battling charges of cupidity, Blaine was now asked to answer an allegation about his sexual rectitude. [. . .]

[. . .] Cleveland's candor persuaded enough voters to secure a November victory. On July 23, he telegraphed a message to his managers in Buffalo, admitting a rendezvous with Halpin and confessing that he might have fathered a child to her. [. . .] Although the Blaine forces kept the Halpin story alive until the eve of the election, Cleveland's timely admission restored much of his credibility.[4]

[. . .] The Halpin affair, however, proved the last major scandal of its kind for more than one hundred years. Sexual rectitude remained a topic for open debate well into the 1890s, but willingness to expose the unsavory habits of influential politicians yielded steadily, haltingly, to a new mood in American political culture – a return of reticence.[5] Partisan rivals and "paul pry" journalists continued to gossip uncharitably about Cleveland, yet both averted their gaze from his successor, Benjamin Harrison, whose moral worthiness suffered no significant assaults. The aloof William McKinley also enjoyed a gossip-free administration. So, too, did William Howard Taft and Woodrow Wilson escape from the discomfort of entering public debate about their sexual peccadilloes. [. . .]

Certainly the case of Warren G. Harding suggests a new mood in political culture. [. . .] That the married Harding had proven morally destitute in his sexual affairs understates the situation. Early in his political career, he embarked on a long-term romance with Carrie Phillips, wife of a Marion, Ohio, department store owner and a family friend. In 1917, while he continued his clandestine assignations with Phillips, Harding found a second paramour, an umnarried eighteen-year-old woman named Nan Britton. In 1919, Britton bore him a daughter. [. . .][6]

[. . .]

If the relentless stream of articles, speeches, and pamphlets probing for hypocrisy and sexual immorality among politicians of national repute had slowed by the 1920s, it had largely stopped by the New Deal years. Franklin Roosevelt ordered a special car to take his mistress, Lucy Mercer Rutherford, to his 1932 inauguration. More than a dozen years later, Rutherford was present at the president's bedside when he died. Correspondents, Republican publishers, and others traded gossip about the relationship but made no mention of either Rutherford or Missy LeHand, another of the president's paramours during Roosevelt's entire time in office. The "friendship" between Rutherford and Roosevelt did not become public knowledge until 1949, the "romance" not until 1966. When John F. Kennedy ascended to the presidency, reticence had become a fixed principle of American political exchange [. . .]. Kennedy, known in certain circles for his habitual and reckless womanizing, enjoyed protection both from the national press corps and from political rivals, who sometimes attempted to document his liaisons but who never organized a public campaign to discredit him – even though, as the Catholic husband of a widely esteemed First Lady, the president was doubly vulnerable to exposure. In 1963 the Profumo sex scandal devastated Harold Macmillan's Conservative government in Great Britain. By contrast, President Kennedy's assignations with Judith Campbell Exner, Marilyn Monroe, Ellen Rometsch, and Durie Malcolm (and many others) remained secrets, their concealment central to the popular image of Camelot. As the 1884 election of Grover Cleveland marked the culmination of one pattern in political speech, so did Kennedy's tenure in the White House mark the apotheosis of another.[7]

[. . .]

Why, then, did indiscretions about sex retreat from popular view? One important explanation centers on the metamorphosis of American journalism. [. . .] As part of this broad disaggregation, reporters and editors broke free from their partisan moorings, established journalism as an autonomous profession, and thereby ended the party monopolies on political information.[8]

Now the most self-conscious and influential purveyors of knowledge about politics, "objective" journalists hastened to elevate their vocation into a profession. [. . .] Reticence about the immoralities of political figures first acquired concerted support in the professionalization of journalism. Ethical codes of conduct constituted "the heart of the whole matter," according to Joseph Pulitzer [. . .]. The American Society of Newspaper Editors (ASNE) crafted the most influential set of ethical guidelines. In 1923 the newly formed group called for "fair play." As formulated by the ASNE, "fair play" meant that "a newspaper should not publish unofficial charges affecting reputation or moral character without opportunity given to the accused to be heard." Furthermore, "a newspaper should not invade private rights or feelings without sure warrant of public right as distinguished from public curiosity." Similar versions of fair play appeared in nearly every guide to professional newspaper practice in the 1910s and 1920s.[9]

Sentiment for such codes had been building for decades. But why did prescriptions of fair play achieve such a broad accord in this period? Essentially, insulation for "well reputed persons" emerged as a reflection of professional journalism's renunciation of popular politics. Beginning in the early decades of the twentieth century, and especially after the bewildering vagaries of public opinion during World War I, a consensus of democratic "realism" coalesced among social scientists, philosophers, businessmen, and reform-minded intellectuals. [. . .]

Led by Lippmann's influential writings, leaders in journalism hewed closely to the realist position, often distinguishing between "giving the public what it wants" and "giving the public what it should have." [. . .]

As democratic realists, editors and reporters assigned themselves the "very great obligation" of managing the opinions of voters. [. . .]

In this respect, the unseemly side of the character question faded from public view as part of a general ideology of insulation. [. . .] Once, evangelicals and republicans appealed to the populace to discipline and monitor the morality of political elites. Now, political elites were charged with the discipline of the populace. [. . .] Reticence emerged as part of a broad operation to protect the workings of government from the sort of "irrational" scrutiny that characterized the popular politics of the nineteenth century.[10]

If reticence originated as part of an ideology of insulation, and, correspondingly, of a concentration of power among early-twentieth-century elites whose authority rested substantially upon their ability to monopolize political knowledge, it proved an ideal especially serviceable for journalism. For the promise of reticence permitted elite reporters to get closer to the instruments of government power. After all, correspondents who endorsed "fair play" demonstrated a willingness to keep secrets from their readers. [. . .] Behind the facade of objective professionalism, new journalistic organizations institutionalized ties to politicians and in consequence legitimated them. [. . .]

By the New Deal years, this sort of "cozy relationship between reporters and officials" extended to the press conference, according to James Reston, who never quite reconciled himself to the "bantering atmosphere of these clubby gatherings." [. . .] Kennedy's charm turned newsmen such as Arthur Krock, Hugh Sidey, and Benjamin Bradlee from putatively objective newsmen into half-confessed sycophants. [. . .][11]

[. . .]

[. . .] Newspapermen, in short, entered the thriving ranks of professional elites by subscribing to the prevailing tenet that political decision making required insulation from "mobbish" and "irrational" voters.

[. . .]

[. . .] The transformation of American journalism constitutes a compelling but an incomplete accounting for the return of reticence. [. . .] The final part of the explanation, accordingly, concerns a general phenomenon: the political psychology of national state building. [. . .] In place of the local controls and party "bossism" that characterized much of nineteenth-century government emerged an increasingly centralized administrative bureaucracy, comprising an expanded federal judiciary and enhanced regulatory mechanisms. A reconstructed state would confront the challenges of industrial capitalism by concentrating power in hierarchical offices staffed by managers, specialists, and other elites. This panoramic nationalization of govern-mental power – which also called forth a muscular chief executive – generated a "sense of the state" heretofore famously absent from American political life.[12]

[. . .]

The preservation of the moral integrity of twentieth-century political elites, one element in this scheme, aspired to unify the nation around the federal state. By adopting reticence, the guideposts of mass communications implied that between the polity and the state lay sacredness and mystification, a symbolic distance.

To many, political authority now appeared not immediate and corporeal, but abstract and intangible, increasingly shrouded in the office of the presidency and other protected images that together functioned as a bulwark against dissent. [. . .]

[. . .]

[. . .] Thus C. Wright Mills witnessed a "penumbra of prestige" shadowing postwar American leaders, who successfully perpetuated and consolidated the "nationalization of status" undertaken by their forebears. In fact, by the time that Mills blasted the "power elite" and Kennedy readied himself to lead it, everyone who held a position in the national firmament – from tabloid journalists to major publishers to partisan officials themselves – had learned to operate according to a tacit understanding guided by a political psychology: exposing certain personal vices of presidents imperiled the legitimacy of the state's claim to concentrated power [. . .]. [13]

[. . .]

[. . .] Contemporary commentators may quarrel over the precise date when the decline of twentieth-century reticence became clear, but I suspect that periodizing the transformation in the 1970s and 1980s – when journalism fragmented and American government suffered renewed challenges to its legitimacy – will meet a general consensus. I suppose, too, that dating the impeachment of Bill Clinton as the consum-mation of the decline of reticence will not cause many disagreements.

[. . .] American history discloses a long and frequently honorable tradition of assailing corrupt personal character in politicians. Today's liberal intellectuals, however, would have us believe otherwise: that inquiries into "private" peccadilloes of political elites demonstrate little except for adolescent sniffing around. [. . .]

[. . .] Much too frequently, advocates for the privacy of high officials begin and end their case simply by invoking the term. But politicians past and present regularly invite attention to favorable features of their ostensibly personal lives, wishing, like other celebrities, to have it both ways as they create, manipulate, and peddle their images in frenzied pursuit of the seats of power. Until the plenteous critics of media invasiveness seriously attend to that side of the problem, they risk fostering the impression that preserving artificial political authority, not privacy, actually motivates their grievances.[14] In the meantime, an important distinction might prove worthwhile for serious debate about this vexed subject. Privacy is not the same as secrecy, and salutary efforts to achieve transparency in government should take care to respect the former while denouncing the latter. Keeping irresponsible power at bay requires sustained and intense scrutiny of officials and quasi officials, but failing to uphold their individual legal rights would rob such publicity of its moral force.

In my view, the most important criterion to consider is whether sex scandals inhibit or promote the free flow of political discussion. This article has observed disturbing connections in this respect. For the same assumptions and developments that drove scandal from the optic of political culture after the 1890s – the decline of political parties and the rise of an ostensibly autonomous journalism, the advent of a version of democratic thought that prized political engineering over political participation, and the construction of nationalized state apparatus – also introduced a sense of enervation and dessication into the twentieth-century polity. As the scope and reach of the federal government enlarged and lengthened, the number and nature of secrets reposed within it also grew, sexual transgressions among them. Organized, effective dissent declined correspondingly, and in many quarters a vague sense of phoniness frustrated would-be political actors. [. . .] Still, contrasting these two long periods in American history ultimately warrants the conclusion that the liberty to gossip in public about the leaders of any society – however tawdry the gossip or however noble the leaders – implies a breadth of freedom of expression that we should not voluntarily constrict anytime soon.[15]

Notes

1   On the "repeal of reticence" and its implications, see Gurstein, R. (1996) *The Repeal of Reticence: A History of America's Cultural and Legal Struggles over Free Speech, Obscenity, Sexual Liberation, and Modern Art*. New York. [. . .] For an informal history of political gossip that furnishes useful documentary evidence but no serious explanatory framework, see Collins, G. (1998) *Scorpion Tongues: Gossip, Celebrity, and American Politics*. New York.

2   Tocqueville, *Democracy in America*, trans. Reeve, 1, 27; Robert H. Wiebe (1995) *Self-Rule: A Cultural History of American Democracy*. Chicago, p. 21. [. . .]

3   La Fevre, B. (1884) *Campaign of '84*. San Francisco, p 27; Welch, D. (1884) *Stephen Grover Cleveland: A Sketch of his Life*. New York. p. iii; *Buffalo Evening Telegraph*, July 21, 1884, p. 1. [. . .]

4   *Buffalo Evening Telegraph*, July 21, 1884, p. 1; Grover Cleveland to Charles W. Goodyear, July 23, 1884, in *Letters of Grover Cleveland, 1850–1908* (ed.) Allan Nevins (Boston, 1933), 37; Nevins, A. (1933) *Grover Cleveland: A Study in Courage*. New York, p. 163. [. . .] See Nevins, *Cleveland*, 166; and Josephson, M. (1938) *The Politicos, 1865–1896*. New York, p. 366. See also Lewis L. Gould, "Election of 1884," in *Running for President: The Candidates and Their Images*. (ed.) Arthur M. Schlesinger Jr (2 vols., New York, 1994), 1, 365–73.

5   Cleveland to Winston S. Bissell, Nov. 13, 1884, in *Letters of Cleveland*, ed. Nevins, 48. [. . .] See Collins, *Scorpion Tongues*, 130.

6   Adams, S.H. (1949) The Timely Death of President Harding. In Isabel Leighton (ed.) *The Aspirin Age*. New York, p. 87; Russell, F. (1968) *The Shadow of Blooming Grove: Warren Harding in His Times*. New York.

7   See Daniels, J. (1966) *The Time between the Wars: Armistice to Pearl Harbor*. Garden City, pp. 208–9, 221; Roberts, C. (1985) Franklin Delano Roosevelt and the Press. In Thompson, K.W. (ed.) *The Credibility of Institutions, Policies, and Leadership*, Vol. V: *The Media*. New York, p. 186; and Hugh A. Bone (1941) *"Smear" Politics: An Analysis of the 1940 Campaign Literature*. Washington. [. . .] Witcover, J. (1998) 'Unshining Moments: What Did Newsmen Know of JFK's Antics – And When Did They Know It?', *Columbia Journalism Review* (Jan./Feb. 1998), p. 76; Seymour M. Hersh (1977) *The Dark Side of Camelot*. New York, esp. pp. 1–12, 24–25, 49, 62, 71, 82–87, 102–20, 129–30, 222–46, 294–340, 344, 386–411. On the Profumo affair, see Gaster, R. (1988) Sex, Spies, and Scandal: The Profumo Affair and British Politics. In Markovits A.S. and Silverstein, M. (eds) *The Politics of Scandal: Power and Process in Liberal Democracies*, New York, pp. 62–88.

8   McGerr, M.E. (1986), *Decline of Popular Politics: The American North, 1865–1928*, New York, 42–137; Robert Westbrook, R. (1983) Politics as Consumption: Managing the Modern American Election. In Richard Wightman Fox and T.J. Jackson Lears (eds) *The Culture of Consumption. Critical Essays in American History, 1880–1980*. New York, pp. 145–73.

9   Joseph Pulitzer, 'The College of Journalism', *North American Review*, 178 (May 1904), 667. [. . .] American Society of Newspaper Editors, *Problems of Journalism: Proceedings of the First Annual Meeting* (Washington, 1923), 17, 1–2. For other press codes and sentiment about their necessity and efficacy, see Crawford, N.A. (1924) *The Ethics of Journalism*. New York, pp. 183–210; M. Lyle Spencer, *Editorial Writing. Ethics, Policy,*

Practice (Boston, 1924), 73; Sorrells, J.H. (1930) *The Working Press*. New York, p. 3; and Koenigsberg, M. (1941) *King News: An Autobiography*. Philadelphia, p. 502.

10   Lasch, C. (1965) *The New Radicalism in America, 1889–1963*; (1965) *The Intellectual as a Social Type*. New York, p. 163; Gladden, W. (1915) "Tainted Journalism: Good and Bad." In Thorpe, M. (ed.) *Coming Newspaper*. New York, 50, 38, 39.

11   Reston, *Deadline*, 102; A. Merriman Smith, Merriman Smith's *Book of Presidents: A White House Memoir* (ed.) Timothy G. Smith (New York, 1972), 38, 221; Hersh, *Dark Side of Camelot*, 25, 49, 62, 71.

12   Skowronek, S. (1982) *Building a New American State: The Expansion of National Administrative Capacities, 1877–1920*. Cambridge, Mass., pp. 3–18, esp. 4, 3.

13   Mills, *Power Elite*, 357, 84. On "sacralization," see Lawrence W. Levine, L.W. (1988) *Highbrow/Lowbrow: The Emergence of Cultural Hierarchy in America*. Cambridge, Mass., esp. pp. 83–168. [. . .]

14   Political speech is only one of many arenas in which the public-private dichotomy is conceptually muddled. For a useful overview, see Weintraub, J. (1997) The Theory and Politics of the Public/Private Distinction. In Weintraub, J. and Kumar, K. (eds) *Public and Private in Thought and Practice: Perspectives on a Grand Dichotomy*. Chicago, pp. 1–42.

15   This point is demonstrated in a brilliant exegesis by a political scientist, useful here as conceptual framework: James C. Scott, J.C. (1985) *Weapons of the Weak: Everyday Forms of Peasant Resistance*. New Haven.

SECTION 8

New media, new politics?

THERE IS AN ONGOING debate among political communication scholars about the extent to which new media, and the Internet in particular, is transforming politics. The pieces selected for this section can be divided into those that think it is altering political advocacy and those that are more circumspect.

The Internet plays a central role in anti-globalisation politics. Its low cost and network characteristics have enabled the formation of global advocacy networks. **Bennett** argues that the Internet has been key in facilitating loosely structured transnational protest movements – ideologically 'thin', but motivated by a series of causes. Futher, in his extract, **Rheingold** argues that new technology has facilitated the emergence of 'smart mobs'. These are technology-linked groups, that can converge ('swarm') on a particular location, anywhere, at any time. Among numerous examples, the extract looks at the case of the SMS-linked smart mob that assembled to protest against the actions of President Estrada of the Philippines, successfully bringing about his downfall.

The role of new media in consciousness raising and activation is revealed by **Danitz and Strobel.** They show how university students in the US were able to use the Internet not only to inform students of multinational Pepsi's ties with Burma's military junta, but also to mobilise support for a boycott of Pepsi on campus. Danitz and Strobel illustrate how the Internet can be utilised to generate and co-ordinate local collective action on global issues.

New technologies are also changing the face of traditional political communication. **Cornfield** *et al.* examine the effects of blogs on the presidential election campaign in the US. The 2004 campaign was the first where online weblogs – easy to use online diaries, in which the author can leave a series of comments – were used. Cornfield *et al.* show that networks of bloggers were able, in certain circumstances, to shape the election campaign agenda. They speculate as to whether 'blogosphere' will become the fifth estate, setting the campaign agenda and allowing citizens to respond to campaign issues.

While the use of the Internet by political advocates in mature democracies has received widespread attention, what about its impact on the political communication systems of consolidating democracies such as Mexico? Will it enhance its democratic status? Wallis shows that the democratising impact of the Internet is significant, but argues it should be considered alongside other democratic reforms that occurred in the 1990s. Finally, **Margolis and Resnick** argue that the utilisation of the web by protest networks has not led to a significant shifts in the exercise of power at a national or global level. They argue that the web is increasingly dominated by many of the traditional holders of power within society, such as government and transnational corporations. So rather than leading to a radical democratic future, as many have claimed, the Internet's impact is marginal, allowing new opportunities for a few – but for the majority it means it will remain politics as usual.

Chapter 49

W. Lance Bennett

COMMUNICATING GLOBAL ACTIVISM
Strengths and vulnerabilities of networked politics

Source: W. Lance Bennett (2003) 'Communicating Global Activism: Strengths and Vulnerabilities of Networked Politics', *Information, Communication & Society*, 6 (2): 143–68.

[. . .]

OBSERVATIONS REPORTED in this article indicate that digital communication practices appear to have a variety of political effects on the growth and forms of global activism. These effects range from organizational dynamics and patterns of change, to strategic political relations between activists, opponents and spectator publics. In addition, patterns of individual participation appear to be affected by hyperlinked communication networks that enable individuals to find multiple points of entry into varieties of political action. Moreover, the redundancy of communication channels in many activist networks creates organizational durability as hub organizations come and go, and as the focus of action shifts across different events, campaigns, and targets. Finally, there appears to be a relationship between communication practices and the evolution of democracy itself. One of the important subtexts of this movement is media democracy, centred on the conversion of media consumers into producers, with the introduction of open publishing and collective editing software – all channelled through personal digital networks.

[. . .]

Talking about such substantial digital media effects flies in the face of the conventional wisdom that the Internet and other digital media typically do little more than amplify or economize communication in political organizations (Davis 1999; Agre 2002). [. . .]

It is easy to see how conceptual confusion surrounds the political impact of the Internet and other digital media. When political networks are viewed at the level of constituent organizations, the implications of Internet communications can vary widely. Political organizations that are older, larger, resource rich, and strategically linked to party and government politics may rely on Internet-based communications mostly to amplify or reduce the costs of pre-existing communication routines. On the other hand, newer, resource-poor organizations that tend to reject conventional politics may be defined in important ways by their Internet presence (Graber *et al.*, forthcoming). In this analysis, I contend that the importance of the Internet in networks of global protest includes – but also goes well beyond – gains that can be documented for particular resource-poor organizations. [. . .]

[. . .]

Internet applications as organizational process

The uses of the Internet may be largely subordinated to existing organizational routines and structures when dedicated to the goals and practices of hierarchical organizations such as parties, interest associations, or election campaigns. However, as noted earlier, the fluid networks of global issue activism enable the Internet to become an organizational force shaping both the relations among organizations and, in some cases, the organizations themselves. Some organizations are even transformed by Inter-networks as they take on new functions and partnerships. At least four distinct organizational dynamics have been identified in our case studies of organizational interaction with communication networks: (1) organizational transformation due to demands of network partners; (2) organizations that 'move on' to other networks to avoid transformation and to maintain their capacity as activist hubs in other campaigns; (3) network organizations created to perform specific tasks that produce successor networks; and (4) organizations that adopt open communication networks and then become transformed by the information exchanges among their members.

Organizational transformation through network demands

Because easy Internet linkages can open organizations to unpredictable traffic patterns, obscure nodes can become more central hubs in networks. As discussed above, the Netaction organization in the Microsoft campaign became such a rich archive of reports and research information about the corporation and the campaign that it became a central hub in the campaign network (as measured, among other things, by overlapping board of directors members). The early mission and identity of the organization were synonymous with Microsoft, even though the mission statement promised engagement with a wide range of electronic policy issues. As noted in the next section, Netaction reclaimed its broader policy agenda only by breaking with the Microsoft campaign and "moving on" to hub positions in other campaign networks.

Another interesting case is the vast network of *Jubilee* debt relief campaigns.

If one follows the origins of these organizations back into the 1990s, they began largely as religious networks proclaiming debt relief a moral and religious issue. For example, one of the largest contingents at the Seattle WTO protests were churches operating under the Jubilee banner. This coalition led the first large march on the evening of 29 November 1999, drawing 10,000–15,000 activists, and setting the stage for the even larger labour-led actions the next day. [. . .]

Moving on to other networks as a protective strategy

Because of the potential to become redefined by location in a communication network, many organizations that provide coordinating or information functions in campaign networks adopt a strategy of periodically 'moving on' to new networks. As noted above, Netaction (www.netaction.org) maintained its identity as a multi-issue organization in the digital communication policy arena by moving on to other campaigns in areas of digital communication regulation and consumer protection. A recent inspection of the website revealed activities in the areas of broadband regulation, electronic privacy, the future of an open Internet, and others.

As indicated in earlier references to the Nike and fair trade coffee campaigns, Global Exchange is another organization that has been careful to leave campaigns before becoming defined by them. During its time as the main hub in the Nike sweatshop campaign (1995–8), Global Exchange used creative communication strategies that produced a deluge of negative press for Nike based largely on a worker's own account of conditions in Indonesian factories (Bullert 2000; Bennett 2003). Global Exchange left the campaign when Nike CEO Phil Knight admitted that Nike had a labour problem and would do something about it.

Just as the 'move on' organization protects itself from transformation by network dynamics, they also tend to make few identity demands on other network organizations. Since Global Exchange, Netaction, and other 'move on' organizations know they will leave networks, they are unlikely to broker collective identity frames or induce other organizations to transformation in ways typically associated with movements when they are viewed from more conventional organization-centred perspectives.

Specific task organizations that produce successor networks

Internet umbrella organizations created to organize issue campaigns and demonstrations often take distinctive network forms based on how they allow users to access and communicate through the site. Many of these organizing networks have survived beyond the action that drew them together because they generally offered networking services and calendars that became useful for future communication and planning. In some cases, these secondary planning features of Internet-only mobilizing networks helped to create successor organizations to mobilize future events. For example, the A 16–2000 umbrella organization that coordinated the demonstrations at the Washington, DC, International Monetary Fund meeting in April 2000 opened its website to announce a constantly changing roster of participants. The site enabled newcomers to post their own rallying messages at the top of the site. The user interface emphasized the political diversity of participating groups, along with an amazing number of different political reasons for opposing the IMF. The list of endorsing and participating groups (692 and still growing at the time I captured the site) was indexed by geographical location so that organizations in different locales could be viewed on the same page. Another page of the site revealed an equally diverse core group of demonstration sponsors: 50 Years is Enough, Alliance for Global Justice, Campaign for Labour Rights, Global Exchange, Mexico Solidarity Network, National Lawyers Guild, Nicaragua Network, and Witness for Peace, among others.

In contrast to the diversity of the A 16 organization, the organizing site for the demonstration against the Free Trade Area of the Americas (FTAA) meeting in Montreal in April 2001 had a much more focused agenda aimed at mobilizing people in localities and training them in direct action and street theatre tactics before they arrived in Montreal. The site listed a different and much smaller set of lead organizations than those involved in the IMF protests above. The Ruckus Society featured prominently in the training and local mobilizing, and the Montreal Anti-Capitalist Convergence was identified as the lead organization at the protest site. A tighter focus on specific protest themes, training, and coordinated action was maintained through much more restricted user features and cross communication opportunities than offered by the A 16 site.

Despite these differences in the communication interfaces created to organize the two demonstrations, both websites offered user features that kept them alive and networked with broader communities of activists beyond those attending the specific demonstrations. [. . .]

Organizations transformed by their internal communication networks

Applications of the Internet and other digital media may also affect the internal development of organizations themselves. As noted in the last section, Le Grignou and Patou's study of ATTAC in France (forthcoming) found that communication practices affected the political identity of the organization. They also find that the structure of the organization is affected by those communication practices [. . .]. [. . .]

A promising approach is Van Aelst and Walgrave's (forthcoming) analysis of organizations that received news coverage surrounding the 2001 protests against the Free Trade Area of the Americas in Montreal. They found that the top seventeen organizations mentioned in the news also maintained substantial cross communication channels on the Internet, and that most of them maintained on-line calendars for the FTAA and other protest activities. By these measures, there was a mutually engaged political action network that operated with a high degree of coordination through digital channels. What is interesting is that the underlying coherence in the digital channels linking these organizations was also reflected in mass media attention to the individual members of the networks. This suggests that digital networks have found paths to jump their communication from relatively personalized digital channels to the mass media. It is important to begin understanding these crossover communication effects of digital networks as well.

New media can alter information flows through mass media

The public spheres created by the Internet and the Web are more than just parallel information universes that exist independently of the traditional mass media. A growing conventional wisdom among communication scholars is that the Internet is changing the way in which news is made. New media provide alternative communication spaces in which information can develop and circulate widely with fewer conventions or editorial filters than in the mainstream media. The gate-keeping capacity of the traditional press is weakened when information appears on the Internet, presenting new material that may prove irresistible to competitors in the world of 24/7 cable news channels that now occupy important niches in the press food chain. Moreover, journalists may actively seek story ideas and information from web sources, thus creating many pathways for information to flow from micro to mass media.

An interesting example of micro-to-mass media crossover in global activism began with an e-mail exchange between a culture jammer named Jonah Peretti and Nike (Peretti 2003). Peretti visited a Nike website that promised greater consumer freedom by inviting customers to order shoes with a name or slogan of their choice on them. He submitted an order to inscribe the term 'sweatshop' on his custom Nikes. Several rounds of amusing exchanges ensued in which Peretti chided the company for breaking its promise of consumer freedom. Successive rounds ended with Nike's awkward and less automated refusals to put any of Peretti's requests for political labels on its shoes. Peretti sent the exchange to a dozen friends, who forwarded it to their friends, and so the Nike-Sweatshop story spread in viral fashion, reaching an audience estimated from several hundred thousand to several million (Peretti 2003).

Based on the flood of responses he received, Peretti tracked the message as it first circulated through the culture jamming community, then the labour activist community, and then, '. . . something interesting happened. The micromedia message worked its way into the mass media . . .' (Peretti 2003). First it reached middle media sites such as weblogs (*slashdot*, *plastic* and others) where it began to resemble news. From there, it was picked up by more conventional middle media sites such as Salon, which are read by journalists. At that point, it was a short journalistic step to *USA Today*, *The Wall Street Journal*, NBC's *Today Show*, and dozens of prominent North American and European news outlets. Whenever Peretti was interviewed about his media adventure, the connection between Nike and sweatshop was communicated again.

[. . .]

While many activist issue campaigns have secured remarkably favourable media coverage, disruptive public demonstrations – the other major power lever of protest politics – have generally received fairly negative coverage. The interesting exception is the Battle in Seattle, which produced fairly extensive coverage of activist messages about globalization. [. . .]

Beyond the characterizations of the activists, the predominant news framing of the overall protest movement is also negative, as in 'anti-globalization'. This is clearly a news construction that is at odds with how many of the activists think of their common cause. If movement media framing could be put to a vote among activists, I suspect that 'democratic globalization' would win over 'anti-globalization' by a wide margin. [. . .] Mass media framing of movements clearly varies from case to case, depending on how activist communication strategies interact with media gatekeeping (Gamson 2001). Gitlin (1980) identified the demand of news organizations for movements to produce leaders and simple messages as part of the explanation why the American new left of the 1960s received considerable media attention, and also fragmented into disunity and internal conflict. A global activist movement that is committed to inclusiveness and diversity over central leadership and issue simplicity should have low expectations of news coverage of demonstrations that display the movement's leaderless diversity in chaotic settings.

Why has a movement that has learned to secure good publicity for particular issue campaigns and organizations not developed more effective media communication strategies for mass demonstrations? I think that the answer here returns us to the opening discussion of the social and personal context in which this activism takes place. Not only are many activists in these broadly distributed protest networks opposed to central leadership and simple collective identity frames, but they may accurately perceive that the interdependence of global politics defies the degree of simplification demanded by most mass media discourse. While issue campaign networks tend to focus on dramatic charges against familiar targets, most of the demonstration organizing networks celebrate the diversity of the movement and resist strategic communication based on core issues or identity frames. For example, Van Aelst and Walgrave (forthcoming) found at least eleven political themes that were shared by substantial portions of the network involved in the FTAA demonstrations in 2001. Thus, demonstrations may be staged mainly as reminders of the human scale, seriousness, and disruptive capacity of this movement, while issue campaigns remain the stealth factor carrying radical messages through the gates of the mass media.

[. . .]

References

Agre, P. (2002) 'Real-time politics: the Internet and the political process', *The Information Society*, 18: 311–31.

Bennett, W.L. (2003) Branded political communication: lifestyle politics, logo campaigns, and the rise of global citizenship. In M. Micheletti, A. Follesdal and D. Stolle (eds) *The Politics Behind Products: Using the Market as a Site for Ethics and Action*. New Brunswick, NJ: Transaction Books.

Bullert, B.J. (2000) 'Strategic Public Relations, Sweatshops, and the Making of a Global Movement', Working Paper #2000-14, Joan Shorenstein Center on the Press, Politics, and Public Policy, Harvard University.

Davis, R. (1999) *The Web of Politics: The Internet's Impact on the American Political System*. New York: Oxford University Press.

Gamson, W. (2001) Promoting political engagement. In W.L. Bennett and R.M. Entman (eds) *Mediated Politics: Communication in the Future of Democracy*. New York: Cambridge University Press, pp. 56–74.

Gitlin, T. (1980) *The Whole World Is Watching: Mass Media in the Making and Unmaking of the New Left*. Berkeley, CA: University of California Press.

Graber, D.A., Bimber, B., Bennett, W.L., Davis, R. and Norris, P. (forthcoming) The Internet and politics: emerging perspectives. In M. Price and H. Nissenbaum (eds) *The Internet and the Academy*. New York: Peter Lang Publishers.

Le Grignou, B. and Patou, C. (forthcoming) The expert always knows best? In W. van de Donk, B.D. Loader, P.G. Nixon and D. Rucht (eds) *Cyberprotest: New Media, Citizens and Social Movement*. London: Routledge.

Peretti, J. (2003) Culture jamming, memes, social networks, and the emerging media ecology: the Nike sweatshop e-mail as object to think with. In M. Micheletti, A. Follesdal and D. Stolle (eds) *The Politics Behind Products*. New Brunswick, NJ: Transaction Books (in press). See also www.engagedcitizen.org under culture jamming.

Van Aelst, P. and Walgrave, S. (forthcoming) New media, new movements? The role of the Internet in shaping the "anti-globalization" movement. In W. van de Donk, B.D. Loader, P.G. Nixon and D. Rucht (eds) *Cyberprotest: New Media, Citizens and Social Movement*. London: Routledge.

Chapter 50

Howard Rheingold

SMART MOBS
The power of the mobile many

Source: Howard Rheingold (2002) *Smart Mobs: The Next Social Revolution,* Cambridge, MA: Basic Books, pp. 157–82.

BYPASSING THE COMPLEX of broadcasting media, cell phone users themselves became broadcasters, receiving and transmitting both news and gossip and often confounding the two. Indeed, one could imagine each user becoming a broadcasting station unto him or herself, a node in a wider network of communication that the state could not possibly even begin to monitor, much less control. Hence, once the call was made for people to mass at Edsa, cell phone users readily forwarded messages they received, even as they followed what was asked of them.

> Cell phones then were invested not only with the power to surpass crowded conditions and congested surroundings brought about by the state's inability to order everyday life. They were also seen to bring a new kind of crowd about, one that was thoroughly conscious of itself as a movement headed towards a common goal.
>
> (Vicente Rafael, "The Cell Phone and the Crowd:
> Messianic Politics in Recent Philippine History")

Netwar—dark and light

On January 20, 2001, President Joseph Estrada of the Philippines became the first head of state in history to lose power to a smart mob. More than 1 million Manila residents, mobilized and coordinated by waves of text messages, assembled at the site of the 1986 "People Power" peaceful demonstrations that had toppled the Marcos regime.[1] Tens of thousands of Filipinos converged on Epifanio de los Santas Avenue, known as "Edsa," within an hour of the first text message volleys: "Go 2EDSA, Wear blck."[2] Over four days, more than a million citizens showed up, mostly dressed in black. Estrada fell. The legend of "Generation Txt" was born.

Bringing down a government without firing a shot was a momentous early eruption of smart mob behavior. It wasn't, however, the only one.

- On November 30, 1999, autonomous but internetworked squads of demonstrators protesting the meeting of the World Trade Organization used "swarming" tactics, mobile phones, Web sites, laptops, and handheld computers to win the "Battle of Seattle."[3]
- In September 2000, thousands of citizens in Britain, outraged by a sudden rise in gasoline prices, used mobile phones, SMS, email from laptop PCs, and CB radios in taxicabs to coordinate dispersed groups that blocked fuel delivery at selected service stations in a wildcat political protest.[4]
- A violent political demonstration in Toronto in the spring of 2000 was chronicled by a group of roving journalist-researchers who webcast digital video of everything they saw.[5]
- Since 1992, thousands of bicycle activists have assembled monthly for "Critical Mass" moving demonstrations, weaving through San Francisco streets en masse. Critical Mass operates through loosely linked networks, alerted by mobile phone and email trees, and breaks up into smaller, tele-coordinated groups when appropriate.[6]

Filipinos were veteran texters long before they toppled Estrada. Short Message Service (SMS) messaging was introduced in 1995 as a promotional gimmick.[7] SMS messaging, free at first, remained inexpensive. Wireline telephone service is more costly than mobile service, and in a country where 40 percent of the population lives on one dollar a day, the fact that text messages are one-tenth the price of a voice call is significant.[8] A personal computer costs twenty times as much as a mobile telephone; only 1 percent of the Philippines' population own PCs, although many more use them in Internet cafes.[9] By 2001, however, 5 million Filipinos owned cell phones out of a total population of 70 million.[10]

Filipinos took to SMS messaging with a uniquely intense fervor. By 2001, more than 70 million text messages were being transmitted among Filipinos every day.[11] The word "mania" was used in the Manila press. The *New York Times* reported in 2001:

> Malls are infested with shoppers who appear to be navigating by cellular compass. Groups of diners sit ignoring one another, staring down at their phones as if fumbling with rosaries. Commuters, jaywalkers, even mourners—everyone in the Philippines seems to be texting over the phone [. . .].[12]

Like the thumb tribes of Tokyo and youth cultures in Scandinavia, Filipino texters took advantage of one of the unique features of texting technology—the ease of forwarding jokes, rumors, and chain letters. Although it requires effort to compose messages on mobile telephone keypads, only a few thumb strokes are required to forward a message to four friends or everybody in your telephone's address book. Filipino texting culture led to a national panic when a false rumor claimed that Pope John Paul II had died.[13]

[. . .]

The "People Power II" demonstrations of 2001 broke out when the impeachment trial of President Estrada was suddenly ended by senators linked to Estrada. Opposition leaders broadcast text messages, and within seventy-five minutes of the abrupt halt of the impeachment proceedings, 20,000 people converged on Edsa.[14] Over four days, more than a million people showed up. The military withdrew support from the regime; the Estrada government fell, as the Marcos regime had fallen a decade previously, largely as a result of massive nonviolent demonstrations.[15] The rapid assembly of the anti-Estrada crowd was a hallmark of early smart mob technology, and the millions of text messages exchanged by the demonstrators in 2001 was, by all accounts, a key to the crowd's esprit de corps.

Professor Rafael sees the SMS-linked crowd that assembled in Manila as the manifestation of a phenomenon that was enabled by a technical infrastructure but that is best understood as a social instrument:

> The power of the crowd thus comes across in its capacity to overwhelm the physical constraints of urban planning in the same way that it tends to blur social distinctions by provoking a sense of estrangement. Its authority rests on its ability to promote restlessness and movement, thereby undermining the pressure from state technocrats, church authorities and corporate interests to regulate and contain such movements. In this sense, the crowd is a sort of medium if by that word one means the means for gathering and transforming elements, objects, people and things. As a medium, the crowd is also the site for the generation of expectations and the circulation of messages. It is in this sense that we might also think of the crowd. . . not merely as an effect of technological devices, but as a kind of technology itself. Centralized urban planning and technologies of policing seek to routinize the sense of contingency generated in crowding. But at moments and in areas where such planning chronically fails, routine can at times give way to the epochal. At such moments, the crowd . . . takes on a kind of telecommunicative power, serving up channels for sending messages at a distance and bringing distances up close. Enmeshed in a crowd, one feels the potential for reaching out across social space and temporal divides.[16]

The Battle of Seattle saw a more deliberate and tactically focused use of wireless communications and mobile social networks in urban political conflict, more than a year before texting mobs assembled in Manila. A broad coalition of demonstrators who represented different interests but were united in opposition to the views of the World Trade Organization planned to disrupt the WTO's 1999 meeting in Seattle. The demonstrators included a wide range of different "affinity groups" who loosely coordinated their actions around their shared objective. The Direct Action Network enabled autonomous groups to choose which levels of action to participate in, from nonviolent support to civil disobedience to joining mass arrests—a kind of dynamic ad hoc alliance that wouldn't have been possible without a mobile, many-to-many, real-time communication network. According to a report dramatically titled, "Black Flag Over Seattle," by Paul de Armond:

> The cohesion of the Direct Action Network was partly due to their improvised communications network assembled out of cell phones, radios, police scanners and portable computers. Protesters in the street with wireless Palm Pilots were able to link into continuously updated web pages giving reports from the streets. Police scanners monitored transmissions and provided some warning of changing police tactics. Cell phones were widely used. [. . .] [17]

From Seattle to Manila, the first "netwars" have already broken out. The term "netwar" was coined by John Arquilla and David Ronfeldt, two analysts for the RAND corporation (birthplace of game theory and experimental economics), who noticed that the same combination of social networks, sophisticated communication technologies, and decentralized organizational structure was surfacing as an effective force in very different kinds of political conflict:

> Netwar is an emerging mode of conflict in which the protagonists—ranging from terrorist and criminal organizations on the dark side, to militant social activists on the bright side—use network forms of organization, doctrine, strategy, and technology attuned to the information age. The practice of netwar is well ahead of theory, as both civil and uncivil society actors are increasingly engaging in this new way of fighting.
>
> From the Battle of Seattle to the "attack on America," these networks are proving very hard to deal with; some are winning. What all have in common is that they operate in small, dispersed units that can deploy nimbly—anywhere, anytime. All feature network forms of organization, doctrine, strategy, and technology attuned to the information age. They know how to swarm and disperse, penetrate and disrupt, as well as elude and evade. The tactics they use range from battles of ideas to acts of sabotage—and many tactics involve the Intenet. [18]

The "swarming" strategies noted by Arquilla and Ronfeldt rely on many small units like the affinity groups in the Battle of Seattle. Individual members of each group remained dispersed until mobile communications drew them to converge on a specific location from all directions simultaneously, in coordination with other groups. Manila, Seattle, San Francisco, Senegal, and Britain were sites of nonviolent political swarming. Arquilla and Ronfeldt cited the nongovernmental organizations associated with the Zapatista movement in Mexico, which mobilized world opinion in support of Indian peasants, and the Nobel Prize-winning effort to enact an anti-landmine treaty as examples of nonviolent netwar actions. Armed and violent swarms are another matter.

The Chechen rebels in Russia, soccer hooligans in Britain, and the FARC guerrillas in Colombia also have used netwar strategy and swarming tactics.[19] The US military is in the forefront of smart mob technology development. The Land Warrior experiment is scheduled to field-test wearable computers with GPS and wireless communications by 2003.[20] The Joint Expeditionary Digital Information (JEDI) program links troops on the ground directly to satellite communications. JEDI handheld devices combine laser range-finding, GPS location awareness, direct satellite telephone, and encrypted text messaging.[21] Remember the DARPA-funded startup MeshNetworks from Chapter 6 [of the original publication], the company whose technology enables military swarms to parachute onto a battlefield and self-organize an ad hoc peer-to-peer wireless network? Small teams of special forces, wirelessly networked and capable of calling in aircraft or missile strikes with increasing accuracy, were introduced by the United States and its allies in Afghanistan: netwar.

Examples later in this chapter [in the original] demonstrate that smart mobs engaging in either violent or nonviolent netwar represent only a few of the many possible varieties of smart mob. Netwars do share similar technical infrastructure with other smart mobs. More importantly, however, they are both animated by a new form of social organization, the network. Networks include nodes and links, use many possible paths to distribute information from any link to any other, and are self-regulated through flat governance hierarchies and distributed power. Arquilla and Ronfeldt are among many who believe networks constitute the newest major social organizational form, after tribes, hierarchies, and markets. Although network-structured communications hold real potential for enabling democratic forms of decision-making and beneficial instances of collective action, that doesn't mean that the transition to networked forms of social organization will be a pleasant one with uniformly benevolent outcomes.

[. . .]

In light of the military applications of netwar tactics, it would be foolish to presume that only benign outcomes should be expected from smart mobs. But any observer who focuses exclusively on the potential for violence would miss evidence of perhaps an even more profoundly disruptive potential—for beneficial as well as malign purposes—of smart mob technologies and techniques. Could cooperation epidemics break out if smart mob media spread beyond warriors—to citizens, journalists, scientists, people looking for fun, friends, mates, customers, or trading partners?

Substitute the word "computers" for the words "smart mobs" in the previous paragraph, and you'll recapitulate the history of computation since its birth in World War II.

[. . .]

Notes

Epigraph: Vincente Rafael, "The Cell Phone and the Crowd: Messianic Politics in Recent Phillipine History," 13 June 2001. http://communication.ucsd.edu/people/F_rafael.cellphone. html.

1   Michael Bociurkiw, "Revolution by Cell Phone," *Forbes*, 10 September 2001, http://www.forbes.comlasap/2001/0910/028.htmb (1 March 2002).

2   Ibid.

3   Paul de Armond, "Black Flag Over Seattle," *Albion Monitor* 72, March 2000, http://www.monitor.netlmonitor/seattlewto/index.htmb (1 March 2002).

4   Alexander MacLeod, "Call to Picket Finds New Ring in Britain's Fuel Crisis," *Christian Science Monitor*, 19 September 2000. See also: Chris Marsden, "Britain's Labour Government and Trade Union Leaders Unite to Crush Fuel Tax Protest," *World Socialist Web Site*, 15 September 2000, http://www.wsws.orglarti_cles/2000/sep2000/fuel-slS.shtmb (1 March 2002).

5   Steve Mann and Hal Niedzviecki, *Cyborg: Digital Destiny and Human Possibility in the Age of the Wearable Computer* (Mississauga: Doubleday Canada, 2001), 177–178.

6   Critical Mass, http://www.Critical-mass.orgl (6 March 2002).

7   Anne Torres, "4 SME, Txtng is Lyf," *TheFeature.com*, 18 April 2001, http://www.thefeature.com (1 March 2002).

8   Bociurkiw, "Revolution by Cell Phone".

9   Rafael, "The Cell Phone and the Crowd".

10   Ibid.

11   Arturo Bariuad, "Text Messaging Becomes a Menace in the Philippines," *Straits Times*, 3 March 2001.

12   Wayne Arnold, "Manila's Talk of the Town Is Text Messaging," *New York Times*, 5 July 2000, C1.

13   Bariuad, "Text Messaging Becomes a Menace".

14   Rafael, 'The Cell Phone and the Crowd'.

15   Richard Lloyd Parry, "The TXT MSG Revolution," *Independent Digital*, 23 January 2001, http://www.independent.co.uklstory.jsp?story=SI748 (1 March 2002).

16   Rafael, "The Cell Phone and the Crowd."

17   de Armond, "Black Flag Over Seattle."

18   David Ronfeldt and John Arquilla, "Networks, Netwars, and the Fight for the Future," *First Monday* 6, 10 (October 2001), http://firstmonday.org/issues/issue6_10/ronfeldt/index.htmb (1 March 2002).

19   John Arquilla and David Ronfeldt (eds), *Networks and Netwars: The Future of Terror, Crime, and Militancy.* (Santa Monica, Calif.: RAND, 2001).

20   Jim Lai, "The Future of Infantry," *Mindjack* 28, January 2002, http://www.mindjack.com/feature/landwarrior.html (1 March 2002).

21   Ian Sample, "Military Palmtop to Cut Collateral Damage," *New Scientist*, 9 March 2002, http://www.newscientist.com/news/news.jsp?id=ns99992005 (29 March 2002).

[. . .]

Chapter 51

Tiffany Danitz and
Warren P. Strobel

NETWORKING DISSENT
Cyber activists use the Internet to promote democracy in Burma

Source: Tiffany Danitz and Warren P. Strobel (2001) 'Networking Dissent: Cyber Activists Use the Internet to Promote Democracy in Burma', in John Arquilla and David Ronfeldt (eds), *Networks and Netwars: The Future of Terror, Crime, and Militancy*, Santa Monica, CA: RAND, pp. 129–69.

[. . .]

The Free Burma Coalition and the Pepsi Boycott
Campaign

[. . .]

THE ADVENT OF COMPUTERS on university campuses linking student groups into national and international networks seems to have invigorated social activism and has transformed the character of student protests. It has also opened up the world to these students, shrinking the globe into a local community that provides a great number of issues on which to campaign. "We are beginning to see the formation of a generic human rights lobby at the grassroots level (on the Internet). People care even though they don't have a personal connection to the country," explained cyber activist Simon Billenness.[1]

[. . .]

In 1990, Pepsi entered Burma through a joint venture with Myanmar Golden Star Co., which is run by Thein Tun, once a small-time exporter of beans. Most Burmese who were working for Pepsi were connected in one way or another to the SLORC regime, said Reed Cooper, of the Burmese Action Group in Canada.[2]

Pepsi ran a bottling operation in Rangoon that grew "from 800,000 bottles a day to 5 million" and added a new plant in Mandalay.[3]

In a Seattle resolution on Burma, which urged an "international economic boycott of Burma until the human rights violations cease and control of the government has been transferred to the winners of the 1990 democratic election," Pepsi was mentioned as one of the companies that supports the military regime and its "cruel measures against the Burmese people."[4] The resolution passed unanimously just after a similar boycott resolution successfully passed in Berkeley, California.[5]

Cyberactivist Billenness was building a campaign with a solid foundation at the local levels. His office was delivering ribbons of circular stickers proclaiming "Boycott Pepsi" across the country to various groups of activists. He had solicited and developed the support of the Nobel Peace laureates who attended the pivotal 1993 fact-finding mission to the border regions of Burma (they were not permitted into the country). The Nobel laureates joined in a call for an international boycott of products exported from Burma. The 1993 trip sparked a campaign that the grass-roots organizers, like Billenness, Cooper, Larry Dohrs, and others, had slowly been orchestrating. The necessary definitive moment that legitimized their efforts had arrived.

"This is how South Africa started," Billenness said. The strategy: to get selective purchasing legislation passed in town councils, then cities, then the states. Congress would be sure to follow, he believed.[6] Most of the roads and Internet lines connecting this network of Burma activists lead back to Billenness. So it is not surprising that he wanted to encourage a university campaign among American colleges to support the growing Burmese student movement.

The Pepsi Campaign at Harvard University

There are few Burmese in the States, and relatively few people who even know where Burma is. But those who care are organized and effective, and it's because of the Internet.

Douglas Steele[7]

Students at Harvard tapped into the Burma Internet network, and soon after, they were successful in preventing a contract between PepsiCo and Harvard's dining services. Their activism also had an influence on the Harvard student body, by raising awareness as well as passing resolutions in the student government that affected the university's investments in Burma.

One of the students who became a ringleader for the Burma campaign on campus was Marco Simons.[8] The summer before his junior year at Harvard, Simons, who had written a paper on the human rights situation in Burma while still in high school, tapped into the Net via the newsgroup *soc.culture.burma*. Soon after, Billenness, who worked at the Franklin Research Institute for Socially Responsible Investing, contacted Simons. Billenness was trying to initiate a Burma group at Harvard. At this same time, autumn 1995, the Free Burma Coalition (FBC) was first appearing online. The FBC's web site was able to attract numerous students across the United States, and it became a hub for the network that would follow.

There were no Burmese undergraduate students at Harvard. There was one native Burmese graduate student and a few students who had either visited Burma or lived there as foreigners. For this reason, the three Harvard students who initiated the Burma group felt their first order of business should be to raise awareness. They set up a table at the political action fair at the start of the fall semester. They tested students who came by on their geographical prowess by asking them where Burma was on a map and which countries bordered it. Those who stopped to play the game were asked to leave their email addresses. Between 40 and 50 addresses were collected that day.

[. . .]

Once they had the student email addresses, members of the fledgling group began encouraging students to join them in letter-writing campaigns calling for university divestment from various companies. They also tried to organize an honorary degree for Aung San Suu Kyi. Harvard became the first student government to pass resolutions supporting the Burmese prodemocracy movement. Since then, many campuses have passed similar resolutions, and many used the Internet to seek advice from Simons on how to engage in this campaign.[9]

Some of the resolutions passed by Harvard's student government required that the university send letters to companies operating in Burma, calling for corporate withdrawal. Simons says the students believed Harvard's name carried a lot of clout in corporate circles. These resolutions passed in January and February 1996.

Harvard University is itself a large investor, with a $7 billion endowment. The students decided to campaign for resolutions requiring Harvard Corp. to write to the companies it owns stock in that deal with Burma and register its desire for divestment.

The Burma activists at Harvard also attempted to localize their campaign whenever possible. Then they stumbled onto a link with Pepsi that allowed them to expand their campaign into a story that would later become a splash with the media.

"At first we didn't think we would have a Pepsi campaign at Harvard because Harvard contracted with Coke for a long time," Simons said.[10] Simons had been aware of the national campaign that Burma activists were waging against PepsiCo from his involvement with Billenness.[11] Billenness held a regular Burma Roundtable that was advocating for a "Boycott Pepsi" campaign, in conjunction with a national group of activists.

It was then that the *Harvard Crimson* ran a story stating that Harvard's dining services were planning on contracting with Pepsi instead of Coca-Cola. "Pepsi was trying to get the beverage contract on campus the whole time," Simons explained. "Coke's dining contract was up for renewal, and they were so dissatisfied with Coke's service, the dining services were thinking of going with Pepsi."[12]

The Burma activists decided to protest this contract on two fronts: first with the student legislature and then with Harvard dining services. As part of the contract, Pepsi would be giving $25,000 to student organizations at Harvard and $15,000 directly to the student government. The activists' strategy with the student legislature would be to attack the Pepsi donations with resolutions. These resolutions called for Harvard to explore investing options for the Pepsi contributions. They could outright refuse the money or, ironically, donate it to Burma-friendly groups like the Boycott Pepsi campaign. When they began investigating these options, the students discovered that dining services had not signed the contract yet.

The students met with dining services in a lobbying effort. They also stayed in contact over the Internet with Michael Berry, then director of dining services, and Purchasing Director John Allegretto. Rand Kaiser, a PepsiCo representative, met with dining services and the activists to explain Pepsi's position. Simons says that Kaiser argued for constructive engagement with the Burmese military junta.[13] Kaiser was successful in casting Pepsi's investments in Burma in a positive light. After the meeting, Simons and Berry contacted one another over the email system. This allowed students to voice opposing arguments to those presented by Pepsi. Simons made a deal: He told dining services that the students would feel that they had adequate information if PepsiCo released a list of their suppliers for countertrade in Burma.[14] Dining services agreed to this request. The Harvard students asked PepsiCo to fax its list of suppliers. Dining services also made a separate request for the information. Simons says neither the students nor dining services ever received a list.

Meanwhile, the 1996 Pepsi shareholders meeting had commenced and a resolution was introduced to withdraw from Burma. PepsiCo's management effectively blocked the filing of the resolution on the basis that Burma did not represent a significant portion of its business. In reaction, Billenness wrote a letter to Pepsi and the shareholders explaining the effects that the Boycott Pepsi campaign had had on the company. He included the clippings from events at Harvard. This proved to be a boost to the students, who felt their efforts were extending beyond their campus.

The Burma student activists requested that their student government pass another resolution that specifically asked dining services to sign a contract with Coca-Cola and not Pepsi. This passed through the student legislature, and dining services renewed their contract with Coca-Cola. Dining services then went on the record explaining that Burma was a factor in its decision.

A media campaign ensued, and the Harvard students were courted by mainstream news organizations. Students downloaded press releases, conferred over the Internet with other student leaders in the FBC, and then sent their statements to the press. Stories appeared in the *Washington Post*, *USA Today*, *Boston Globe*, on the Associated Press wire, and in local newspapers.[15] In addition, Simons said he received overseas calls from the BBC and from a Belgian news outlet.

Other students who subscribed to the FBC web site and email list were able to follow what was happening at Harvard and use information generated there for campaigns on their own campuses. They also emailed and conversed with other students to discuss techniques and strategy, while learning from past mistakes.

Even with the help of the Internet, not every student campaign on Burma was a success. An effort at Georgetown University in Washington, DC, did not go very far.[16] Another Boston university, Tufts, also saw a spark of student activism on the Burma issue. The Tufts activists were hooked up to the Net, which they used to communicate with the Harvard group. But the Tufts students were unable to convince their student government to pass a resolution that would end their dining services' contract with Pepsi. Kaiser had been to the student government to lobby in favor of PepsiCo in the wake of the Harvard campaign. Tufts students also admit that they did not have as good a relationship with dining services as the Harvard students did. The director of dining services deferred the Pepsi decision to the university president, who renewed Pepsi's contract.

The network

The Harvard group worked closely with several activists who have come to define a core for the Burma prodemocracy campaign. They are Billenness, Father Joe Lamar, Zar Ni of the FBC, and Larry Dohrs.

As noted, the bulk of the Harvard campaign was conducted over the Internet. Simons would post condensed versions of the Free Burma daily digest (a news-like account of events in Burma and developments in the Free Burma campaign, similar to BurmaNet) for the Harvard students. Previously written press releases, with quotes chosen through collaboration, were used throughout the campaign. Furthermore, most of the Harvard group's meetings were held over the Internet via email. "This would not have happened without the Internet," Simons said of the Pepsi campaign. "The Free Burma Coalition and possibly the whole movement would not have been nearly as successful this far and would look completely different," he added.[17]

The FBC, which is a network of student organizations, organized three international days of coordinated protest, one in October 1995, another in March 1996, and a fast in October 1996. These were coordinated almost exclusively on the Internet. The Harvard students joined in these events.

The Boston student network grew from contact with FBC and through outreach between local groups. Harvard University, Tufts University, Boston College, Brandeis, the Massachusetts Institute of Technology, and Boston University are all in contact with the Burma Roundtable set up by Billenness. Now the Boston network is reaching into the high schools. The Madison, Wisconsin-area groups are the only others reaching into the high school level. Boston and Madison are using the Internet to coordinate an organized effort to bring activism on Burma to the public schools.

The FBC provides information, advice, and an organized framework for these students to plug in and perform very simple tasks that help push the campaign along. The Internet is appealing to the students because (1) they have easy access through their university; (2) information is available quickly; (3) it is affordable; (4) things that make a difference can be done quickly and with few individuals; (5) the network has the ability to coordinate internationally; and (6) it is social. The three students who initiated the Burma campaign at Harvard remained the core group, producing most of the work on Burma. Because of the group's small size, they say there is no way they could have been so successful and effective without the larger outside network.

"Phone trees and snail mail are suboptimal because they are labor intensive and expensive," explained Simons, who spends an average of a couple of hours a day on the Internet. He thinks another advantage to the web of "spiders," as the activists call themselves, is the up-to-the-minute information that comes from people in Rangoon or the surrounding areas. Zar Ni's updates hit the web immediately.[18]

There was a preexisting network of activists that the FBC has drawn on. For instance, Simons was in his high school Amnesty International group. The actions were planned to raise awareness and strengthen the growing network of people. Very few activists are working on Burma exclusively. They may begin with the Southeast Asian nation but then expand to work on East Timor, Sri Lanka, environmental issues, and the like. Many of these smaller networks are relying on the FBC and the Burma campaign as a model for their own actions.

[. . .]

Notes

1   Interview with Billenness, 1997.
2   Telephone interview with Reed Cooper, Washington, D.C., March 1995.
3   Michael Hirsh and Ron Moreau, 'Making It in Mandalay', *Newsweek*, June 19, 1995, p. 24.
4   Press release by The Seattle Campaign for a Free Burma, April 24, 1995. Also in Seattle City Council Resolution 29077.
5   Ibid.
6   Billenness interview, 1997.
7   Quoted in Neumann, 'The Resistance Network', 1996.
8   This section is based on interviews with Marco Simons in Boston, January 1997, and Zar Ni in Washington, DC, February 1997.
9   Simons and Billenness interviews, 1997.
10   Simons interview, 1997.
11   Selective purchasing laws were being considered across the country by local city councils.
12   Simons interview, 1997.
13   Constructive engagement is the free-market argument for investment in troubled regions. The argument goes that with investment, the standard of living is raised for the average person. This in turn raises the expectations for rights and freedoms from the government. At the same time, the heightened economy requires a free flow of information, which boils down to technology and freedoms of press and speech. These then open up a previously closed society.
14   In Burma, the currency is virtually worthless, so foreign investors have to repatriate their profits before taking them out of the country. The human rights community firmly believed that PepsiCo was buying agricultural goods to sell to recoup its profits and that those goods were harvested with state-enforced slave labor. Macy's department stores had published a similar list, and the resulting pressure proved destructive to its investment.
15   The many such articles include a front-page report by Joe Urschel, 'College Cry: 'Free Burma' Activists Make Inroads with US Companies', *USA Today*, April 29, 1996, p. lA.
16   Steele interview, 1997.
17   Simons interview, 1997.
18   Ibid.

Chapter 52

Michael Cornfield, Jonathan Carson, Alison Kalis and Emily Simon

BUZZ, BLOGS, AND BEYOND
The Internet and the national discourse in the fall of 2004

Source: Michael Cornfield, Jonathan Carson, Alison Kalis and Emily Simon (2005) 'Buzz, Blogs, and Beyond: The Internet and the National Discourse in the Fall of 2004', *Pew Internet & American Life Project*, 16 May, www.pewinternet.org.

[. . .]

Political bloggers and the power of buzz

BLOGS ARE HOT. Two Pew surveys conducted in early 2005 show that 16% of US adults (32 million) are blog readers. [. . .] [T]he blogger audience now commands respect: it stands at 20% of the newspaper audience and 40% of the talk radio audience. Meanwhile, 6% of the entire US adult population has created a blog. That's 11 million people, or one out of every 17 American citizens.[1]

[. . .]

To understand why blogs are hot, it helps to consider the concept of buzz. Buzz is the sound heard in public when a lot of people are talking about the same thing at the same time. Some buzz forms around trivial topics, as the Yahoo! "Buzz Index" illustrates in abundance.[2] But buzz can alter social behavior and perceptions. It can embolden or embarrass its subjects. It can affect sales, donations, and campaign coffers. It can move issues up, down, and across institutional agendas (across being issue reconceptualization or re-framing). When these changes occur, buzz can shift the balance of forces arrayed in a political struggle, and so affect its outcome.

Today, bloggers have buzz partly because a few dozen of them, known as the "A-list" or "political blogs," have been hailed as a new force in national politics.[3] [. . .] The blog set up by the Howard Dean campaign was instrumental to its candidate's rise from obscurity to front-runner for the Democratic nomination in 2003. Bloggers were the new kids on the block during the 2004 national conventions, as both parties accommodated them with credentials, arena space, and interviews. [. . .] Most notably, bloggers sparked a public outcry against the authenticity of memos cited in a CBS News report about George W. Bush's service in the National Guard, a buzz which culminated in an apology from the media giant and the early retirement of its most prominent figure, Dan Rather.

Positing a blog-buzz connection

There are several reasons to think that the force wielded by the political blogs has a lot to do with buzzmaking. First, the internet is a great place to roam for buzzworthy topics. All sorts of social and political communication occur online, from commercial advertising to educational symposia, concerted rabble-rousing to casual chewing the fat, technical databases to home-made cartoons. [. . .]

Second, the blog as a net form is conducive to buzz. A blog is basically a web site consisting of a collection of entries in reverse chronological order. It is more personal and informal than institutional web sites, more accessible to web roamers and searchers than email, more spontaneous than advertisements, and more open to discussion than video, audio, textual, and statistical files. At the same time, a blog can be linked to all these other internet forms. So whatever is buzzworthy anywhere can be brought to the attention of a blog readership.

Then conversation may commence. Often, a blog contains features interlacing it with other blogs, whence the concept of a network of blogs, or blogosphere, existing within the internet. These connective features include a "blogroll" of favorite blogs, a "permalink" identifying a blog entry, or post, for ready reference elsewhere, a "track back" capacity whereby outsiders who link to the entry are listed and given a reciprocal link, and "RSS feed" capability to deliver an entry automatically to those who have requested its type. These features assure that whatever one blog buzzes about, adjacent blogs are readily able to amplify.

Third, adjacency develops out of shared interests, as do audience followings. Internet users do not go to blogs out of obligation, [. . .]. Blogs are perused voluntarily, and returned to automatically or habitually, because readers are disposed to want information on the same topics as fascinate the blogger. [. . .]

Fourth, the A-list bloggers occupy key positions in the mediascape. Journalists, activists, and political decision-makers have learned to consult political blogs as a guide to what is going on in the rest of the internet.[4] The bloggers are fast to spot items of interest; they link to sources so that items may be verified and inspected at length; and they embroider items with witty captions and frequently passionate commentaries. Accordingly, when bloggers buzz, the big mouthpieces of society notice.

Finally, it is hard to see what other than buzzmaking that blogger power could spring from. The political blogs don't have big promotion budgets, statutory or propriety authority over information, large staffs, mass audiences[5], social respectability, or armored divisions. They do have access to a lot of information, the appeal of the individual voice, a devotion to the subject of politics, and tools to share what they see, hear, and say with others possessing similar devotion.

Research framework and techniques

In this report we examine the political power of buzz as manifest in blogs, and on the internet as a whole, during the last two months of the 2004 presidential campaign season. Instead of looking solely at blogs, we developed a comparative four-channel framework, such that on any day topics mentioned in blogs could be compared with those in mainstream media, the presidential and national party campaign organs, and online citizen chat forums. We tracked the frequency of posts by keywords on a variety of buzz topics in the time period 9/1/2004–11/3/2004. We coded message topics for comparative analysis in the time period 9/27/2004– 10/31/2004. [. . .]

[. . .]

Tracking buzz across the mediascape

During the last two months of the 2004 presidential campaign, numerous topics attracted buzz. Iraq, of course, was a consistently popular subject. [*See* Figure 52.1.]

The release of the videotape with a pre-election statement from Osama Bin Laden garnered a great deal of attention from the media, but relatively little from the blogs and chatterers. [*See* Figure 52.2.]

Another late October "surprise," the disclosure about missing explosives in Iraq, stirred more buzz among the blogs, although probably not as much as the Kerry campaign would have liked. [*See* Figure 52.3.]

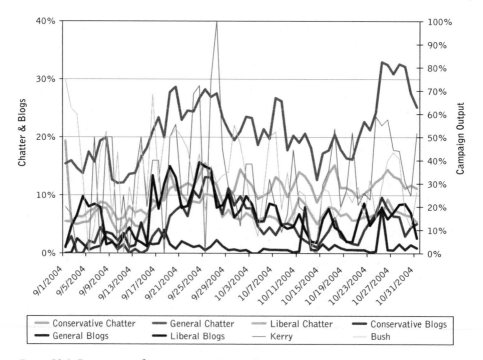

Figure 52.1 Percentage of messages mentioning Iraq

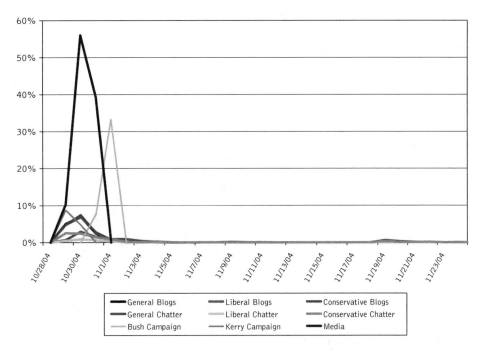

Figure 52.2 Percentage of messages mentioning Osama Bin Laden tape

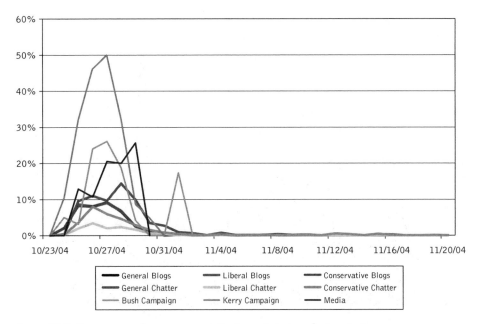

Figure 52.3 Percentage of messages mentioning missing explosives in Iraq

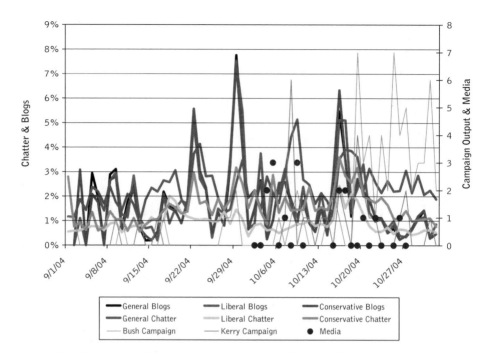

Figure 52.4 Percentage of messages mentioning the military draft

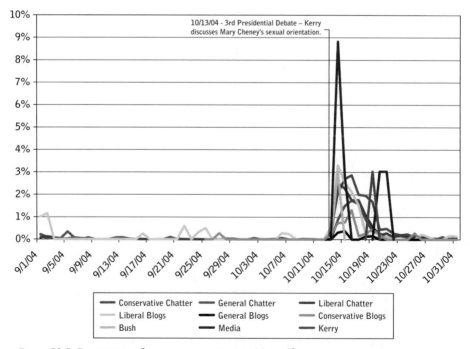

Figure 52.5 Percentage of messages mentioning Mary Cheney

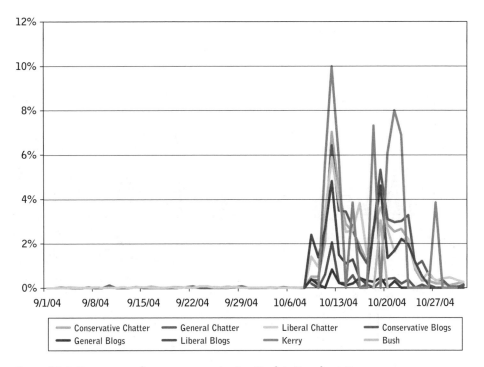

Figure 52.6 Percentage of messages mentioning Sinclair Broadcast Group

The Kerry campaign devoted a couple of days to pushing concerns about the draft into the limelight in mid-September, and there was low-level buzz on the topic well into November, with a media spike after it came up in a presidential debate, and push-back from the Bush campaign in late October. [*See* Figure 52.4.]

The next two charts are much lower on the buzz scale than the previous three. [See Figures 52.5, 52.6.] There was a week of buzz about Mary Cheney, the Vice-President's lesbian daughter, after the third presidential debate. [*See* Figure 52.5.]

Liberals talked about the Sinclair Broadcast Group more than conservatives in October; the media corporation retreated from plans to broadcast a program critical of Kerry in the face of mounting plans for an advertising boycott. [*See* Figure 52.6.]

Finally, on a very low scale, there was a little buzz about the mysterious bulge detected in the back of Bush's jacket after the first debate, especially in general chatter. [*See* Figure 52.7.]

The buzz peaks, mountain ranges, valleys and other patterns on display in these mediascape charts are clues to what Jamieson and Campbell once called "the interplay of influence."[6] As can be seen from these examples, there are multiple pattern possibilities. We have not compiled enough cases or data to start cataloging buzz events, much less developing hypotheses about the dynamics of buzz. But it is clear that during the 2004 fall campaign buzz started (in the sense of a big spike followed by heavier activity in the other channels) in several channels, not just with bloggers. The same was true for sustaining buzz. If bloggers, or media, or presidential campaigns, were buzz makers plenipotentiary, that is, heavyweight agenda-setters and issue-framers, then there would be a recurring pattern in which one channeled and

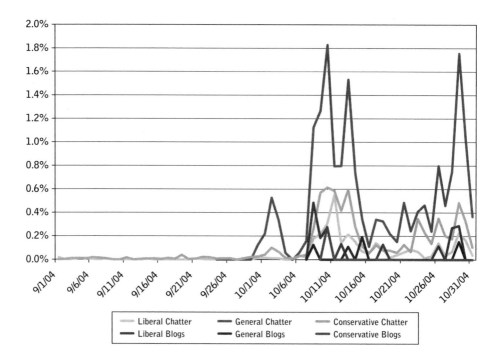

Figure 52.7 Percentage of messages mentioning Bush's jacket bulge

the others followed. This was not what we detected. Still, there must be something special about the relationship between bloggers and political buzz to account for all the attention paid to blogs in 2004 and 2005.

Do blogs constitute a "Fifth Estate"?

One possibility is that bloggers have a distinct set of priorities and proclivities, that they have emerged as a sort of Fifth Estate. Recall from French history that the four estates consist of the political "nobility" (today, that would be government, parties, and top advocacy groups), the knowledge "clergy" (academia, think tanks, foundations, research institutes), the popular "citizenry," and the "press" (infotainment media). Our study does not include a knowledge channel. However, we did look closely at buzzmaking relationships among the campaigns, the media, the bloggers, and the online citizens. Both internet channels were subdivided ideologically as well as considered as a whole, to explore the possibility that the way people online process information is somehow related to a trans-ideological unity of perspective on national discourse priorities during the general election phase of a presidential election. Such a perspective would make certain topics particularly interesting to bloggers, and/or chatters, and/or internet users, regardless of their ideological outlooks. (Lacking an offline chat component, we could not explore the opposite possibility, that being online reinforces ideological perspectives. Another Pew Internet & American Life study has examined this question.[7])

Topical priorities and buzz influence: a look at correspondences

Our analysis of how closely preferred topics in one channel or subdivision corresponded with those in other channels, like our mediascape charts for particular topics, suggests that the bloggers did not have their own agenda.

BuzzMetrics examined the political issues most frequently discussed in the media, among bloggers, among users in citizen chatter sites, and from the Bush and Kerry campaigns, from September 27 – October 31, 2004.

We developed a set of topical categories and measured how frequently they were mentioned by various channel constituents.[8] The resulting frequency count was then converted into a percentage of sample size. We then determined the top 20 issues in each channel, and correlated those top 20 issues to the corresponding percentages of those issues in the other channels. Again, our four channels of data were:

- Political blogs: commentary from 40 top political pundit bloggers. Citizen Chatter: conversations from politically-engaged citizens.
- Campaign releases: news distributions from Bush and Kerry campaign websites, newsletters, and blogs.
- Media coverage: 16 key national media outlets.

Strong correlations among the various channels and subdivisions may be seen throughout the flow chart. The bloggers were agenda followers as leaders. No single, mono-directional path of influence is discernible.

Looking at the 38 pairings in various combinations yields some interesting observations.[9] [. . .] [*See* Figure 52.8.]

The strongest two combinations existed between general citizen chat groups and ideological chat groups (.89) with conservatives, (.79) with liberals. The weakest two combinations both involved the Kerry campaign, which had small topic preference correspondences with the priorities of the media (.13) and the Bush campaign (.09). The Bush campaign did not follow media priorities strongly either (.26), but it did speak much more to the priorities of the Kerry campaign (.45) than vice versa (again, .09).

For both the Kerry and Bush campaigns, the most frequent topic of mention was the character of the opponent. The online chatter reflected similar priorities: character came in at the number one and two positions for general, conservative, and liberal. However, conservatives and liberals talked about the media almost as much as the candidates' characters, while the general chat groups talked more about Iraq and the debates than the media.[10]

The strength of the correspondences between the blogs and the media, on one hand, and the blogs and the online chat groups, on the other, lends credence to the contention that blogs are positioned between the two other channels as a sort of guide for the media to the rest of the internet. [. . .] Media to blogs (.78) was slightly stronger than blogs to media (.65), with the topic preferences of liberal blogs corresponding more with the media than conservative blogs, (.83) to (.54). Blogs to chatter correlated at (.81), and chatter to blogs was practically the same (.78). Media and chatter, in contrast, exhibited a weaker pair of correspondence coefficients,

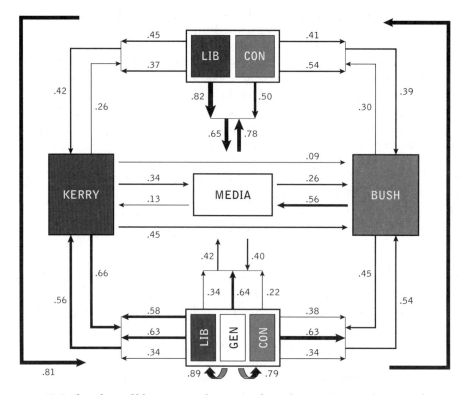

Figure 52.8 Flowchart of blog, citizen chatter, media and campaign correlations

with media to chatter at (.40) and chatter to media at (.43). The correlation of conservative chat priorities to the media was weaker still, at (.22). These numbers encourage us to test the blog-positioning hypothesis for our database through rigorous correlation analysis, pending the completion of methodological refinements. We are also interested in assembling a second data base, to see how these relationships correspond without the supervening focal point of a presidential campaign (although the agenda of the president may also provide a common focus).

[. . .]

The blogs and the media talked about aspects of the campaign horserace (polls, voters, strategy, campaign activities, and swing states) more than the online chat groups, with the exception of the debates, which was a commonly popular topic.

In terms of topical priorities, then, the political blogosphere seems less an entity unto itself than a well integrated part of the national discourse. The levels of its topical correspondences with the other channels do not cluster at the top of the rank orderings (which would point to a separate and strongly influential estate). Nor do they cluster at the bottom (which would suggest a world apart). Instead, blog correspondences are marbled throughout the rank order list. And while there are differences among liberal, conservative, and overall blog correlations with respect to the other voices in the discourse, again there does not seem to be a clustering pattern for anyone of the ideological subdivisions.

So let us turn to another possibility: that the current high reputation of bloggers as buzz-makers of consequence rests on their proclivities. Perhaps it's not that they have a separate agenda, but that they have a distinct role to play on a topic of common interest. Different methods of processing information are, after all, a large part of what distinguishes the traditional four estates. [. . .]

Notes

1   Lee Rainie, 'The State of Blogging," Pew Internet & American Life Project Data Memo, January 2, 2005, and "New Data on Blogs and Blogging', *Commentary* May 2, 2005, www.pewinternet.org .

2   The Yahoo! Buzz Index is calculated based on the percentage of Yahoo! users who search for a subject on a given day. (The presumption built into this metric is that people look for more information about topics they have just heard about and want to talk about knowledgeably.) The Index may be found at buzz.yahoo.com.

3   A political blog is a species of the "filter blog," in which the blogger supplies interesting content found elsewhere online to readers (and viewers and listeners, since the content may be multimedia in form). [. . .] The "A-list" consists of those political filters with the greatest traffic.

4   On the emergent role of A-list bloggers as gatekeepers for the gatekeepers, so to speak, see Lada Adamic and Natalie Clance, "The Political Blogosphere and the 2004 US Election: Divided They Blog," blogpulse.com/papers/2005/AdamicGlanceBlog WWW.pdf. Daniel W. Drezner and Henry Farrell, "Web of Influence," *Foreign Policy*, November–December 2004; Dan Gillmor, *We the Media: Grassroots Journalism by the People, For the People* (Sebastopol, CA: O'Reilly Publishing, 2004).

5   Only five political blogs average more than 100,000 visitors per day, according to SiteMeter. See www.truthlaidbear.com for traffic rankings.

6   Kathleen Hall Jamieson and Karlyn Kohrs Campbell, *The Interplay of Influence: News, Advertising, Politics, and the Mass Media*. 5th Edition (Belmont, CA: Wadsworth Publishing, 2000.)

7   John Horrigan, Kelly Garrett, and Paul Resnick, "The Internet and Democratic Debate," *Pew Internet & American Life Project*, October 27,2004. www.pewinternet. org.jpPF/r/141/report_display.asp. [. . .]

8   BuzzMetrics defines message as a single message board post or a single blog posting, and a single article from campaign output or a single article from a giyen media outlet.

9   We think it premature to draw any inferences about internal correlation patterns from just one data set.

10   Data presenting the topical preferences of each channel and subchannel are available upon request.

Chapter 53

Darren Wallis

DEMOCRATISATION, PARTIES AND THE NET

Mexico – model or aberration?

Source: Darren Wallis (2003) 'Democratisation, Parties and the Net: Mexico – Model or Aberration', in Rachel Gibson, Paul Nixon and Stephen Ward (eds), *Political Parties and the Internet: Net Gain?*, London and New York: Routledge, pp. 175–94.

Introduction

R ECENT CONTRIBUTIONS TO debates on electronic democracy have challenged two perceived biases in the literature. According to Hoff *et al.* (2000a: 1–2) debate has focused 'too greatly on the technology itself and has been 'highly Americano-centric'.[1] Their own work, along with that of a number of other authors, has sought to address this dual distortion, bringing human agency back into the equation and drawing on case studies beyond the United States, especially from Western Europe. Nevertheless, it is reasonable to argue that the literature continues to exhibit a narrow empirical focus, inasmuch as it is concerned principally with developments in the established democracies. There are two compelling reasons why this should be the case. First, the established democracies are generally the most technologically advanced countries, and they evince the greatest degree of penetration of information and communications technologies (ICTs). Second, they exhibit the classic symptoms of malaise of representative democracy that ICTs are purported to help cure or transform.[2] The technology needs to be there before it can have an impact; political systems have to be democratic before they can suffer a 'crisis of democracy'. Put the other way around, the reason why countries like Mexico have not been analysed to date is that they are insufficiently electronic and insufficiently democratic.[3]

[. . .]

Democratising Mexico

For most of the twentieth century, Mexico was governed by a hegemonic party, semi-authoritarian regime, which was neither as repressive nor as closed as its military and communist counterparts.[4] [. . .]

The watershed election of 1988 set the stage for a series of political reforms that gradually led to freer and fairer elections. Electoral and party reforms of 1990, 1993, 1994 and 1996 allowed the opposition to compete more effectively. In 1997 the opposition managed to keep the PRI [Institutional Revolutionary Party] from control of the Chamber of Deputies for the first time in its history, and in 2000 an alliance of the right-wing National Action Party (PAN) and the Greens (PVEM) took the presidency under Vicente Fox. In between 1988 and 2000 rapidly expanding opposition representation at the state and local level reduced voters' fear of the unknown and boosted confidence in the competence of the opposition. [. . .]

What role can be attributed to ICTs in bringing about democratisation in Mexico? In an obvious sense, the role was minimal. Mexico's technological base following the economic crisis of the debt years lagged badly. Democratisation initially responded more to long-term shifts in the social structure than to short-term developments in technology. Parties appeared preoccupied with more pressing matters – the PAN with internal divisions and the PRD with its (and its members') survival. Moreover, all opposition parties faced resource constraints in investing seriously in information technology. The playing field was slanted heavily towards the ruling party and the use of technology by the mainstream parties was slow to start. A partial exception can be found in the computer centres established by PAN president Castillo Peraza between 1993 and 1996 to conduct opinion polls, gather and process electoral results and prevent electoral fraud (Mizrahi, 1998). For the PRI, the Internet represented a potential threat to the way in which it traditionally garnered its vote; its approach to the Internet was conditioned by the fierce battle for the soul of the party raging between 'the dinosaurs' and the modernisers.

[. . .]

Social movements

A second illustration of the use of ICTs in democratising Mexico comes from social movement activity. [. . .] These groups quickly latched on to the opportunities offered by new technologies in the early 1990s to construct networks, alliances and common identities through which they could challenge the regime and advance their political position. Many of these groups were linked to sympathisers abroad, especially in the United States, and used Peacenet and Usenet bulletin boards, discussion groups and email to create networks of resistance to state power and in support of democratic reform (Cleaver, 1998). [. . .]

A particularly stark illustration of the potential of ICTs in this context, even allowing for its generally low level of penetration, can be had from the Zapatista rebellion that erupted in January 1994. This was a low-intensity insurgency among the indigenous population in the impoverished state of Chiapas. Lacking substantial military or financial capability, the Zapatistas have managed to hold domestic and international audiences in thrall for eight years. [. . .]

That the Zapatistas were able to achieve so much with such sparse resources is due in no small part to their use of the Internet as a communication tool to spread their message to domestic and international sympathisers. [. . .] Earlier rebellions in Mexico had met with the familiar, repressive state response. Now, the government found itself obliged to maintain at least a facade of negotiation (although atrocities still occurred). Its attempts to control the flow of information and remove Chiapas from public consciousness have been largely ineffective. Government sites have not been able to successfully counteract the war of words emanating from the Zapatistas.
[. . .]

Parties and campaigns

Mexican election and party websites evince a degree of comprehensiveness and technical sophistication that is comparable with that of many established democracies. We have already raised some clues as to why this might be the case: public financing means that the parties have sufficient resources; the Internet is mainly used by the young, whose membership and votes will be open to capture in subsequent elections; rapid growth is anticipated; parties wish to be seen as in touch with the latest technological developments; parties have a keen eye on their overseas audiences; and technology and expertise can be harboured from the United States more easily by Mexico than by other Latin-American countries. Despite very low levels of penetration, parties gave serious thought to their web presence in the 2000 election and there has been ongoing development subsequently.

Party presence

[. . .]

Because the universe of competing parties is fixed by the national registration requirements, all official and non-official political sites provide links to each of these parties. On official sites, such as IFE's, parties were simply listed in alphabetical order. On most sites, however, the big three parties – PRI, PAN and PRD – were listed first, usually in that order, a reflection of opinion-poll ratings rather than support in the previous election (where the PRD gained more seats than the PAN). Once the alliances were approved, links to alliance websites were included.

In an obvious sense, the Internet has facilitated a general increase in exposure for minor parties, whose voice has rarely been heard through the conventional media. All minor parties, including the new Social Democracy (DS) and Centre (PCD) parties had web presence, with basic information on the party's background and principles and its candidate's proposals available. As mentioned, these parties were not differentiated in any way on official sites. In the past, fringe parties have tended to be either pro-government satellite parties or parties of the left that have struggled to find a stable organisational identity. The Internet at least presents some opportunities for genuinely independent minor parties to develop a public presence.

It is not just the presence of minor parties, however, that has been at issue in Mexico. Until quite recently, information about, and the public presence of, the opposition generally was limited. Whereas the concern in established democratic contexts has been the informational balance between minor parties and the established parties, in a democratising context it is more the balance between a ruling party on the one hand and the opposition as a whole on the other. In order to try to make their voices heard, both the PRD and the PAN have invested substantial resources in creating and maintaining comprehensive websites that provide voters and analysts with information on alternatives to PRI rule. The Internet evinced greater exposure for all opposition parties than had previously been the case with exposure on radio and television.

[. . .]

Campaigning in Mexico

A rapid 'Americanisation' of campaigning has been evident in Mexico since 1996, which I have elsewhere labelled a shift from a 'tortilla' model of campaigns to a 'coca-cola' model (Wallis, 2001). [. . .] Parties have focused more heavily on communicating messages through the media than on traditional set-piece rallies around the country. [. . .]

In terms of attempting to capture undecided voters, party and alliance websites provided constituency-level information on candidates, previous results and trends in support. However, there was no evidence of parties narrowcasting and there was only limited use of websites as a recruitment tool for new members. [. . .] Chat rooms are available on some of these pages and there are specially designed pages for children on the PRI website, featuring graphics, cartoons and games. [. . .]

There is some evidence of opportunities for interactivity, rather than a one-way flow of information from the top down. We have already mentioned the use of chat rooms. Some parties provided opportunities for voters to send their opinions to the party or candidate through electronic forms. There were general opportunities for 'comments or suggestions' on all relevant sites, although in the main these are simply directed to webmasters.

Independent political discussion sites

Finally, one further feature of the 1997 and, especially, the 2000 campaigns has been the proliferation of independent political websites, lists and discussion groups, such as *presidenciables.com* and *Elector2000.com*, as well as pages within the sites of the mainstream press, such as *Reforma* and *Proceso*. All of these sites provided voters with a comprehensive array of information on parties and candidates, as well as offering analyses and comments from specialists and users alike. [. . .]

Conclusions

The development of these sites is indicative of a general information explosion that has occurred in Mexico as the shackles of the dictatorship have gradually been released. Many of the sites are unsurprisingly biased, and many contain scathing criticisms of politicians, but they also evince engagement among the citizenry with the political process. In a democratising context, of course, technology should not be required to invigorate engagement with the political process, but it may have a critical role to play in consolidating that engagement and providing alternative sources of information and analysis. There is evidence that this is already happening in Mexico.

Engagement with the Internet among party-political actors in Mexico was contingent upon changes in the institutional rules of the game. Although a democratising force in some respects throughout the 1990s, its move into mainstream democratic politics required the reforms of 1996. As we have stressed repeatedly, political behaviour has been so clearly structured by the issue of the regime's future in recent years, that future projections on the role and use of the Internet by Mexican parties and candidates must remain tentative. However, as we have also stressed, the embracing of the technology by parties is very real and the demographic and technological outlooks such that we may confidently anticipate a more central role in subsequent elections.

Notes

1   'Electronic democracy' remains a useful shorthand for what Hoff, Horrocks and Tops and collaborators prefer to term Technologically Mediated Innovations in Political Practice (Hoff, Horrocks and Tops, 2000b). To a Latin Americanist, 'Americano-centric' implies a continent-wide centrism that does not square easily with the focus in the literature. 'US-centric' would be more politically correct.

2   Theories of the pathology of established democracies are summarised in Kaase and Newton (1994). Whether ICTs are viewed as a mechanism by which to reinvigorate 'politics as usual' or as a contribution to a radically new way of conducting politics depends upon whether political changes in the advanced democracies are viewed through the pessimistic lenses of the 'crisis of democracy' (Crozier, Huntington and Watanaki, 1975) and 'overload' (King, 1975; Olson, 1982) schools prevalent in the 1970s and 1980s, or through the more optimistic lenses of radical democracy (Laclau and Mouffe, 1985) or the 'silent revolution' (Inglehart, 1977) schools, among others. [. . .]

3   Ironically, the sub-set of established democracies has often been defined by membership of the Organisation for Economic Cooperation and Development (OECD), which Mexico joined in 1992.

4   The post-revolutionary regime dates to the 1917 Constitution and developed its classical features with the establishment of the official party in 1929 and the creation of corporatist interest mediation structures within that party in the 1930s.

References

Crozier, M., Huntington, S. and Watanaki, J. (1975) *The Crisis of Democracy: A Report on the Governability of Democracies to the Trilateral Commission*. New York: New York University Press.

Cleaver, H. (1998) 'The Zapatistas and the electronic fabric of struggle,' in Holloway, J. and Peláez, E. (eds), *Zapatista: Reinventing Revolution in Mexico*. London: Pluto Press.

Hoff, J., Horrocks, I. and Tops, P. (2000a) 'Introduction: New Technology and the crises of democracy,' in Hoff, J., Horrocks I. and Tops, P. (eds), *Democratic Governance and New Technology: Technologically Mediated Innovations in Political Practice in Western Europe*. London: Routledge.

Hoff, J., Horrocks, I. and Tops, P. (eds) (2000b) *Democratic Governance and New Technology: Technologically Mediated Innovations in Political Practice in Western Europe*. London: Routledge.

Inglehart, R. (1977) *The Silent Revolution: Changing Values and Political Styles among Western Publics*. Princeton: Princeton University Press.

Kaase, M. and Newton, K. (1994) *Beliefs in Government*. Oxford: Oxford University Press.

King, A. (1975) 'Overload: The problems of governing in the 1970s', *Political Studies*, XXIII: 283–296.

Laclau, E. and Mouffe, C. (1985) *Hegemony and Socialist Strategy: Towards a Radical Democratic Politics*. London: Verso.

Mizrahi, Y. (1998) 'The costs of electoral success: The Partido Accion Nacional in Mexico', in Serrano, M. (ed.), *Governing Mexico: Political Parties and Elections*. London: Institute of Latin American Studies, 95–113.

Olson, M. (1982) *The Rise and Decline of Nations*. New Haven: Yale University Press.

Wallis, D. (2001) 'Outfoxing Leviathan: On the campaign trail down Mexico way', *Journal of Public Affairs*, 1(3).

Chapter 54

Michael Margolis and David Resnick

HOW THE NET WILL NOT CONTRIBUTE TO DEMOCRACY

Source: M. Margolis and D. Resnick (2000) *Politics as Usual: The Cyberspace 'Revolution'*, London; Thousand Oaks, CA; New Dehli: Sage Publications, pp. 207–12.

W E EXPECT THAT the Internet will foster democracy in the long run but not in the way utopians have trumpeted. It will influence politics and democratic government, but before we can focus on which changes are likely, we must be clear about which are not. It is unlikely that there will be a massive increase in political participation because of the Internet. There has been a tremendous increase in the number of people now on the Net, but there is no indication that their presence will inaugurate a new era in mass politics. The Internet has become a mass medium, but the numbers tallied by those who estimate the growth of the Internet have not been translated into comparable growth in political participation.

The Net is a new means of participating in politics because it provides new conduits for the expression of public opinion. The future undoubtedly will bring some form of voting online. It may provide instant public feedback about the events of the day, but it is unlikely to lead to the triumph of popular sovereignty and direct democracy.

[. . .]

Direct democracy is not appropriate for a complex industrial or postindustrial society. The unity, equality, and devotion to the public good, which are the prerequisites for a successful participatory democracy, according to traditional democratic theory, are not present. [. . .] The changes that the Internet will bring to modern democracies will be important, but hardly revolutionary.

Another radical democratic vision sees the Internet as empowering the powerless by providing them with a new voice and leverage that will shift power away from entrenched economic interests. In the past, democratic power, the power of numbers, has been used to redistribute resources and opportunities formerly monopolized by elites. Many have seen the Internet as a way to combat elite domination. Even if the Net will not initiate a new golden age of direct democratic participation, at least it could be used to magnify the power of the powerless. More concretely, some believe that the democratic process in advanced societies could be invigorated if the minor parties of today used the Internet to get their message of hope and change across to the broad mass of the citizenry. Unfortunately, there is little evidence to support that belief. The access of marginal movements to a new and powerful medium of mass communication has not led them to make significant headway in the real world. The problem seems to lie more in the message than in the medium. In any case, the evidence shows that those who have been powerful in the past – the established organizations, the wealthy, and the privileged – are moving into cyberspace and taking their advantages with them .

Whatever new exposure minor parties and movements have gotten by entering cyberspace has yet to be translated into real-world shifts of power and resources (Margolis, Resnick, & Lu, 1997; Margolis, Resnick, & Wolfe, 1999; Roper, 1998). Most Net surfers today pay little attention to the radical fringe in cyberspace. If one or more new radical parties emerge into prominence in the twenty-first century, no doubt they, or their ancestors, will have been on the Web. However, it is doubtful that the Internet will have been directly responsible for their rise to prominence. Almost certainly, no significant shift in power from the haves to the have-nots will occur simply because the have-nots are able to exploit the democratic potential of the Internet. Indeed, the evidence reviewed [. . .] indicates that the parties, interests, news media, bureaucracies, and public officials who dominate politics in the real world have become more adept at exploiting the Web for political purposes than have their real-world rivals who lie outside the mainstream.

The Internet also will not create the global village, at least in any meaningful political sense. True, cyberspace is a realm without borders. [. . .] Marvellous though this is, people and computers are located in real space, and real space is divided into national sovereignties, The Internet undoubtedly creates new difficulties for nation-states asserting their sovereign authority, but the aspects of the Internet that now evade national jurisdictions are unlikely to be the foundations for a worldwide erosion of the power of the nation-state. There are many processes connected with international economic trends that lead some observers to claim that the days of the nation-state are doomed, but we doubt that it will cease to be the dominant form of organized political life in our lifetimes or those of our children.

The Internet will further those trends that have made it more difficult for nations to control what flows across their borders. Certainly, they can no longer so easily police what their citizens see and think. If nations wish to participate in the modern world, they must accept the inevitable invasion of their space by ideas, attitudes, and lifestyles that they might otherwise prefer to keep at bay. It will be more difficult to run a closed society and still benefit from the fruits of modern technology, but that is a long way from having a world without borders. As we have pointed out in (earlier chapters) [of the original publication] [. . .] the Internet poses new difficulties for the fight against international crime and for regulating international trade, but none of these difficulties is insurmountable. Nation-states have been around for a long time, and they possess deep reservoirs of power and legitimacy. The Internet presents challenges to them,but in our judgment, nation-states will meet the challenges and incorporate solutions within the existing structures of governance.

How the Net will contribute to democracy

Some pundits look to a newly energized wired citizenry to spread democracy. Although it is true that the Internet can be used as a tool for democratic participation, it also has great potential to stimulate economic development and create wealth. A modern telecommunication infrastructure is a great aid to economic development, and the Internet is becoming a crucial component of that infrastructure. Economic development, in turn, promotes and stabilizes democratic regimes. Ironically, it may be the commercial aspect of cyberspace, its ability to connect individuals and businesses to each other for commercial purposes, that will have a more profound effect on the increase and stabilization of democratic regimes than its ability to nurture online political life.

We believe that a more mundane but ultimately more powerful effect of the Internet holds out a greater chance of fostering democracy. The Internet will help to spread democracy, but not because more people will conduct more of their politics online. Rather, as we enter an age in which information will be at the center of new forms of economic wealth, the Net will facilitate the spread of that wealth. Areas of the world lacking old-fashioned sources of wealth rooted in natural resources, such as vast tracts of arable land or scarce minerals, can now compete with nations more abundantly endowed. As the world as a whole becomes increasingly information-rich, this richness will have profound effects on many nations that are now both poor and governed despotically. Because the information spread via the Internet will contribute to general world economic wealth, and because economic wealth facilitates the rise of democratic government, the Internet will contribute to the spread of democracy.

The Internet also will help dissident groups in authoritarian societies. The Net adds to the technological arsenal of the communications revolution, whose weapons, such as the fax and the cell phone, already have breached national barriers to the flow of information. [. . .] With these new types of decentralized technological innovations – the Net being but the latest and most powerful – it is difficult for an authoritarian regime to monopolize the sources of public information.

[. . .] Its real radical political potential lies in the less-developed areas of the world. The liberating aspect of criticism directed at repressive regimes will help spread democracy, but only in countries where the ordinary means of public dissent are stifled.

Governments in the developed world now have a very visible presence in cyberspace. Elected officials have their own Web sites and email addresses, and so do agencies at all levels of government. We can clearly document this change, but its exact significance for the future of democratic politics is not clear. The greatly increased presence of government agencies online is an achievement. Although it represents a genuine effort on the part of government officials to provide better service and to bring government closer to the people, it represents no significant increase in citizen participation in public policy development [. . .].

Democratic government should be responsive to the will of the people, but there are two levels of responsiveness. The first is responsiveness to policy initiatives. [. . .] The second type is responsiveness to how government implements its existing policies. [. . .]

For many, the Internet promises increased responsiveness to citizens' policy initiatives. Email and Web pages enable citizens to wage campaigns for change in new ways. The Internet makes it easier to organize, to bring pressure on legislators and government officials, and to make them aware of what citizens want. Yet, despite the advantages, so far there is little evidence that initiatives organized through the Internet to have government adopt significant new policies or alter existing ones have been successful (Gurak, 1997). No doubt in the future, efforts to lobby government via the Internet will become more sophisticated and more successful, but this process is essentially an extension of ordinary democratic politics. Some public policies will change because some always change. There will probably be online activity crucial to these changes in particular cases, but a systematic increase in governmental responsiveness to policy initiatives due to political activity on the Internet seems unlikely.

The argument for the Internet bringing about an increase in responsiveness in the second sense, implementing government policies, is much stronger. Most of the increased presence of government in cyberspace is an attempt to be responsive to citizens as clients and customers. The Internet provides new ways for government to interface with citizens. [. . .] Thanks to the Internet, government in the future will be more responsive, more efficient, and less bureaucratic.

Paradoxically, one of the hardest things to predict is whether the Internet will improve the quality of democracy by creating a more informed citizenry. We say paradoxically, because it seems obvious that because the Internet provides instant and almost cost-free information, it should enable the ordinary citizen to be fully informed about all relevant policy areas. Citizens also can follow government activity in ways that never were possible in the past. Will the dream of an enlightened citizenry finally be realized? We remain skeptical – not about the Internet as a source of information, but about the predilection of ordinary citizens to use it to better inform themselves about public issues. To be sure, the Net is now and will continue to be a boon to those who already have an active and sustained interest in public affairs, but there is little evidence that the Internet by itself will increase the attentive public.

References

Gurak, L.J. (1997). *Persuasion and Privacy in Cyberspace: The Online Protests over Lotus Marketplace and the Clipper Chip*. New Haven, CT: Yale University Press.

Margolis, M., Resnick, D., & Lu, C.C. (1997, Winter) Campaigning on the Internet: Parties and candidates on the World Wide Web in the 1996 primary season. *Harvard International Journal of Press/Politics*, 2(1), 59–78.

Margolis, M., Resnick, D., & Wolfe, J. (1999, Fall) Party competition on the Internet: Minor versus major parties in the UK and USA. *Harvard International Journal of Press/Politics*, 4(3), 24–27.

Roper, J. (1998). New Zealand political parties online: The World Wide Web as a tool for democratization or for political marketing? In C. Toulouse & T.W. Luke (eds), *The Politics of Cyberspace* (pp. 69–83). New York: Routledge.

Index

Page references in *italics* indicate illustrations.